SUPER 10

CBSE Class 10

Mathematics (Standard)

2023 Exam Sample Papers

with 2021-22 Previous Year Solved Papers, CBSE Sample Paper & 2020 Topper Answer Sheet

DISHA Publications Inc.
45, 2nd Floor, Maharishi Dayanand Marg,
Corner Market, Malviya Nagar, new Delhi -110017
Tel: 49842349/ 49842350

Typeset By
DISHA DTP Team

Write To Us At
feedback_disha@aiets.co.in

Contents

Latest Syllabus Issued by CBSE for Academic Year (2022-2023)

COURSE STRUCTURE
CLASS X
(Annual Examination)

Time: 03 Hours **Max. Marks: 80**

Unit No.	Unit	Marks
I.	Number Systems	06
II.	Algebra	20
III.	Coordinate Geometry	06
IV.	Geometry	12
V.	Trigonometry	15
VI.	Mensuration	10
VII.	Statistics & Probability	11
	Total	**80**

UNIT I: NUMBER SYSTEMS

1. REAL NUMBER (15) Periods

Fundamental Theorem of Arithmetic - statements after reviewing work done earlier and after illustrating and motivating through examples, Proofs of irrationality of $\sqrt{2}, \sqrt{3}\sqrt{5}$

UNIT II: ALGEBRA

1. POLYNOMIALS (8) Periods

Zeros of a polynomial. Relationship between zeros and coefficients of quadratic polynomials.

2. PAIR OF LINEAR EQUATIONS IN TWO VARIABLES (15) Periods

Pair of linear equations in two variables and graphical method of their solution, consistency/ inconsistency.

Algebraic conditions for number of solutions. Solution of a pair of linear equations in two variables algebraically - by substitution, by elimination. Simple situational problems.

3. QUADRATIC EQUATIONS (15) Periods

Standard form of a quadratic equation $ax^2 + bx + c = 0, (a \neq 0)$. Solutions of quadratic equations (only real roots) by factorization, and by using quadratic formula. Relationship between discriminant and nature of roots.

Situational problems based on quadratic equations related to day to day activities to be incorporated.

4. ARITHMETIC PROGRESSIONS (10) Periods

Motivation for studying Arithmetic Progression Derivation of the nth term and sum of the first n terms of A.P. and their application in solving daily life problems.

UNIT III: COORDINATE GEOMETRY

Coordinate Geometry (15) Periods

Review: Concepts of coordinate geometry, graphs of linear equations. Distance formula. Section formula (internal division).

UNIT IV: GEOMETRY

1. TRIANGLES (15) Periods

Definitions, examples, counter examples of similar triangles.

1. (Prove) If a line is drawn parallel to one side of a triangle to intersect the other two sides in distinct points, the other two sides are divided in the same ratio.
2. (Motivate) If a line divides two sides of a triangle in the same ratio, the line is parallel to the third side.
3. (Motivate) If in two triangles, the corresponding angles are equal, their corresponding sides are proportional and the triangles are similar.
4. (Motivate) If the corresponding sides of two triangles are proportional, their corresponding angles are equal and the two triangles are similar.
5. (Motivate) If one angle of a triangle is equal to one angle of another triangle and the sides including these angles are proportional, the two triangles are similar.

2. CIRCLES (10) Periods

Tangent to a circle at, point of contact

1. (Prove) The tangent at any point of a circle is perpendicular to the radius through the point of contact.
2. (Prove) The lengths of tangents drawn from an external point to a circle are equal.

UNIT V: TRIGONOMETRY

1. INTRODUCTION TO TRIGONOMETRY (10) Periods

Trigonometric ratios of an acute angle of a right-angled triangle. Proof of their existence (well defined); motivate the ratios whichever are defined at 0° and 90°. Values of the trigonometric ratios of 30°, 45° and 60°. Relationships between the ratios.

2. TRIGONOMETRIC IDENTITIES (15) Periods

Proof and applications of the identity $\sin^2 A + \cos^2 A = 1$. Only simple identities to be given.

3. HEIGHTS AND DISTANCES: Angle of elevation, Angle of Depression. (10) Periods

Simple problems on heights and distances. Problems should not involve more than two right triangles. Angles of elevation / depression should be only 30°, 45°, and 60°.

UNIT VI: MENSURATION

1. AREAS RELATED TO CIRCLES (12) Periods

Area of sectors and segments of a circle. Problems based on areas and perimeter / circumference of the above said plane figures. (In calculating area of segment of a circle, problems should be restricted to central angle of 60°, 90° and 120° only.

2. SURFACE AREAS AND VOLUMES (12) Periods

Surface areas and volumes of combinations of any two of the following: cubes, cuboids, spheres, hemispheres and right circular cylinders/cones.

UNIT VII: STATISTICS AND PROBABILITY

1. STATISTICS (18) Periods

Mean, median and mode of grouped data (bimodal situation to be avoided).

2. PROBABILITY (10) Periods

Classical definition of probability. Simple problems on finding the probability of an event.

A Foundation Series with 3 Goals
Bring Concept Clarity, Sharpen Problem Solving & Build a Strong Foundation.

The theory is followed by the Exercise part which covers in total **1800 questions divided into 4 levels of fully solved exercises,** which are graded as per their level of difficulty.

- **Exercise 1: Master Boards: MCQs**, FIB, True-False, Assertion-Reason, Passage, Matching, Very Short, Short & Long Answer Type Questions including Past Years Board Qns. This Exercise also includes - Reasoning Based, HOTS and Case Based MCQs.
- **Exercise 2: Master the NCERT:** All Textbook & Exemplar Questions
- **Exercise 3: Foundation Builder:** Question Bank on NCERT chapter including MCQs 1 Correct, MCQs>1 Correct, Passage, Assertion-Reason, Multiple Matching and Numeric/ Integer Type Questions with past years - NTSE, JSTSE & KVPY considering Syllabus and Level of difficulty.
- **Exercise 4: Foundation Builder+ :** Question Bank on Connecting Topics/ Chapters including MCQs 1 Correct, MCQs>1 Correct, Passage, Assertion-Reason, Multiple Matching and Numeric/ Integer Type Questions with past years - NTSE, JSTSE & KVPY considering Syllabus and Level of difficulty.

The book adheres to the latest syllabus set by the NCERT, going beyond by incorporating those topics which will assist the students to scale-up in the next classes to achieve their academic dreams of Medicine or Engineering.

CBSE SAMPLE QUESTION PAPER (THEORY)

SESSION : 2022-2023

Time Allowed : 3 Hours **Max. Marks : 80**

General Instructions

1. This Question Paper has 5 Sections A-E.
2. **Section A** has 20 MCQs carrying 1 mark each
3. **Section B** has 5 questions carrying 02 marks each.
4. **Section C** has 6 questions carrying 03 marks each.
5. **Section D** has 4 questions carrying 05 marks each.
6. **Section E** has 3 case based integrated units of assessment (04 marks each) with sub-parts of the values of 1, 1 and 2 marks each respectively.
7. All Questions are compulsory. However, an internal choice in 2 Qs of 5 marks, 2 Qs of 3 marks and 2 Questions of 2 marks has been provided. An internal choice has been provided in the 2marks questions of Section E
8. Draw neat figures wherever required. Take π =22/7 wherever required if not stated.

SECTION-A

Section A consists of 20 questions of 1 mark each.

1. Let a and b be two positive integers such that $a = p^3q^4$ and $b = p^2q^3$, where p and q are prime numbers. If HCF(a,b) = p^mq^n and LCM(a,b) = p^rq^s, then (m + n) (r + s) =

(a) 15 (b) 30 (c) 35 (d) 72

2. Let p be a prime number. The quadratic equation having its roots as factors of p is

(a) $x^2 - px + p = 0$ (b) $x^2 - (p+1)x + p = 0$ (c) $x^2 + (p+1)x + p = 0$ (d) $x^2 - px + p + 1 = 0$

3. If α and β are the zeros of a polynomial $f(x) = px^2 - 2x + 3p$ and $\alpha + \beta = \alpha\beta$, then p is

(a) –2/3 (b) 2/3 (c) 1/3 (d) –1/3

4. If the system of equations $3x + y = 1$ and $(2k - 1)x + (k - 1)y = 2k + 1$ is inconsistent, then k =

(a) –1 (b) 0 (c) 1 (d) 2

5. If the vertices of a parallelogram PQRS taken in order are P(3,4), Q(–2,3) and R(–3,–2), then the coordinates of its fourth vertex S are

(a) (–2,–1) (b) (–2,–3) (c) (2,–1) (d) (1,2)

6. $\Delta ABC \sim \Delta PQR$. If AM and PN are altitudes of ΔABC and ΔPQR respectively and $AB^2 : PQ^2 = 4 : 9$, then AM : PN =

(a) 3 : 2 (b) 16 : 81 (c) 4 : 9 (d) 2 : 3

7. If $x \tan 60° \cos 60° = \sin 60° \cot 60°$, then x =

(a) cos30° (b) tan30° (c) sin30° (d) cot30°

8. If $\sin\theta + \cos\theta = \sqrt{2}$, then $\tan\theta + \cot\theta$ =

(a) 1 (b) 2 (c) 3 (d) 4

9. In the given figure, DE || BC, AE = a units, EC –b units, DE = x units and BC = y units. Which of the following is true?

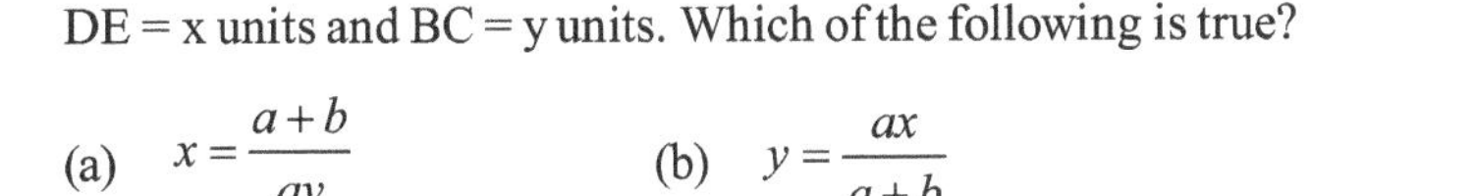

(a) $x = \frac{a+b}{ay}$ (b) $y = \frac{ax}{a+b}$

(c) $x = \frac{ay}{a+b}$ (d) $\frac{x}{y} = \frac{a}{b}$

A, D, E, B, C

10. ABCD is a trapezium with AD || BC and AD = 4cm. If the diagonals AC and BD intersect each other at O such that AO/OC = DO/OB = 1/2, then BC =
(a) 6cm (b) 7cm (c) 8cm (d) 9cm

11. If two tangents inclined at an angle of 60° are drawn to a circle of radius 3cm, then the length of each tangent is equal to
(a) $\frac{3\sqrt{3}}{2}$ cm (b) 3cm (c) 6cm (d) $3\sqrt{3}$ cm

12. The area of the circle that can be inscribed in a square of 6cm is
(a) $36\pi cm^2$ (b) $18\pi cm^2$ (c) $12\pi cm^2$ (d) $9\pi cm^2$

13. The sum of the length, breadth and height of a cuboid is $6\sqrt{3}$ cm and the length of its diagonal is $2\sqrt{3}$ cm. The total surface area of the cuboid is
(a) $48 cm^2$ (b) $72 cm^2$ (c) $96 cm^2$ (d) $108 cm^2$

14. If the difference of Mode and Median of a data is 24, then the difference of median and mean is
(a) 8 (b) 12 (c) 24 (d) 36

15. The number of revolutions made by a circular wheel of radius 0.25m in rolling a distance of 11km is
(a) 2800 (b) 4000 (c) 5500 (d) 7000

16. For the following distribution,

Class	0-5	5-10	10-15	15-20	20-25
Frequency	10	15	12	20	9

the sum of the lower limits of the median and modal class is
(a) 15 (b) 25 (c) 30 (d) 35

17. Two dice are rolled simultaneously. What is the probability that 6 will come up at least once?
(a) 1/6 (b) 7/36 (c) 11/36 (d) 13/36

18. If 5 tanβ = 4, then $\frac{5\sin\beta - 2\cos\beta}{5\sin\beta + 2\cos\beta} =$
(a) 1/3 (b) 2/5 (c) 3/5 (d) 6

DIRECTION: In the question number 19 and 20, a statement of Assertion (A) is followed by a statement of Reason (R). Choose the correct option.

(a) Both Assertion (A) and Reason (R) are true and Reason (R) is the correct explanation of Assertion (A).
(b) Both Assertion (A) and Reason (R) are true and Reason (R) is not the correct explanation of Assertion (A).
(c) Assertion (A) is true but Reason (R) is false.
(d) Assertion (A) is false but Reason (R) is true.

19. **Assertion (A):** If product of two numbers is 5780 and their HCF is 17, then their LCM is 340
Reason (R): HCF is always a factor of LCM

20. **Assertion (A):** If the co-ordinates of the mid-points of the sides AB and AC of ΔABC are D(3,5) and E(-3,-3) respectively, then BC = 20 units
Reason (R): The line joining the mid points of two sides of a triangle is parallel to the third side and equal to half of it.

SECTION-B

Section B consists of 5 questions of 2 marks each.

21. If 49x + 51y = 499, 51x + 49y = 501, then find the value of x and y.

22. In the given figure below, $\frac{AD}{AE} = \frac{AC}{BD}$ and $\angle 1 = \angle 2$. Show that $\Delta BAE \sim \Delta CAD$.

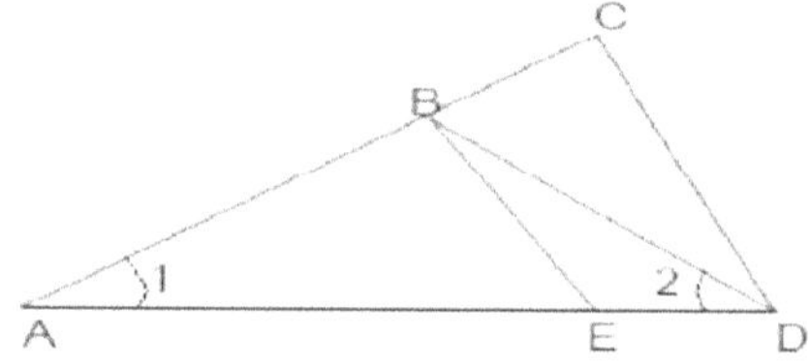

23. In the given figure, O is the centre of circle. Find $\angle AQB$, given that PA and PB are tangents to the circle and $\angle APB = 75°$.

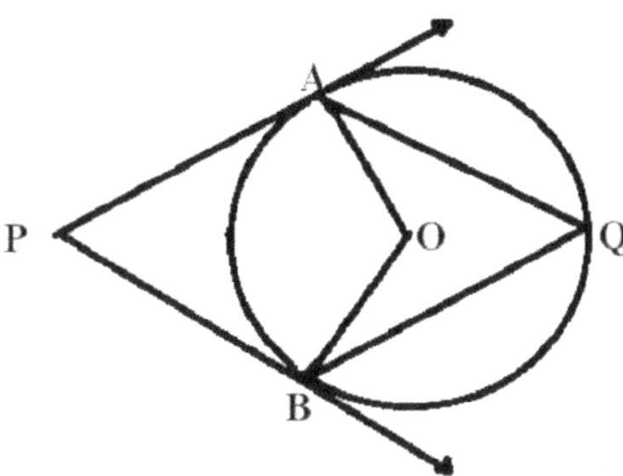

24. The length of the minute hand of a clock is 6cm. Find the area swept by it when it moves from 7:05 p.m. to 7:40 p.m.

OR

In the given figure, arcs have been drawn of radius 7cm each with vertices A, B, C and D of quadrilateral ABCD as centres. Find the area of the shaded region.

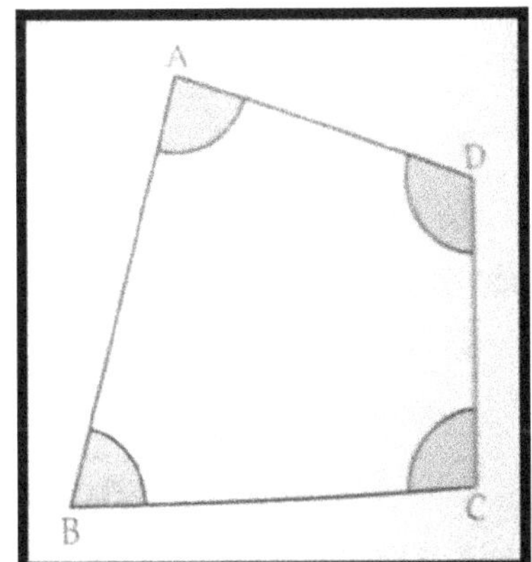

25. If $\sin(A+B)=1$ and $\cos(A-B)=\sqrt{3}/2$, $0° < A+B \leq 90°$ and $A > B$, then find the measures of angles A and B.

OR

Find an acute angle θ when $\dfrac{\cos\theta - \sin\theta}{\cos\theta + \sin\theta} = \dfrac{1-\sqrt{3}}{1+\sqrt{3}}$

SECTION-C

Section C consists of 6 questions of 3 marks each.

26. Given that $\sqrt{3}$ is irrational, prove that $5+2\sqrt{3}$ is irrational.

27. If the zeroes of the polynomial x^2+px+q are double in value to the zeroes of the polynomial $2x^2-5x-3$, then find the values of p and q.

28. A train covered a certain distance at a uniform speed. If the train would have been 6 km/h faster, it would have taken 4 hours less than the scheduled time. And, if the train were slower by 6 km/hr ; it would have taken 6 hours more than the scheduled time. Find the length of the journey.

OR

Anuj had some chocolates, and he divided them into two lots A and B. He sold the first lot at the rate of ₹2 for 3 chocolates and the second lot at the rate of ₹1 per chocolate, and got a total of ₹400. If he had sold the first lot at the rate of ₹1 per chocolate, and the second lot at the rate of ₹4 for 5 chocolates, his total collection would have been ₹460. Find the total number of chocolates he had.

29. Prove the following that-

$$\frac{\tan^3\theta}{1+\tan^2\theta}+\frac{\cot^3\theta}{1+\cot^2\theta} = \sec\theta\,\text{cosec}\theta - 2\sin\theta\cos\theta$$

30. Prove that a parallelogram circumscribing a circle is a rhombus

OR

In the figure XY and X'Y' are two parallel tangents to a circle with centre O and another tangent AB with point of contact C interesting XY at A and X'Y' at B, what is the measure of $\angle AOB$.

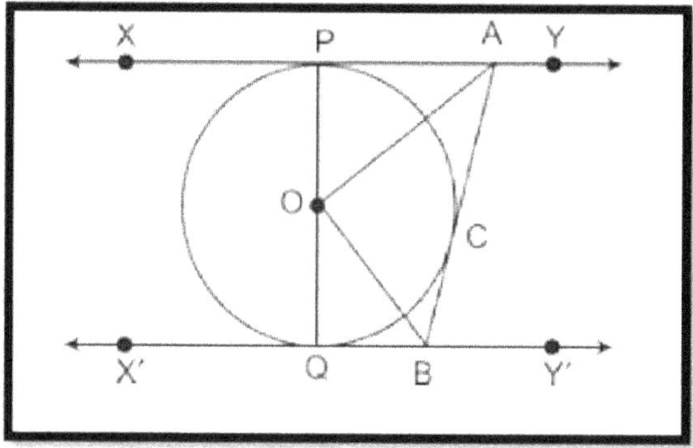

31. Two coins are tossed simultaneously. What is the probability of getting

(i) At least one head? (ii) At most one tail? (iii) head and a tail?

SECTION-D

Section D consists of 4 questions of 5 marks each.

32. To fill a swimming pool two pipes are used. If the pipe of larger diameter used for 4 hours and the pipe of smaller diameter for 9 hours, only half of the pool can be filled. Find, how long it would take for each pipe to fill the pool separately, if the pipe of smaller diameter takes 10 hours more than the pipe of larger diameter to fill the pool?

OR

In a flight of 600km, an aircraft was slowed down due to bad weather. Its average speed for the trip was reduced by 200 km/hr from its usual speed and the time of the flight increased by 30 min. Find the scheduled duration of the flight.

33. Prove that if a line is drawn parallel to one side of a triangle intersecting the other two sides in distinct points, then the other two sides are divided in the same ratio.

Using the above theorem prove that a line through the point of intersection of the diagonals and parallel to the base of the trapezium divides the non parallel sides in the same ratio.

34. Due to heavy floods in a state, thousands were rendered homeless. 50 schools collectively decided to provide place and the canvas for 1500 tents and share the whole expenditure equally. The lower part of each tent is cylindrical with base radius 2.8 m and height 3.5 m and the upper part is conical with the same base radius, but of height 2.1 m. If the canvas used to make the tents costs ₹120 per m^2, find the amount shared by each school to set up the tents.

OR

There are two identical solid cubical boxes of side 7cm. From the top face of the first cube a hemisphere of diameter equal to the side of the cube is scooped out. This hemisphere is inverted and placed on the top of the second cube fs surface to form a dome. Find

(i) the ratio of the total surface area of the two new solids formed.

(ii) volume of each new solid formed.

35. The median of the following data is 525. Find the values of x and y, if the total frequency is 100

Class interval	0-100	100-200	200-300	300-400	400-500	500-600	600-700	700-800	800-900	900-1000
Frequency	2	5	x	12	17	20	y	9	7	4

SECTION-E

Case study based questions are compulsory.

36. A tiling or tessellation of a flat surface is the covering of a plane using one or more geometric shapes, called tiles, with no overlaps and no gaps. Historically, tessellations were used in ancient Rome and in Islamic art. You may find tessellation patterns on floors, walls, paintings etc. Shown below is a tiled floor in the archaeological Museum of Seville, made using squares, triangles and hexagons.

A craftsman thought of making a floor pattern after being inspired by the above design. To ensure accuracy in his work, he made the pattern on the Cartesian plane. He used regular octagons, squares and triangles for his floor tessellation pattern

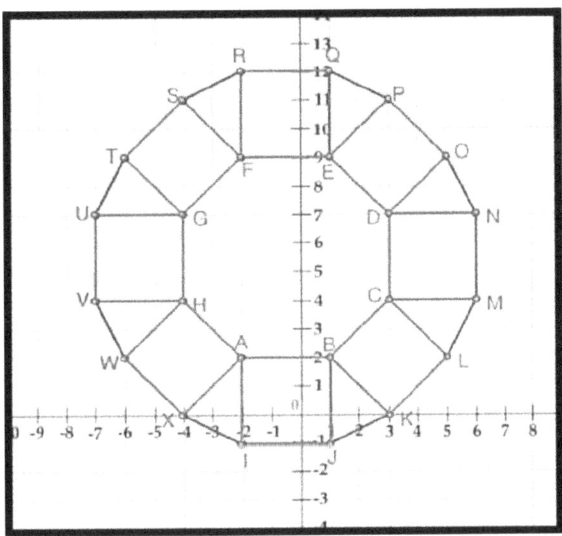

Use the above figure to answer the questions that follow:

(i) What is the length of the line segment joining points B and F?

(ii) The centre 'Z' of the figure will be the point of intersection of the diagonals of quadrilateral WXOP. Then what are the coordinates of Z?

(iii) What are the coordinates of the point on y axis equidistant from A and G?

OR

What is the area of Trapezium AFGH?

37. The school auditorium was to be constructed to accommodate at least 1500 people. The chairs are to be placed in concentric circular arrangement in such a way that each succeeding circular row has 10 seats more than the previous one.

(i) If the first circular row has 30 seats, how many seats will be there in the 10th row?

(ii) For 1500 seats in the auditorium, how many rows need to be there?

OR

If 1500 seats are to be arranged in the auditorium, how many seats are still left to be put after 10th row?

(iii) If there were 17 rows in the auditorium, how many seats will be there in the middle row?

38. We all have seen the airplanes flying in the sky but might have not thought of how they actually reach the correct destination. Air Traffic Control (ATC) is a service provided by ground-based air traffic controllers who direct aircraft on the ground and through a given section of controlled airspace, and can provide advisory services to aircraft in non-controlled airspace. Actually, all this air traffic is managed and regulated by using various concepts based on coordinate geometry and trigonometry.

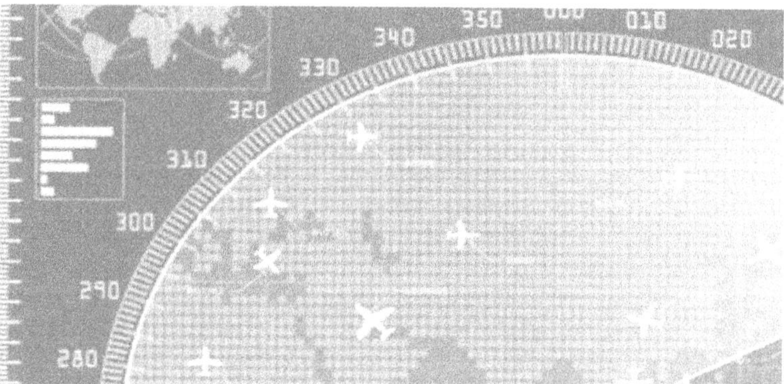

At a given instance, ATC finds that the angle of elevation of an airplane from a point on the ground is 60°. After a flight of 30 seconds, it is observed that the angle of elevation changes to 30°. The height of the plane remains constantly as $3000\sqrt{3}$ m. Use the above information to answer the questions that follow-

(i) Draw a neat labelled figure to show the above situation diagrammatically.

(ii) What is the distance travelled by the plane in 30 seconds?

OR

Keeping the height constant, during the above flight, it was observed that after $15(\sqrt{3}-1)$ seconds, the angle of elevation changed to 45°. How much is the distance travelled in that duration.

(iii) What is the speed of the plane in km/hr.

SOLUTIONS

1. (c) 35
2. (b) $x^2-(p+1)x+p=0$
3. (b) 2/3
4. (d) 2
5. (c) (2,–1)
6. (d) 2 : 3
7. (b) tan 30°
8. (b) 2
9. (c) $x=\frac{ay}{a+b}$
10. (c) 8cm
11. (d) $3\sqrt{3}$ cm
12. (d) $9\pi\,cm^2$
13. (c) $96\,cm^2$
14. (b) 12
15. (d) 7000
16. (b) 25
17. (c) 11/36
18. (a) 1/3
19. (b) Both Assertion (A) and Reason (R) are true and Reason (R) is not the correct explanation of Assertion (A)
20. (a) Both Assertion (A) and Reason (R) are true and Reason (R) is the correct explanation of Assertion (A)
21. Adding the two equations and dividing by 10, we get :
$x+y=10$ (½ mark)
Subtracting the two equations and dividing by –2, we get:
$x-y=1$ (½ mark)
Solving these two new equations, we get, **x = 11/2** (½ mark)
y = 9/2 (½ mark)
22. In ΔABC, $\angle 1=\angle 2$
∴ AB = BD ....(i) (½ mark)
Given,
AD / AE = AC / BD (½ mark)
Using equation (i), we get
AD / AE = AC / AB ....(ii)
In ΔBAE and ΔCAD, by equation (ii),
AC / AB = AD / AE (½ mark)
$\angle A=\angle A$ (common)
∴ $\Delta BAE \sim \Delta CAD$ [By SAS similarity criterion] (½ mark)
23. $\angle PAO=\angle PBO=90°$ (angle b/w radius and tangent) (½ mark)
$\angle AOB=105°$ (By angle sum property of a triangle) (½ mark)
$\angle AQB=½\times105°=52.5°$ (Angle at the remaining part of the circle is half the angle subtended by the arc at the centre) (1 mark)
24. We know that, in 60 minutes, the tip of minute hand moves 360°
In 1 minute, it will move = 360°/60 = 6° (½ mark)
∴ From 7 : 05 pm to 7: 40 pm i.e. 35 min, it will move through = 35 × 6° = 210° (½ mark)
∴ Area of swept by the minute hand in 35 min = Area of sector with sectorial angle θ of 210° and radius of 6 cm
$=\frac{210}{360}\times\pi\times6^2$ (½ mark)
$=\frac{7}{12}\times\frac{22}{7}\times6\times6=66\text{ cm}^2$ (½ mark)

OR

Let the measure of $\angle A$, $\angle B$, $\angle C$ and $\angle D$ be $\theta_1, \theta_2, \theta_3$ and θ_4 respectively
Required area = Area of sector with centre A + Area of sector with centre B + Area of sector with centre C + Area of sector with centre D (½ mark)
$=\frac{\theta_1}{360}\times\pi\times7^2+\frac{\theta_2}{360}\times\pi\times7^2+\frac{\theta_3}{360}\times\pi\times7^2+\frac{\theta_4}{360}\times\pi\times7^2$ (½ mark)
$=\frac{(\theta_1+\theta_2+\theta_3+\theta_4)}{360}\times\pi\times7^2$ (½ mark)
(By angle sum property of a triangle)
$=154\text{ cm}^2$ (½ mark)
25. $\sin(A+B)=1=\sin 90$, so $A+B=90$ ....(i) (½ mark)
$\cos(A-B)=\sqrt{3}/2=\cos 30$, so $A-B=30$ ....(ii) (½ mark)
From (i) & (ii) $\angle A=60°$ (½ mark)
And $\angle B=30°$ (½ mark)

OR

$\frac{\cos\theta-\sin\theta}{\cos\theta+\sin\theta}=\frac{1-\sqrt{3}}{1+\sqrt{3}}$ (½ mark)
Dividing the numerator and denominator of LHS by cosθ, we get
$\frac{1-\tan\theta}{1+\tan\theta}=\frac{1-\sqrt{3}}{1+\sqrt{3}}$ (½ mark)
Which on simplification (or comparison) gives $\tan\theta=\sqrt{3}$ (½ mark)
Or $\theta=60°$ (½ mark)
26. Let us assume $5+2\sqrt{3}$ is rational, then it must be in the form of p/q where p and q are co-prime integers and $q\neq0$ (½ mark)

i.e $5+2\sqrt{3}=p/q$ (1 mark)

So $\sqrt{3}=\dfrac{p-5q}{2q}$ ....(i)

(½ mark)

Since p, q, 5 and 2 are integers and $q\neq 0$, HS of equation (i) is rational. But LHS of (i) is $\sqrt{3}$ which is irrational.(½ mark) This is not possible. This contradiction has arisen due to our wrong assumption that $5+2\sqrt{3}$ is rational. So, $5+2\sqrt{3}$ is irrational. (½ mark)

27. Let α and β be the zeros of the polynomial $2x^2-5x-3$

Then $\alpha+\beta=5/2$ (½ mark)

And $\alpha\beta=-3/2$. (½ mark)

Let 2α and 2β be the zeros x^2+px+q (½ mark)

Then $2\alpha+2\beta=-p$

$2(\alpha+\beta)=-p$

$2\times 5/2=-p$ (½ mark)

So $p=-5$ (½ mark)

And $2\alpha\times 2\beta=q$

$4\alpha\beta=q$

So $q=4\times -3/2=-6$ (½ mark)

28. Let the actual speed of the train be x km/hr and let the actual time taken be y hours. (½ mark)

Distance covered is xy km If the speed is increased by 6 km/hr, then time of journey is reduced by 4 hours i.e., when speed is (x + 6)km/hr, time of journey is (y – 4) hours.

∴ Distance covered $=(x+6)(y-4)$

⇒ $xy=(x+6)(y-4)$

⇒ $4x+6y-24=0$

⇒ $2x+3y-12=0$ ....(i)

(½ mark)

Similarly $xy=(x-6)(y+6)$

⇒ $6x-6y-36=0$

⇒ $x-y-6=0$ ....(ii)

(½ mark)

Solving (i) and (ii) we get x = 30 and y = 24 (1 mark)

Putting the values of x and y in equation (i), we obtain Distance = (30 × 24) km = 720 km.

Hence, the length of the journey is 720 km. (½ mark)

OR

Let the number of chocolates in lot A be x

And let the number of chocolates in lot B be y (½ mark)

∴ Total number of chocolates = x + y

Price of 1 chocolate = ₹2/3 , so for x chocolates $=\dfrac{2}{3}x$ and price of y chocolates at the rate of ₹1 per chocolate = y.

∴ by the given condition $\dfrac{2}{3}x+y=400$ (½ mark)

⇒ $2x+3y=1200$ ....(i)

Similarly $= x+\dfrac{4}{5}y=460$ (½ mark)

⇒ $5x+4y=2300$ .... (ii)

Solving (i) and (ii) we get

x = 300 and y = 200

∴ $x+y=300+200=500$ (1 mark)

So, Anuj had 500 chocolates. (½ mark)

29. LHS: $\dfrac{\sin^3\theta/\cos^3\theta}{1+\sin^2\theta/\cos^2\theta}+\dfrac{\cos^3\theta/\sin^3\theta}{1+\cos^2\theta/\sin^2\theta}$ (½ mark)

$=\dfrac{\sin^3\theta/\cos^3\theta}{(\cos^2\theta+\sin^2\theta)/\cos^2\theta}+\dfrac{\cos^3\theta/\sin^3\theta}{(\sin^2\theta+\cos^2\theta)/\sin^2\theta}$

$=\dfrac{\sin^3\theta}{\cos\theta}+\dfrac{\cos^3\theta}{\sin\theta}$ (½ mark)

$=\dfrac{\sin^4\theta+\cos^4\theta}{\cos\theta\sin\theta}$ (½ mark)

$=\dfrac{(\sin^2\theta+\cos^2\theta)^2-2\sin^2\theta\cos^2\theta}{\cos\theta\sin\theta}$ (½ mark)

$=\dfrac{1-2\sin^2\theta\cos^2\theta}{\cos\theta\sin\theta}$ (½ mark)

$=\dfrac{1}{\cos\theta\sin\theta}-\dfrac{2\sin^2\theta\cos^2\theta}{\cos\theta\sin\theta}$

$\sec\theta\operatorname{cosec}\theta - 2\sin\theta\cos\theta$

= RHS (½ mark)

30. Let ABCD be the rhombus circumscribing the circle with centre O, such that AB, BC, CD and DA touch the circle at points P, Q, R and S respectively.

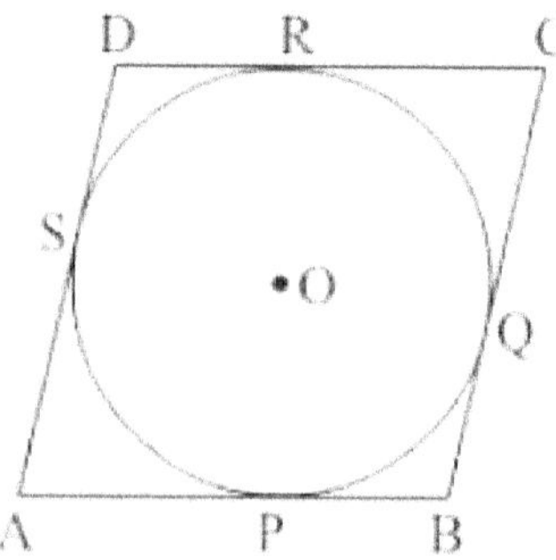

We know that the tangents drawn to a circle from an exterior point are equal in length.

$\therefore$ AP = AS ....(1)
BP = BQ ....(2)
CR = CQ ....(3)
DR = DS ....(4)
(1 mark)

Adding (1), (2), (3) and (4) we get
AP + BP + CR + DR = AS + BQ + CQ + DS
(AP + BP) + (CR + DR) = (AS + DS) + (BQ + CQ)
$\therefore$ AB + CD = AD + BC ....(5)
(1 mark)

Since AB = DC and AD = BC (opposite sides of parallelogram ABCD) putting in (5) we get, 2AB = 2AD or AB = AD.
(½ mark)

$\therefore$ AB=BC=DC=AD
Since a parallelogram with equal adjacent sides is a rhombus, so ABCD is a rhombus (½ mark)

OR

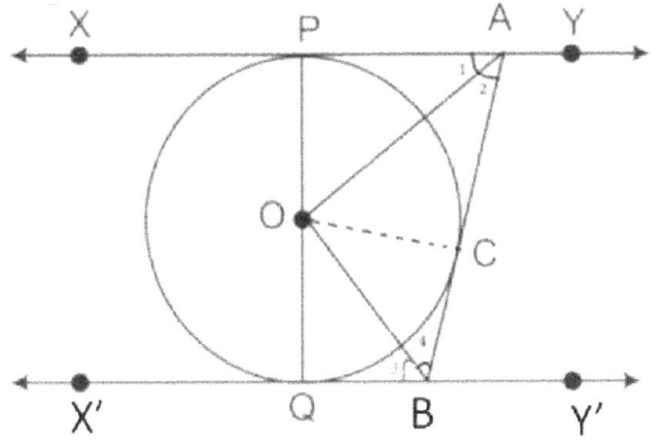

Join OC In ΔOPA and ΔOCA
OP = OC (radii of same circle)
PA = CA (length of two tangents from an external point)
(½ mark)

AO = AO (Common)
Therefore, ΔOPA ≅ ΔOCA (By SSS congruency criterion)
(½ mark)

Hence, $\angle 1 = \angle 2$ (CPCT)
Similarly $\angle 3 = \angle 4$ (½ mark)
$\angle PAB + \angle QBA = 180°$ (co interior angles are supplementary as XY ∥ X'Y') (½ mark)
$2\angle 2 + 2\angle 4 = 180°$
$\angle 2 + \angle 4 = 90°$ ....(1)
(½ mark)

$\angle 2 + \angle 4 + \angle AOB = 180°$ (Angle sum property)
Using (1), we get, $\angle AOB = 90°$

31. (i) P (At least one head) = 3/4 (1 mark)
(ii) P(At most one tail) = 3/4 (1 mark)
(iii) P(A head and a tail) = 2/4 = 1/2 (1 mark)

32. Let the time taken by larger pipe alone to fill the tank = x hours
Therefore, the time taken by the smaller pipe = x + 10 hours
(½ mark)

Water filled by larger pipe running for 4 hours = $\frac{4}{x}$ litres

Water filled by smaller pipe running for 9 hours = $\frac{9}{x+10}$ litres

We know that

$\frac{4}{x} + \frac{9}{x+10} = \frac{1}{2}$ (1 mark)

Which on simplification gives: (1 mark)
$x^2 - 16x - 80 = 0$
$x^2 - 20x + 4x - 80 = 0$
$x(x - 20) + 4(x - 20) = 0$
$(x + 4)(x - 20) = 0$
$x = -4, 20$ (1 mark)
x cannot be negative.
Thus, x = 20
x + 10 = 30 (½ mark)
Larger pipe would alone fill the tank in 20 hours and smaller pipe would fill the tank alone in 30 hours. (½ mark)

OR

Let the usual speed of plane be x km/hr (½ mark)
and the reduced speed of the plane be (x – 200) km/hr
Distance = 600 km [Given]
According to the question,
(time taken at reduced speed) - (Schedule time) = 30 minutes = 0.5 hours.

$\frac{600}{x-200} - \frac{600}{x} = \frac{1}{2}$ (1 mark)

Which on simplification gives: (1 mark)
$x^2 - 200x - 240000 = 0$
$x^2 - 600x + 400x - 240000 = 0$
$x(x - 600) + 400(x - 600) = 0$
$(x - 600)(x + 400) - 0$
$x = 600$ or $x = -400$ (1 mark)
But speed cannot be negative. (½ mark)
$\therefore$ The usual speed is 600 km/hr and (½ mark)

the scheduled duration of the flight is $\frac{600}{600}$ = 1hour (½ mark)

33. For the Theorem :

Given, To prove, Construction and figure (1½ marks)

Proof (1½ marks)

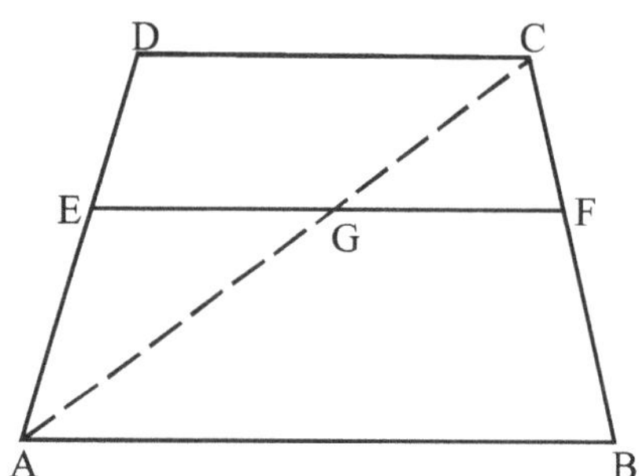

(½ mark)

Let ABCD be a trapezium DC || AB and EF is a line parallel to AB and hence to DC.

To prove: $\frac{DE}{EA} = \frac{CF}{FB}$

Construction : Join AC, meeting EF in G.

Proof :

In ΔABC, we have

GF || AB

CG/GA = CF/FB [By BPT] .....(1)

(½ mark)

In ΔADC, we have

EG || DC (EF || AB & AB || DC)

DE/EA = CG/GA [By BPT] .....(2)

(½ mark)

From (1) & (2), we get,

$\frac{DE}{EA} = \frac{CF}{FB}$ (½ mark)

34. Radius of the base of cylinder (r) = 2.8 m = Radius of the base of the cone (r)

Height of the cylinder (h) = 3.5 m

Height of the cone (H) = 2.1 m.

Slant height of conical part (l) = $\sqrt{r^2 + H^2}$

$= \sqrt{(2.8)^2 + (2.1)^2}$

$= \sqrt{7.84 + 4.41}$ (1 mark)

$= \sqrt{12.25} = 3.5$ m (1 mark)

Area of canvas used to make tent = CSA of cylinder + CSA of cone = $2 \times \pi \times 2.8 \times 3.5 + \pi \times 2.8 \times 3.5$ (1 mark)

$= 61.6 + 30.8 = 92.4 \text{m}^2$ (1 mark)

Cost of 1500 tents at ₹120 per sq.m (1 mark)

$= 1500 \times 120 \times 92.4$

= 16,632,000

Share of each school to set up the tents = 16632000/50

= ₹332,640

OR

First Solid Second Solid

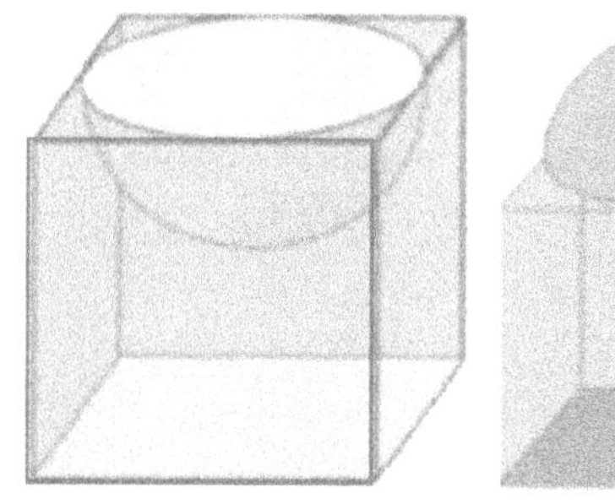

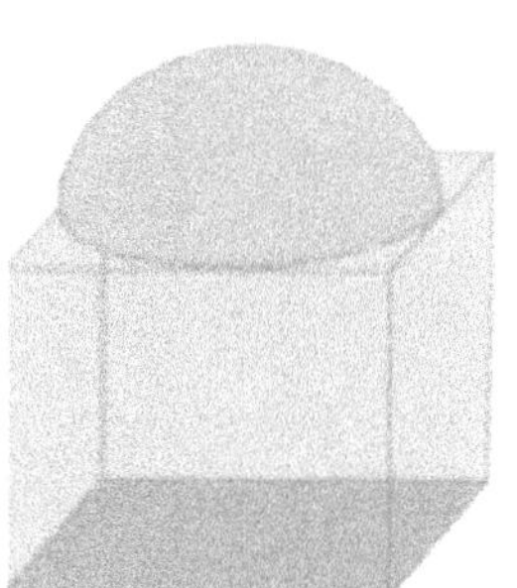

(i) SA for first new solid (S.): (1 mark)

$6 \times 7 \times 7 + 2\pi \times 3.5^2 - \pi \times 3.5^2$

$= 294 + 77 - 38.5 = 332.5 \text{ cm}^2$

SA for second new solid (S.): (1 mark)

$6 \times 7 \times 7 + 2\pi \times 3.5^2 - \pi \times 3.5^2$

$= 294 + 77 - 38.5 = 332.5 \text{ cm}^2$ (1 mark)

So $S_1 : S_2 = 1:1$

(ii) Volume for first new solid (V_1) = $7 \times 7 \times 7 - \frac{2}{3}\pi \times 3.5^3$

$= 343 - \frac{539}{6} = \frac{1519}{6} \text{cm}^2$ (1 mark)

Volume for second new solid (V_2) = $7 \times 7 \times 7 + \frac{2}{3}\pi \times 3.5^3$

$= 343 + \frac{539}{6} = \frac{2597}{6} \text{cm}^2$ (1 mark)

35. Median = 525, so Median Class = 500 – 600 (½ mark)

Class interval	Frequency	Cumulative Frequency
0-100	2	2
100-200	5	7
200-300	x	7 + x
300-400	12	19 + x
400-500	17	36 + x
500-600	20	56 + x
600-700	y	56 + x + y
700-800	9	65 + x + y
800-900	7	72 + x + y
900-1000	4	76 + x + y

(1½ marks)

$76+x+y=100 \Rightarrow x+y=24$ ....(i)
(1 mark)

$$\text{Median} = l+\frac{\frac{n}{2}-cf}{f}\times h$$ (½ mark)

Since, $l=500$, $h=100$, $f=20$, $cf=36+x$ and $n=100$
Therefore, putting the value in the Median formula, we get;

$$525 = 200+\frac{50-(36+x)}{20}\times 100$$ (½ mark)

so $x=9$
$y=24-x$ (from eq.i)
$y=24-9=15$
Therefore, the value of $x=9$ (½ mark)
and $y=15$. (½ mark)

36. (i) B(1,2), F(-2,9)
$BF^2=(-2-1)^2+(9-2)^2$
$=(-3)^2+(7)^2$
$=9+49=58$
So, $BF=\sqrt{58}$ units (1 mark)

(ii)

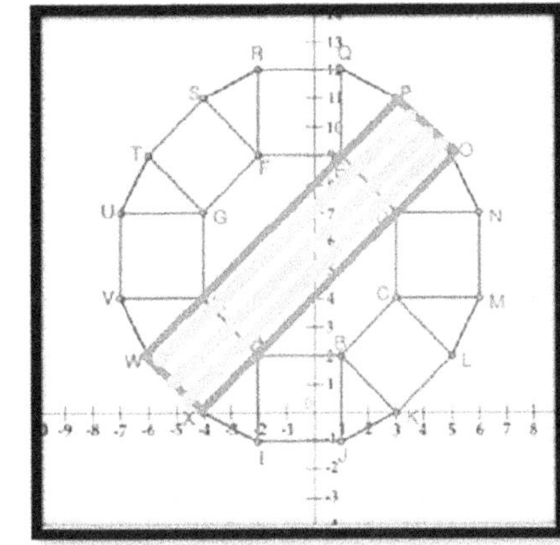

W(–6, 2), X(–4, 0), O(5, 9), P(3, 11) (½ mark)
Clearly WXOP is a rectangle
Point of intersection of diagonals of a rectangle is the mid point of the diagonals. So the required point is mid point of WO or XP

$$=\left(\frac{-6+5}{2},\frac{2+9}{2}\right)$$ (½ mark)

$$=\left(\frac{-1}{2},\frac{11}{2}\right)$$

(iii) A(–2, 2), G(–4, 7)
Let the point on y-axis be Z(0,y) (½ mark)
$AZ^2=GZ^2$ (½ mark)
$(0+2)^2+(y-2)^2=(0+4)^2+(y-7)^2$
$(2)^2+y^2+4-4y=(4)^2+y^2+49-14y$
$8-4y=65-14y$
$10y=57$
So, $y=5.7$
i.e. the required point is (0, 5.7)

OR

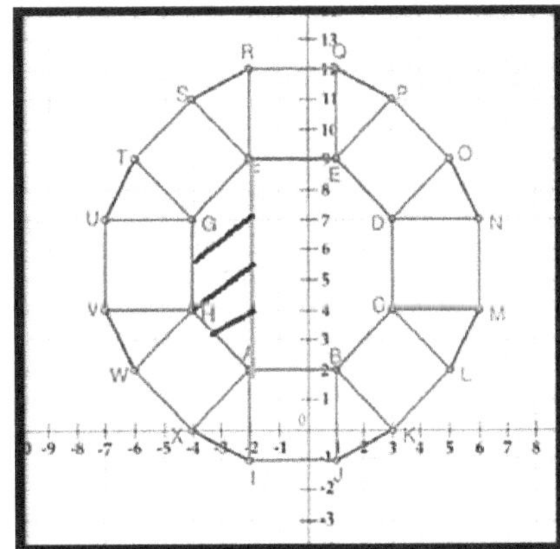

A(–2, 2), F(–2, 9), G(–4, 7), H(–4, 4)
Clearly $GH=7-4=3$units (½ mark)
$AF=9-2=7$ units (½ mark)
So, height of the trapezium AFGH = 2 units

$$\text{So, area of AFGH} = \frac{1}{2}(AF+GH)\times \text{height}$$

$$=\frac{1}{2}(7+3)\times 2$$ (½ mark)

= 10 sq. units (½ mark)

37. (i) Since each row is increasing by 10 seats, so it is an AP with first term $a=30$, and common difference $d=10$.
(½ mark)

So number of seats in 10th row $= a_{10} = a+9d$
$=30+9\times10=120$

(ii) $S_n=\frac{n}{2}(2a+(n-1)d)$ (½ mark)

$$1500=\frac{n}{2}(2\times 30+(n-1)10)$$

$3000=50n+10n^2$
$n^2+5n-300=0$ (½ mark)
$n^2+20n-15n-300=0$
$(n+20)(n-15)=0$ (½ mark)
Rejecting the negative value, $n=15$ (½ mark)

OR

No. of seats already put up to the 10th row = S_{10}

$S_{10} = \frac{10}{2}\{2 \times 30 + (10-1)10)\}$

$= 5(60 + 90) = 750$ (½ mark)

So, the number of seats still required to be put are $1500 - 750 = 750$ (½ mark)

(iii) If no. of rows = 17

then the middle row is the 9th row (½ mark)

$a_8 = a + 8d$

$= 30 + 80$

$= 110$ seats (½ mark)

38. (i)

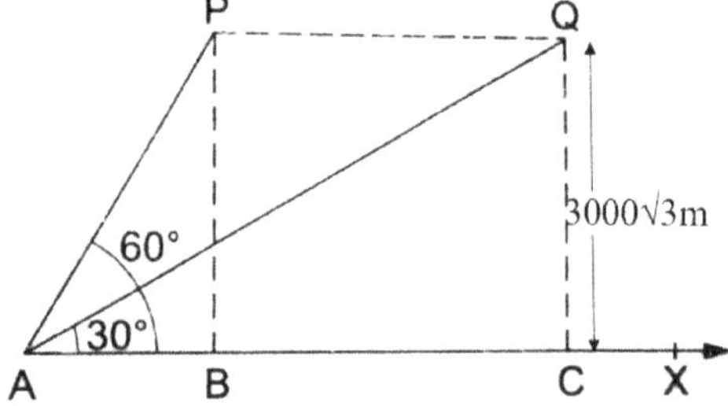

P and Q are the two positions of the plane flying at a height of $3000\sqrt{3}$ m. A is the point of observation.

(ii) In Δ PAB, tan 60° = PB/AB

Or $\sqrt{3} = 3000\sqrt{3}/AB$

So AB = 3000 m (1 mark)

tan 30° = QC/AC

$1/\sqrt{3} = 3000\sqrt{3}/AC$

AC = 9000 m (½ mark)

distance covered = 9000 – 3000

= 6000 m. (½ mark)

OR

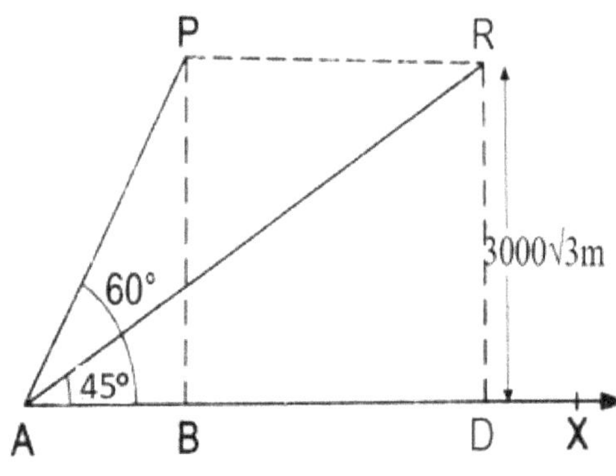

In ΔPAB, tan 60° = PB/AB

Or $\sqrt{3} = 3000\sqrt{3}/AB$ (½ mark)

So AB = 3000 m

tan 45° = RD/AD

$1 = 3000\sqrt{3}/AD$ (½ mark)

$AD = 3000\sqrt{3}$ m

distance covered = $3000\sqrt{3} - 3000$ (½ mark)

$= 3000(\sqrt{3} - 1)$ m.

(iii) speed = 6000/30 (½ mark)

= 200 m/s

= 200 × 3600/1000 (½ mark)

= 720 km/hr

Alternatively: speed = $\frac{3000(\sqrt{3}-1)}{15(\sqrt{3}-1)}$ (½ mark)

= 200 m/s

= 200 × 3600/1000 (½ mark)

= 720 km/hr

All India 2022
CBSE Board Solved Paper
Term-II

Time Allowed : 2 Hours ***Maximum Marks : 40***

General Instructions:

(i) This question paper contains **14** questions. **All** questions are compulsory.

(ii) This question paper is divided into **3** Sections - Section - A, B and C.

(iii) **Section - A** comprises of **6** questions (Q. Nos. **1 to 6**) **2** marks each. Internal choice has been provided in two questions.

(iv) **Section - B** comprises of **4** questions (Q. Nos. **7 to 10**) of **3** marks each. Internal choice has been provided in one question.

(v) **Section - C** comprises of **4** questions (Q. Nos. **11 to 14**) of **4** marks each. An internal choice has been provided in one question. It also contains two case study based questions.

(vi) Use of calculator is not permitted.

SECTION - A

Question Numbers 1 to 6 carry 2 marks each.

1. A solid piece of metal in the form of a cuboid of dimensions 11 cm × 7 cm × 7 cm is melted to form 'n' number of solid spheres of radii $\frac{7}{2}$ cm each. Find the value of n.

2. (a) In Fig., AB is diameter of a circle centered at O. BC is tangent to the circle at B. If OP bisects the chord AD and ∠AOP = 60°, then find m∠C.

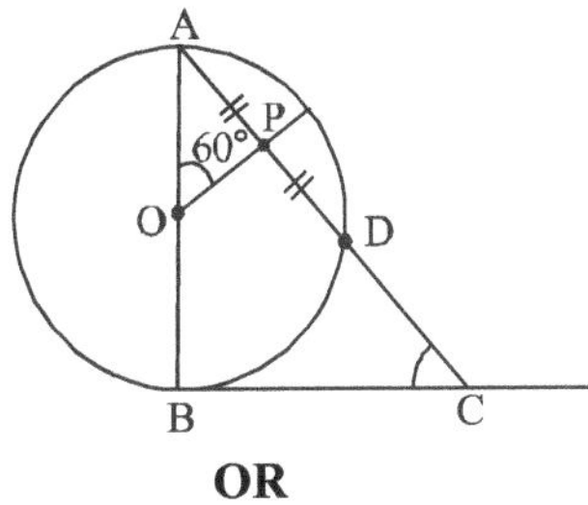

OR

(b) In Fig., XAY is a tangent to the circle centered at O. If ∠ABO = 40°, then find m∠BAY and m∠AOB.

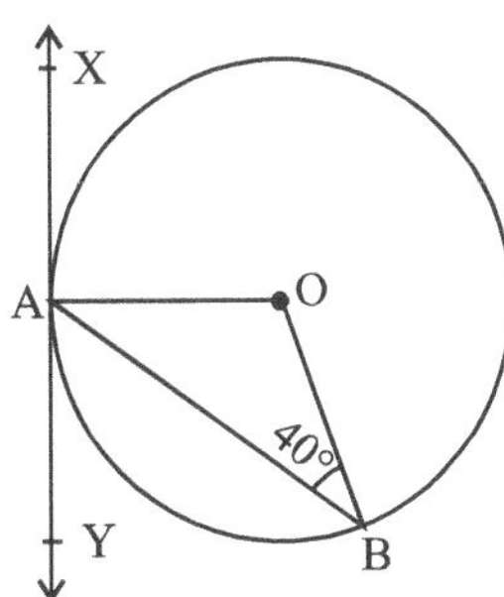

3. (a) Which term of the A.P. $-\frac{11}{2}, -3, -\frac{1}{2}, ...$ is $\frac{49}{2}$?

OR

(b) Find a and b so that the numbers

a, 7, b, 23 are in A.P.

4. Find the sum of first 20 terms of an A.P. whose n^{th} term is given as $a_n = 5 - 2n$.

5. Solve the quadratic equation: $x^2 - 2ax + (a^2 - b^2) = 0$ for x.

6. If mode of the following frequency distribution is 55, then find the value of x.

Class:	0-15	15-30	30-45	45-60	60-75	75-90
Frequency:	10	7	x	15	10	12

SECTION - B

Question Numbers from 7 to 10 carry 3 marks each.

7. Heights of 50 students of class X of a school are recorded and following data is obtained:

Height (in cm):	130-135	135-140	140-145	145-150	150-155	155-160
Number of students:	4	11	12	7	10	6

Find the median height of the students.

8. (a) The mean of the following frequency distribution is 25. Find the value of f.

Class:	0-10	10-20	20-30	30-40	40-50
Frequency:	5	18	15	f	6

OR

(b) Find the mean of the following data using assumed mean method:

Class:	0-5	5-10	10-15	15-20	20-25
Frequency:	8	7	10	13	12

9. Two men on either side of a cliff 75 m high observe the angles of elevation of the top of the cliff to be 30° and 60°. Find the distance between the two men.

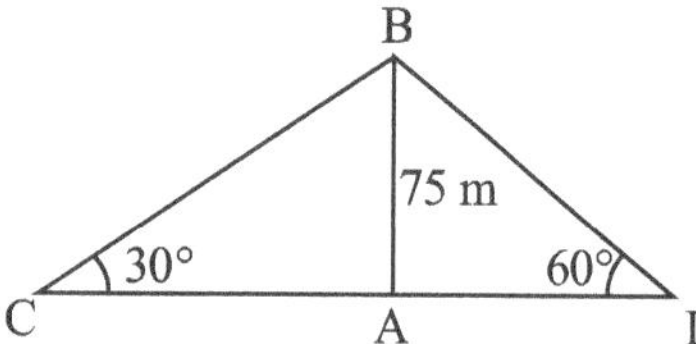

10. Construct a pair of tangents to a circle of radius 3 cm which are inclined to each other at an angle of 60°.

SECTION - C

Question Numbers from 11 to 14 carry 4 marks each.

11. (a) The sum of two numbers is 34. If 3 is subtracted from one number and 2 is added to another, the product of these two numbers becomes 260. Find the numbers.

OR

(b) The hypotenuse (in cm) of a right angled triangle is 6 cm more than twice the length of the shortest side. If the length of third side is 6 cm less than thrice the length of shortest side, then find the dimensions of the triangle.

12. In Fig., PQ is a chord of length 8 cm of a circle of radius 5 cm. The tangents at P and Q meet at a point T. Find the length of TP.

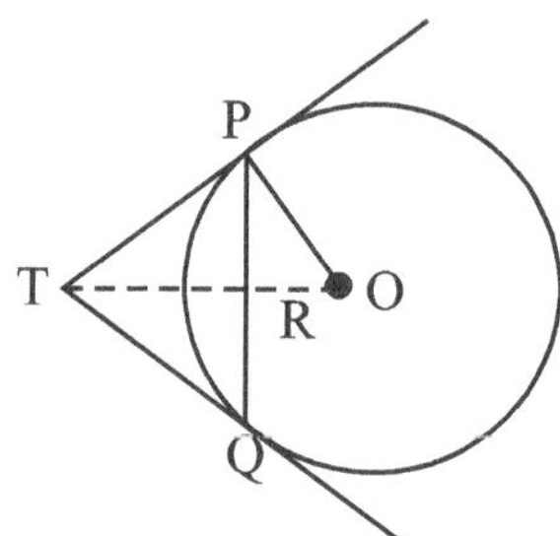

13. **Case Study-1**:

Kite Festival

Kite festival is celebrated in many countries at different times of the year. In India, every year 14th January is celebrated as International Kite Day. On this day many people visit India and participate in the festival by flying various kinds of kites.

The picture given below, shows three kites flying together.

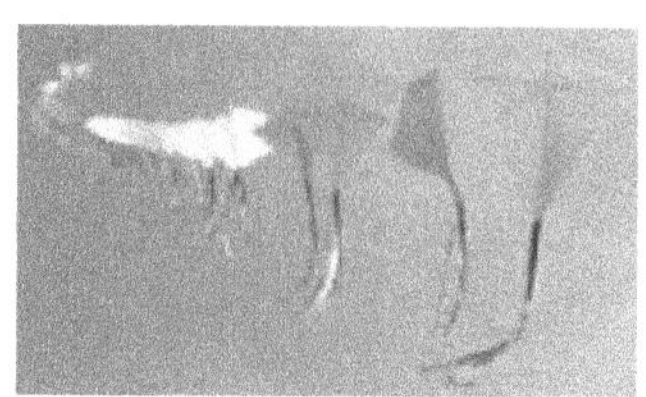

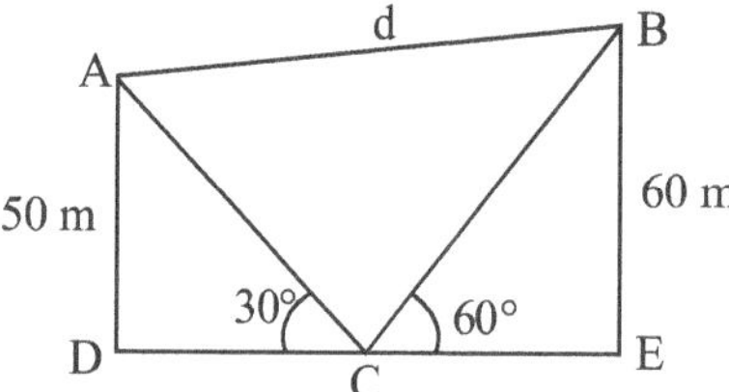

In Fig., the angles of elevation of two kites (Points A and B) from the hands of a man (Point C) are found to be 30° and 60° respectively. Taking AD = 50 m and BE = 60 m, find

(1) the lengths of strings used (take them straight) for kites A and B as shown in the figure.

(2) the distance 'd' between these two kites.

14. **Case Study-2**

A 'circus' is a company of performers who put on shows of acrobats, clowns etc. to entertain people started around 250 years back, in open fields, now generally performed in tents.

One such 'Circus tent' is shown below.

The tent is in the shape of a cylinder surmounted by a conical top. If the height and diameter of cylindrical part are 9 m and 30 m respectively and height of conical part is 8 m with same diameter as that of the cylindrical part, then find

(1) the area of the canvas used in making the tent;

(2) the cost of the canvas bought for the tent at the rate ₹ 200 per sq. m, if 30 sq m canvas was wasted during stitching.

Solutions

1. Given, the length = 11 cm, breadth = 7cm, height = 7 cm and radius of sphere = $\frac{7}{2}$ cm.

According to question,
Volume of cuboid = n × volume of sphere

$$l \times b \times h = n \times \frac{4}{3}\pi r^3$$ [1 Mark]

$$11 \times 7 \times 7 = n \times \frac{4}{3} \times \frac{22}{7} \times \frac{7}{2} \times \frac{7}{2} \times \frac{7}{2}$$

$n = 3$ [1 Mark]

Therefore, the value of n is 3.

When one solid is converted into another solid then their volume will be equal.

2(a). Since, OP bisects the chord AD.
So OP will be perpendicular to AD.

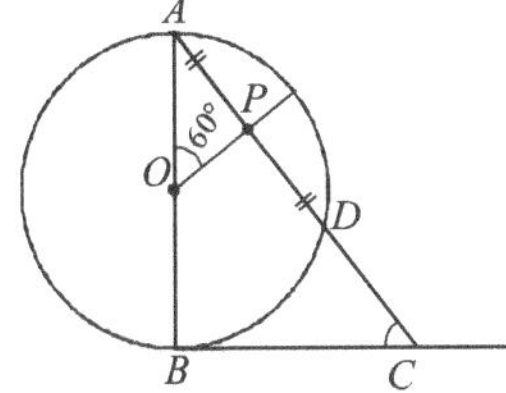

In ΔAOP

Thus $\angle OAP = 180° - 60° - 90° = 30°$ [1 Mark]

Now In ΔABC

$\angle A = 30°$

$\angle B = 90°$ (∴ BC is tangent to AB)

Thus $\angle ACB = 180 - 90 - 30 = 60°$ [1 Mark]

OR

2(b). From the given figure

$OA = OB$ (Radii of a circle)

so $\angle A = \angle B = 40°$ (each)

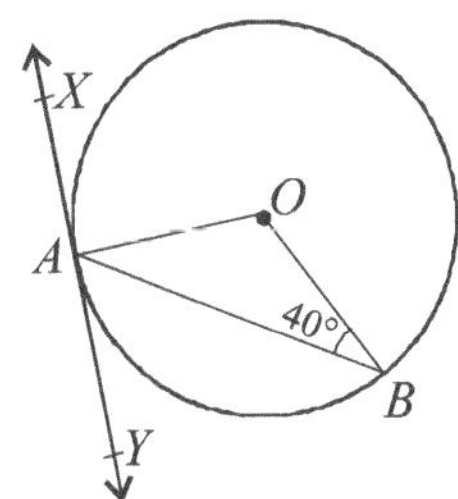

Hence $\angle A + \angle B + \angle AOB = 180°$

$M\angle AOB = 180° - 40° - 40°$

$= 100°$ [1 Mark]

Here, $\angle OAY = 90°$ (∵ XAY is tangent of OA)

and $M\angle BAY = \angle OAY - \angle OAB$

$= 90° - 40° = 50°$ [1 Mark]

3(a). Given, AP = $-\frac{11}{2}, -3, -\frac{1}{2}$, ..., Let $a_n = \frac{49}{2}$

where, $a = -\frac{11}{2}$, $d = -3 + \frac{11}{2} = \frac{5}{2}$

Apply a_n term formula,

$a_n = a + (n-1) \times d$ [1 Mark]

$$\frac{49}{2} = -\frac{11}{2} + (n-1) \times \frac{5}{2}$$

$n = 12 + 1 = 13.$ [1 Mark]

OR

3(b). Given a, 7, b, 23 are in A.P.

Then, there common difference will be equal.

$d = 7 - a = b - 7$

$7 - a = b - 7$

$a + b = 14$ .... (i) [1 Mark]

Similarly,

$b - 7 = 23 - b$

$2b = 30$

$b = 15$

From (i)

$a + 15 = 14$

$\boxed{a = -1}$ [1 Mark]

Required A.P = –1, 7, 15, 23

4. Given, $a_n = 5 - 2n$

Put $n = 1$

$a_1 = 5 - 2 \times 1 = 5 - 2 = 3$

Put $n = 20$

$a_{20} = 5 - 2 \times 20 = 5 - 40 = -35$

$$S_n = \frac{n}{2}[a + a_n]$$ [1 Mark]

Here, $n = 20$

$$S_{20} = \frac{20}{2}[3 - 35]$$

$$= \frac{20}{2} \times (-32) = -320$$

$S_{20} = -320$ [1 Mark]

5. Given, quadratic equation $x^2 - 2ax + (a^2 - b^2) = 0$.
Compare the above equation with general quadratic equation $ax^2 + bx + c = 0$
Here, $a = 1, b = -2a, c = (a^2 - b^2)$
$D = b^2 - 4ac$
$= (-2a)^2 - 4 \times 1 \times (a^2 - b^2)$ [1 Mark]
$= 4a^2 - 4a^2 + 4b^2 = 4b^2 > 0$ {real & distinct roots}
Apply quadratic formula,

$$x = \frac{-b \pm \sqrt{D}}{2a} = \frac{-(-2a) \pm \sqrt{4b^2}}{2 \times 1}$$

$$x = \frac{2a \pm 2b}{2} = a \pm b$$

Hence, $x = a + b$ and $x = a - b$ [1 Mark]

6. Given, mode = 55
Then, the modal class in the given class interval is 45–60.
Here, $l = 45, f_1 = 45, f_0 = x, f_2 = 10, h = 15$

$$\text{Mode} = l + \frac{f_1 - f_0}{2f_1 - f_0 - f_2} \times h$$ [1 Mark]

$$55 = 45 + \frac{15 - x}{(2 \times 15 - x - 10)} \times 15$$

$$10 = \frac{15(15 - x)}{(30 - x - 10)}$$

$$\frac{2}{3} = \frac{(15 - x)}{(20 - x)}$$

$40 - 2x = 45 - 3x$

$\boxed{x = 5}$ [1 Mark]

Therefore, the value of x is 5.

7.

Class interval	f_i	(C.f)	
130 – 135	4	4	
135 – 140	11	15	→ (C. f)
140 – 145	12	27	→ Median class
145 – 150	7	34	$\frac{N}{2} = \frac{50}{2} = 25$
150 – 155	10	44	
155 – 160	6	50	$l = 140$

Apply Median formula, [1 Mark]

$$\text{Median} = l + \frac{\left(\frac{N}{2} - \text{C.f}\right)}{f} \times h$$ [1 Mark]

$$= 140 + \frac{(25 - 15)}{12} \times 5$$

$$= 140 + \frac{10}{12} \times 5$$

$$= 140 + \frac{25}{6} = 140 + 4.16$$

Median = 144.16 [1 Mark]

8(a). Given, Mean = 25

Class interval	f_i	x_i	f_ix_i
0 – 10	5	5	25
10 – 20	18	15	270
20 – 30	15	25	375
30 – 40	f	35	35f
40 – 50	6	45	270
	$44 + f$		$940 + 35f$

[1 Mark]

$$\bar{x} = \frac{\sum f_ix_i}{\sum f_i} = \frac{940 + 35f}{44 + f}$$ [1 Mark]

$$25 = \frac{5(188 + 7f)}{44 + f}$$

$$5 = \frac{188 + 7f}{44 + f}$$

$220 + 5f = 188 + 7f$
$32 = 2f$

$\boxed{f = 16}$ [1 Mark]

Therefore, the value of $f = 16$

OR

8(b).

Class interval	frequency	x_i	$d_i = x_i - A$	f_id_i
0 – 5	8	2.5	–10	–80
5 – 10	7	7.5	–5	–35
10 – 15	10 A ←	12.5	0	0
15 – 20	13	17.5	5	65
20 – 25	12	22.5	10	120
	50			70

[1 Mark]

$$\bar{x} = A + \frac{\sum f_id_i}{\sum f_i}$$ [1 Mark]

$$= 12.5 + \frac{70}{50} = 12.5 + 1.4$$

$\bar{x} = 13.9$ [1 Mark]

Suppose the assume mean to middle class mark among all the class mark.

9. Let AD = 'x'm & AC = 'y'm.

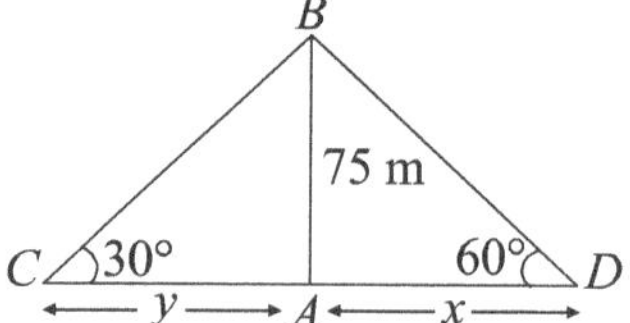

In ΔBAD

$\tan 60° = \frac{AB}{AD}$

$\sqrt{3} = \frac{75}{x}$

$x = \frac{75}{\sqrt{3}}$ m. [1 Mark]

In ΔBAC

$\tan 30° = \frac{AB}{AC}$

$\frac{1}{\sqrt{3}} = \frac{75}{y}$

$y = 75\sqrt{3}$ m. [1 Mark]

Required distance $AC = x + y$

$= \frac{75}{\sqrt{3}} \times \frac{\sqrt{3}}{\sqrt{3}} + 75\sqrt{3}$

$= 100\sqrt{3}$ m [1 Mark]

10. Steps :- [3 Marks]

(i) Draw circle of radius 3 cm.
(ii) Given, a pair of tangents construct 60° angle, then two radius construct 120° angle at the centre.
(iii) Draw tangents from points of contacts of both radii
(iv) These two tangents will intersect each other at the angle of 60°.

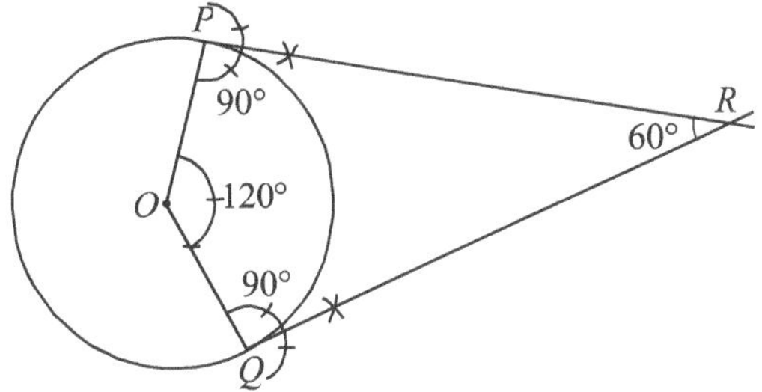

Pair of tangents PR & QR.

11(a). Let the two numbers are x and y.

$x + y = 34$ ... (i)

$(x - 3)(y + 2) = 260$

$xy + 2x - 3y - 6 = 260$

$xy + 2x - 3y = 266$ ... (ii) [1 Mark]

Multiply eq. (i) with (iii).

$3x + 3y = 102$ ... (iii)

Add equations (ii) & (iii)

$$\begin{array}{r} xy + 2x - 3y = 266 \\ 3x + 3y = 102 \\ \hline xy + 5x = 368 \end{array}$$ [1 Mark]

$x(y + 5) = 368$

$x(34 - x + 5) = 368$ $\left\{\begin{array}{l}\text{from (i)} \\ y = 34 - x\end{array}\right.$

$x(39 - x) = 368$

$-x^2 + 39x - 368 = 0$

$x^2 - 39x + 368 = 0$

$x^2 - 23x - 16x + 368 = 0$

$x(x - 23) - 16(x - 23) = 0$

$(x - 16)(x - 23) = 0$

$(x - 16) = 0, x - 23 = 0$

$x = 16, x = 23.$

From (i)

$x + y = 34$

put $x = 16, y = 34 - 16 = 18$

put $x = 23, y = 34 - 23 = 11$ [2 Marks]

Therefore, two numbers are (16, 18) and (23, 11).

OR

11(b). Let the shortest side be x cm. (Let b)

hypotenuse $= (2x + 6)$ cm.

third side $= (3x - 6)$ cm $= p$ (Let) [1 Mark]

Apply pythagoras theorem,

$H^2 = p^2 + b^2$ [2 Marks]

$(2x + 6)^2 = (3x - 6)^2 + x^2$

$4x^2 + 3b + 24x = 9x^2 + 3b - 3bx + x^2$

$10x^2 - 4x^2 - 36x - 24x = 0$

$6x^2 - 60x = 0$

$6x(x - 10) = 0$

$x = 0, x - 10 = 0$

$x = 10.$

Hence $b = 10$ cm [1 Mark]

hypotenuse $= (2x + 6) = 2 \times 10 + 6 = 26$ cm.

and, $p = (3x - 6) = 3 \times 10 - 6 = 24$ cm.

Note

We need to assume the shortest side as base 'b'. So, third side will be perpendicular 'p'.

12. Given, $PQ = 8$ cm, $OP = 5$ cm.

Since, A line joining external point to centre of circle bisect the angle between tangents drawn from that point. Here, TP & TQ are tangents with equal lengths. If join PQ then ΔTPQ is an isosceles triangle and $OT \perp PQ$.

So, $PR = RQ$.

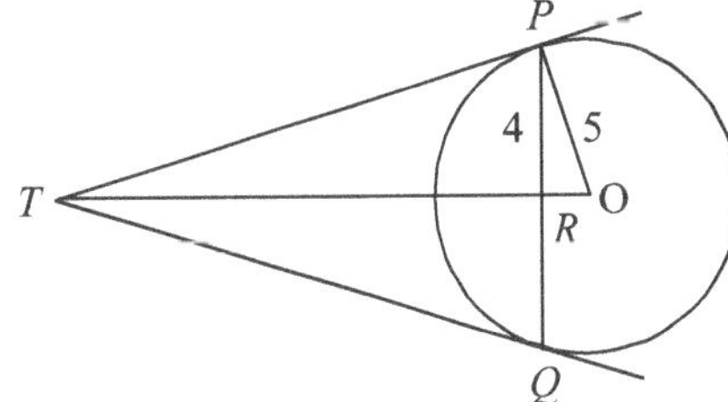

$PR = \frac{PQ}{2} = \frac{8}{2} = 4$ cm.

In ΔPRO

$PO^2 = PR^2 + RO^2$

$5^2 = 4^2 + RO^2$
$25 = 16 + RO^2$
$RO^2 = 9.$
$RO = 3$ cm. [2 Marks]
Let $TP = x$ cm, $TR = y$ cm.
In ΔPRT
$TP^2 = TR^2 + PR^2$
$x^2 = y^2 + 16$ ... (i)
In ΔTPO
$TO^2 = TP^2 + OP^2$
$(y + 3)^2 = x^2 + 25$
$y^2 + 9 + by = y^2 + 16 + 25$ {from (i)}
$6y = 32$

$$y = \frac{16}{3}$$

From (i)
$x^2 = y^2 + 16$

$$x^2 = \frac{256}{9} + 16 = \frac{256+144}{9}$$

$$x^2 = \frac{400}{9}$$

$$x = \frac{20}{3}\text{cm.}$$ [2 Marks]

Therefore, the length of TP is $\frac{20}{3}$ cm.

Case Study-1:

13(1). Given, figure of two flying kites is represented as:

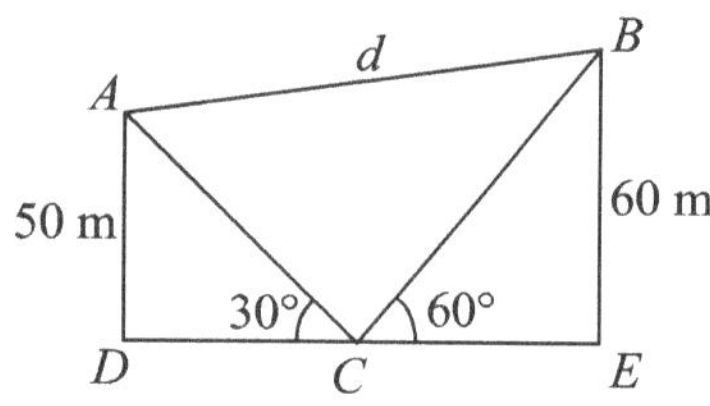

[2 Marks]

In ΔADC	In ΔBEC
$\sin 30° = \frac{P}{H} = \frac{AD}{AC}$	$\sin 60° = \frac{P}{H} = \frac{BE}{BC}$
$\frac{1}{2} = \frac{50}{AC}$	$\frac{\sqrt{3}}{2} = \frac{60}{BC}$
$AC = 100$ cm	$BC = \frac{120}{\sqrt{3}} \times \frac{\sqrt{3}}{\sqrt{3}}$
	Hence $BC = 40\sqrt{3}$m.

13(2). In the above figure $\angle ACB = 180 - (60 + 30) = 90°$
In ΔACB
$AB^2 = AC^2 + BC^2$
$d^2 = (100)^2 + (40\sqrt{3})^2$
$d^2 = 10000 + 1600 \times 3$
$d^2 = 10000 + 4800$
$d^2 = 14800$ [2 Marks]
$d = 20\sqrt{37}$m.

Case Study-2:

14(1). Given diameter of cylinder = 30 m

hence, $r = \frac{30}{2} = 15$cm.
In ΔABC
$AC^2 = AB^2 + BC^2$
$AC^2 = (8)^2 + (15)^2$
$= 64 + 225$
or $AC = 17$ m. (say, 'l') [1 Mark]
Area of canvas used = C.S.A of cone + C.S.A of cylinder.
$= \pi rl + 2\pi rh$
$= \pi r\,(l + 2h)$

$$= \frac{22}{7} \times 15\,(17 + 2 \times 9)$$

$$= \frac{22}{7} \times 15 \times 35 = 110 \times 15 = 1650\text{m}^2$$ [2 Marks]

14(2). Cost of the canvas bought of $1\text{m}^2 \rightarrow$ ₹ 200
Total area of canvas bought = $(1650 + 30)$ m^2
$= 1680$ m^2
Cost of total canvas = 1680×200
= ₹ 3,36,000 [1 Mark]

Wasted area of canvas will be included in the area of canvas used in the tent to find the total cost of canvas bought.

All India 2022 CBSE Board Solved Paper Term-I

Time Allowed : 90 Minutes *Maximum Marks : 40*

General Instructions:

(i) This question paper contains **50** questions out of which **40** questions are to be attempted. **All** questions carry equal marks.

(ii) The question paper consists of **three** Sections – Section A, B and C.

(iii) **Section - A** contains of **20** questions. Attempt any **16** questions from Q. No. **01** to **20**.

(iv) **Section - B** also contains of **20** questions. Attempt any **16** questions from Q. No. **21** to **40**.

(v) **Section - C** contains of two Case Studies containing **5** questions in each case. Attempt any **4** questions from Q. No. **41** to **45** and another **4** from Q. No. **46** to **50**.

(vi) There is only one correct option for every Multiple Choice Question (MCQ). Marks will not be awarded for answering more than one option.

(vii) There is no negative marking.

SECTION - A

Q. No. 1 to 20 are of 1 mark each. Attempt any 16 from Q. 1 to 20

1. The exponent of 5 in the prime factorisation of 3750 is
(a) 3 (b) 4 (c) 5 (d) 6

2. The graph of a polynomial P(x) cuts the x-axis at 3 points and touches it at 2 other points. The number of zeroes of P(x) is
(a) 1 (b) 2 (c) 3 (d) 5

3. The values of x and y satisfying the two equations $32x+33y=34, 33x+32y=31$ respectively are:
(a) $-1, 2$ (b) $-1, 4$ (c) $1, -2$ (d) $-1, -4$

4. If A(3, $\sqrt{3}$); B(0, 0) and C(3, k) are the three vertices of an equilateral triangle ABC, then the value of k is
(a) 2 (b) -3 (c) $-\sqrt{3}$ (d) $-\sqrt{2}$

5. In figure, DE || BC, AD = 2 cm and BD = 3 cm, then ar (ΔABC) : ar (ΔADE) is equal to

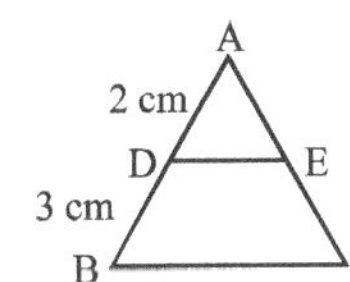

(a) 4:25 (b) 2:3 (c) 9:4 (d) 25:4

6. If $\cot\theta = \frac{1}{\sqrt{3}}$, then value of $\sec^2\theta + \text{cosec}^2\theta$ is
(a) 1 (b) $\frac{40}{9}$ (c) $\frac{38}{9}$ (d) $5\frac{1}{3}$

7. The area of a quadrant of a circle where the circumference of circle is 176 m, is
(a) 2464 m^2 (b) 1232 m^2 (c) 616 m^2 (d) 308 m^2

8. For an event E, $P(E)+P(\bar{E})=x$, then the valur of x^3-3 is
(a) -2 (b) 2 (c) 1 (d) -1

9. What is the greatest possible speed at which a girl can walk 95 m and 171 m in an exact number of minutes ?
(a) 17 m/min (b) 19 m/min
(c) 23 m/min (d) 13 m/min

10. In figure, the graph of a polynomial P(x) is shown. The number of zeroes of P(x) is

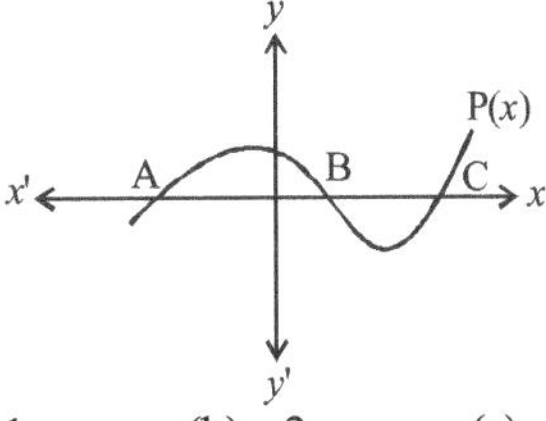

(a) 1 (b) 2 (c) 3 (d) 4

11. Two lines are given to be parallel. The equation of one of the lines is $3x - 2y = 5$. The equation of the second line can be
(a) $9x+8y=7$ (b) $-12x-8y=7$
(c) $-12x+8y=7$ (d) $12x+8y=7$

12. Three vertices of a parallelogram ABCD are A(1, 4), B(−2, 3) and C(5, 8). The ordinate of the fourth vertex D is
(a) 8 (b) 9 (c) 7 (d) 6

13. In ΔABC and ΔDEF, $\angle F = \angle C$, $\angle B = \angle E$ and $AB = \frac{1}{2}DE$.

Then the two triangles are
(a) Congruent, but not similar
(b) Similar but not congruent
(c) Neither congruent nor similar
(d) Congruent as well as similar

14. In ΔABC right angled at B, $\sin A = \frac{7}{25}$, then the value of $\cos C$ is

(a) $\frac{7}{25}$ (b) $\frac{24}{25}$ (c) $\frac{7}{24}$ (d) $\frac{24}{7}$

15. The minute hand of a clock is 84 cm long. The distance covered by the tip of minute hand from 10:10 am to 10:25 am is
(a) 44 cm (b) 88 cm (c) 132 cm (d) 176 cm

16. The probability that the drawn card from a pack of 52 cards is neither an ace nor a spade is

(a) $\frac{9}{13}$ (b) $\frac{35}{52}$ (c) $\frac{10}{13}$ (d) $\frac{19}{26}$

17. Three alarm clocks ring their alarms at regular intervals of 20 min, 25 min and 30 min respectively. If they first beep together at 12 noon, at what time will they beep again for the first time ?
(a) 4 : 00 pm (b) 4 : 30 pm
(c) 5 : 00 pm (d) 5 : 30 pm

18. A quadratic polynomial, the product and sum of whose zeroes are 5 and 8 respectively is
(a) $k[x^2 - 8x + 5]$ (b) $k[x^2 + 8x + 5]$
(c) $k[x^2 - 5x + 8]$ (d) $k[x^2 + 5x + 8]$

19. Points A(–1, y) and B(5, 7) lie on a circle with centre O(2, –3y). The values of y are
(a) 1, –7 (b) –1, 7 (c) 2, 7 (d) –2, –7

20. Given that $\sec\theta = \sqrt{2}$, the value of $\frac{1+\tan\theta}{\sin\theta}$ is

(a) $2\sqrt{2}$ (b) $\sqrt{2}$ (c) $3\sqrt{2}$ (d) 2

SECTION - B

Q. No. 21 to 40 are of 1 mark each. Attempt any 16 from Q. 21 to 40

21. The greatest number which when divides 1251, 9377 and 15628 leaves remainder 1, 2 and 3 respectively is
(a) 575 (b) 450 (c) 750 (d) 625

22. Which of the following cannot be the probability of an event ?

(a) 0.01 (b) 3% (c) $\frac{16}{17}$ (d) $\frac{17}{16}$

23. The diameter of a car wheel is 42 cm. The number of complete revolutions it will make in moving 132 km is
(a) 10^4 (b) 10^5 (c) 10^6 (d) 10^3

24. If θ is an acute angle and $\tan\theta + \cot\theta = 2$, then the value of $\sin^3\theta + \cos^3\theta$ is

(a) 1 (b) $\frac{1}{2}$ (c) $\frac{\sqrt{2}}{2}$ (d) $\sqrt{2}$

25. The ratio in which the line $3x + y - 9 = 0$ divides the line segment joining the points (1, 3) and (2, 7) is
(a) 3 : 2 (b) 2 : 3 (c) 3 : 4 (d) 4 : 3

26. If $x - 1$ is a factor of the polynomial $p(x) = x^3 + ax^2 + 2b$ and $a + b = 4$, then
(a) $a = 5, b = -1$ (b) $a = 9, b = -5$
(c) $a = 7, b = -3$ (d) $a = 3, b = 1$

27. If a and b are two coprime numbers, then a^3 and b^3 are
(a) Coprime (b) Not coprime
(c) Even (d) Odd

28. The area of a square that can be inscribed in a circle of area $\frac{1408}{7}$ cm^2 is

(a) 321 cm^2 (b) 642 cm^2 (c) 128 cm^2 (d) 256 cm^2

29. If A(4, –2), B(7, –2) and C(7, 9) are the vertices of a ΔABC, then ΔABC is
(a) equilateral triangle
(b) isosceles triangle
(c) right angled triangle
(d) isosceles right angled triangle

30. If α, β are the zeroes of the quadratic polynomial $p(x) = x^2 - (k + 6)x + 2(2k - 1)$, then the value of k, if $\alpha + \beta = \frac{1}{2}\alpha\beta$, is

(a) –7 (b) 7 (c) –3 (d) 3

31. If n is a natural number, then $2(5^n + 6^n)$ always ends with
(a) 1 (b) 4 (c) 3 (d) 2

32. The line segment joining the points P(–3, 2) and Q(5, 7) is divided by the y-axis in the ratio
(a) 3 : 1 (b) 3 : 4 (c) 3 : 2 (d) 3 : 5

33. If $a\cot\theta + b\operatorname{cosec}\theta = p$ and $b\cot\theta + a\operatorname{cosec}\theta = q$, then $p^2 - q^2 =$
(a) $a^2 - b^2$ (b) $b^2 - a^2$ (c) $a^2 + b^2$ (d) $b - a$

34. If the perimeter of a circle is half to that of a square, then the ratio of the area of the circle to the area of the square is
(a) 22 : 7 (b) 11 : 7 (c) 7 : 11 (d) 7 : 22

35. A dice is rolled twice. The probability that 5 will not come up either time is

(a) $\frac{11}{36}$ (b) $\frac{1}{3}$ (c) $\frac{13}{36}$ (d) $\frac{25}{36}$

36. The LCM of two numbers is 2400. Which of the following cannot be their HCF ?
(a) 300 (b) 400 (c) 500 (d) 600

37. In fig., PA, QB and RC are each perpendicular to AC. If $x = 8$ cm and $z = 6$ cm, then y is equal to

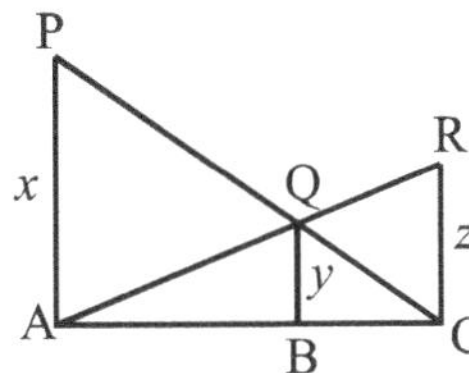

(a) $\frac{56}{7}$ cm (b) $\frac{7}{56}$ cm (c) $\frac{25}{7}$ cm (d) $\frac{24}{7}$ cm

38. In a ΔABC, $\angle A = x°$, $\angle B = (3x - 2°)$, $\angle C = y°$. Also $\angle C - \angle B = 9°$, The sum of the greatest and the smallest angles of this triangle is

(a) 107° (b) 135° (c) 155° (d) 145°

39. If $\sec\theta + \tan\theta = p$, then $\tan\theta$ is

(a) $\frac{p^2+1}{2p}$ (b) $\frac{p^2-1}{2p}$ (c) $\frac{p^2-1}{p^2+1}$ (d) $\frac{p^2+1}{p^2-1}$

40. The base BC of an equilateral ΔABC lies on the y-axis. The co-ordinates of C are (0, –3). If the origin is the mid-point of the base BC, what are the co-ordinates of A and B?

(a) $A(\sqrt{3}, 0)$; B(0, 3) (b) $A(\pm 3\sqrt{3}, 0)$; B(3, 0)

(c) $A(\pm 3\sqrt{3}, 0)$; B(0, 3) (d) $A(-\sqrt{3}, 0)$; B(3, 0)

SECTION - C

Q. No. 41 to 45 are based on Case Study-I, you have to answer any (4) four questions. Q. No. 46-50 are based on Case Study-II, you have to answer any (4) four questions.

Case Study-I

A book store shopkeeper gives books on rent for reading. He has variety of books in his store related to fiction, stories and quizzes etc. He takes a fixed charge for the first two days and an additional charge for subsequent day. Amruta paid ₹ 22 for a book and kept for 6 days, while Radhika paid ₹ 16 for keeping the book for 4 days.

Assume that the fixed charge be ₹ x and additional charge (per day) be ₹ y.

Based on the above information, answer any four of the following questions.

41. The situation of amount paid by Radhika, is algebraically represented by

(a) $x - 4y = 16$ (b) $x + 4y = 16$

(c) $x - 2y = 16$ (d) $x + 2y = 16$

42. The situation of amount paid by Amruta, is algebraically represented by

(a) $x - 2y = 11$ (b) $x - 2y = 22$

(c) $x + 4y = 22$ (d) $x - 4y = 11$

43. What are the fixed charges for a book?

(a) ₹ 9 (b) ₹ 10 (c) ₹ 13 (d) ₹ 15

44. What ar=e the additional charges for each subsequent day for a book ?

(a) ₹ 6 (b) ₹ 5 (c) ₹ 4 (d) ₹ 3

45. What is the total amount paid by both, if both of them have kept the book for 2 more days ?

(a) ₹ 35 (b) ₹ 52 (c) ₹ 50 (d) ₹ 58

Case Study-II

A farmer has a field in the shape of trapezium. whose map with scale 1 cm = 20 m, is given below :

The field is divided into four parts by joining the opposite vertices.

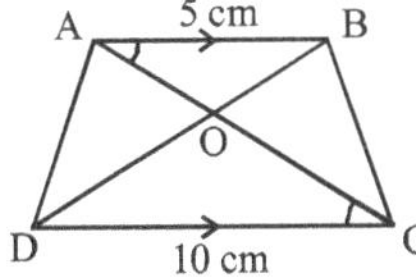

Based on the above information, answer any four of the following questions.

46. The two triangular regions AOB and COD are

(a) Similar by AA criterion

(b) Similar by SAS criterion

(c) Similar by RHS criterion

(d) Not similar

47. The ratio of the area of the ΔAOB to the area of ΔCOD, is

(a) 4 : 1 (b) 1 : 4 (c) 1 : 2 (d) 2 : 1

48. If the ratio of the perimeter of ΔAOB to the perimeter of ΔCOD would have been 1 : 4, then

(a) AB = 2 CD (b) AB = 4 CD

(c) CD = 2 AB (d) CD = 4 AB

49. If in Δs AOD and BOC, $\frac{AO}{BC} = \frac{AD}{BO} = \frac{OD}{OC}$, then

(a) $\Delta AOD \sim \Delta BOC$ (b) $\Delta AOD \sim \Delta BCO$

(c) $\Delta ADO \sim \Delta BCO$ (d) $\Delta ODA \sim \Delta OBC$

50. If the ratio of areas of two similar triangles AOB and COD is 1 : 4, then which of the following statements is true?

(a) The ratio of their perimeters is 3 : 4.

(b) The corresponding altitudes have a ratio 1 : 2.

(c) The medians have a ratio 1 : 4.

(d) The angle bisectors have a ratio 1 : 16.

Solutions

1. **(b)** Given number is 3750. [1 Mark]

Prime factorisation of $3750 = 5 \times 5 \times 5 \times 5 \times 2 \times 3$

$= 5^4 \times 2^1 \times 3^1$

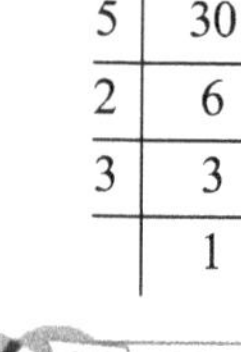

5	3750
5	750
5	150
5	30
2	6
3	3
	1

Exponent of 5 = 4.

Note

a^m, a = base

m = exponent

2. **(d)** When polynomial $P(x)$ cuts the x-axis at 3 points and touches the x-axis at 2 points, then there are two pairs of equal roots of the polynomial $P(x)$.

Intersecting graph with x-axis, then the total number of roots = 3.

Total number of distinct roots when touches the x-axis = 2.

Total number of zeroes = 3 + 2 = 5. [1 Mark]

When graph cuts the x-axis then it is considered as one zero & when touches it considered as two equal zeroes.

3. **(a)** $32x + 33y = 34$ ...(i)

$33x + 32y = 31$ ...(ii)

Apply substitution method.

$32x + 33y = 34$ {from (i)}

$33y = 34 - 32x$

$y = \frac{34}{33} - \frac{32}{33}x$ ...(iii)

Substitute the value of y in eq. (ii)

$33x + 32y = 31$

$33x + 32\left(\frac{34}{33} - \frac{32}{33}x\right) = 31$

$33x + \frac{1088 - 1024x}{33} = 31$

$1089x + 1088 - 1024x = 1023$

$65x = -65$

$x = -1$

From (iii)

$y = \frac{34}{33} - \frac{32}{33} \times (-1)$

$y = \frac{34 + 32}{33} = \frac{66}{33} = 2$ [1 Mark]

Therefore, the value of x and y are –1 and 2 respectively.

4. **(c)** Given, vertices of equilateral triangle $A(3, \sqrt{3})$; $B(0, 0)$ and $C(3, k)$.

So, AC = CB

$\sqrt{(3-3)^2 + (k - \sqrt{3})^2}$

$= \sqrt{(0-3)^2 + (0-k)^2}$

$\sqrt{(k - \sqrt{3})^2} = \sqrt{9 + k^2}$

Take square both sides,

$k^2 + 3 - 2\sqrt{3}k = 9 + k^2$

$-2\sqrt{3}k = 6$

$-\sqrt{3}k = 3$

$k = \frac{-3}{\sqrt{3}} \times \frac{\sqrt{3}}{\sqrt{3}}$

$k = -\sqrt{3}$

Therefore, the value of k is $-\sqrt{3}$. [1 Mark]

All three sides of equilateral triangle are equal.

5. **(d)** Given, DE ∥ BC

Then, $\Delta ADE \sim \Delta ABC$

Apply ratio of area theorem

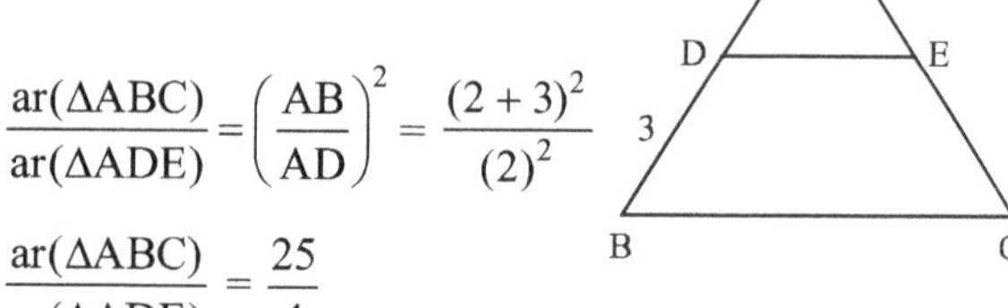

$\frac{ar(\Delta ABC)}{ar(\Delta ADE)} = \left(\frac{AB}{AD}\right)^2 = \frac{(2+3)^2}{(2)^2}$

$\frac{ar(\Delta ABC)}{ar(\Delta ADE)} = \frac{25}{4}$

Therefere, $ar(\Delta ABC) : ar(\Delta ADE) = 25 : 4$. [1 Mark]

6. **(d)** Given, $\cot\theta = \frac{1}{\sqrt{3}}$

$\cot\theta = \cot 60°$

$\theta = 60°$

$\sec^2\theta + \text{cosec}^2\theta = \sec^2 60 + \text{cosec}^2 60$

$= (2)^2 + \left(\frac{2}{\sqrt{3}}\right)^2$

$= 4 + \frac{4}{3} = \frac{12+4}{3} = \frac{16}{3} = 5\frac{1}{3}$ [1 Mark]

7. **(c)** Given, circumference of circle = 176

$2\pi r = 176$

$2 \times \frac{22}{7} \times r = 176$

$r = 28$ m

Area of quadrant $= \frac{\theta}{360} \times \pi r^2$

$= \frac{90}{360} \times \frac{22}{7} \times 28 \times 28$

$= 616$ m^2. [1 Mark]

8. **(a)** Given, $P(E) + P(\bar{E}) = x$

Sum of probabilities is 1.

so, $P(E) + P(\bar{E}) = 1$

$x^3 - 3 = (1)^3 - 3 = 1 - 3 = -2.$ [1 Mark]

Note

Sum of all probabilities is 1.

Then, x = 1.

9. **(b)** Given, distances covered by girl are 95m and 171m.

$95 = 5 \times 19$

$171 = 3 \times 3 \times 19$

H.C.F of (95, 171) = 19

Girl can cover maximum distance 19m in 1 min. Therefore, the speed is 19m/min. [1 Mark]

10. **(c)**

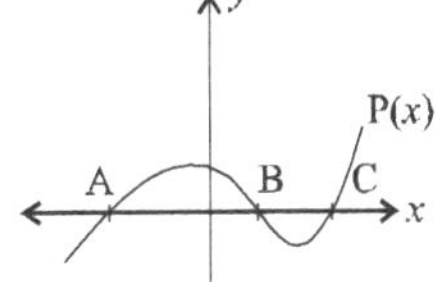

Graphs intersects at three points A, B and C. Then, the number of zeroes are 3. [1 Mark]

11. **(c)** Given, line is $3x - 2y = 5$

Take line $-12x + 8y = 7$

$-4(3x - 2y) = 7$

$3x - 2y = -\frac{7}{4}$

General form

$ax + by = c$

$ax + by = c'$

[1 Mark]

Therefore, the other parallel line is $-12x + 8y = 7$.

12. **(b)** Let D(x, y)

Mid point O $= \left(\frac{1+5}{2}, \frac{4+8}{2}\right)$

$= \left(\frac{6}{2}, \frac{12}{2}\right) = (3, 6)$

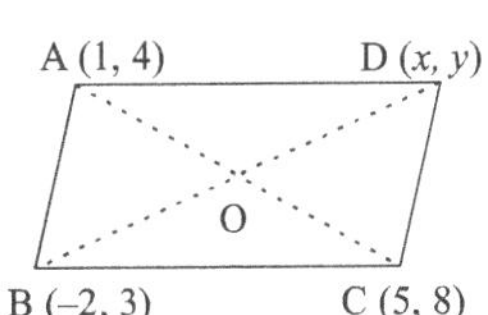

Coordinate O will also the midpoint of BD.

$3 = \frac{x-2}{2}$

$6 = x - 2$

$x = 8$

$\frac{x+3}{2} = 6$

$x + 3 = 12$

$x = 9$ [1 Mark]

Coordinate D$(x, y) \rightarrow$ D(8, 9), ordinate = 9.

Note

Ordinate stands for 'y' coordinate of the ordered pair.

13. **(b)**

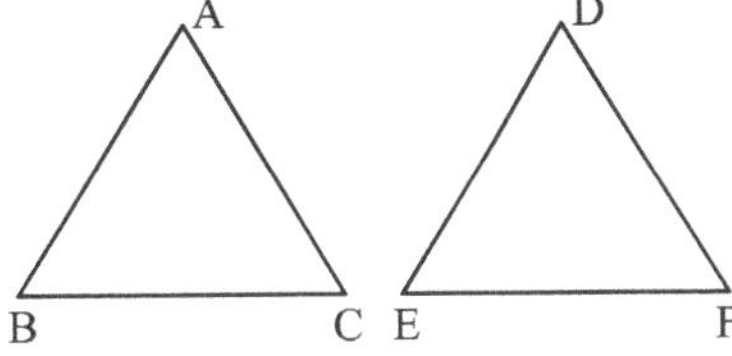

Given, $\angle T = \angle C$

$\angle B = \angle E$

Then $\Delta ABC \sim \Delta DEF$ (by AA criterion)

Then, $\frac{AB}{DE} = \frac{BC}{EF} = \frac{AC}{DF} = \frac{1}{2}$

For congruent sides should be equal. [1 Mark]

Therefore, triangles are similar but not congruent.

14. **(a)** $\sin A = \frac{7}{25} = \frac{P}{H}$

Apply pythagoras theorem

$\cos C = \frac{B}{H} = \frac{BC}{AC}$

$= \frac{7}{25}$

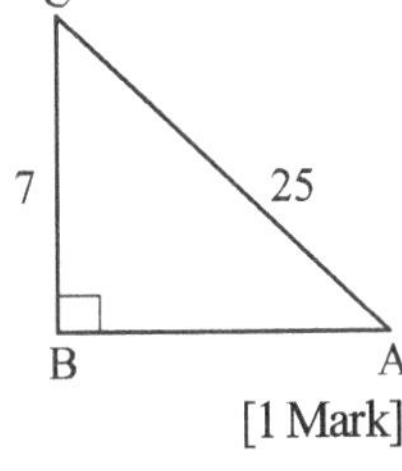

[1 Mark]

15. **(a)** Angle of 1 division $= \frac{360}{12} = 30°$

Angle between 10 : 10 am to 10 : 25 am $= 30 \times 3 = 90°$

Distance covered by minute tip $= \frac{\theta}{360} \times 2\pi r$

$= \frac{30}{360} \times 2 \times \frac{22}{7} \times 84$

$= 44$ cm [1 Mark]

Note

There are 3 divisions in the given time interval.

16. **(a)** There are total 4 ace and 13 spade in a well shuffled card.

Number of cards other than ace and spade

$= 52 - (4 + 12) = 52 - 16 = 36$

Probability $\overline{\text{(ace and spade)}} = \frac{36}{52} = \frac{9}{13}$ [1 Mark]

17. **(c)** Given, regular intervals are 20 min, 25 min and 30 min.

L.C.M of (20, 25, 30) = 2 × 5 × 2 ×3 × 5 = 300 min.

2	20, 25, 30
5	10, 25, 15
2	2, 5, 3
3	1, 5, 3
5	1, 5, 2
	1, 1, 1

They beep together at 12 noon, then they beep after 300 minutes again.

$300 \text{ min} = \frac{300}{60} = 5 \text{ h}$

All clocks will beep again together at 5 : 00 pm. [1 Mark]

18. **(c)** Given product and sum of zeroes are 5 and 8 respectively.

$P(x) = x^2 - Sx + P$

Here, S = 5, P = 8

$P(x) = x^2 - 5x + 8$ [1 Mark]

Therefore, $k[x^2 - 5x + 8]$ is the required polynomial.

When we multiply the quadratic polynomial with 'k' then it will also considered as quadratic polynomial.

19. **(b)** Centre O(2, –3y) and point A(–1, y) and B (5, 7).

OA and OB are radii of circle.

OA = OB

$$\sqrt{(-1-2)^2 + (y+3y)^2} = \sqrt{(5-2)^2 + (7+3y)^2}$$

Take square both sides.

$9 + 16y^2 = 9 + 49 + 9y^2 + 42y$

$7y^2 - 42y - 49 = 0$

$7(y^2 - 6y - 7) = 0$

$y^2 - 6y - 7 = 0$

$y^2 - 7y + y - 7 = 0$

$y(y-7) + 1(y-7) = 0$

$(y-7)(y+1) = 0$

$y = 7, -1$ [1 Mark]

Therefore, the values of y are 7 and –1.

(2 – 3y)
O

20. **(a)** $\sec\theta = \sqrt{2}$

$\sec\theta = \sec 45°$

$\theta = 45°$

Put θ = 45° in the given expression,

$$\frac{1+\tan\theta}{\sin\theta} = \frac{1+\tan 45°}{\sin 45°} = \frac{1+1}{\frac{1}{\sqrt{2}}} = 2\sqrt{2}$$ [1 Mark]

21. **(d)** Three numbers are 1251, 9377, 15628 and the respective remainders are 1, 2 & 3.

(1251 – 1) = 1250

(9377 – 2) = 9375

(15628 – 3) = 15625

H.C.F of (1250, 9375, 15625) is shown below.

1250 = 2 × 5 × 5 × 5 × 5

9375 = 3 × 5 × 5 × 5 × 5 × 5

15625 = 5 × 5 × 5 × 5 × 5× 5

H.C.F of (1250, 9375, 15625) = 5 × 5 × 5 × 5 = 625

Therefore, the greatest no. is 625. [1 Mark]

22. **(b)** Probability of an event cannot be in the percentage and cannot be greater than one. [1 Mark]

23. **(b)** Diameter of car wheel = 42 cm

$\text{radius} = \frac{42}{2} = 21 \text{ cm.}$

Let the number of revolutions is n

$n \times 2\pi r = 10^5 \times 132$ cm

$n \times 2 \times \frac{22}{7} \times 21 = 10^5 \times 132$

$n = 10^5$ [1 Mark]

Therefore, the number of revolutions are 10^5.

24. **(c)** $\tan\theta + \cot\theta = 2$

$$\frac{\sin\theta}{\cos\theta} + \frac{\cos\theta}{\sin\theta} = 2$$

$$\frac{\sin^2\theta + \cos^2\theta}{\sin\theta\cos\theta} = 2$$

$$\frac{1}{2\sin\theta\cos\theta} = 1$$

$\Rightarrow \sin 2\theta = 1$

$\sin 2\theta = \sin 90°$

$2\theta = 90°$

$\theta = 45°$

$$\sin^3\theta + \cos^3\theta = (\sin 45°)^3 + (\cos 45°)^3$$

$$= \left(\frac{1}{\sqrt{2}}\right)^3 + \left(\frac{1}{\sqrt{2}}\right)^3$$

$$= \frac{1}{2\sqrt{2}} + \frac{1}{2\sqrt{2}} = \frac{2}{2\sqrt{2}} = \frac{\sqrt{2}}{2}$$ [1 Mark]

25. **(c)** (1, 3) ———— (2, 7)

Let the ratio be $k : 1$

Apply section formula,

$$x = \frac{2k+1}{k+1}, \quad y = \frac{7k+3}{k+1}$$

These two coordinates also satisfied the line 3x + y – 9 = 0

$$3\left(\frac{2k+1}{k+1}\right) + \left(\frac{7k+3}{k+1}\right) - 9 = 0$$

$6k + 3 + 7k + 3 - 9k - 9 = 0$

$4k = 3$

$k = \frac{3}{4}$

Therefore, the required ratio is 3 : 4. [1 Mark]

26. **(b)** $p(x) = x^3 + ax^2 + 2b$

If $(x - 1)$ is the factor of the polynomial $p(x)$ then $x = 1$ is the zero of the polynomial & $p(1) = 0$ put $x = 1$ in the polynomial $p(x)$.

$p(1) = 1 + a + 2b = 0$

$a + 2b = -1$ ....(i)

$a + b = 4$ ....(ii)

Subtract (ii) from (i)

$$\begin{array}{r} a + 2b = -1 \\ a + \ \ b = 4 \\ \hline b = -5 \end{array}$$

From (ii)

$a + b = 4$

$a - 5 = 4$

$\boxed{a = 9}$ [1 Mark]

27. **(a)** Given a and b are coprime, whose H.C.F is 1.

Then, a^3 & b^3 also the coprime numbers.

Whose H.C.F is 1. [1 Mark]

28. **(c)** Area of circle $= \dfrac{1408}{7}$ cm^2

$\pi r^2 = \dfrac{1408}{7}$

$\dfrac{22}{7} \times r^2 = \dfrac{1408}{7}$

$r = 8$cm

In ΔAOB

Apply pythagoras theorem,

$AB^2 = OA^2 + OB^2$

$AB^2 = 8^2 + 8^2 = 64 + 64 = 128$

$AB = 8\sqrt{2}$ cm

Area of square $= (\text{side})^2 = \left(8\sqrt{2}\right)^2$

$= 128$ cm^2 [1 Mark]

29. **(c)** Given vertices of triangle ABC is $A(4, -2)$; $B(7, -2)$ and $C(7, 9)$

$AB = \sqrt{(-2+2)^2 + (7-4)^2} = 3$

$BC = \sqrt{(7-7)^2 + (9+2)^2} = 11$

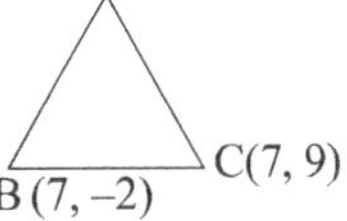

$AC = \sqrt{(7-4)^2 + (9+2)^2} = \sqrt{130}$

Apply pythagoras theorem,

$AC^2 = AB^2 + BC^2$

$\left(\sqrt{130}\right)^2 = (3)^2 + (11)^2$

$130 = 9 + 121$

$130 = 130$ [1 Mark]

So, these vertices forms the right angle triangle.

We cannot say anything about triangle by coordinates. So, we need to find distances by using the coordinates.

30. **(b)** $p(x) = x^2 - (k + 6)x + 2(2k - 1)$

$\alpha + \beta = \dfrac{-b}{a}$

$\alpha + \beta = \dfrac{(k+6)}{1} = k + 6$

$\alpha\beta = \dfrac{c}{a} = 2(2k - 1)$

$\alpha + \beta = \dfrac{1}{2}\alpha\beta$

$(k+6) = \dfrac{1}{2} \times 2(2k-1)$

$k + 6 = 2k - 1$

$\boxed{7 = k}$

Therefore, the value of k is 7. [1 Mark]

31. **(d)** Number $2(5^n + 6^n)$ contains power n to the base 5 and 6. For every $n \in N$ 5^n ends with 5 and 6^n ends with 6. Sum of 5 & 6 is 11, then $2 \times 11 = 22$. [1 Mark]

Therefore, the number always ends with 2.

32. **(d)** Given points of the line PQ is $P(-3, 2)$ & $Q(5, 7)$

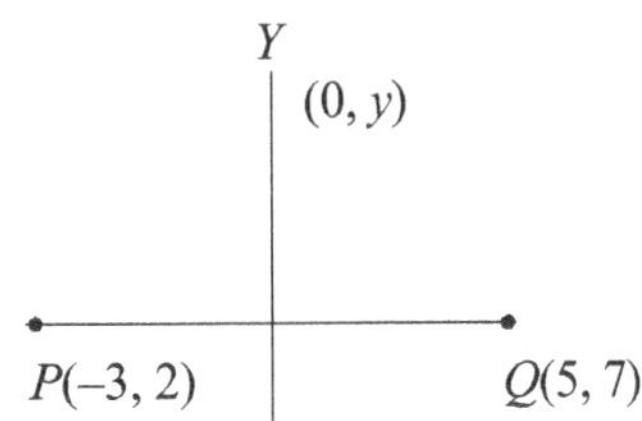

Let the ratio be $k : 1$

$x = \dfrac{k \times 5 + 1 \times (-3)}{k+1}$

$0 = \dfrac{5k - 3}{k+1}$

$5k - 3 = 0$

$5k = 3$

$k = \dfrac{3}{5}$

Therefore, the ratio is 3 : 5 [1 Mark]

33. **(b)** $a \cot\theta + b \operatorname{cosec}\theta = p$ ..... (i)

$b \cot\theta + a \operatorname{cosec}\theta = q$ ..... (ii)

$p^2 - q^2 = (p - q)(p + q)$ .....(iii)

Add (i) & (ii)

$p + q = (a + b)\cot\theta + (a + b)\operatorname{cosec}\theta$

$p + q = (a + b)(\cot\theta - \operatorname{cosec}\theta)$

Subtract (i) & (ii)

$p - q = (a - b)(\cot\theta - \operatorname{cosec}\theta)$

Substitute the values in eq. (iii)

$(p^2 - q^2) = (p - q)(p + q)$

$= [(a - b)(\cot\theta - \operatorname{cosec}\theta)][(a + b)(\cot\theta + \operatorname{cosec}\theta)]$

$= (a^2 - b^2)(\cot^2\theta - \operatorname{cosec}^2\theta)$

$p^2 - q^2 = -(a^2 - b^2) = b^2 - a^2$ [1 Mark]

34. **(d)** Perimeter of circle $= \frac{1}{2}$(Perimeter of square)

$$2\pi r = \frac{1}{2} \times a \times 4$$

$$\frac{a}{r} = \frac{22}{7} \Rightarrow \frac{r}{a} = \frac{7}{22} \quad \text{......(i)}$$

$$\frac{\textit{area of circle}}{\textit{area of square}} = \frac{\pi r^2}{a^2}$$

$$= \frac{22}{7} \times \frac{7}{22} \times \frac{7}{22} \quad \text{[from (i)]}$$

$$= \frac{7}{22}$$

Required ratio is 7 : 22 [1 Mark]

35. **(d)** Total sample space $= 6^2 = 36$

$$S = \begin{cases} (1, 1)\ (1, 2)\ (1, 3)\ (1, 4)\ (1, 5)\ (1, 6) \\ (2, 1)\ (2, 2)\ (2, 3)\ (2, 4)\ (2, 5)\ (2, 6) \\ (3, 1)\ (3, 2)\ (3, 3)\ (3, 4)\ (3, 5)\ (3, 6) \\ (4, 1)\ (4, 2)\ (4, 3)\ (4, 4)\ (4, 5)\ (4, 6) \\ (5, 1)\ (5, 2)\ (5, 3)\ (5, 4)\ (5, 5)\ (5, 6) \\ (6, 1)\ (6, 2)\ (6, 3)\ (6, 4)\ (6, 5)\ (6, 6) \end{cases}$$

P(5 not come either time) $= \frac{25}{36}$ [1 Mark]

36. **(c)** LCM = 2400

HCF of two numbers will always divide the LCM of two numbers.

Factors of 2400 = 2 × 2 × 2 × 2 × 2 × 3 × 5 × 5

2 × 2 × 5 × 5 × 3 = 300

2 × 2 × 5 × 5 × 3 × 2 = 600

2 × 2 × 5 × 5 × 2 × 2 = 400

As per options, it will give all numbers except 500.

[1 Mark]

37. **(d)**

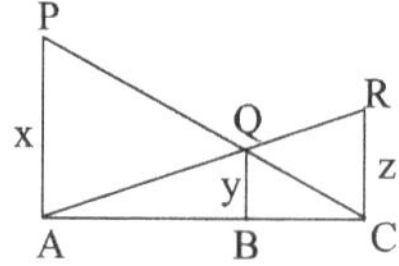

Here, AP ⊥ AC, QB ⊥ AC, RC ⊥ AC

Then AP || BQ, BQ || RC, AP || RC.

Given, $x = 8$ cm, $z = 6$ cm.

In ΔAQP & ΔRQC.

∠PQA = ∠RQC [vertically opp. angle]

∠QPA = ∠QCR [alternate interior angle]

ΔAQP ~ ΔRQC [by AA criterion]

So, $\frac{AP}{CR} = \frac{AQ}{RQ}$

$$\frac{x}{z} = \frac{AQ}{RQ}$$

$$\frac{8}{6} = \frac{AQ}{RQ} \quad \text{..... (i)}$$

In ΔABQ & ΔACR.

∠A = ∠A [common]

∠AQB = ∠ARC [corresponding angle]

ΔABQ ~ ΔACR [by AA criterion]

$$\frac{BQ}{CR} = \frac{AQ}{AR} \quad \text{..... (ii)}$$

from (i)

$$\frac{8}{6} = \frac{AQ}{RQ} \Rightarrow \frac{RQ}{AQ} = \frac{6}{8}$$

Add both side 1

$$\frac{8+6}{8} = \frac{AQ+RQ}{AQ}$$

$$\frac{14}{8} = \frac{AR}{AQ} \Rightarrow \frac{AQ}{AR} = \frac{8}{14}$$

Substitute the value in eq. (ii)

$$\frac{y}{z} = \frac{8}{14}$$

$$\frac{y}{6} = \frac{8}{14}$$

$y = \frac{24}{7}$ cm. [1 Mark]

38. **(a)** Sum of all angles of triangle is 180°

∠A + ∠B + ∠C = 180°

$x + 3x - 2 + y = 180°$

$4x + y = 182$ .... (i)

∠C – ∠B = 9° (Given)

$y - 3x + 2 = 9$

$-3x + y = 7$

$3x - y = -7$ .... (ii)

Add (i) and (ii)

$4x + y = 182$

$3x - y = -7$

$7x = 175$

$x = 25$

From (ii)

$3x - y = -7$

$3 \times 25 - y = -7$

$75 + 7 = y$

$y = 82°$

∠A = $x°$ = 25° → Smallest angle

∠B = $(3x - 2)°$ = 3 × 25 – 2 = 75 – 2 = 73°

∠C = $y°$ = 82° → Greatest angle

Sum of ∠A + ∠C = $x + y$

= 25 + 82

= 107° [1 Mark]

39. **(b)** $\sec\theta + \tan\theta = p$ ...(i)

$$\frac{1}{\sec\theta + \tan\theta} = \frac{1}{p}$$

$$\frac{1}{\sec\theta + \tan\theta} \times \frac{\sec\theta - \tan\theta}{\sec\theta - \tan\theta} = \frac{1}{p}$$

$$\frac{\sec\theta - \tan\theta}{\sec^2\theta - \tan^2\theta} = \frac{1}{p} \quad \therefore \{\sec^2\theta - \tan^2\theta = 1\}$$

$\sec\theta - \tan\theta = \frac{1}{p}$ ...(ii)

Subtract (ii) from (i)

$\sec\theta + \tan\theta = p$

$\sec\theta - \tan\theta = \frac{1}{p}$

$-\quad + \quad -$

$2\tan\theta = p - \frac{1}{p}$

$\tan\theta = \left(\frac{p^2-1}{2p}\right)$ [1 Mark]

40. **(c)** Given origin is the midpoint of the line BC.

Let B(0, y) and A(x, 0).

Apply midpoint formula.

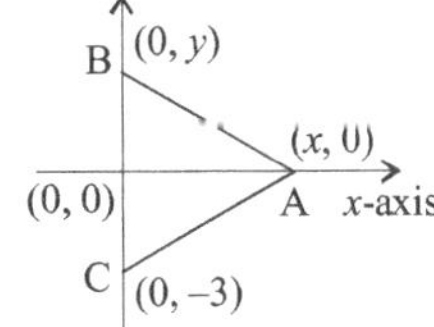

$0 = \frac{y-3}{2} \Rightarrow y = 3$

$\Rightarrow B \rightarrow (0, 3)$

ΔABC is an equilateral triangle.

AB = BC

$\sqrt{(x-0)^2 + (0-3)^2} = \sqrt{(0-0)^2 + (-3-3)^2}$

$\sqrt{x^2+9} = \sqrt{36}$

Take square both sides,

$x^2 + 9 = 36$

$x^2 = 27 \Rightarrow x \pm 3\sqrt{3}$

$A = (\pm 3\sqrt{3}, 0)$ [1 Mark]

Case Study - I

41. **(d)** Let the fixed charge for first two days be ₹ x and additional charges be ₹ y per day.

Radhika situation algebraically represented as

$x + 2y = 16.$ [1 Mark]

42. **(c)** According to question, Amruta situation represented as $x + 4y = 22$. [1 Mark]

43. **(b)** System of linear equations are represented as:

$x + 4y = 22$ ...(i)

$x + 2y = 16$ ...(ii)

Subtract (ii) from (i) by using elimination method,

$x + 4y = 22$

$x + 2y = 16$

$-\quad -$

$2y = 6$

$y = 3$

From (ii)

$x + 2y = 16$

$x + 2 \times 3 = 16$

$x + 6 = 16$

$x = 10$

Fixed charges is ₹ 10. [1 Mark]

44. **(d)** From solution Q. 43, the value of additional charges $y = 3$. [1 Mark]

45. **(c)** If both of them kept book for 2 more day at ₹ 3 per day then the total amount paid by both is represented as.

Amount of 2 more days for Amruta = 2 × 3 = ₹ 6

Amount of 2 more days for Radhika = 2 × 3 = ₹ 6

Total amount paid by both = 22 + 16 + 6 + 6

= ₹ 50. [1 Mark]

Case Study - II

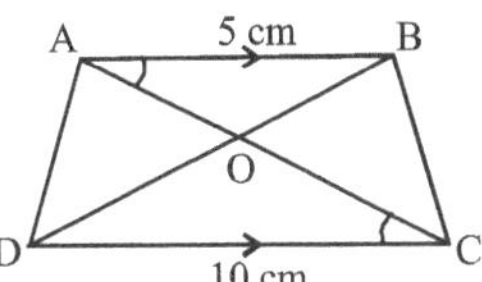

Common solution:

In ΔAOB and ΔCOD

$\angle$AOB = $\angle$COD (Vertically opposite angle)

$\angle$OAB = $\angle$OCD (Alternate interior angle)

ΔAOB ~ ΔCOD (by AA criterion)

So, $\frac{AB}{CD} = \frac{AO}{CO} = \frac{OB}{OD}, \frac{AB}{CD} = \frac{5}{10} = \frac{1}{2}$.

46. **(a)** Given ΔAOB and ΔCOD are similar by AA criterion. [1 Mark]

47. **(b)** As ΔAOB and ΔCOD are similar, then the ratio their corresponding sides will also equal.

So, $\frac{AO}{CO} = \frac{OB}{OD} = \frac{AB}{CD} = \frac{5}{10} = \frac{1}{2}$

By ratio of area of similar triangle theorem,

$\frac{ar(\Delta AOB)}{ar(\Delta COD)} = \left(\frac{AB}{CD}\right)^2 = \left(\frac{1}{2}\right)^2 = \frac{1}{4}$

ar(ΔAOB) : ar (ΔCOD) = 1 : 4 [1 Mark]

48. **(d)** Given $\frac{OA + OB + AB}{OC + OD + CD} = \frac{1}{4}$, then the ratio of their corresponding sides also be 1 : 4.

So, $\frac{AB}{CD} = \frac{1}{4}$ {If we add numerator and denominator. individually of the ratio of sides then, it will give the same ratio of the perimeter.}

CD = 4AB [1 Mark]

Ratio of corresponding sides of two similar triangles will also equal to the ratio of their perimeters.

49. **(b)** In ΔAOD and ΔBOC,

$$\frac{AO}{BC}=\frac{AD}{BO}=\frac{OD}{OC} \text{ (Given)}$$

So, the representation of triangles would be:

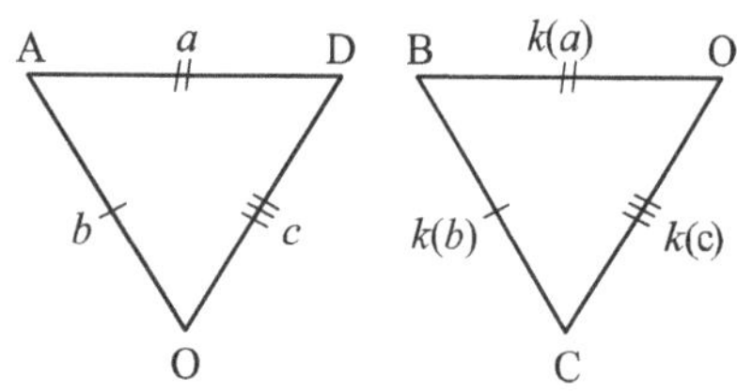

Therefore, $\Delta AOD \sim \Delta BCO$
(by SSS proportional criterion). [1 Mark]

50. **(b)** Given, ratio of areas of two similar triangles is 1 : 4.

$$\frac{ar(\Delta AOB)}{ar(\Delta COD)}=\left(\frac{AB}{CD}\right)^2$$

$$\frac{1}{4}=\left(\frac{AB}{CD}\right)^2$$

$$\frac{AB}{CD}=\frac{1}{2}=\frac{\text{alt. of } \Delta AOB}{\text{alt. of } \Delta COD}$$ [1 Mark]

The ratio of sides of two similar triangles will also equal to the ratio of their corresponding altitudes.

CBSE TOPPER-2020

Answer Sheet

परीक्षार्थी प्रवेश-पत्र के अनुसार भरें

Subject: MATHEMATICS STANDARD

Subject Code: 041

Day & Date of the Examination: THURSDAY 12.3.2020

Medium of answering the paper: ENGLISH

Code Number	Set Number
30/5/2	① ● ③ ④

No. of supplementary answer-book(s) used: –

Person with Benchmark Disabilities Yes / No: NO

Category of Disability: –

Whether writer provided Yes / No: NO

If Visually challenged, name of software used: –

Each letter be written in one box and one box be left blank between each part of the name. In case Candidate's Name exceeds 24 letters, write first 24 letters.

Space for office use

3

SECTION - D

(40) choice - ①

$P(x) = 2x^4 - x^3 - 11x^2 + 5x + 5.$

Given zeroes: $\sqrt{5}, -\sqrt{5}.$

Sum of zeroes $= \sqrt{5} - \sqrt{5} = 0$

Product of zeroes $= \sqrt{5} \times -\sqrt{5} = -5.$

$g(x) = x^2 + 0x - 5$

$$\begin{array}{r} 2x^2 - 1x - 1 \\ x^2+0x-5 \overline{\smash{)}\, 2x^4 - x^3 - 11x^2 + 5x + 5} \\ -2x^4 + 0x^3 + 10x^2 \\ \hline 0 - x^3 - 1x^2 + 5x + 5 \\ + x^3 + 0x^2 \mp 5x \\ \hline 0 - 1x^2 \pm 0x + 5 \\ +1x^2 + 0x \mp 5 \\ \hline 0 \quad 0 \quad 0 \end{array}$$

$g(x) = 2x^2 - 1x - 1$

$g(x) = 0$

$2x^2 - 1x - 1 = 0$

$2x^2 - 2x + 1x - 1 = 0$

$2x(x-1) + 1(x-1) = 0$

$x = 1$

$x = \frac{-1}{2}$

Ans: The other zeroes of $P(x)$ are: $1, \frac{-1}{2}$

Zeroes of $P(x)$: $\sqrt{5}, -\sqrt{5}, 1, \frac{-1}{2}$

9) A, B, C, D, 1, 2

Given: Right ΔABC, $\angle B = 90^\circ$

To Prove: $AC^2 = AB^2 + BC^2$

Construction:

Draw $BD \perp AC$.

Proof:

In ΔABC and ΔADB,

$\angle ABC = \angle ADB = 90^\circ$

$\angle 1 = \angle 1$ (common)

$\therefore \Delta ABC \sim \Delta ADB$ (AA)

by CPST, $\frac{AB}{AD} = \frac{BC}{DB} = \frac{AC}{AB}$

$\Rightarrow \frac{AB}{AD} = \frac{AC}{AB}$

$AB^2 = AC . AD \rightarrow (1)$

In ΔABC and ΔBDC

$\angle ABC = \angle BDC = 90^\circ$

$\angle 2 = \angle 2$ (common)

$\therefore \Delta ABC \sim \Delta BDC$ (AA)

by CPST, $\frac{AB}{BD} = \frac{BC}{DC} = \frac{AC}{BC}$

$\frac{BC}{DC} = \frac{AC}{BC} \Rightarrow BC^2 = AC . DC \rightarrow (2)$

Adding (1) and (2),

$$AB^2 + BC^2 = AC.AD + AC.DC$$

$$AB^2 + BC^2 = AC(AD + DC)$$

$$AB^2 + BC^2 = AC^2 \text{ //}$$

Hence Proved.

(8)

A, h, B, 20m, 60°, 45°, P, x, C

Let AB → Transmission tower

BC → Building - 20m

P → Point on the ground.

In ΔPBC, $\angle C = 90°$

$\tan 45° = \frac{20}{x} \Rightarrow 1 = \frac{20}{x}$

$x = 20m.$

In ΔPAC, $\angle C = 90°$

$\tan 60° = \frac{h+20}{x}$

$\frac{20+h}{20} = \sqrt{3}$

$h = 20\sqrt{3} - 20$

7

$h = 20(\sqrt{3}-1)$

$h = 14.64m.$

Ans :- Height of transmission tower = 14.64m

Choice-1

(37)

Age (in yrs) (C.I)	No. of persons (f)	Less than	c.f
0 - 10	5	< 10	5
10 - 20	15	< 20	20
20 - 30	20	< 30	40
30 - 40	25	< 40	65
40 - 50	15	< 50	80
50 - 60	11	< 60	91
60 - 70	9	< 70	100
	100		

$65 + 15 = 80$

Median Age :

$$L + \left(\frac{\frac{n}{2} - cf}{f}\right) \times h \Rightarrow 30 + \frac{50-40}{25} \times 10$$

$$\Rightarrow 30 + \frac{100}{25} \Rightarrow 34 \text{ years}$$

2020

Median of the distribution: 34 years (by graph and calculation)

(36)

10cm

7cm

For Hemisphere:

$r = 7cm$

For cone:

$h = 10cm$

$r = 7cm$

$l = \sqrt{100+49} = 12.2 cm$

Volume of the toy: Volume of cone + Volume of hemisphere

$\frac{1}{3}\pi r^2 h + \frac{2}{3}\pi r^3$

$\frac{1}{3}\pi r^2 (h + 2r)$

$\frac{1}{3} \times \frac{22}{7} \times 7 \times 7 (10 + 14)$

$\frac{1}{3} \times \frac{22}{7} \times 7 \times 7 \times 24^{8}$

$\Rightarrow 1232 cm^3$

9

Area of coloured sheet required : CSA of cone + CSA of hemisphere

$\Rightarrow \pi r l + 2\pi r^2$

$\Rightarrow \pi r(l+2r)$

$\Rightarrow \frac{22}{7} \times 7 (12.2 + 14)$

$\Rightarrow \frac{22}{7} \times 7 \times 26.2$

$\Rightarrow 576.4 \text{ cm}^2$

Ans: Volume of the toy = 1232 cm^3

Area of coloured sheet required = 576.4 cm^2.

(35) For motorboat:

Speed in still water = 18 km/hr

let speed of stream = x km/hr

upstream speed = $18 - x$ km/hr

downstream speed = $18 + x$ km/hr.

10

$t = \frac{d}{s}$

$\frac{24}{18-x} - \frac{24}{18+x} = 1$

$24\left(\frac{1}{18-x} - \frac{1}{18+x}\right) = 1$

$\frac{18+x-18+x}{(18-x)(18+x)} = \frac{1}{24}$

$\frac{2x}{324-x^2} = \frac{1}{24}$

$48x = 324 - x^2$

$x^2 + 48x - 324 = 0.$

$(x+54)(x-6) = 0.$

$x = -54$ (invalid - speed cannot be negative)

$x = 6$

Ans: Speed of the stream = 6 km/hr.

11

SECTION-C

(34) (i) Total numbers of 'Numbers' on spinner = 6
'Even numbers' = 5

P(Shweta being allowed to pick a marble) = $\frac{\text{No. of favourable outcomes}}{\text{Total number of outcomes}}$

Ans: Probability of being allowed to pick a marble $\Rightarrow \frac{5}{6}$

(ii) Total numbers of marbles = 20
black marbles = 6.

P(Sweta winning a prize) = $\frac{6}{20} \Rightarrow \frac{3}{10} \Rightarrow 0.3$ $\left\{\frac{\text{Number of favourable outcomes}}{\text{Total number of outcomes}}\right\}$

Ans: Probability of getting a prize = $\frac{3}{10}$

(33) $a = 54$

$d = -3$

$a_n = 0$

$a_n = 0$

$a + (n-1)d = 0$

$54 - 3(n-1) = 0$

$3(n-1) = 54$

$n = 19$

Ans: $n = 19$

$a_{19} = 0$

$S_n = \frac{n}{2}[2a + (n-1)d]$

$S_n = \frac{n}{2}[108 - 3(n-1)]$

$S_n = \frac{n}{2}[108 - 3n + 3] \Rightarrow \frac{n}{2}(111 - 3n)$

WITH GRAPH PAPER

13

Here, $n = 19$

$S_{19} = \frac{19}{2}[111 - 57]$

$S_{19} = \frac{19}{2} \times 54$ (27)

Ans: $S_{19} = 513$

Ans: $n = 19$

$S_n = S_{19} = 513.$

(33) choice - (1)

k : 1

A(6, -4) P(0, y) B(-2, -7)

Let the y axis meet the line segment joining points A(6, -4) and B(-2, -7) be P(0, y).

Let P divide AB in the ratio k:1.

14 A P(x, y)

coordinates of P: $P\left(\frac{-2k+6}{k+1}, \frac{-7k-4}{k+1}\right)$

$\frac{-2k+6}{k+1} = 0$

$-2k+6=0$

$2k=6$

$k=\frac{3}{1}$

Ans: Ratio in which y axis divides AB = 3 : 1

$y = \frac{-7(3)-4}{(3)+1}$

$y = \frac{-21-4}{4}$

$y = \frac{-25}{4}$

Ans: Point of intersection of y axis and line segment = $P\left(0, \frac{-25}{4}\right)$.

15

(31) $870 - 3 = 867$

$258 - 3 = 255$

HCF(867, 255) by Euclid's Division Algorithm:

$867 = 255 \times 3 + 102$

$255 = 102 \times 2 + 51$

$102 = (51) \times 2 + 0$

HCF(867, 255) = 51.

Ans: The largest number which divides 870 and 258 leaving remainder 3 in each case is 51.

16

Choice - (2)

(30) Let the Present age of

Father = x years

Son = y years.

$x = 3y + 3$

$x - 3y - 3 = 0 \rightarrow (1)$

~~$x + 3 = 2y + 10$~~

$x + 3 = 2(y+3) + 10$

$x + 3 = 2y + 6 + 10$

$x - 2y = 16 - 3$

$x - 2y - 13 = 0 \rightarrow (2)$

Solving (1) and (2),

$x - 3y - 3 = 0$

$-x + 2y + 13 = 0$

$-y + 10 = 0$

$y = 10$

$x = 33$

17

Ans: Present age of father = 33 years

son = 10 years

(29) $\frac{2\cos^3\theta - \cos\theta}{\sin\theta - 2\sin^3\theta} = \cot\theta$

LHS:

$\frac{\cos\theta\,(2\cos^2\theta - 1)}{\sin\theta\,(1 - 2\sin^2\theta)}$

$\frac{\cos\theta\,[2(1-\sin^2\theta) - 1]}{\sin\theta\,(1 - 2\sin^2\theta)}$

$\frac{\cos\theta\,[2 - 2\sin^2\theta - 1]}{\sin\theta\,(1 - 2\sin^2\theta)} \Rightarrow \frac{\cos\theta}{\sin\theta} \times \frac{(1-2\sin^2\theta)}{(1-2\sin^2\theta)} \Rightarrow \cot\theta$

LHS = RHS = $\cot\theta$ //

Proved.

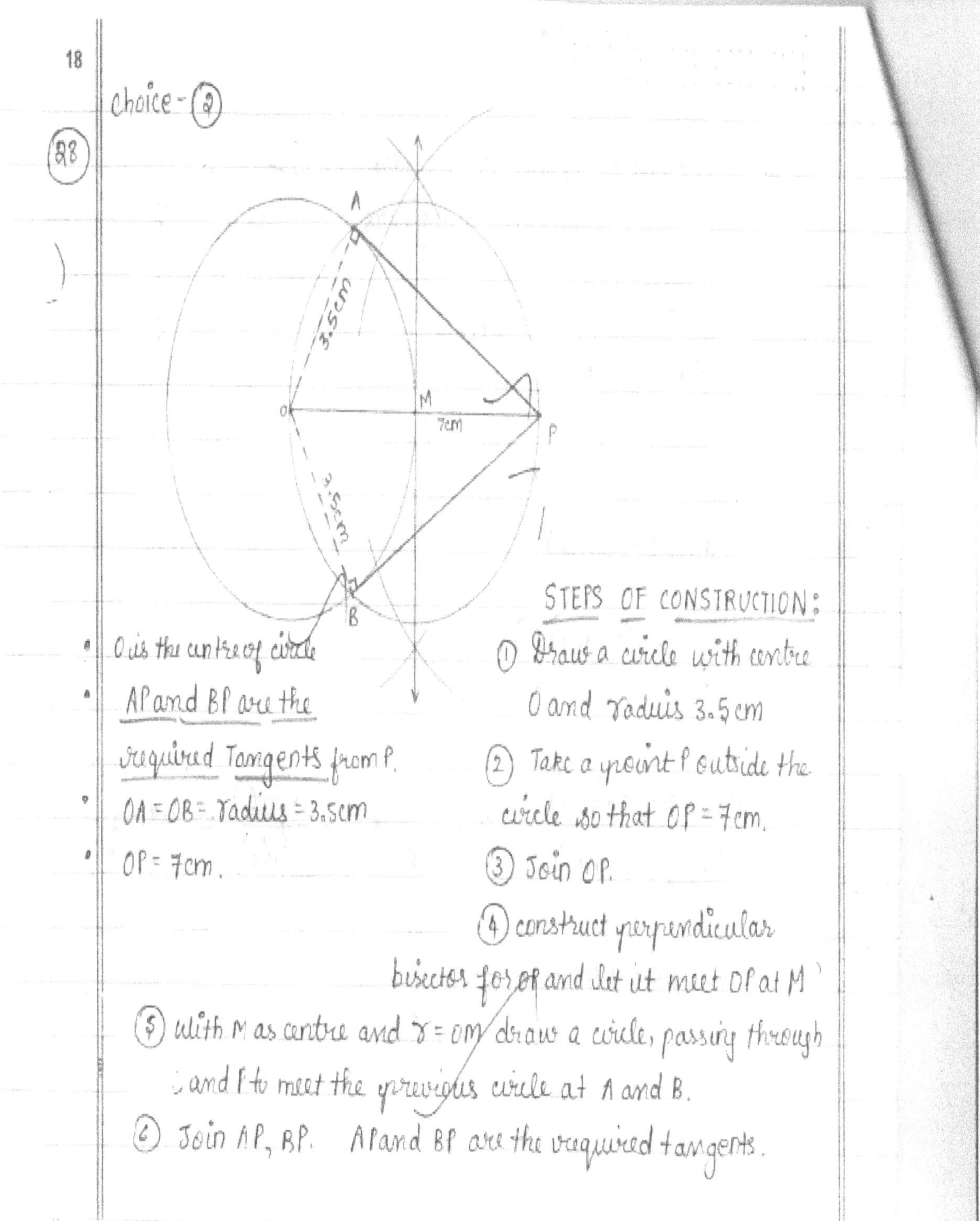

18

choice - (2)

(28)

- O is the centre of circle
- AP and BP are the required Tangents from P.
- OA = OB = radius = 3.5cm
- OP = 7cm.

STEPS OF CONSTRUCTION:

(1) Draw a circle with centre O and radius 3.5 cm

(2) Take a point P outside the circle so that OP = 7cm.

(3) Join OP.

(4) construct perpendicular bisector for OP and let it meet OP at M

(5) With M as centre and r = OM draw a circle, passing through O and P to meet the previous circle at A and B.

(6) Join AP, BP. AP and BP are the required tangents.

$\frac{11}{7} \times 36 \times 2$

19

rea of Quadrant − Area of square.

$\frac{22}{7} \times 6 \times 6 \times 2 - 6 \times 6$

$6 \times 6 \left[\frac{11}{7} - 1\right]$

$6 \times 6 \times \frac{4}{7} \Rightarrow 20.57\ cm^2$ (approx)

.57 cm^2 (approx)

20

SECTION - B

(26) Since A, B, C are interior angles of ΔABC,

$\angle A + \angle B + \angle C = 180^\circ$ (ASP).

$\frac{\angle A + \angle B + \angle C}{2} = 90^\circ$

$\frac{\angle B + \angle C}{2} = 90^\circ - \frac{\angle A}{2} \rightarrow (1)$

$\cot\left(\frac{B+C}{2}\right) = \tan\left(\frac{A}{2}\right) \rightarrow$ To Prove:

LHS:

$\cot\left(\frac{B+C}{2}\right)$

sub (1),

$\cot\left(90^\circ - \frac{\angle A}{2}\right)$ $\left\{\because \cot(90^\circ - \theta) = \tan\theta\right\}$

$\tan\left(\frac{\angle A}{2}\right) = RHS$

// Proved.

21

i) Let us assume to the contrary that $5+2\sqrt{7}$ is rational.

Then $5+2\sqrt{7}$ is of the form $\frac{p}{q}$ where p and q are co-primes and $q \neq 0$.

$$\frac{p}{q} = 5+2\sqrt{7}$$

$$\frac{p}{q} - 5 = 2\sqrt{7}$$

$$\frac{p-5q}{2q} = \sqrt{7}$$

$\frac{p-5q}{2q}$ is rational as p and q are integers

This contradicts the given fact that $\sqrt{7}$ is irrational.

$\therefore$ Our assumption is wrong.

$5+2\sqrt{7}$ is irrational //

Proved.

22

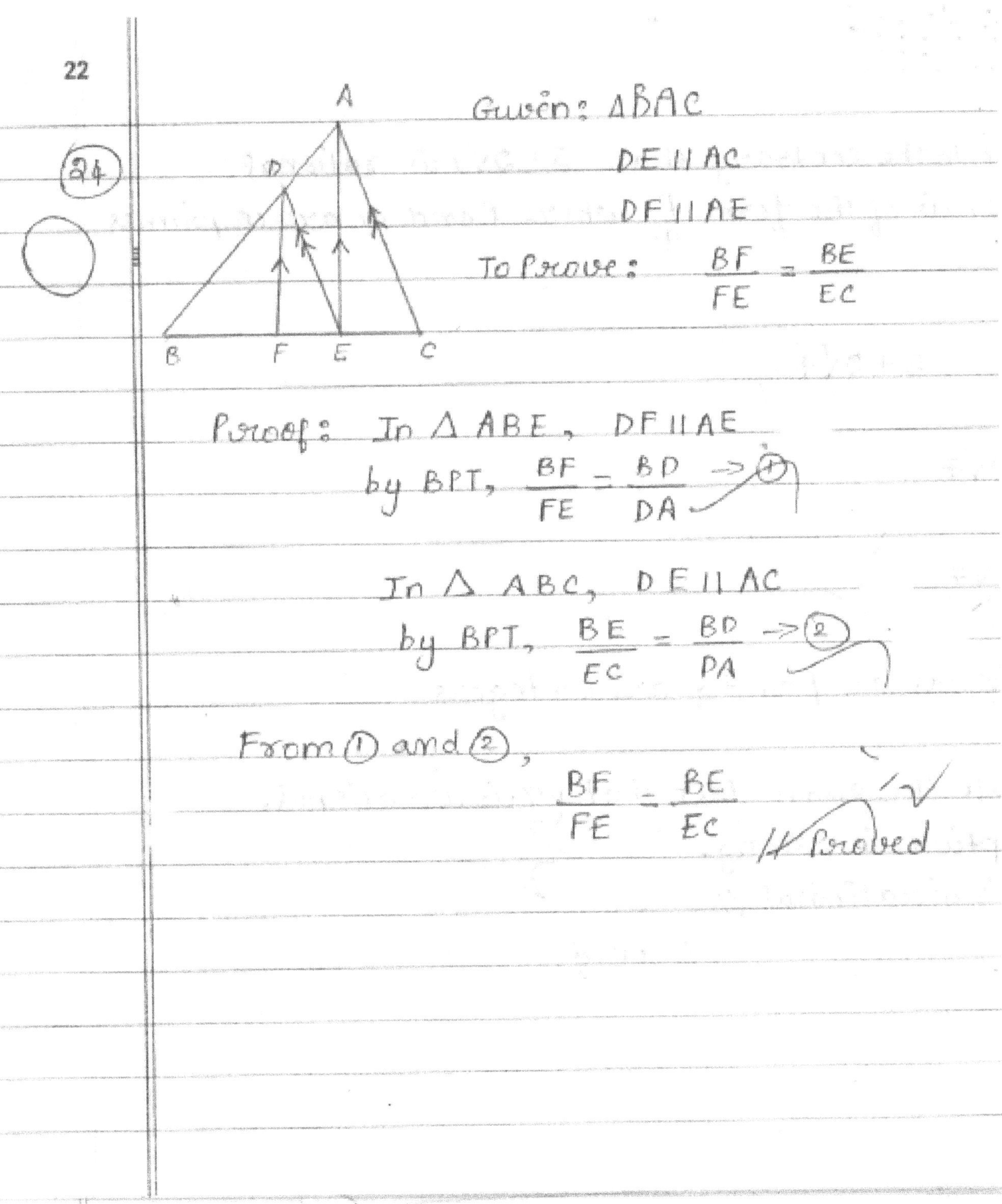
24
A
D
B
F
E
C
Given: ΔBAC
DE ∥ AC
DF ∥ AE
To Prove: BF/FE = BE/EC
Proof: In Δ ABE, DF ∥ AE
by BPT, BF/FE = BD/DA → (1)
In Δ ABC, DE ∥ AC
by BPT, BE/EC = BD/DA → (2)
From (1) and (2),
BF/FE = BE/EC
Hence Proved

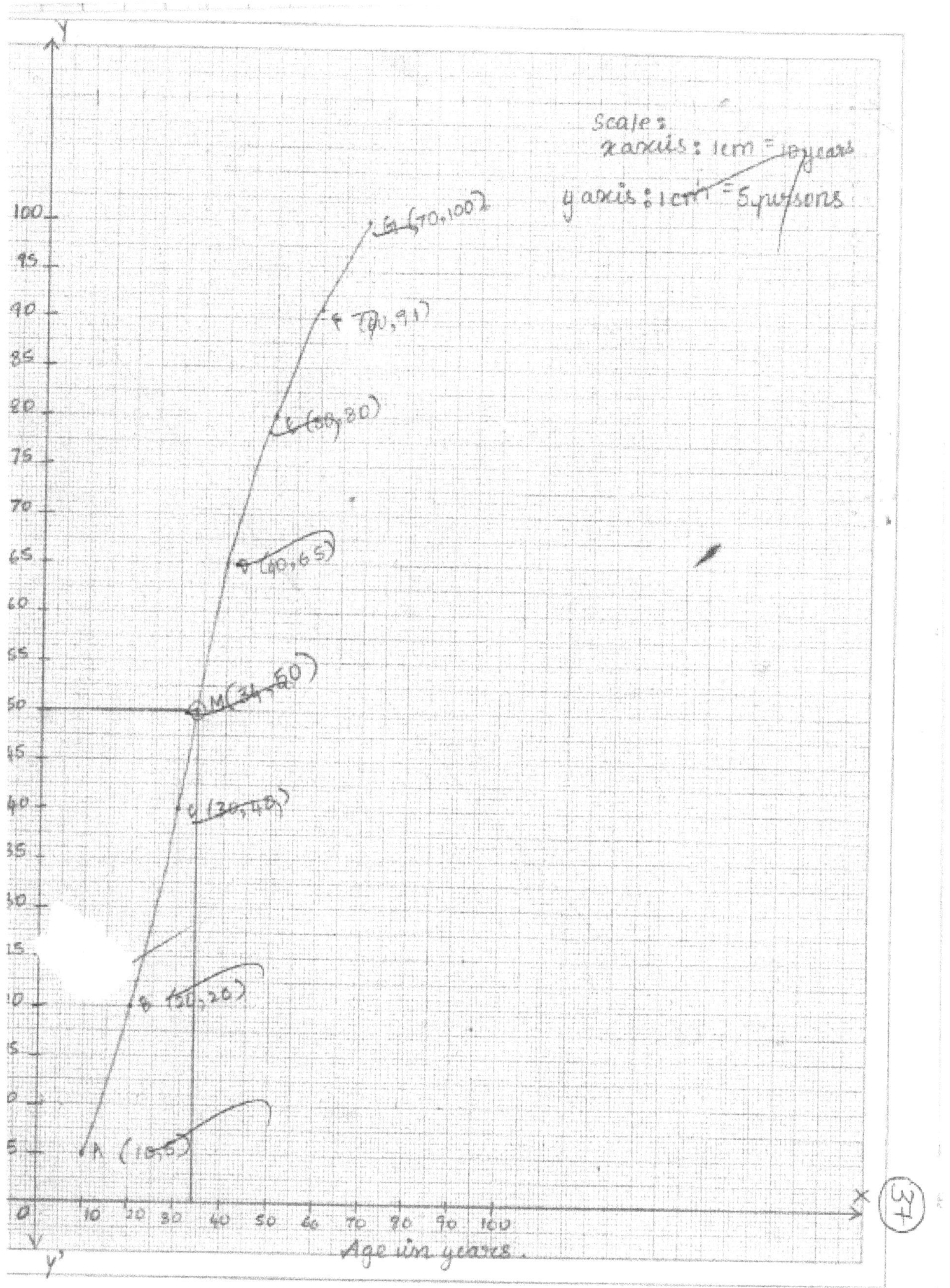
Scale:
x axis: 1cm = 10 years
y axis: 1cm = 5 persons
G (70,100)
F (60,91)
E (50,80)
D (40,65)
M (34,50)
C (30,40)
B (20,20)
A (10,5)
Age in years
X
Y
Y'
0

27

(23) For Small cube : $a = 2cm$

large cube : $A = 10cm$

let number of cubes = n.

$A^3 = n \times a^3$

$n = \frac{A^3}{a^3}$

$n = \frac{1000}{8} = 125$

Ans: Number of cubes that can be made = 125 cubes

(22) choice-(1)

Let the circle and quadrilateral meet at P, Q, R, S.

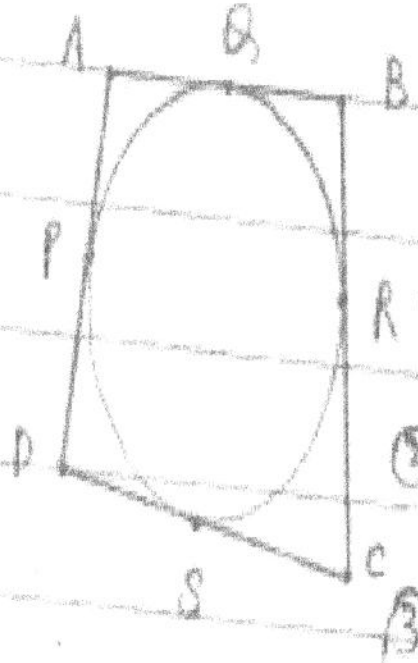

① AP = AQ

② DP = DS

③ BR = BQ

④ CR = CS

} lengths of Tangents from external points A, B, C, D to the circle are equal

28

Adding ①, ②, ③, ④,

$AP + DP + BR + CR = AQ + BQ + DS + CS$

$AD + BC = AB + DC$ //

Proved.

(21)

Marks	No. of students (f)
0 - 10	4
10 - 20	6
20 - 30	7
30 - 40	12
40 - 50	5
50 - 60	6

modal class

Mode : $L + \frac{f_1 - f_0}{2f_1 - f_0 - f_2} \times h$

$30 + \frac{12-7}{14-7-5} \times 10$

$30 + \frac{5}{2} \times 10^5 \Rightarrow$ 55 marks

$30 + \frac{12-7}{24-7-10}$

$30 + \frac{12-7}{24-12} \times 10$

$30 + \frac{5}{12} \times h = 30 +$

$h = 10$

Mode: $30 + \frac{12-7}{24-7-5} \times 10$

$30 + \frac{5}{12} \times 10 \Rightarrow 34.17$ (approx)

Ans: Modal marks = 34.17 marks (approx)

SECTION-A

(20)

Let ht of tower - AB = h m

In right ΔABC,

$\tan 30° = \frac{h}{30}$

$\frac{1}{\sqrt{3}} = \frac{h}{30} \Rightarrow h = \frac{30\sqrt{3}}{3}$

$h = 10\sqrt{3} \Rightarrow 17.32$ m.

Ans- Height of tower = 17.32m (approx)

30

(19) $2\sec 30^\circ \times \tan 60^\circ$

$\frac{2 \times 2}{\sqrt{3}} \times \sqrt{3} = 4$

(18) $n = 100$

Sum of first 100 natural numbers $= \frac{n(n+1)}{2}$

Ans: Sum of 1st 100 natural nos. $\Rightarrow \frac{100 \times 101}{2} = 5050$

(17) Sum of zeroes $= -3$

Product of zeroes $= 2$.

Ans: The required Polynomial:

$P(x) = k(x^2 + 3x + 2)$

(16)

Product of 2 nos. = LCM × HCF

Let other number be x

$x \times 26 = 182 \times 13$

$x = 91$

Ans: other number is 91

31

(15) $(1-\cos^2 A)(1+\cot^2 A)$

$(1-\cos^2 A)\left(1+\frac{\cos^2 A}{\sin^2 A}\right)$

$(1-\cos^2 A)\left(\frac{\sin^2 A+\cos^2 A}{\sin^2 A}\right)$

$\frac{(1-\cos^2 A)}{\sin^2 A} \Rightarrow \frac{\sin^2 A}{\sin^2 A} =$

Ans 1

(14) P(Sure event) = 1

(13) Similar

(12) $u_i = \frac{x_i - a}{h}$

(11) A(0,-3), C, O(0,0), B(4,0)

Length of diagonal AB $= \sqrt{(x_2-x_1)^2+(y_2-y_1)^2}$

$= \sqrt{(0-4)^2+(-3-0)^2} = \sqrt{16+9} = 5$ units

Ans: Length of diagonal of rectangle AOBC is 5 units

(10) Volume = 12π

$\frac{4}{3}\pi r^3 = 12\pi$

$r^3 = 9$

$r = 3^{\frac{2}{3}}$ cm.

Ans: (c) $3^{\frac{2}{3}}$ cm

(9) (A) 50°

(8) $\frac{3}{2}x + \frac{5}{3}y = 7$

$9x + 10y = 14$

$\frac{a_1}{a_2} = \frac{3}{2} \times \frac{1}{9} = \frac{1}{6}$

$\frac{b_1}{b_2} = \frac{5}{3} \times \frac{1}{10} = \frac{1}{6}$

$\frac{c_1}{c_2} = \frac{+7}{+14} = \frac{1}{2}$

$\frac{a_1}{a_2} = \frac{b_1}{b_2} \neq \frac{c_1}{c_2}$

Ans (B) Inconsistent

(7) $A(-6,3)$

$B(6,4)$

$O = \left(\frac{-6+6}{2}, \frac{3+4}{2}\right)$

$O = \left(0, \frac{7}{2}\right)$

Ans - (c) $\left[0, \frac{7}{2}\right]$

(6) $AB^2 = AC^2 + BC^2$

$AB^2 = 2AC^2$

Ans (A) $AB^2 = 2AC^2$

34

(5) (A) 2

(4) A(m, −n)
B(−m, n)

$AB = \sqrt{(m+m)^2 + (-n-n)^2}$

$AB = \sqrt{4m^2 + 4n^2}$

$AB = 2\sqrt{m^2 + n^2}$

Ans- (c) $2\sqrt{m^2+n^2}$

(3) (B) 4cm

(2) (c) $\frac{4}{3}, \frac{7}{3}, \frac{9}{3}, \frac{12}{3}$

$3+\sqrt{2}-3 = \sqrt{2}$

$\frac{7}{3} - \frac{4}{3} = 1$, $\frac{9}{3} - \frac{7}{3} = \frac{2}{3}$

35

$2x^2 + kx + 2 = 0$

For equal roots;

$b^2 - 4ac = 0$

$k^2 - 16 = 0$

$k^2 = 16$

$k = \pm 4$

Ans (B) ± 4

1 Sample Paper

LATEST PATTERN

BLUE PRINT

Ch. No.	Chapter Name	Per Unit Marks	Section-A (1 Mark)		Section-B (2 Marks)	Section-C (3 Marks)	Section-D (5 Marks)	Section-E (4 Marks)	Total Marks
			MCQ	A/R	VSA	SA	LA	Case-Study	
1	Real Number	6	2(Q1,5)	1(Q19)		1(Q26)			**6**
2	Polynomials	20	1(Q4)			1(Q27)			**4**
3	Pair of Linear Equations in Two Variables		1(Q3)		1(Q21)	1(Q28)			**6**
4	Quadratic Equations		1(Q2)				1(Q34)		**6**
5	Arithmetic Progression							1(Q36)	**4**
6	Triangles	15	2(Q6,8)		1(Q22)		1(Q32)		**9**
7	Circles		1(Q13)		1(Q24)	1(Q30)			**6**
8	Coordinate Geometry	6	2(Q9,11)					1(Q38)	**6**
9	Introduction to Trigonometry	12	2(Q7,10)	1(Q20)	1(Q23)	1(Q29)			**8**
10	Some Applications of Trigonometry							1(Q37)	**4**
11	Areas Related to Circles	10	2(Q12,14)		1(Q25)				**4**
12	Surface Areas and Volumes		1(Q16)				1(Q33)		**6**
13	Statistics	11	2(Q15,17)				1(Q35)		**7**
14	Probability		1(Q18)			1(Q31)			**4**
Total Marks (Total Questions)		**80**	**18(18)**	**2(2)**	**10(5)**	**18(6)**	**20(4)**	**12(3)**	**80(38)**

Note : The number given inside the bracket denotes question number, asked in the sample paper, while the number given outside the bracket are the number of questions from that particular chapter.

Time : 3 Hours **Max. Marks : 80**

General Instructions

1. *This Question paper contains - five sections A, B, C, D and E. Each section is compulsory. However, there are internal choices in some questions.*
2. *Section A has 18 MCQ's and 02 Assertion-Reason based questions of 1 mark each.*
3. *Section B has 5 Very Short Answer (VSA)-type questions of 2 marks each.*
4. *Section C has 6 Short Answer (SA)-type questions of 3 marks each.*
5. *Section D has 4 Long Answer (LA)-type questions of 5 marks each.*
6. *Section E has 3 case based integrated units of assessment (4 marks each) with sub parts of values of 1, 1 and 2 marks each respectively.*

SECTION-A (Multiple Choice Questions)

Each question carries 1 mark.

1. I. The L.C.M. of x and 18 is 36.
II. The H.C.F. of x and 18 is 2.
What is the number x ?
(a) 1 (b) 2 (c) 3 (d) 4

2. If the sum of the roots of a quadratic equation is 6 and their product is 6, the equation is
(a) $x^2 - 6x + 6 = 0$ (b) $x^2 + 6x - 6 = 0$
(c) $x^2 - 6x - 6 = 0$ (d) $x^2 + 6x + 6 = 0$

3. For what values of k will the following pair of linear equations have infinitely many solutions?
$kx + 3y - (k - 3) = 0$
$12x + ky - k = 0$
(a) $k = 4$ (b) $k = 3$ (c) $k = 6$ (d) $k = 2$

4. If the zeroes of the polynomial $f(x) = k^2x^2 - 17x + k + 2$, $(k > 0)$ are reciprocal of each other than value of k is
(a) 2 (b) –1 (c) –2 (d) 1

5. Given that L.C.M. (91, 26) = 182, then H.C.F. (91, 26) is
(a) 13 (b) 26 (c) 17 (d) 9

6. Two triangles are similar if
(a) their corresponding angles are equal.
(b) their corresponding sides are equal.
(c) both are right triangle.
(d) None of the above

7. If $\tan^2\theta = 1 - a^2$, then the value of $\sec\theta + \tan^3\theta \operatorname{cosec}\theta$ is
(a) $(2 - a^2)$ (b) $(2 - a^2)^{1/2}$
(c) $(2 - a^2)^{2/3}$ (d) $(2 - a^2)^{3/2}$

8. If in two ΔDEF and ΔPQR, $\angle D = \angle Q$ and $\angle R = \angle E$, then which of the following is not true?
(a) $\frac{EF}{PR} = \frac{DF}{PQ}$ (b) $\frac{DE}{PQ} = \frac{EF}{RP}$ (c) $\frac{DE}{QR} = \frac{DF}{PQ}$ (d) $\frac{EF}{RP} = \frac{DE}{QR}$

9. If P = (2, 5), Q = (x, –7) and PQ = 13, what is the value of 'x'?
(a) 5 (b) 3 (c) –3 (d) –5

10. If $b\tan\theta = a$, the value of $\frac{a\sin\theta - b\cos\theta}{a\sin\theta + b\cos\theta}$ is
(a) $\frac{a-b}{a^2+b^2}$ (b) $\frac{a+b}{a^2+b^2}$ (c) $\frac{a^2+b^2}{a^2-b^2}$ (d) $\frac{a^2-b^2}{a^2+b^2}$

11. In what ratio does the point (–2, 3) divide the line-segment joining the points (–3, 5) and (4, –9) ?
(a) 2 : 3 (b) 1 : 6 (c) 6 : 1 (d) 2 : 1

12. The figure shows two concentric circleswith centre O and radii 3.5 m and 7 m. If $\angle BOA = 40°$, find the area of the shaded region.

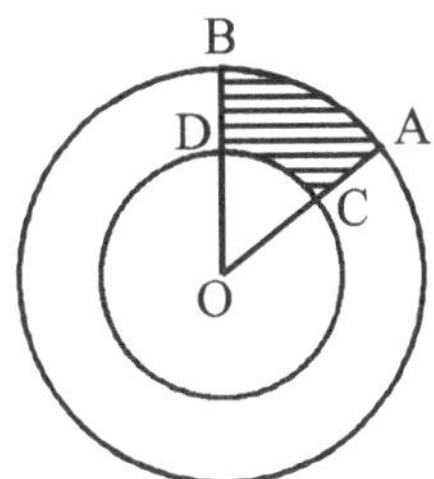

(a) $\frac{77}{6} cm^2$ (b) $\frac{76}{5}$

(c) $\frac{73}{6}$ (d) None of these

13. In the figure below (not to scale), AB = CD and $\overline{AB}$ and $\overline{CD}$ are produced to meet at the point p.

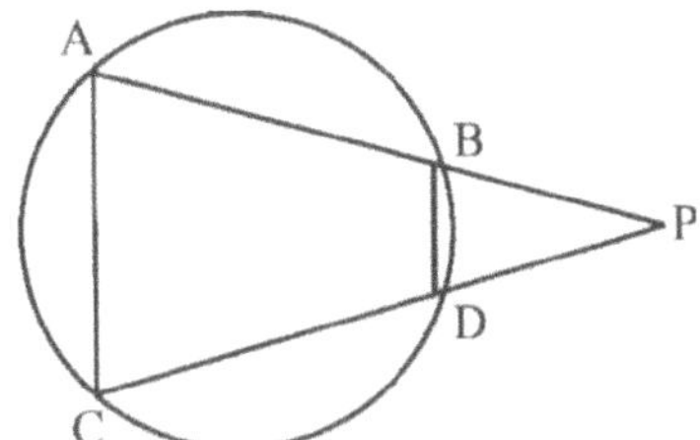

If $\angle BAC = 70°$, then $\angle P$ is

(a) 30° (b) 40° (c) 45° (d) 50°

14. The area of a circular ring formed by two concentric circles whose radii are 5.7 cm and 4.3 cm respectively is (Take $\pi = 3.1416$)

(a) 43.98 sq.cm (b) 53.67 sq. cm

(c) 47.24 sq.cm (d) 38.54 sq.cm

15. The mean weight of a class of 35 students is 45kg. If the weight of a teacher be included, the mean weight increases by 500 grams. Find the weight of the teacher.

(a) 63 kg (b) 61 kg

(c) 64 kg (d) 70 kg

16. Volume of a spherical shell is given by

(a) $4\pi(R^2 - r^2)$ (b) $\pi(R^3 - r^3)$

(c) $4\pi(R^3 - r^3)$ (d) $\pi(R^3 - r^3)$

17. In the following distribution

Monthly income range (in ₹)	Number of families
Income more than ₹ 10,000	100
Income more than ₹ 13,000	85
Income more than ₹ 16,000	69
Income more than ₹ 19,000	50
Income more than ₹ 22,000	33
Income more than ₹ 25,000	15

the number of families having income range (in ₹) 16000 – 19000 is

(a) 15 (b) 16 (c) 17 (d) 19

18. For an event E, P (E) + $P(\overline{E})$ = q, then

(a) $0 \le q < 1$ (b) $0 < q \le 1$

(c) $0 < q < 1$ (d) None of these

(ASSERTION-REASON BASED QUESTIONS)

In the following questions, a statement of Assertion (A) is followed by a statement of Reason (R). Choose the correct answer out of the following choices.

(a) ***Both A and R are true and R is the correct explanation of A.***
(b) ***Both A and R are true but R is not the correct explanation of A.***
(c) ***A is true but R is false.***
(d) ***A is false but R is true.***

19. **Assertion :** $n^2 - n$ is divisible by 2 for every positive integer.

Reason : $\sqrt{2}$ is not a rational number.

20. **Assertion:** In a right angled triangle, if $\tan\theta = \frac{3}{4}$, the greatest side of the triangle is 5 units.

Reason: (greatest side)^2 = (hypotenuse)^2 = (perpendicular)^2 + (base)^2.

SECTION-B

This section comprises of very short answer type-questions (VSA) of 2 marks each.

21. Which type of equations $x + 2y = 4$ and $2x + y = 5$ will be?

OR

For what value of k, the equations $3x - y + 8 = 0$ and $6x - ky = -16$ represent coincident lines?

22. Sides AB and BC and median AD of a triangle ABC are respectively proportional to sides PQ and QR and median PM of triangle PQR. Prove that $\Delta ABC \sim \Delta PQR$.

23. Prove that $\frac{\tan^2\theta}{\tan^2\theta - 1} + \frac{\operatorname{cosec}^2\theta}{\sec^2\theta - \operatorname{cosec}^2\theta} = \frac{1}{\sin^2\theta - \cos^2\theta}$

24. A ball is in the rest position against a step PQ. If PQ = 10 cm and QR = 15 cm, then the diameter of the ball is ____________.

P
Q R

OR

In the diagram, PQ and QR are tangents to the circle centre O, at P and R respectively. Find the value of x.

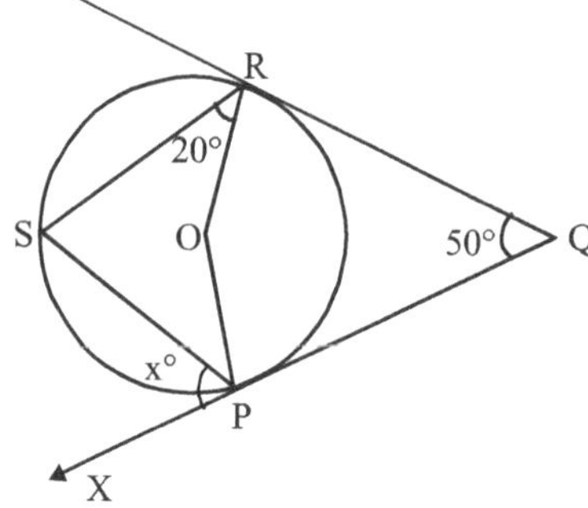

25. In figure, two concentric circles with centre O, have radii 21 cm and 42 cm. If $\angle AOB = 60°$, find the area of the shaded region.

[Use $\pi = \frac{22}{7}$].

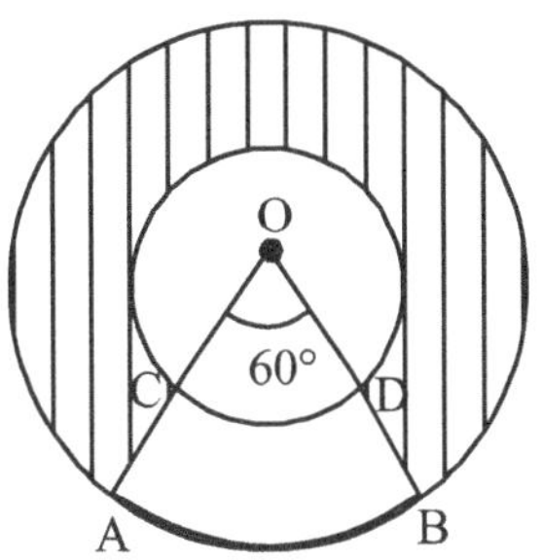

SECTION-C

This section comprises of short answer type questions (SA) of 3 marks each.

26. Prove that $\sqrt{2} + \sqrt{5}$ is irrational.

27. Quadratic polynomial $2x^2 - 3x + 1$ has zeroes as α and β. Now form a quadratic polynomial whose zeroes are 3α and 3β.

28. Solve the following system of equations :

$$\frac{4}{x} + 5y = 7; \quad \frac{3}{x} + 4y = 5$$

29. If $\tan(A+B) = \sqrt{3}$ and $\tan(A-B) = \frac{1}{\sqrt{3}}$; $0° < A+B \leq 90°$; $A > B$, find A and B.

30. In fig. a circle touches the side BC of ΔABC at P and touches AB and AC produced at Q and R respectively. If AQ = 5 cm, find the perimeter of ΔABC.

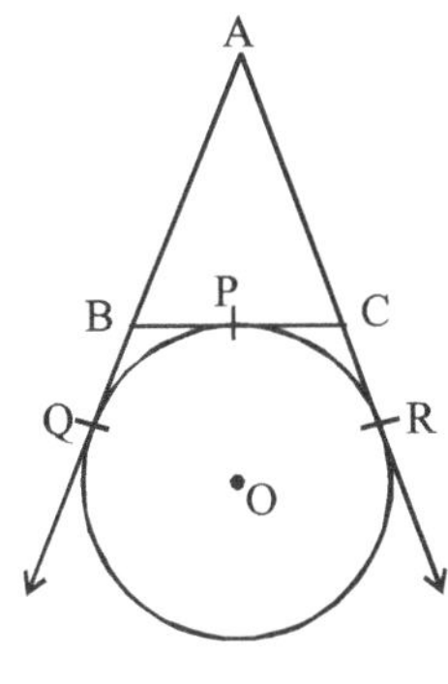

OR

In the given figure, ΔABC and ΔDBC are on the same base BC. AD and BC intersect at O. Prove that $\frac{AE}{DF} = \frac{AO}{DO}$.

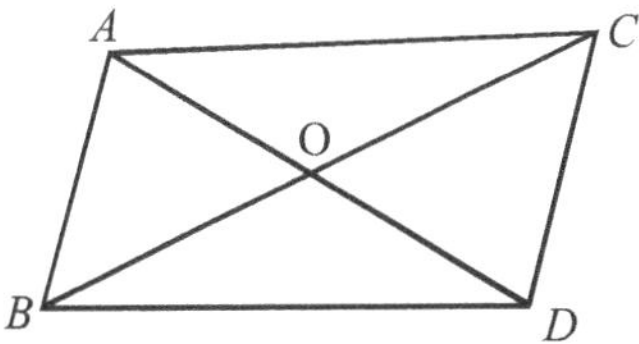

31. In a single throw of a pair of different dice, what is the probability of getting (i) a prime number on each dice ? (ii) a total of 9 or 11 ?

OR

Three different coins are tossed together. Find the probability of getting (i) exactly two heads (ii) at least two heads (iii) at least two tails.

SECTION-D

This section comprises of long answer-type questions (LA) of 5 marks each.

32.

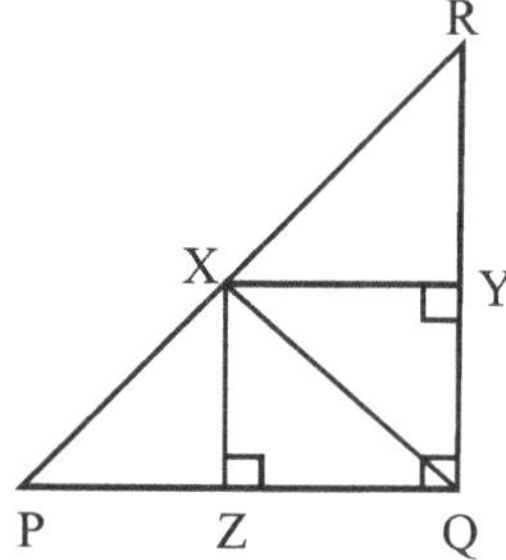

ΔPQR is right angled at Q. $QX \perp PR$, $XY \perp RQ$ and $XZ \perp PQ$ are drawn. Prove that $XZ^2 = PZ \times ZQ$.

33. A solid metallic right circular cone 20 cm high and whose vertical angle is 60°, is cut into two parts at the middle of its height by a plane parallel to its base. Find volume of small cone.

OR

From a solid cylinder of height 2.8 cm and diameter 4.2 cm, a conical cavity of the same height and same diameter is hollowed out. Find the total surface area of the remaining solid. [Take $\pi = \frac{22}{7}$].

34. Roots of the quadratic equation $36x^2 - 12ax + (a^2 - b^2) = 0$ are $\frac{a+b}{c}$ and $\frac{a-b}{c}$. Then, find the value of c.

OR

Find the real roots of the equation $x^{2/3} + x^{1/3} - 2 = 0$.

35. Find the median of the following data :

Height (in cm)	Less than 120	Less than 140	Less than 160	Less than 180	Less than 200
Number of students	12	26	34	40	50

SECTION-E

This section comprises of 3 case study/passage - based questions of 4 marks each with three sub-parts (i), (ii), (iii) of marks 1, 1, 2 respectively.

36. **Case - Study 1:** Read the following passage and answer the questions given below.

India is competitive manufacturing location due to the low cost of manpower and strong technical and engineering capabilities contributing to higher quality production runs. The production of TV sets in a factory increases uniformly by a fixed number every year. It produced 16000 sets in 6th year and 22600 in 9th year.

Based on the above information, answer the following questions:

(i) Find the production during first year.

(ii) Find the production during 8th year.

(iii) Find the production during first 3 years.

OR

In which year, the production is Rs 29,200.

37. **Case - Study 2:** Read the following passage and answer the questions given below.
An electrician has to repair an electric fault on a pole of height 5m. He needs to reach a point 1.3 m below the top of the pole to under take the repair work. He place the ladder of length 7.4 m at that position.

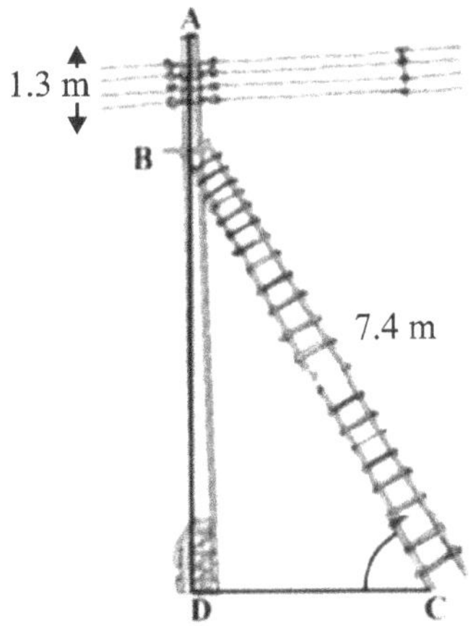

Then answer the following questions.

(i) Find measure of $\angle C$.

(ii) Find measure of $\angle B$.

(iii) Find distance between foot of ladder and pole.

OR

The value of $\sin^2 B + \sin^2 C$ is

38. **Case - Study 3:** Read the following passage and answer the questions given below.
A **hockey field** is the playing surface for the game of hockey. Historically, the game was played on natural turf (grass) but nowadays it is predominantly played on an artificial turf.
It is rectangular in shape - 100 yards by 60 yards. Goals consist of two upright posts placed equidistant from the centre of the backline, joined at the top by a horizontal crossbar. The inner edges of the posts must be 3.66 metres (4 yards) apart, and the lower edge of the crossbar must be 2.14 metres (7 feet) above the ground.
Each team plays with 11 players on the field during the game including the goalie.
Positions you might play include-

- **Forward :** As shown by players A, B, C and D.
- **Midfielders:** As shown by players E, F and G.
- **Fullbacks:** As shown by players H, I and J.

Goalie: As shown by players H, I and J.
Using the picture of a hockey field below, answer the questions that follow:

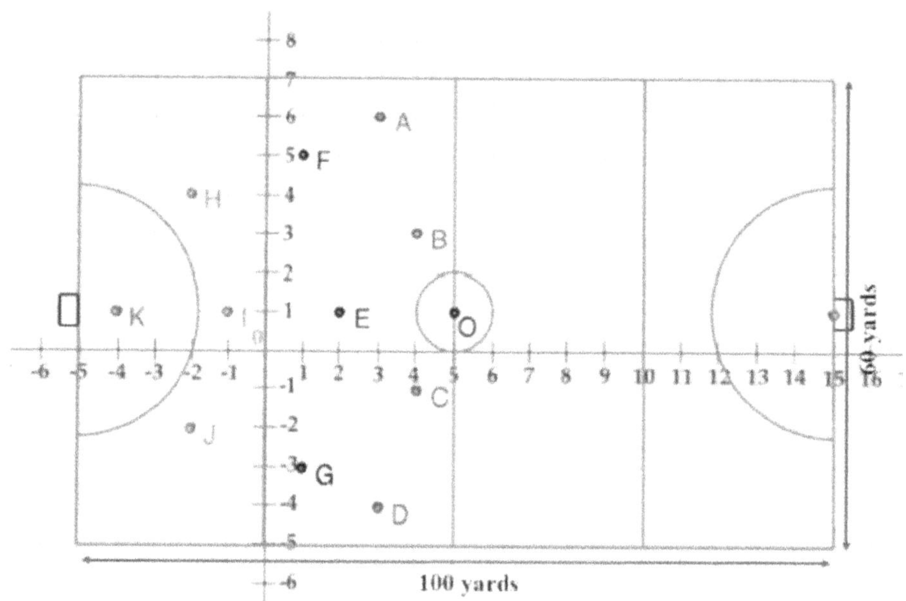

(i) Find the coordinates of the centroid of ΔEHJ.

(ii) If a player P needs to be at equal distances from A and G, such that A, P and G are in straight line, then find the position of P.

(iii) Find the point on x axis equidistant from I and E.

OR

What are the coordinates of the position of a player Q such that his distance from K is twice his distance from E and K, Q and E are collinear?

2 Sample Paper

LATEST PATTERN

BLUE PRINT

Ch. No.	Chapter Name	Per Unit Marks	Section-A (1 Mark)		Section-B (2 Marks)	Section-C (3 Marks)	Section-D (5 Marks)	Section-E (4 Marks)	Total Marks
			MCQ	A/R	VSA	SA	LA	Case-Study	
1	Real Number	6	1(Q1)	1(Q19)				1(Q36)	6
2	Polynomials	20	1(Q3)		1(Q21)	1(Q26)			6
3	Pair of Linear Equations in Two Variables		1(Q2)		1(Q22)				3
4	Quadratic Equations		1(Q4)				1(Q32)		6
5	Arithmetic Progression		2(Q5, 8)			1(Q27)			5
6	Triangles	15	2(Q6, 9)		1(Q23)			1(Q37)	8
7	Circles		2(Q10, 18)		1(Q25)	1(Q30)			7
8	Coordinate Geometry	6	3(Q7, 12, 14)	1(Q20)	1(Q24)				6
9	Introduction to Trigonometry	12	1(Q11)			1(Q28)	1(Q33)		9
10	Some Applications of Trigonometry					1(Q29)			3
11	Areas Related to Circles	10					1(Q34)		5
12	Surface Areas and Volumes		1(Q13)					1(Q38)	5
13	Statistics	11					1(Q35)		5
14	Probability		3(Q15, 16, 17)			1(Q31)			6
Total Marks (Total Questions)		**80**	**18(18)**	**2(2)**	**10(5)**	**18(6)**	**20(4)**	**12(3)**	**80(38)**

Note : The number given inside the bracket denotes question number, asked in the sample paper, while the number given outside the bracket are the number of questions from that particular chapter.

Time : 3 Hours **Max. Marks : 80**

General Instructions

1. *This Question paper contains - five sections A, B, C, D and E. Each section is compulsory. However, there are internal choices in some questions.*
2. *Section A has 18 MCQ's and 02 Assertion-Reason based questions of 1 mark each.*
3. *Section B has 5 Very Short Answer (VSA)-type questions of 2 marks each.*
4. *Section C has 6 Short Answer (SA)-type questions of 3 marks each.*
5. *Section D has 4 Long Answer (LA)-type questions of 5 marks each.*
6. *Section E has 3 case based integrated units of assessment (4 marks each) with sub parts of values of 1, 1 and 2 marks each respectively.*

SECTION-A (Multiple Choice Questions)

Each question carries 1 mark.

1. A class of 20 boys and 15 girls is divided into n groups so that each group has x boys and y girls. Values of x, y and n respectively are
(a) 3, 4 and 8 (b) 4, 3 and 6 (c) 4, 3 and 7 (d) 7, 4 and 3

2. Which of the following is the other name for a pair of linear equations in two variables?
(a) Consistent equations (b) Simultaneous equations
(c) Inconsistent equations (d) Dependent equations

3. Let $f(x) = x^2 - 27x + 196$. If $f(a) = a$, then what is the value of a.
(a) 7 (b) 14 (c) 21 (d) 6

4. If the roots of $5x^2 - kx + 1 = 0$ are real and distinct, then
(a) $-2\sqrt{5} < k < 2\sqrt{5}$ (b) $k > 2\sqrt{5}$ only
(c) $k < -2\sqrt{5}$ only (d) either $k > 2\sqrt{5}$ or $k < -2\sqrt{5}$

5. The first term of an A.P. is 5 and its 100th term is –292. The 50th term of this A.P. will be
(a) 142 (b) –142 (c) 130 (d) –140

6. If in ΔABC and ΔDEF, $\frac{AB}{DE} = \frac{BC}{FD}$, then they will be similar, when
(a) ∠B = ∠E (b) ∠A = ∠D (c) ∠B = ∠D (d) ∠A = ∠F

7. If the point $P(p, q)$ is equidistant from the points $A(a+b, b-a)$ and $B(a-b, a+b)$, then
(a) $ap = by$ (b) $bp = ay$ (c) $ap + bq = 0$ (d) $bp + aq = 0$

8. The nth term of the A.P. a, $3a$, $5a$, ..., is
(a) na (b) $(2n-1)a$ (c) $(2n+1)a$ (d) $2na$

9. If ΔABC is an equilateral triangle such that $AD \perp BC$, then $AD^2 =$
A. $\frac{3a^2}{4}$ B. $\frac{3a^2}{2}$ C. $\frac{3}{4}BC^2$ D. $\frac{\sqrt{3}}{2}a$
(a) A and C (b) A (c) D (d) B and C

10. In the adjoining figure, TP and TQ are the two tangents to a circle with centre O. If ∠POQ = 110°, then ∠PTQ is

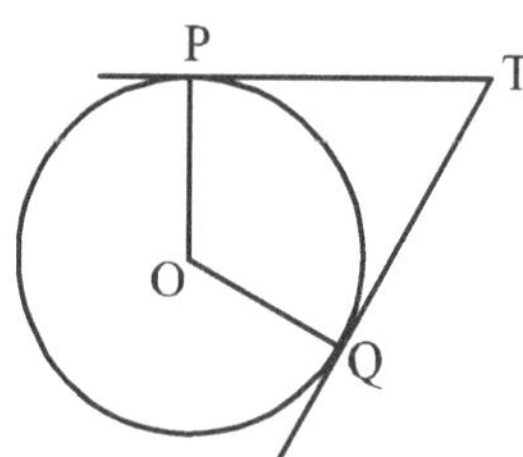

(a) 60° (b) 70° (c) 80° (d) 90°

11. If cosec x – cot $x = \frac{1}{3}$, where $x \neq 0$, then the value of $\cos^2 x - \sin^2 x$ is

(a) $\frac{16}{25}$ (b) $\frac{9}{25}$ (c) $\frac{8}{25}$ (d) $\frac{7}{25}$

12. The point which divides the line joining the points $A(1, 2)$ and $B(-1, 1)$ internally in the ratio 1 : 2 is

(a) $\left(\frac{-1}{3}, \frac{5}{3}\right)$ (b) $\left(\frac{1}{3}, \frac{5}{3}\right)$ (c) $(-1, 5)$ (d) $(1, 5)$

13. The radii of the top and bottom of a bucket of slant height 45 cm are 28 cm and 7 cm, respectively. The curved surface area of the bucket is

(a) 4950 cm^2 (b) 4951 cm^2 (c) 4952 cm^2 (d) 4953 cm^2

14. If the points (a, 0), (0, b) and (1, 1) are collinear then which of the following is true :

(a) $\frac{1}{a}+\frac{1}{b}=2$ (b) $\frac{1}{a}-\frac{1}{b}=1$ (c) $\frac{1}{a}-\frac{1}{b}=2$ (d) $\frac{1}{a}+\frac{1}{b}=1$

15. The probability of getting a number greater than 2 in throwing a die is

(a) 2/3 (b) 1/3 (c) 4/3 (d) 1/4

16. A bag contains card numbers 3, 4, 5, 6, 7....27. One card is drawn, then probability of prime number card is

(a) $\frac{9}{25}$ (b) $\frac{8}{27}$ (c) $\frac{8}{25}$ (d) $\frac{1}{5}$

17. A coin is tossed. Then the probability of getting either head or tail is

(a) 1 (b) $\frac{1}{3}$ (c) $\frac{1}{2}$ (d) $\frac{1}{4}$

18. In figure, AT is a tangent to the circle with centre O such that OT = 4 cm and ∠OTA = 30°. Then, AT is equal to

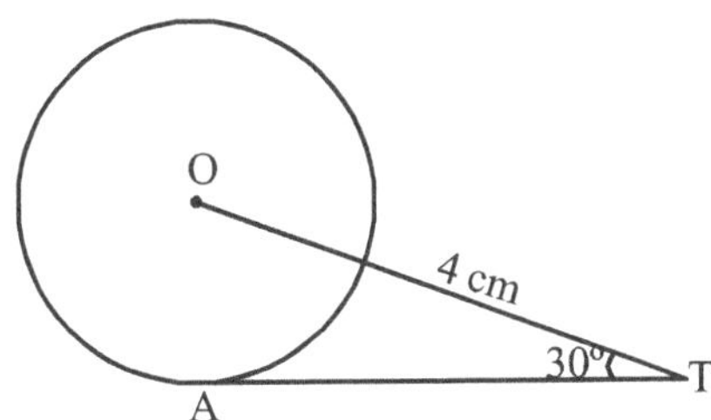

(a) 4 cm (b) 2 cm (c) $2\sqrt{3}$ cm (d) $4\sqrt{3}$ cm

(ASSERTION-REASON BASED QUESTIONS)

In the following questions, a statement of Assertion (A) is followed by a statement of Reason (R). Choose the correct answer out of the following choices.

(a) ***Both A and R are true and R is the correct explanation of A.***

(b) ***Both A and R are true but R is not the correct explanation of A.***

(c) ***A is true but R is false.***

(d) ***A is false but R is true.***

19. **Assertion :** The H.C.F. of two numbers is 16 and their product is 3072. Then, their L.C.M = 162.

Reason : If a, b are two positive integers, then H.C.F × L.C.M. = $a \times b$.

20. **Assertion :** If $A(2a, 4a)$ and $B(2a, 6a)$ are two vertices of an equilateral triangle ABC then, the vertex C is given by $(2a + a\sqrt{3}, 5a)$.

Reason : In equilateral triangle, all the coordinates of three vertices can be rational.

SECTION-B

This section comprises of very short answer type-questions (VSA) of 2 marks each.

21. If α and β are the zeroes of the quadratic polynomial $f(x) = ax^2 + bx + c$ then evaluate $\frac{\alpha^2}{\beta^2} + \frac{\beta^2}{\alpha^2}$

22. Find the solution of the pair equations $\frac{x}{10}+\frac{y}{5}-1=0$ and $\frac{x}{8}+\frac{y}{6}=15$. Hence, find λ, if $y=\lambda x+5$.

OR

A part of monthly hostel charge is fixed and the remaining depends on the number of days one has taken food in the mess. When Swati takes food for 20 days, she has to pay ₹ 3,000 as hostel charges whereas Mansi who takes food for 25 days ₹ 3,500 as hostel charges. Find the fixed charges and the cost of food per day.

23. In the given fig, $BD \perp AC$ and $CE \perp AB$. Prove that

(i) $\Delta AEC \sim \Delta ADB$

(ii) $\frac{CA}{AB} = \frac{CE}{DB}$

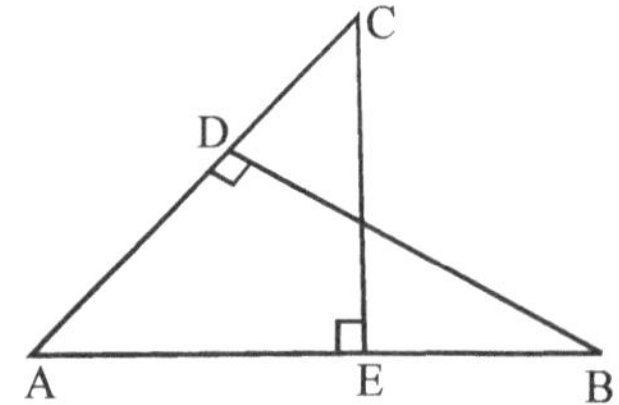

OR

In the given fig, $\frac{OA}{OC} = \frac{OD}{OB}$, prove that $\angle A = \angle C$ and $\angle B = \angle D$

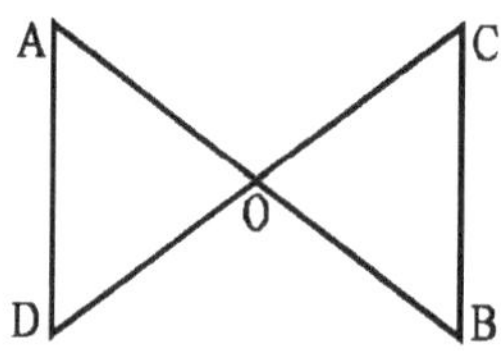

24. In what ratio, the line segment joining the points (3, 5) & (–4, 2) is divided by y-axis?

25. Prove that the line segment joining the points of contact of two parallel tangents of a circle, passes through its centre.

SECTION-C

This section comprises of short answer type questions (SA) of 3 marks each.

26. If α, β are the roots of the polynomial $f(x)=2x^2+5x+k$ satisfying the relation $\alpha^2+\beta^2+\alpha\beta=\frac{21}{4}$, then find the value of k for this to be possible.

27. If $a\left(\frac{1}{b}+\frac{1}{c}\right), b\left(\frac{1}{a}+\frac{1}{c}\right), c\left(\frac{1}{a}+\frac{1}{b}\right)$, are in A.P., prove that a, b, c are in A.P.

28. Prove that : $\frac{\cot A+\operatorname{cosec} A-1}{\cot A-\operatorname{cosec} A+1}=\frac{1+\cos A}{\sin A}=\operatorname{cosec} A+\cot A$

29. The angle of elevation of the top of a tower at a distance of 120 m from a point A on the ground is 45°. If the angle of elevation of the top of a flagstaff fixed at the top of the tower, at A is 60°, then find the height of the flagstaff. [Use $\sqrt{3}=1.73$]

30. Prove that the tangent at any point of a circle is perpendicular to the radius through the point of contact.

OR

Prove that the length of the tangents drawn from an external point to a circle are equal.

31. A piggy bank contains hundred 50p coins, fifty ₹ 1 coins, twenty ₹ 2 coins and ten ₹ 5 coins. If it is equally likely that one of the coins will fall out when the bank is turned upside down, what is the probability that the coin (i) will be a 50 p coin ? (ii) will not be a ₹ 5 coin?

OR

A book containing 100 pages is opened at random. Find the probability that a doublet page is found.

SECTION-D

This section comprises of long answer-type questions (LA) of 5 marks each.

32. Solve the equation by using quadratic formula : $(x + 4)(x + 5) = 3(x + 1)(x + 2) + 2x$

OR

If the roots of the equation $(c^2 - ab)x^2 - 2(a^2 - bc)x + (b^2 - ac) = 0$ are equal, prove that either $a = 0$ or $a^3 + b^3 + c^3 = 3abc$

33. If $\cos\theta + \sqrt{3}\sin\theta = 2\sin\theta$. Show that $\sin\theta - \sqrt{3}\cos\theta = 2\cos\theta$.

34. In fig., a circle is inscribed in an equilateral triangle ABC of side 12 cm. Find the radius of inscribed circle and the area of the shaded region.

[Use $\pi = 3.14$ and $\sqrt{3} = 1.73$]

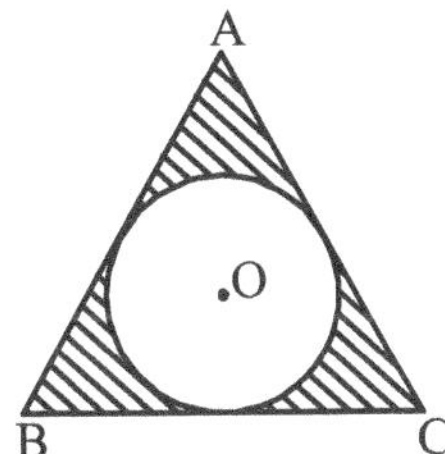

35. Following frequency distribution shows the daily expenditure on milk of 30 households in a locality:

Daily expenditure on milk (in ₹)	0 – 30	30 – 60	60 – 90	90 – 120	120 – 150
Number of households	5	6	9	6	4

Find the mode for the above data.

OR

If the mean of the following data is 14.7, find the value of p and q.

Class	0 – 6	6 – 12	12 – 18	18 – 24	24 – 30	30 – 36	36 – 42	Total
Frequency	10	p	4	7	q	4	1	40

SECTION-E

This section comprises of 3 case study/passage - based questions of 4 marks each with three sub-parts (i), (ii), (iii) of marks 1, 1, 2 respectively.

36. **Case - Study 1:** Read the following passage and answer the questions given below.

A seminar is being conducted by an Educational Organisation, where the participants will be educators of different subjects. The number of participants in Hindi, English and Mathematics are 60, 84 and 108 respectively.

(i) What is the LCM of 60, 84 and 108?

(ii) How 108 can be expressed as a product of its primes?

(iii) In each room the same number of participants are to be seated and all of them being in the same subject. What are the maximum number of participants that can accommodated in each room?

OR

What is the minimum number of rooms required during the event?

37. **Case - Study 2:** Read the following passage and answer the questions given below.

Rohan wants to measure the distance of a pond during the visit to his native. He marks points A and B on the opposite edges of a pond as shown in the figure below. To find the distance between the points, he makes a right-angled triangle using rope connecting B with another point C are a distance of 12m, connecting C to point D at a distance of 40m from point C and the connecting D to the point A which is are a distance of 30m from D such the $\angle ADC = 90°$.

(i) What is the distance AC?

(ii) Find the length of the rope used.

(iii) Which is the following does not form a Pythagoras triplet?

OR

Find the length AB?

38. **Case - Study 3:** Read the following passage and answer the questions given below.

The Great Stupa at Sanchi is one of the oldest stone structures in India, and an important monument of Indian Architecture. It was originally commissioned by the emperor Ashoka in the 3rd century BCE. Its nucleus was a simple hemispherical brick structure built over the relics of the Buddha. .It is a perfect example of combination of solid figures. A big hemispherical dome with a cuboidal structure mounted on it. $\left(\text{Take } \pi = \frac{22}{7}\right)$

(i) Calculate the volume of the hemispherical dome if the height of the dome is 21 m?

(ii) What is the lateral surface area of cuboidal shaped top with dimensions $10\text{m} \times 8\text{m} \times 6\text{m}$?

(iii) How much the cloth require to cover the hemispherical dome if the radius of its base is 14m?

OR

What is the total surface area of the combined figure i.e. hemispherical dome with radius 14m and cuboidal shaped top with dimensions $8\text{m} \times 6\text{m} \times 4\text{m}$?

3 Sample Paper

LATEST PATTERN

BLUE PRINT

Ch. No.	Chapter Name	Per Unit Marks	Section-A (1 Mark)		Section-B (2 Marks)	Section-C (3 Marks)	Section-D (5 Marks)	Section-E (4 Marks)	Total Marks
			MCQ	A/R	VSA	SA	LA	Case-Study	
1	Real Number	6	3(Q1, 5, 8)	1(Q19)	1(Q21)				**6**
2	Polynomials	20	2(Q2, 3)						**2**
3	Pair of Linear Equations in Two Variables		2(Q4, 6)				1(Q34)		**7**
4	Quadratic Equations		1(Q7)				1(Q32)		**6**
5	Arithmetic Progression		2(Q9, 10)			1(Q26)			**5**
6	Triangles	15	1(Q11)		1(Q22)				**3**
7	Circles		1(Q17)		1(Q25)		1(Q35)	1(Q36)	**12**
8	Coordinate Geometry	6	3(Q12, 13, 14)	1(Q20)	1(Q23)				**6**
9	Introduction to Trigonometry	12	2(Q15, 16)		1(Q24)	1(Q27)			**7**
10	Some Applications of Trigonometry						1(Q33)		**5**
11	Areas Related to Circles	10				1(Q28)		1(Q37)	**7**
12	Surface Areas and Volumes					1(Q29)			**3**
13	Statistics	11				1(Q30)			**8**
14	Probability		1(Q18)			1(Q31)		1(Q38)	**8**
Total Marks (Total Questions)		**80**	**18(18)**	**2(2)**	**10(5)**	**18(6)**	**20(4)**	**12(3)**	**80(38)**

Note : The number given inside the bracket denotes question number, asked in the sample paper, while the number given outside the bracket are the number of questions from that particular chapter.

Time : 3 Hours **Max. Marks : 80**

General Instructions

1. *This Question paper contains - five sections A, B, C, D and E. Each section is compulsory. However, there are internal choices in some questions.*
2. *Section A has 18 MCQ's and 02 Assertion-Reason based questions of 1 mark each.*
3. *Section B has 5 Very Short Answer (VSA)-type questions of 2 marks each.*
4. *Section C has 6 Short Answer (SA)-type questions of 3 marks each.*
5. *Section D has 4 Long Answer (LA)-type questions of 5 marks each.*
6. *Section E has 3 case based integrated units of assessment (4 marks each) with sub parts of values of 1, 1 and 2 marks each respectively.*

SECTION-A (Multiple Choice Questions)

Each question carries 1 mark.

1. The sum of three non-zero prime numbers is 100. One of them exceeds the other by 36. Then, the largest number is

(a) 73 (b) 91 (c) 67 (d) 57

2. Let $p(y) = y^4 - 3y^2 + 2y + 5$, then the remainder when $p(y)$ is divided by $(y - 1)$.

(a) 2 (b) 3 (c) –5 (d) 5

3. If $x^2 - 4$ is the factor of $2x^3 + k_1x^2 + k_2x + 12$, where k_1, k_2 are constant, then the value of $k_1 + k_2$ is

(a) 11 (b) 5 (c) –11 (d) –5

4. The difference between two numbers is 26 and one number is three times the other. Find them.

(a) 39, 13 (b) 41, 67 (c) 96, 70 (d) 52, 26

5. The value of $0.\overline{235}$ is :

(a) $\frac{233}{900}$ (b) $\frac{233}{990}$ (c) $\frac{235}{999}$ (d) $\frac{235}{990}$

6. ₹49 was divided among 150 children. Each girl got 50 paise and each boy got 25 paise. How many boys were there?

(a) 100 (b) 102 (c) 104 (d) 105

7. If $x^2 + y^2 = 25$, $xy = 12$, then $x =$

(a) $\{3, 4\}$ (b) $\{3, -3\}$ (c) $\{3, 4, -3, -4\}$ (d) $\{-3, -3\}$

8. The unit digit in the expression $55^{725} + 73^{5810} + 22^{853}$ is

(a) 0 (b) 4 (c) 5 (d) 6

9. Sum of n terms of the series $\sqrt{2} + \sqrt{8} + \sqrt{18} + \sqrt{32} + ...$ is

(a) $\frac{n(n+1)}{2}$ (b) $2n((n+1)$ (c) $\frac{n(n+1)}{\sqrt{2}}$ (d) 1

10. If eight times the 8th term of an A.P. is equal to 12 times the 12th term of the A.P. then its 20th term will be

(a) –1 (b) 1 (c) 0 (d) 2

11. The diagonal BD of a parallelogram ABCD intersects the segment AE at the point F, where E is any point on the side BC. Then

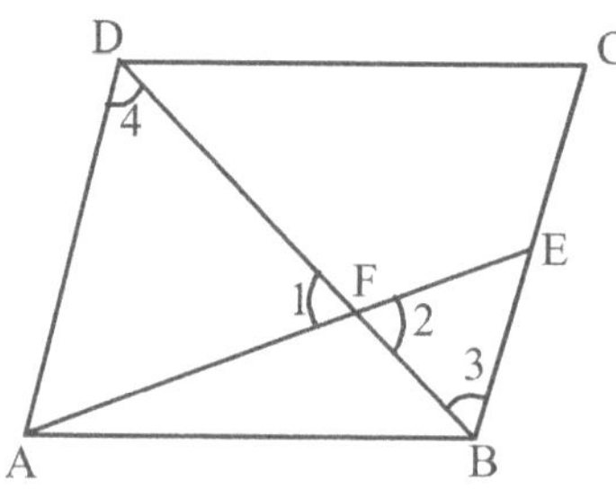

(a) $\frac{EF}{FA}=\frac{FB}{AB}$ (b) $DF\times EF=FB\times FA$ (c) $DF\times EF=(FB)^2$ (d) None of these

12. The perimeter of a triangle with vertices (0, 4), (0, 0) and (3, 0) is

(a) 5 (b) 12 (c) 11 (d) $7+\sqrt{5}$

13. If the point P(6, 2) divides the line segment joining A(6, 5) and B(4, y) in the ratio 3 : 1, then the value of y is

(a) 4 (b) 3 (c) 2 (d) 1

14. The points A (– 4, – 1), B (–2, – 4), C (4, 0) and D (2, 3) are the vertices of a

(a) Parallelogram (b) Rectangle (c) Rhombus (d) Square

15. If $\sin(A+B)=\frac{\sqrt{3}}{2}$ and $\sin 2B=\frac{1}{2}$, then

(a) $\tan B=1$ (b) $B=30°$ (c) $B=45°$ (d) $\cos A=\frac{1}{2}$

16. If $\frac{\cos\theta}{1-\sin\theta}+\frac{\cos\theta}{1+\sin\theta}=4$, then

(a) $\cos\theta=\frac{\sqrt{3}}{2}$ (b) $\sin\theta=\frac{1}{2}$ (c) $\theta=60°$ (d) $\tan\theta=\frac{1}{\sqrt{3}}$

17. In fig. the pair of tangents AP and AQ drawn from an external point A to a circle with centre O are perpendicular to each other and length of each tangent is 5 cm.

Then, the radius of the circle is

P
5 cm
A
O
Q

(a) 2 (b) 3 (c) 5 (d) 1

18. A bag contains 40 coins, consisting of '₹2, '₹5 and ₹10 denominations. If a coin is drawn at random, the probability of drawing a '₹2 coin is $\frac{5}{8}$. If x number of ₹2 coins are removed from the bag and then a coin is drawn at random, the probability of drawing a ₹2 coin is $\frac{1}{2}$. Find the value of x.

(a) 5 (b) 2 (c) 10 (d) 8

(ASSERTION-REASON BASED QUESTIONS)

In the following questions, a statement of Assertion (A) is followed by a statement of Reason (R). Choose the correct answer out of the following choices.

(a) ***Both A and R are true and R is the correct explanation of A.***

(b) ***Both A and R are true but R is not the correct explanation of A.***

(c) ***A is true but R is false.***

(d) ***A is false but R is true.***

19. **Assertion :** If L.C.M. $\{p, q\}=30$ and H.C.F $\{p, q\}=5$, then $p.q=150$.

Reason : L.C.M. of $(a, b)\times$ H.C.F of $(a, b)=a.b.$

20. **Assertion :** Mid-point of a line segment divides line in the ratio 1 : 1.

Reason : If area of triangle is zero that means points are collinear.

SECTION-B

This section comprises of very short answer type-questions (VSA) of 2 marks each.

21. Prove that $\frac{1}{3+\sqrt{11}}$ is irrational.

22. AD is the median of ΔABC. The bisector of $\angle ADB$ and $\angle ADC$ meet AB and AC at points E and F. Prove that $EF \,||\, BC$.

23. If (3,0), (2, a) and (b, 6) are the vertices of a ΔABC, whose centroid is (2, 5). Find the values of a and b.

OR

Using distance formula show that the points A(8,1), B(3, –4) and C(2, –5) are collinear.

24. If $\tan\theta + \sin\theta = m$ and $\tan\theta - \sin\theta = n$, then prove that $m^2 - n^2 = 4\sqrt{mn}$

OR

Solve : $\dfrac{\cos^2\theta}{\cot^2\theta - \cos^2\theta} = 3;\ (\theta < 90°)$

25. In figure, AB is a chord of circle, and PQ is a tangent at point B of the circle. If $\angle AOB = 110°$, then find $\angle ABQ$.

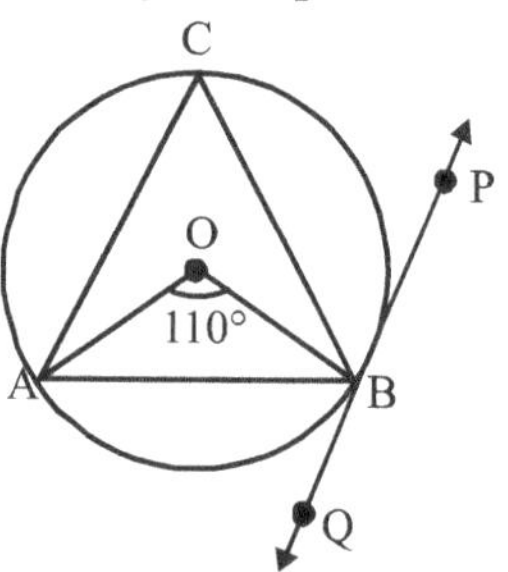

SECTION-C

This section comprises of short answer type questions (SA) of 3 marks each.

26. Find the sum of first 24 terms of the sequence whose n^{th} term is $a_n = 3 + \dfrac{2n}{3}$

OR

The first and the last terms of an AP are 5 and 45 respectively. If the sum of all its terms is 400, find its common difference.

27. If $4\tan\theta = 3$, then $\left(\dfrac{4\sin\theta - \cos\theta}{4\sin\theta + \cos\theta}\right)$ is equal to

28. In figure find the area of the shaded region [Use $\pi = 3.14$]

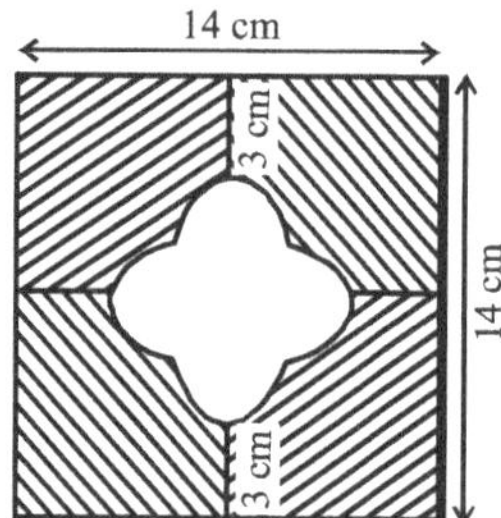

29. In figure, a tent is in the shape of a cylinder surmounted by a conical top of same diameter. If the height and diameter of cylindrical part are 2.1 m and 3 m respectively and the slant height of conical part is 2.8 m, find the cost of canvas needed to make the tent if the canvas is available at the rate of ₹ 500/sq. metre. (Use $\pi = \dfrac{22}{7}$]

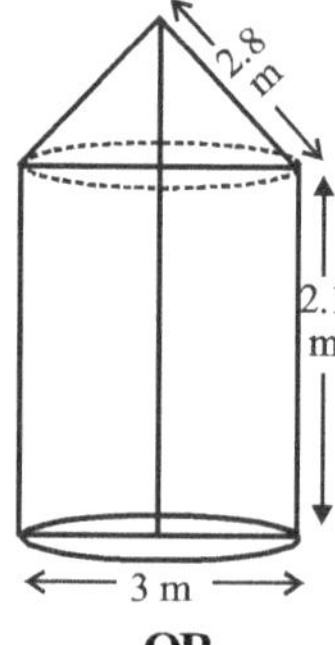

OR

Show that the points A (1, 0), B (5, 3), C (2, 7) and D (–2, 4) are the vertices of a parallelogram.

30. The data regarding marks obtained by 48 students of a class in a class test is given below. Calculate the modal marks of students.

Marks Obtained	0 – 5	5 – 10	10 – 15	15 – 20	20 – 25	25 – 30	30 – 35	35 – 40	40 – 45	45 – 50
Number of students	1	0	2	0	0	10	25	7	2	1

31. Find the chance that a non-leap year contains 53 Saturdays.

SECTION-D

This section comprises of long answer-type questions (LA) of 5 marks each.

32. Sove for x : $\frac{1}{x+1}+\frac{3}{5x+1}=\frac{5}{x+4}, x \neq -1, -\frac{1}{5}, -4$

33. The angle of elevation of an aeroplane from a point A on the ground is 60°. After a flight of 15 seconds, the angle of elevation changes to 30°. If the aeroplane is flying at a constant height of $1500\sqrt{3}$ m, find the speed of the plane in km/hr.

34. Solve the following pair of linear equations graphically :

$$x+3y=6,\ 2x-3y=12$$

Also shade the region bounded by the line $2x - 3y = 12$ and both the co-ordinate axes

OR

Determine graphically whether the following pair of linear equations has :

$$3x - y = 7$$
$$2x + 5y + 1 = 0 \text{ has :}$$

(i) a unique solution (ii) infinitely many solutions or (iii) no solution

35. In figure, a circle is inscribed in a Δ ABC, such that it touches the sides AB, BC and CA at points D, E and F respectively. If the lengths of sides AB, BC and CA are 12 cm, 8 cm and 10 cm respectively, find the lengths of AD, BE and CF.

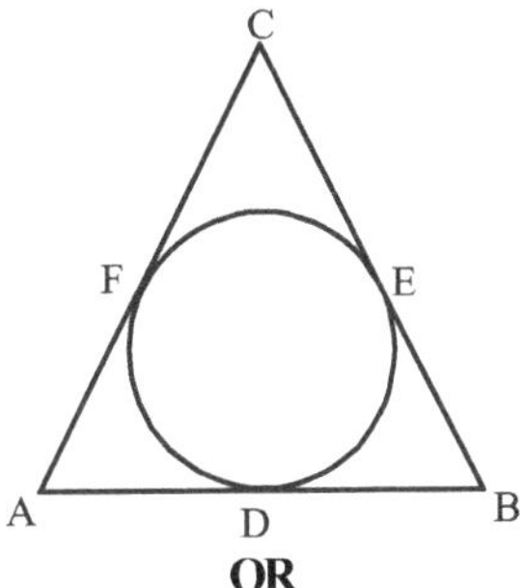

OR

In figure, AP and BP are tangents to a circle with centre O, such that AP = 5 cm and ∠APB = 60°. Find the length of chord AB.

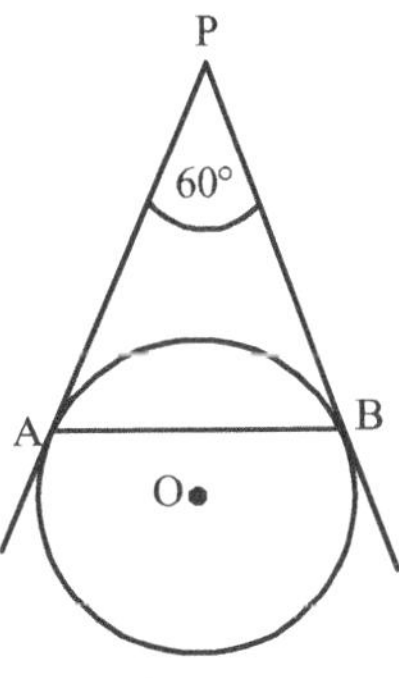

SECTION-E

This section comprises of 3 case study/passage - based questions of 4 marks each with three sub-parts (i), (ii), (iii) of marks 1, 1, 2 respectively.

36. **Case - Study 1:** Read the following passage and answer the questions given below.
Varun has been selected by his School to design logo for Sports Day T-shirts for students and staff. The logo design is as given in the figure and he is working on the fonts and different colours according to the theme.

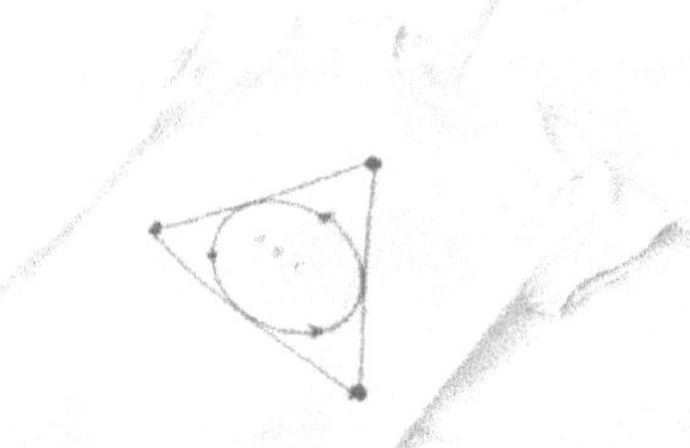

In given figure, a circle with centre O is inscribed in a "ABC, such that it touches the sides AB, BC and CA at points D, E and F respectively. The lengths of sides AB, BC and CA are 12 cm, 8 cm and 10 cm respectively.

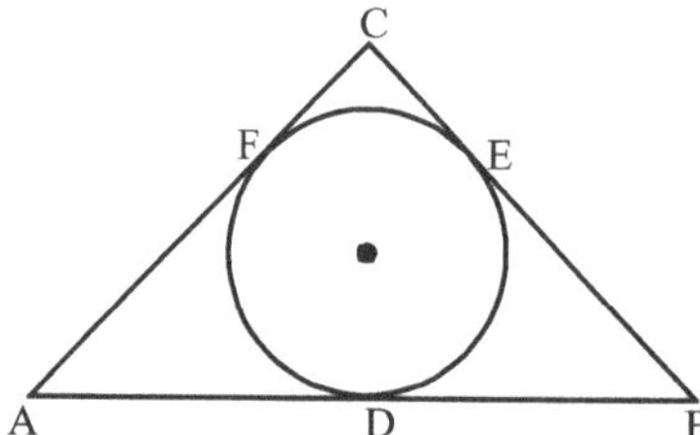

(i) Find the length of AD (ii) Find the Length of BE (iii) Find the length of CF

OR

If radius of the circle is 4cm, Find the area of "OAB

37. Case - Study 2: Read the following passage and answer the questions given below.

On school sport day, a sport teacher make a racing track whose left and right ends are semicircular shown in figure.

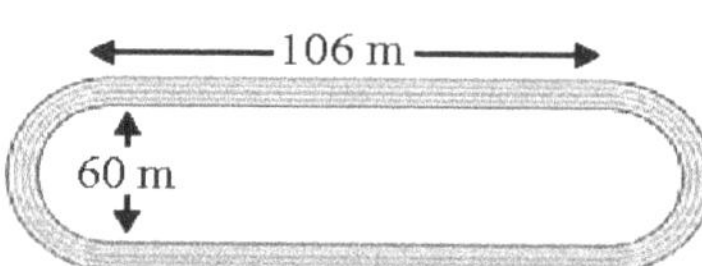

The distance between the two inner parallel line segments is 60 m and they are each 106 m long. If the track is 10 m wide then answer the following questions.

(i) Find the radius of inner semicircular end. (ii) Find the radius of outer semicircular end

(iii) The distance around the track along its inner edge is:

OR

The distance around the track along its outer edge is:

38. Case - Study 3: Read the following passage and answer the questions given below.

Rakesh and Mohit playing a card game. Rakesh picked up a card from properly mixed cards numbered from 1 to 25. Then answer the following questions :

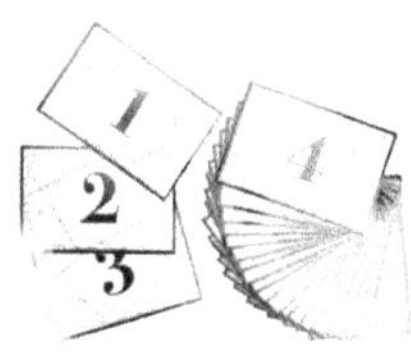

(i) The probability of getting prime numbers is :

(ii) The probability of getting multiple of 3 is :

(iii) The probability of getting multiple of 2 is :

OR

The probability of getting multiple of 2 and 3 is :

4 Sample Paper

LATEST PATTERN

BLUE PRINT

Ch. No.	Chapter Name	Per Unit Marks	Section-A (1 Mark)		Section-B (2 Marks)	Section-C (3 Marks)	Section-D (5 Marks)	Section-E (4 Marks)	Total Marks
			MCQ	A/R	VSA	SA	LA	Case-Study	
1	Real Number	6	2(Q1,5)	1(Q19)		1(Q26)			**6**
2	Polynomials	20	1(Q4)			1(Q28)			**4**
3	Pair of Linear Equations in Two Variables		1(Q2)		1(Q25)				**3**
4	Quadratic Equations		1(Q3)				1(Q32)		**6**
5	Arithmetic Progression					1(Q29)		1(Q36)	**7**
6	Triangles	15	2(Q6,9)		1(Q21)		1(Q33)		**9**
7	Circles		1(Q13)		1(Q23)	1(Q30)			**6**
8	Coordinate Geometry	6	2(Q8,11)					1(Q37)	**6**
9	Introduction to Trigonometry	12	2(Q7,10)	1(Q20)	1(Q22)	1(Q27)			**8**
10	Some Applications of Trigonometry							1(Q38)	**4**
11	Areas Related to Circles	10	3(Q12,14,16)		1(Q24)				**5**
12	Surface Areas and Volumes						1(Q34)		**5**
13	Statistics	11	2(Q15,18)			1(Q31)	1(Q35)		**10**
14	Probability		1(Q17)						**1**
Total Marks (Total Questions)		**80**	**18(18)**	**2(2)**	**10(5)**	**18(6)**	**20(4)**	**12(3)**	**80(38)**

Note : The number given inside the bracket denotes question number, asked in the sample paper, while the number given outside the bracket are the number of questions from that particular chapter.

Time : 3 Hours **Max. Marks : 80**

General Instructions

1. *This Question paper contains - five sections A, B, C, D and E. Each section is compulsory. However, there are internal choices in some questions.*
2. *Section A has 18 MCQ's and 02 Assertion-Reason based questions of 1 mark each.*
3. *Section B has 5 Very Short Answer (VSA)-type questions of 2 marks each.*
4. *Section C has 6 Short Answer (SA)-type questions of 3 marks each.*
5. *Section D has 4 Long Answer (LA)-type questions of 5 marks each.*
6. *Section E has 3 case based/integrated units of assessment (4 marks each) with sub parts of values of 1, 1 and 2 marks each respectively.*

SECTION-A (Multiple Choice Questions)

Each question carries 1 mark.

1. The number 313 – 310 is divisible by
(a) 2 and 3 (b) 3 and 10 (c) 2, 3 and 10 (d) 2, 3 and 13

2. which of the following is true if following pair of linear equations has unique solution?
$3x-2y=-8$
$(2m-5)x+7y-6=0$
(a) $m=\frac{11}{4}$ (b) $m=-\frac{11}{4}$ (c) $m\neq-\frac{11}{4}$ (d) $m\neq\frac{11}{4}$

3. If the equation $x^2+2(k+2)x+9k=0$ has equal roots, then $k=$?
(a) 1 or 4 (b) –1 or 4 (c) 1 or –4 (d) –1 or –4

4. The zeroes of the polynomial $x^2-3x-m(m+3)$ are
(a) $m, m+3$ (b) $-m, m+3$ (c) $m, -(m+3)$ (d) $-m, -(m+3)$

5. Which of the following statement(s) is/are always true?
(a) The sum of two distinct irrational numbers is rational.
(b) The rationalising factor of a number is unique.
(c) Every irrational number is a surd.
(d) None of these

6. In ΔABC, $\frac{AB}{AC}=\frac{BD}{DC}$, $\angle B=70°$ and $\angle C=50°$. Then, $\angle BAD=$_______.

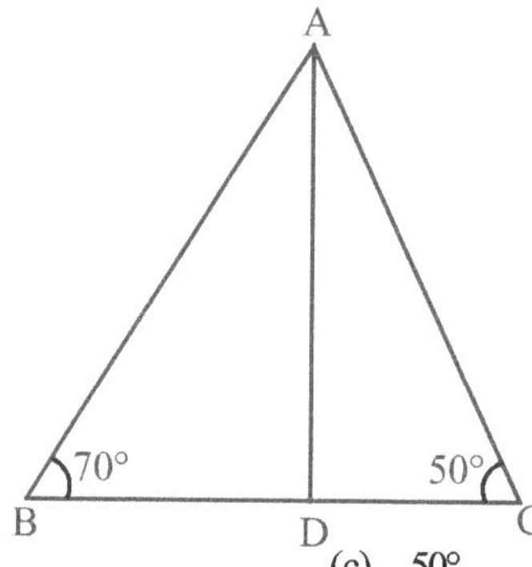

(a) 30° (b) 40° (c) 50° (d) 45°

7. If $x=a(\operatorname{cosec}\theta+\cot\theta)$ and $y=\frac{b(1-\cos\theta)}{\sin\theta}$, then $xy=$
(a) $\frac{a^2+b^2}{a^2-b^2}$ (b) a^2-b^2 (c) ab (d) $\frac{a}{b}$

8. If $\left(\frac{a}{3},4\right)$ is the midpoint of the line segment joining A(–6, 5) and B(–2, 3), then what is the value of 'a'?
(a) –4 (b) –12 (c) 12 (d) –6

9. In the figure, ABC is a triangle in which AD bisects $\angle A$, AC = BC, $\angle B = 72°$ and CD = 1cm. Length of BD (in cm) is

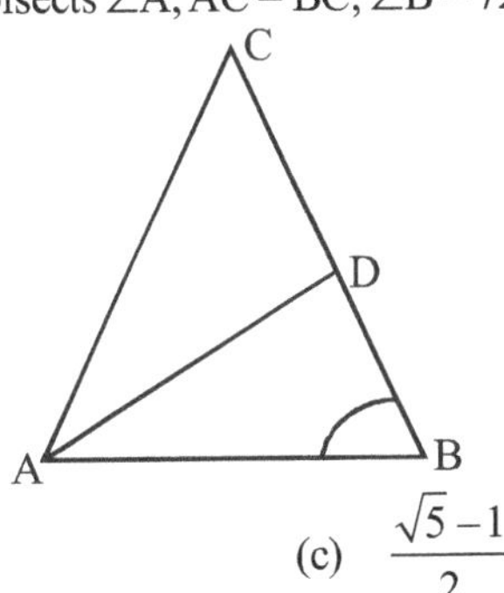

(a) 1 (b) $\frac{1}{2}$ (c) $\frac{\sqrt{5}-1}{2}$ (d) $\frac{\sqrt{3}+1}{2}$

10. If $\cot\theta = \left(\frac{15}{8}\right)$, then evaluate $\frac{(2+2\sin\theta)(1-\sin\theta)}{(1+\cos\theta)(2-2\cos\theta)}$

(a) 1 (b) $\frac{225}{64}$ (c) $\frac{156}{7}$ (d) –1

11. The points (a, b), (a^1, b^1) and $(a-a^1, b-b^1)$ are collinear if

(a) $ab = a^1b^1$ (b) $ab^1 = a^1b$ (c) a = b (d) $a^1 = b^1$

12. If the sum of the circumferences of two circles with diameters d_1 and d_2 is equal to the circumference of a circle of diameter d, then

(a) $d_1^2 + d_2^2 = d^2$ (b) $d_1 + d_2 = d$ (c) $d_1 + d_2 > d$ (d) $d_1 + d_2 < d$

13. In the given figure, PA and PB are two tangents to the circle with centre O. If $\angle APB = 40°$, find $\angle AQB$ and $\angle AMB$.

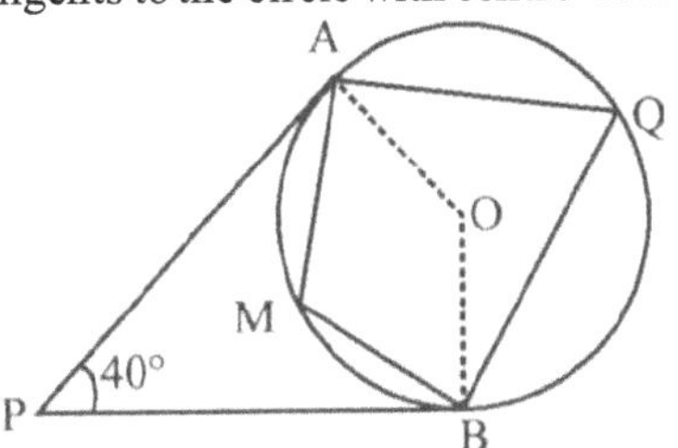

(a) $\angle AQB = 70°, \angle AMB = 110°$ (b) $\angle AQB = 110°, \angle AMB = 70°$
(c) $\angle AQB = 100°, \angle AMB = 50°$ (d) $\angle AQB = 60°, \angle AMB = 40°$

14. Find area of minor segment made by a chord which subtends right-angle at the centre of a circle of radius 10 cm.

(a) 24.5 cm^2 (b) 25.5 cm^2 (c) 24.5 cm^2 (d) 28.5 cm^2

15. There are three sections A, B and C in class X with 25, 40 and 35 students respectively. The average marks obtained by section A, B and C are 70%, 65% and 50% respectively. Find the average marks of entire class X.

(a) 59% (b) 56% (c) 63% (d) 61%

16. The diameter of a garden roller is 1.4 m, and 2m long. How much area will it cover in 5 revolutions.

(a) 44 m^2 (b) 140 m^2 (c) 440 m^2 (d) 220 m^2

17. Two dice are thrown at a time, then find the probability that the difference of the numbers shown on the dice is 1.

(a) $\frac{3}{16}$ (b) $\frac{5}{18}$ (c) $\frac{7}{36}$ (d) $\frac{7}{18}$

18. Calculate the mean of the following frequency distribution:

C. I.	0–80	80–160	160–240	240–320	320–400
Frequency	22	35	44	25	24

(a) 195.5 (b) 198.8 (c) 196.8 (d) 195

(ASSERTION-REASON BASED QUESTIONS)

In the following questions, a statement of Assertion (A) is followed by a statement of Reason (R). Choose the correct answer out of the following choices.

(a) ***Both A and R are true and R is the correct explanation of A.***
(b) ***Both A and R are true but R is not the correct explanation of A.***
(c) ***A is true but R is false.***
(d) ***A is false but R is true.***

19. **Assertion:** $n^2 - n$ is divisible by 2 for every positive integer.
Reason: $\sqrt{2}$ is not a rational number.

20. **Assertion:** In a right angled triangle, if $\cos\theta = \frac{1}{2}$ and $\sin\theta = \frac{\sqrt{3}}{2}$, then $\tan\theta = \sqrt{3}$.
Reason: $\tan\theta = \frac{\sin\theta}{\cos\theta}$

SECTION-B

This section comprises of very short answer type-questions (VSA) of 2 marks each.

21. In a ΔXYZ, if the internal bisector of $\angle X$ meets YZ at 'P', then prove $\frac{XY + XZ}{XZ} = \frac{YZ}{PZ}$

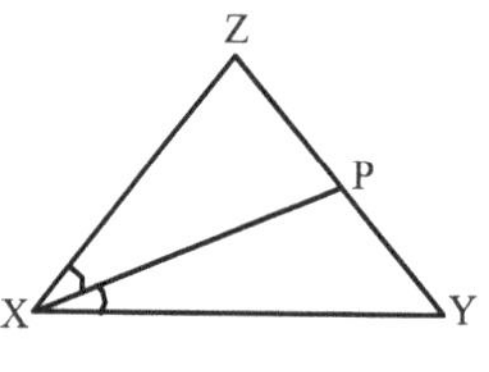

22. If $\sec\theta.\sin\theta = 0$, then find the value of θ.

OR

If $5\tan\theta = 4$, then find the value of $\frac{5\sin\theta - 3\cos\theta}{5\sin\theta + 2\cos\theta}$

23. In the given figure, PA and PB are tangents to the circle from an external point P. CD is another tangent touching the circle at Q. If PA = 12 cm, QC = QD = 3 cm, then find PC + PD.

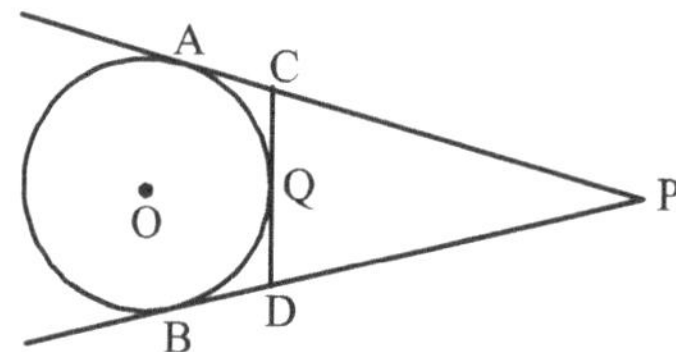

24. Find the radius of the circle inscribed in a square of side 10cm.

25. Solve the following pair of equations : $\frac{2}{\sqrt{x}} + \frac{3}{\sqrt{y}} = 2$ and $\frac{4}{\sqrt{x}} - \frac{9}{\sqrt{y}} = -1$

OR

Solve the system of equations : $\frac{2}{x} + \frac{2}{3y} = \frac{1}{6}$ and $\frac{3}{x} + \frac{2}{y} = 0$ and hence find 'p' for which $y = px - 4$.

SECTION-C

This section comprises of short answer type questions (SA) of 3 marks each.

26. Prove that $\sqrt{5}$ is irrational.

27. If $\sec\theta + \tan\theta = p$, show that $\sec\theta - \tan\theta = \frac{1}{p}$. Hence, find the values of $\cos\theta$ and $\sin\theta$.

OR

If $3\cot A = 4$, check whether $\frac{1 - \tan^2 A}{1 + \tan^2 A} = \cos^2 A - \sin^2 A$ or not.

28. Quadratic polynomial $2x^2 - 3x + 1$ has zeroes as α and β. Now form a quadratic polynomial whose zeroes are 3α and 3β.

29. The first three terms of an AP respectively are $3y - 1$, $3y + 5$ and $5y + 1$. Then y equals:

OR

If k, $2k - 1$ and $2k + 1$ are three consecutive terms of an AP the value of k is

30. In the adjoining figure, PA and PB are tangents to a circle with centre O. If OP is equal to the diameter of the circle, prove that ΔABP is an equilateral triangle.

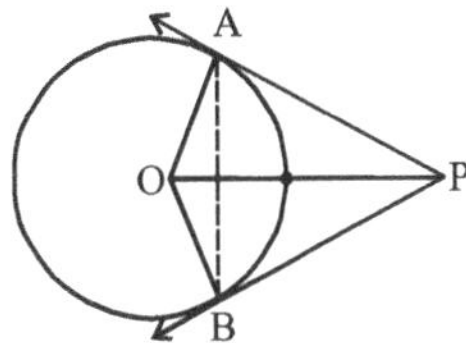

31. If the median for the following frequency distribution is 28.5, find the values of x and y:

Class Interval	Frequencies
0 – 10	5
10 – 20	x
20 – 30	20
30 – 40	15
40 – 50	y
50 – 60	5
Total	**60**

SECTION-D

This section comprises of long answer-type questions (LA) of 5 marks each.

32. A thief runs with a uniform speed of 100 m/minute. After one minute a policeman runs after the thief to catch him. He goes with a speed of 100 m/minute in the first minute and increases his speed by 10 m/minute every succeeding minute. After how many minutes the policeman will catch the thief.

33. In ΔABC, AD is the median to BC and in ΔPQR, PM is the median to QR. If $\frac{AB}{PQ} = \frac{BC}{QR} = \frac{AD}{PM}$. Prove that $\Delta ABC \sim \Delta PQR$.

OR

If the corresponding sides of two triangles are proportional (i.e., in the same ratio), then prove that their corresponding angles are equal and hence the two triangles are similar.

34. 150 spherical marbles, each of diameter 1.4 cm, are dropped in a cylindrical vessel of diameter 7 cm containing some water, which are completely immersed in water. Find the rise in the level of water in the vessel.

OR

Volume and surface area of a solid hemisphere are numerically equal. What is the diameter of hemisphere?

35. The median of the following data is 525. Find the values of x and y if the total frequency is 100.

Class Interval	0–100	100–200	200–300	300–400	400–500	500–600	600–700	700–800	800–900	900–1000
Frequency	2	5	x	12	17	20	y	9	7	4

SECTION-E

This section comprises of 3 case study/passage - based questions of 4 marks each with three sub-parts (i), (ii), (iii) of marks 1, 1, 2 respectively.

36. Case - Study 1: Read the following passage and answer the questions given below.

Students of class X were given a task to observe the application of arithmetic progression for the construction of staiyers at a football ground.

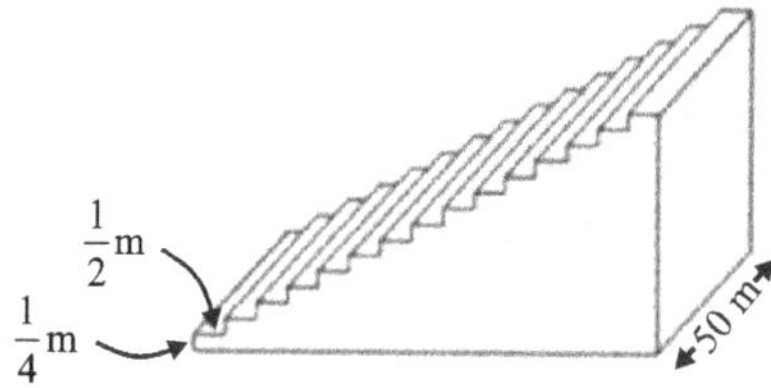

In the figure a small terrace at a football ground comprises of 15 steps each of which is 50 m long and built of solid concrete.

Each step has a rise of $\frac{1}{4}m$ and a tread of $\frac{1}{2}m$

Then, answer the following questions

(i) Find volume of the concrete for the first step of terrace.

(ii) Find volume of the concrete for the 8th step of terrace.

(iii) Find the common difference of A.P formed by the volume of steps of terrace.

OR

Find total volume of concrete required to build the terrace.

37. Case - Study 2: Read the following passage and answer the questions given below.

Class X students of a secondary school in Krishnagar have been allotted a rectangular plot of a land for gardening activity. Saplings of Gulmohar are planted on the boundary at a distance of 1m from each other. There is a triangular grassy lawn in the plot as shown in the fig. The students are to sow seeds of flowering plants on the remaining area of the plot.

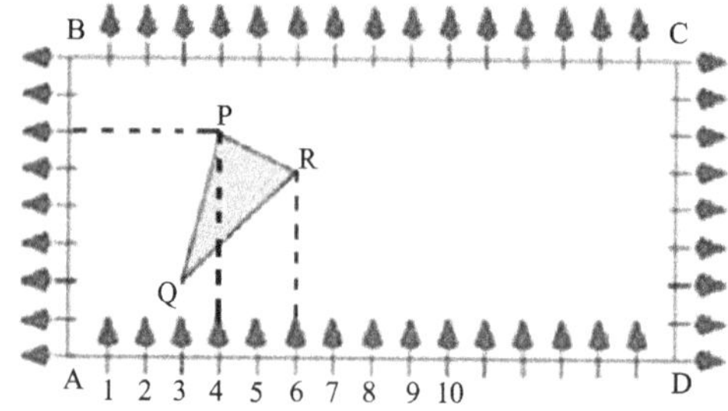

Considering A as origin, answer following questions.

(i) Considering A as the origin, what are the coordinates of A?

(ii) What are the coordinates of P?

(iii) What are the coordinates of R?

OR

What are the coordinates of D?

38. Case - Study 3: Read the following passage and answer the questions given below.

Two pillars of equal height are one either side of a road, which is 100 m wide. The angles of elevation of the top of the pillars are 60° and 30° at a point on the road between the pillars, then

(i) Find distance of the point from a pillar making an angle of 60° is

(ii) Find distance of the point from a pillar making an angle of 30° is

(iii) Find the height of each pillar is

OR

Find the sum of distance of point from both tops.

5 Sample Paper

LATEST PATTERN

BLUE PRINT

Ch. No.	Chapter Name	Per Unit Marks	Section-A (1 Mark)		Section-B (2 Marks)	Section-C (3 Marks)	Section-D (5 Marks)	Section-E (4 Marks)	Total Marks
			MCQ	A/R	VSA	SA	LA	Case-Study	
1	Real Number	6	2(Q1, 4)					1(Q36)	6
2	Polynomials	20				1(Q26)			3
3	Pair of Linear Equations in Two Variables							1(Q37)	4
4	Quadratic Equations						1(Q32)		5
5	Arithmetic Progression					1(Q27)	1(Q33)		8
6	Triangles	15	2(Q2, 5)	1(Q19)			1(Q34)		8
7	Circles		2(Q11, 14)		1(Q22)	1(Q30)			7
8	Coordinate Geometry	6	3(Q3, 6, 8)	1(Q20)	1(Q25)				6
9	Introduction to Trigonometry	12	3(Q7, 10, 13)		1(Q21)	1(Q28)			8
10	Some Applications of Trigonometry		1(Q9)			1(Q29)			4
11	Areas Related to Circles	10			1(Q23)	1(Q31)			5
12	Surface Areas and Volumes		1(Q12)					1(Q38)	5
13	Statistics	11	2(Q17, 18)				1(Q35)		7
14	Probability		2(Q16, 15)		1(Q24)				4
Total Marks (Total Questions)		**80**	**18(18)**	**2(2)**	**10(5)**	**18(6)**	**20(4)**	**12(3)**	**80(38)**

Note : The number given inside the bracket denotes question number, asked in the sample paper, while the number given outside the bracket are the number of questions from that particular chapter.

Time : 3 Hours **Max. Marks : 80**

General Instructions

1. *This Question paper contains - five sections A, B, C, D and E. Each section is compulsory. However, there are internal choices in some questions.*
2. *Section A has 18 MCQ's and 02 Assertion-Reason based questions of 1 mark each.*
3. *Section B has 5 Very Short Answer (VSA)-type questions of 2 marks each.*
4. *Section C has 6 Short Answer (SA)-type questions of 3 marks each.*
5. *Section D has 4 Long Answer (LA)-type questions of 5 marks each.*
6. *Section E has 3 case based integrated units of assessment (4 marks each) with sub parts of values of 1, 1 and 2 marks each respectively.*

SECTION-A (Multiple Choice Questions)

Each question carries 1 mark.

1. The least number which is a perfect square and is divisible by each of 16, 20 and 24 is
(a) 240 (b) 1600 (c) 2400 (d) 3600

2. If the lengths of the diagonals of rhombus are 16 cm and 12 cm. Then, the length of the sides of the rhombus is
(a) 9 cm (b) 10 cm (c) 8 cm (d) 20 cm

3. P, Q, R are three collinear points. The coordinates of P and R are (3, 4) and (11, 10) respectively and PQ is equal to 2.5 units. Coordinates of Q are
(a) (5, 11/2) (b) (11, 5/2) (c) (5, –11/2) (d) (–5, 11/2)

4. If $m = n^2 - n$, where n is an integer, then $m^2 - 2m$ is divisible by
(a) 20 (b) 24 (c) 30 (d) 16

5. In figure, two line segments AC and BD intersect each other at the point P such that PA = 6 cm, PB = 3 cm, PC = 2.5 cm, PD = 5 cm, $\angle APB = 50°$ and $\angle CDP = 30°$. Then, $\angle PBA$ is equal to

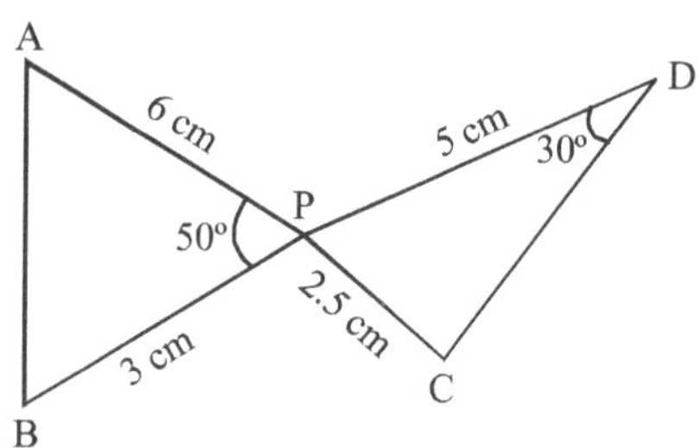

(a) 50° (b) 30° (c) 60° (d) 100°

6. The coordinates of the point which is reflection of point (–3, 5) in x-axis are
(a) (3, 5) (b) (3, –5) (c) (–3, –5) (d) (–3, 5)

7. If cosec x + sin $x = a$ and sec x + cos $x = b$, then
(a) $(a^2b)^{\frac{2}{3}} + (ab^2)^{\frac{2}{3}} = 1$ (b) $(ab^2)^{\frac{2}{3}} + (a^2b^2)^{\frac{2}{3}} = 1$ (c) $a^2 + b^2 = 1$ (d) $b^2 - a^2 = 1$

8. C is the mid-point of PQ, if P is $(4, x)$, C is $(y, -1)$ and Q is $(-2, 4)$, then x and y respectively are
(a) – 6 and 1 (b) – 6 and 2 (c) 6 and – 1 (d) 6 and – 2

9. If the angle of depression of an object from a 75 m high tower is 30°, then the distance of the object from the tower is
(a) $25\sqrt{3}$ m (b) $50\sqrt{3}$ m (c) $75\sqrt{3}$ m (d) 150 m

10. $\dfrac{1+\tan^2 A}{1+\cot^2 A} = L$
(a) $\sec^2 A$ (b) –1 (c) $\cot^2 A$ (d) $\tan^2 A$

11. In the below diagram, O is the centre of the circle, AC is the diameter and if ∠APB = 120°, then ∠BQC is

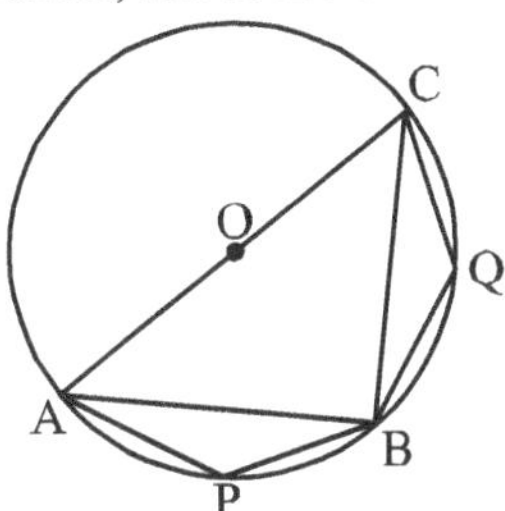

(a) 30° (b) 150° (c) 90° (d) 120°

12. If four times the sum of the areas of two circular faces of a cylinder of height 8 cm is equal to twice the curve surface area, then diameter of the cylinder is
(a) 4 cm (b) 8 cm (c) 2 cm (d) 6 cm

13. (sec A + tan A) (1 – sin A) =
(a) sec A (b) sin A (c) cosec A (d) cos A

14. In two concentric circles, if chords are drawn in the outer circle which touch the inner circle, then
(a) all chords are of different lengths.
(b) all chords are of same length.
(c) only parallel chords are of same length.
(d) only perpendicular chords are of same length.

15. A school has five houses A, B, C, D and E. A class has 23 students, 4 from house A, 8 from house B, 5 from house C, 2 from house D and rest from house E. A single student is selected at random to be the class monitor. The probability that the selected student is not from A, B and C is
(a) $\frac{4}{23}$ (b) $\frac{6}{23}$ (c) $\frac{8}{23}$ (d) $\frac{17}{23}$

16. A box contains a number of marbles with serial number 18 to 38. A marble is picked at a random. Find the probability that it is a multiple of 3.
(a) $\frac{3}{5}$ (b) $\frac{7}{20}$ (c) $\frac{3}{4}$ (d) $\frac{1}{3}$

17. The median of a set of 9 distinct observations is 20.5. If each of the largest 4 observation of the set is increased by 2, then the median of the new set
(a) is increased by 2
(b) is decreased by 2
(c) is two times the original median
(d) remains the same as that of the original set

18. The mean of a group of eleven consecutive natural numbers is m. What will be the percentage change in the mean when next six consecutive natural numbers are included in the group ?
(a) m % (b) $\frac{m}{3}$ % (c) $\frac{m}{300}$ % (d) $\frac{300}{m}$ %

(ASSERTION-REASON BASED QUESTIONS)

In the following questions, a statement of Assertion (A) is followed by a statement of Reason (R). Choose the correct answer out of the following choices.

(a) *Both A and R are true and R is the correct explanation of A.*
(b) *Both A and R are true but R is not the correct explanation of A.*
(c) *A is true but R is false.*
(d) *A is false but R is true.*

19. **Assertion :** ABC is an isosceles, right triangle, right angled at C. Then $AB^2 = 3AC^2$.
Reason : In an isosceles triangle ABC if $AC = BC$ and $AB^2 = 2AC^2$, then $\angle C = 90°$.

20. **Assertion :** The points $(k, 2 - 2k)$, $(-k + 1, 2k)$ and $(-4 - k, 6 - 2k)$ are collinear if $k = \frac{1}{2}$.
Reason : Three points A, B and C are collinear in same straight line, if $AB + BC = AC$.

SECTION-B

This section comprises of very short answer type-questions (VSA) of 2 marks each.

21. If sin A + cosec A = 3 then the value of $\frac{\sin^4 A + 1}{\sin^2 A}$ is ________.

22. Find the length of the tangent drawn from a point, whose distance from the centre of a circle is 5 cm and radius of the circle is 3 cm.

23. An umbrella has 8 ribs which are equally spaced (see Fig.). Assuming umbrella to be a flat circle of radius 45 cm, find the area between the two consecutive ribs of the umbrella.

24. 90% of the mangoes in a bag are good. If a mango is chosen randomly from the box, find the probability of getting a bad mango.

OR

A bag contains 40 coins, consisting of ₹ 2, ₹ 5 and ₹ 10 denominations. If a coin is drawn at random, the probability of drawing a ₹ 2 coin is $\frac{5}{8}$. If x ₹ 2 coins are removed from the bag and then a coin is drawn at random, the probability of drawing a ₹ 2 coin is $\frac{1}{2}$. Find the value of x.

25. Find 'k' so that the points (7, –2), (5, 1) and (3, k) are collinear.

OR

Find the value of a, if the distance between the points A(–3, –14) and B(a, –5) is 9 units.

SECTION-C

This section comprises of short answer type questions (SA) of 3 marks each.

26. Verify whether 2, 3 and $\frac{1}{2}$ are the zeroes of the polynomial $p(x) = 2x^3 - 11x^2 + 17x - 6$.

OR

Find the zeroes of the quadratic polynomial $5x^2 + 8x - 4$ and verify the relationship between the zeroes and the coefficients of the polynomial.

27. If p, q, r are in A.P. then find the value of $p^3 + r^3 - 8q^3$.

OR

Find the number of terms of the AP 18, 15½, 13, ..., – 49½ and find the sum of all its terms.

28. If $a \cos \theta + b \sin\theta = m$ and $a \sin \theta - b\cos \theta = n$, prove that $a^2 + b^2 = m^2 + n^2$

29. Two ships are there in the sea on either side of a light house in such a way that the ships and the light house are in the same straight line. The angles of depression of two ships as observed from the top of the light house are 60° and 45°. If the height of the light house is 200m, find the distance between the two ships. [Use $\sqrt{3}$ = 1.73].

30. A circle touches all the four sides of a quadrilateral ABCD. Prove that AB + CD = BC + DA.

31. In figure, PQRS is a square lawn with side PQ = 42 metres. Two circular flower beds are there on the sides PS and QR with centre at O, the intersection of its diagonals. Find the total area of the two flower beds (shaded parts).

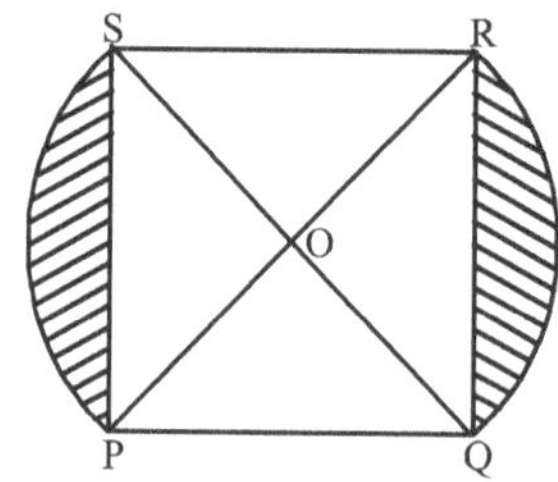

SECTION-D

This section comprises of long answer-type questions (LA) of 5 marks each.

32. Solve the equation : $\left(\frac{2x-3}{x-1}\right)-4\left(\frac{x-1}{2x-3}\right)=3, x \neq 1, 3/2$

OR

The sum of the reciprocals of Rehman's ages, (in years) 3 years ago and 5 years from now is $\frac{1}{3}$. Find his present age.

33. If the sum of p terms of an A.P. is q and the sum of q terms is p then, show that sum of $(p-q)$ terms is equal to $(p-q)\left(1+\frac{2q}{p}\right)$.

OR

If S_1, S_2, S_3, be the sum of n, 2n and 3n terms respectively of an A.P., prove that $S_3 = 3(S_2 - S_1)$

34. Prove that if a line is drawn parallel to one side of a triangle to intersect the other two sides in distinct points, then other two sides are divided in the same ratio.

35. On the sports day of a school, 300 students participated. Their ages are given in the following distribution:

Age (in years)	5 - 7	7 - 9	9 - 11	11 - 13	13 - 15	15 - 17	17 - 19
Number of students	67	33	41	95	36	13	15

Find the mode of the data.

SECTION-E

This section comprises of 3 case study/passage - based questions of 4 marks each with three sub-parts (i), (ii), (iii) of marks 1, 1, 2 respectively.

36. Case - Study 1: Read the following passage and answer the questions given below.

Situation-1

H.C.F. × L.C.M. = Product of two integers.

(i) The H.C.F. of two numbers is 16 and their product is 3072. Find their L.C.M.

(ii) The sum of two numbers is 135 and their H.C.F. is 27. If their L.C.M. is 162, then what will be the numbers?

Situation-2

HCF of natural numbers is the largest factor which is common to all the number and LCM of natural numbers is the smallest natural number which is multiple of all the numbers.

(iii) The LCM and HCF of two rational numbers are equal. Which types of numbers satisfy the given condition ?

OR

If two positive integers a and b are expressible in the form $a = pq^2$ and $b = p^3q$; p, q being prime number, then what will be the LCM of (a, b) ?

37. Case - Study 2: Read the following passage and answer the questions given below.

A two digit number is obtained by either multiplying sum of the digits by 8 and adding 1 or by multiplying the difference of the digits by 13 and adding 2.

If x be the digit in ten's place and y be the digit at unit place with x > y, then answer the following questions.

(i) Find the equation corresponding to multiplying sum of the digits by 8 and adding 1.

(ii) Find the equation corresponding to multiplying the difference of the digits by 13 and adding 2.

(iii) What is the value of y ?

OR

What is the value of x ?

38. Case - Study 3: Read the following passage and answer the questions given below.

Adventure camps are the perfect place for the children to practice decision making for themselves without parents and teachers guiding their every move. Some students of a school reached for adventure at Sakleshpur. At the camp, the waiters served some students with a welcome drink in a cylindrical glass and some students in a hemispherical cup whose dimensions are shown below. After that they went for a jungle trek. The jungle trek was enjoyable but tiring. As dusk fell, it was time to take shelter. Each group of four students was given a canvas of area $551 m^2$. Each group had to make a conical tent to accommodate all the four students. Assuming that all the stitching and wasting incurred while cutting, would amount to $1 m^2$, the students put the tents. The radius of the tent is 7 m.

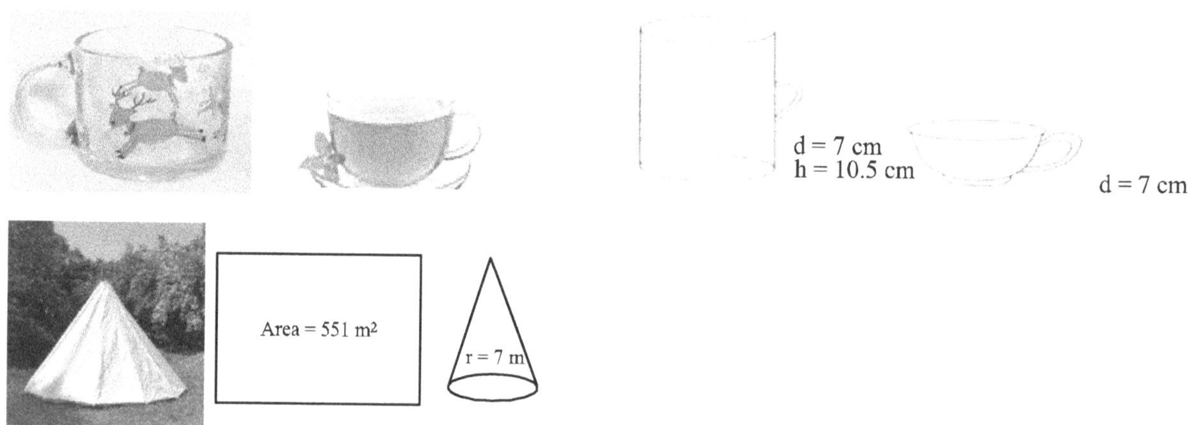

(i) What will be the volume of cylindrical cup ?

(ii) What will be the volume of hemispherical cup ?

(iii) What is the height of the conical tent prepared to accommodate four students ?

OR

How much space on the ground is occupied by each student in the conical tent.

6 Sample Paper

LATEST PATTERN

BLUE PRINT

Ch. No.	Chapter Name	Per Unit Marks	Section-A (1 Mark)		Section-B (2 Marks)	Section-C (3 Marks)	Section-D (5 Marks)	Section-E (4 Marks)	Total Marks
			MCQ	A/R	VSA	SA	LA	Case-Study	
1	Real Number	6	4(Q1, 2, 7, 15)		1(Q21)				6
2	Polynomials	20						1(Q36)	4
3	Pair of Linear Equations in Two Variables		1(Q4)	1(Q19)					2
4	Quadratic Equations					1(Q26)	1(Q32)		8
5	Arithmetic Progression		1(Q3)				1(Q33)		6
6	Triangles	15	3(Q5, 9, 14)	1(Q20)		1(Q27)			7
7	Circles		1(Q17)		1(Q25)		1(Q34)		8
8	Coordinate Geometry	6	2(Q6, 12)		2(Q22, 23)				6
9	Introduction to Trigonometry	12	3(Q8, 16, 18)			2(Q28, 30)			9
10	Some Applications of Trigonometry					1(Q31)			3
11	Areas Related to Circles	10	1(Q11)						1
12	Surface Areas and Volumes						1(Q35)	1(Q37)	9
13	Statistics	11	1(Q13)			1(Q29)			4
14	Probability		1(Q10)		1(Q24)			1(Q38)	7
Total Marks (Total Questions)		**80**	**18(18)**	**2(2)**	**10(5)**	**18(6)**	**20(4)**	**12(3)**	**80(38)**

Note : The number given inside the bracket denotes question number, asked in the sample paper, while the number given outside the bracket are the number of questions from that particular chapter.

Time : 3 Hours **Max. Marks : 80**

General Instructions

1. *This Question paper contains - five sections A, B, C, D and E. Each section is compulsory. However, there are internal choices in some questions.*
2. *Section A has 18 MCQ's and 02 Assertion-Reason based questions of 1 mark each.*
3. *Section B has 5 Very Short Answer (VSA)-type questions of 2 marks each.*
4. *Section C has 6 Short Answer (SA)-type questions of 3 marks each.*
5. *Section D has 4 Long Answer (LA)-type questions of 5 marks each.*
6. *Section E has 3 case based/integrated units of assessment (4 marks each) with sub parts of values of 1, 1 and 2 marks each respectively.*

SECTION-A (Multiple Choice Questions)

Each question carries 1 mark.

1. The sum of exponents of prime factors in the prime-factorisation of 196 is

(a) 3 (b) 4 (c) 5 (d) 2

2. If , then $2x$ is

(a) $1.\overline{4}$ (b) $1.\overline{5}$ (c) $1.\overline{54}$ (d) $1.\overline{45}$

3. If eight times the 8th term of an A.P. is equal to 12 times the 12th term of the A.P. then its 20th term will be

(a) –1 (b) 1 (c) 0 (d) 2

4. At present ages of a father and his son are in the ratio 7 : 3, and they will be in the ratio 2 : 1 after 10 years. Then the present age of father (in years) is

(a) 42 (b) 56 (c) 70 (d) 77

5. ΔABC is an isosceles triangle right angled at B. Similar triangles ACD and ABE are constructed on sides AC and AB. Ratio between the sides AB and AC

(a) 1 : 4 (b) 2 : 1 (c) $1 : \sqrt{2}$ (d) 4 : 3

6. The coordinates of the point which is reflection of point (–3, 5) in x-axis are

(a) (3, 5) (b) (3, –5) (c) (–3, –5) (d) (–3, 5)

7. If n is an even natural number, then the largest natural number by which $n(n+1)(n+2)$ is divisible is

(a) 6 (b) 8 (c) 12 (d) 24

8. $\cos 1° . \cos 2° . \cos 3°$ .... $\cos 179°$ is equal to

(a) –1 (b) 0 (c) 1 (d) $1/\sqrt{2}$

9. The diagonal BD of a parallelogram ABCD intersects the segment AE at the point F, where E is any point on the side BC. Then

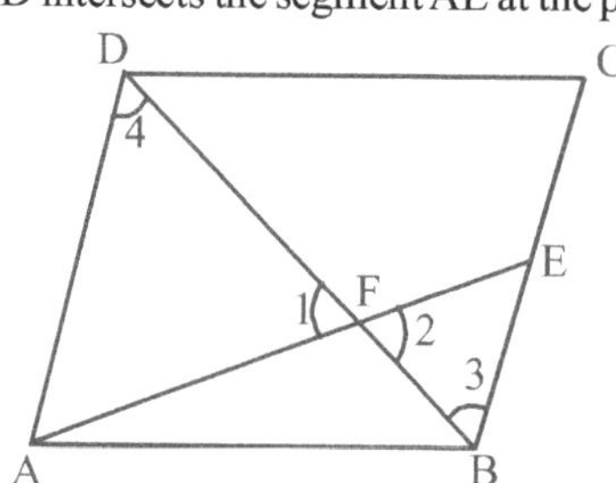

(a) $\frac{EF}{FA} = \frac{FB}{AB}$ (b) $DF \times EF = FB \times FA$ (c) $DF \times EF = (FB)^2$ (d) None of these

10. Which of the following cannot be the probability of an event?

(a) 2/3 (b) – 1/5 (c) 15% (d) 0.7

11. A race track is in the form of a ring whose inner and outer circumference are 437m and 503m respectively. The area of the track is

(a) 66 sq. cm (b) 4935 sq. cm (c) 9870 sq. cm (d) None of these

12. C is the mid-point of PQ, if P is $(4, x)$, C is $(y, -1)$ and Q is $(-2, 4)$, then x and y respectively are
(a) -6 and 1 (b) -6 and 2 (c) 6 and -1 (d) 6 and -2

13. The numbers 3, 5, 7 and 9 have their respective frequencies $x-2$, $x+2$, $x-3$ and $x+3$. If the arithmetic mean is 6.5, then the value of x is
(a) 3 (b) 4 (c) 5 (d) 6

14. From the given figure, then length of the sides AB and BD.

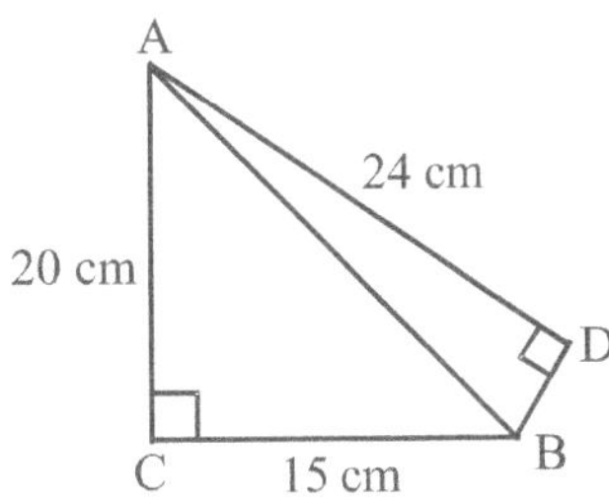

(a) 25 cm and 7 cm (b) 25 cm and 17 cm (c) 7 cm and 15 cm (d) 18 cm and 7 cm

15. The least number which when divided by 15, leaves a remainder of 5, when divided by 25, leaves a remainder of 15 and when divided by 35, leaves a remainder of 25, is
(a) 515 (b) 525 (c) 1040 (d) 1050

16. The value of $\frac{\tan 30°}{\cot 60°}$ is
(a) $\frac{1}{\sqrt{2}}$ (b) $\frac{1}{\sqrt{3}}$ (c) $\sqrt{3}$ (d) 1

17. A tangent CQ touches a circle with centre O at P. Diameter AB is produced to meet the tangent at C. If $\angle ACP = a°$ and $\angle BPC = b°$, the relation connecting a and b is

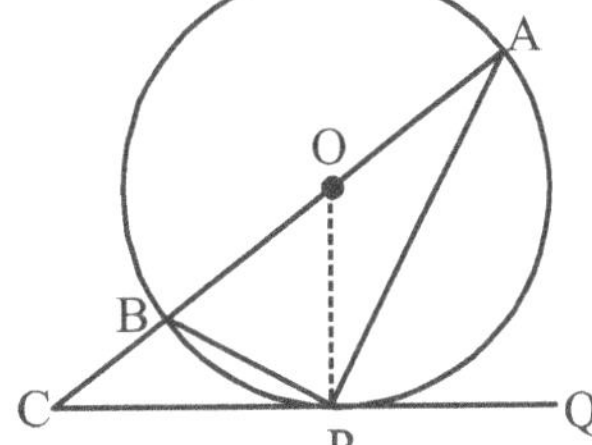

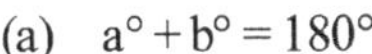
(a) $a° + b° = 180°$ (b) $a° + 2b° = 90°$
(c) $a° - b° = 60°$ (d) $2a° + b° = 100°$

18. If $\cos A = \frac{4}{5}$, then the value of tan A is
(a) $\frac{3}{5}$ (b) $\frac{3}{4}$ (c) $\frac{4}{3}$ (d) $\frac{5}{3}$

(ASSERTION-REASON BASED QUESTIONS)

In the following questions, a statement of Assertion (A) is followed by a statement of Reason (R). Choose the correct answer out of the following choices.

(a) ***Both A and R are true and R is the correct explanation of A.***
(b) ***Both A and R are true but R is not the correct explanation of A.***
(c) ***A is true but R is false.***
(d) ***A is false but R is true.***

19. **Assertion :** The value of $q = \pm 2$, if $x = 3, y = 1$ is the solution of the line $2x + y - q^2 - 3 = 0$
Reason : The solution of the line will satisfy the equation of the line

20. **Assertion :** If in a ΔABC, a line $DE \parallel BC$, intersects AB in D and AC in E, then $\frac{AB}{AD} = \frac{AC}{AE}$.
Reason : If a line is drawn parallel to one side of a triangle intersecting the other two sides, then the other two sides are divided in the same ratio.

SECTION-B

This section comprises of very short answer type-questions (VSA) of 2 marks each.

21. Explain why 13233343563715 is a composite number?

22. If the point P $(k-1, 2)$ is equidistant from the points A $(3, k)$ and B $(k, 5)$, find the values of k.

23. In fig., the area of triangle ABC (in sq. units) is :

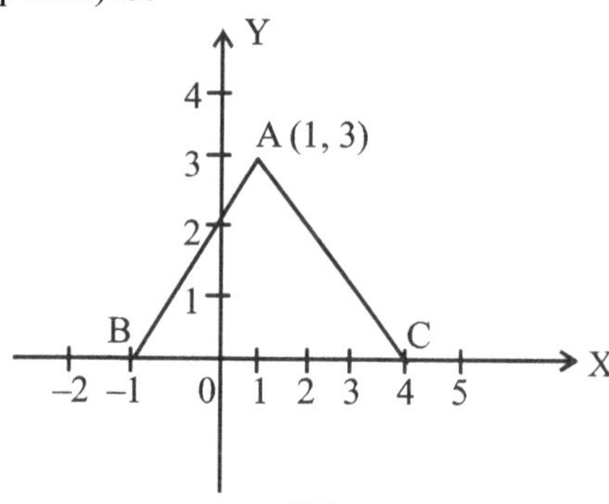

OR

Find the value of a, if the distance between the points A(–3, –14) and B(a, –5) is 9 units.

24. In ΔABC, if X and Y are points on AB and AC respectively such that $\frac{AX}{XB} = \frac{3}{4}$, $AY = 5$ cm and $YC = 9$ cm, then state whether XY and BC parallel or not.

OR

In an equilateral triangle of side 24 cm, find the length of the altitude.

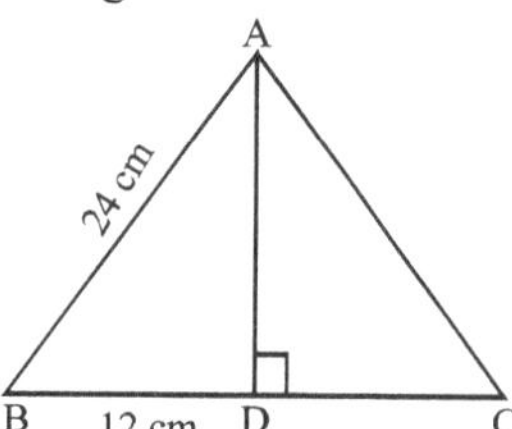

25. If the difference between the circumference and the radius of a circle is 37 cm, then using $\pi = \frac{22}{7}$, the circumference (in cm) of the circle is:

SECTION-C

This section comprises of short answer type questions (SA) of 3 marks each.

26. Sum of the areas of two squares is 400 cm^2. If the difference of their perimeters is 16 cm, find the sides of the two squares.

OR

Solve the following pair of linear equations by substitution method:

$$3x + 2y - 7 = 0$$
$$4x + y - 6 = 0$$

27. In given figure $DE \parallel BC$. If $AD = 3$ cm, $DB = 4$cm and $AE = 6$ cm, then find EC.

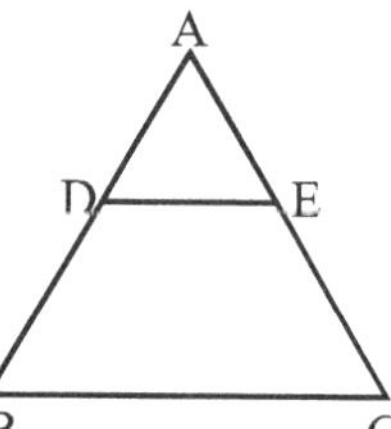

28. Evaluate : $\dfrac{5\cos^2 60° + 4\cos^2 30° - \tan^2 45°}{\sin^2 30° + \cos^2 60°}$

29. If the mean of the following data is 14.7, find the value of p and q.

Class	0 – 6	6 – 12	12 –18	18 – 24	24 –30	30 –36	36 – 42	Total
Frequency	10	p	4	7	q	4	1	40

OR

On the sports day of a school, 300 students participated. Their ages are given in the following distribution:

Age (in years)	5 – 7	7 – 9	9 – 11	11 – 13	13 – 15	15 – 17	17 – 19
Number of students	67	33	41	95	36	13	15

Find the mean and mode of the data.

30. Evaluate : $\tan^2 30° \sin 30° + \cos 60° \sin^2 90° \tan^2 60° - 2\tan 45° \cos^2 0° \sin 90°$

31. The angle of elevation of an aeroplane from a point on the ground is 60°. After a flight of 30 seconds the angle of elevation becomes 30°. If the aeroplane is flying at a constant height of $3000\sqrt{3}$ m, find the speed of the aeroplane.

SECTION-D

This section comprises of long answer-type questions (LA) of 5 marks each.

32. Solve for x : $\frac{1}{x+1}+\frac{2}{x+2}=\frac{4}{x+4}, x \neq -1, -2, -4$

OR

A motor boat whose speed is 24 km/h in still water takes 1 hour more to go 32 km upstream than to return downstream to the same spot. Find the speed of the stream.

33. In a school, students decided to plant trees in and around the school to reduce air pollution. It was decided that the number of trees, that each section of each class will plant, will be double of the class in which they are studying. If there are 1 to 12 classes in the school and each class has two sections, find how many trees were planted by the students. Which value is shown in this question?

34. In figure tangents PQ and PR are drawn from an external point P to a circle with centre O, such that ∠RPQ = 30°. A chord RS is drawn parallel to the tangent PQ. Find ∠RQS.

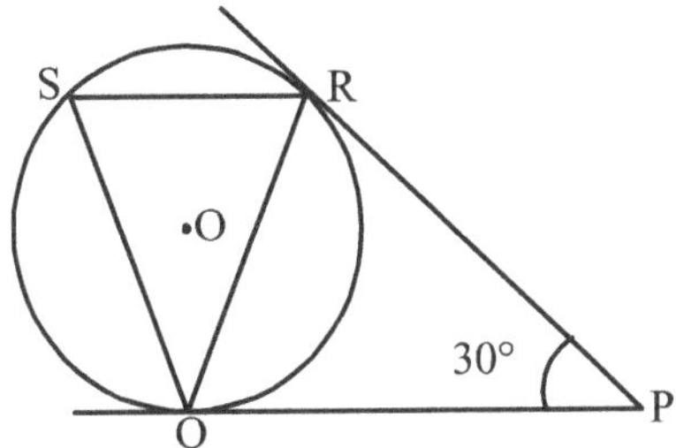

35. In a rain water harvesting system, the rain water from a roof of 22 m × 20 m drains into a cylindrical tank having diameter of base 2 m and height 3.5 m. If the tank is full, find the rainfall in cm. Write your views on water conservation.

OR

A well of diameter 4 m is dug 14 m deep. The earth taken out is spread evenly all around the well to form a 40 cm high embankment. Find the width of the embankment.

SECTION-E

This section comprises of 3 case study/passage - based questions of 4 marks each with three sub-parts (i), (ii), (iii) of marks 1, 1, 2 respectively.

36. **Case - Study 1:** Read the following passage and answer the questions given below.

An asana is a body posture, originally and still a general term for a sitting meditation pose, and later extended in hatha yoga and modern yoga as exercise, to any type of pose or position, adding reclining, standing, inverted, twisting, and balancing poses. In the figure, one can observe that poses can be related to representation of quadratic polynomial.

TRIKONASANA

ADHOMUKHA SAVASANA

ADHO MUKHA SVANA

(i) The shape of the poses shown is

(ii) The graph of parabola opens downwards, and expression $f(x) = ax^2 + bx + c$ if

(iii) In the graph, how many zeroes are there for the polynomial?

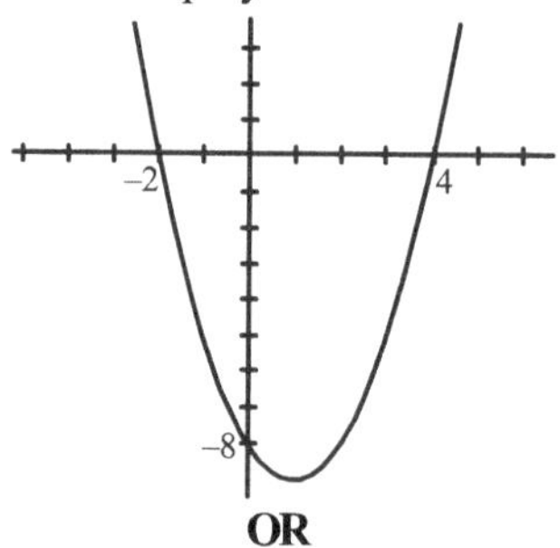

OR

According to graph zeros are

37. Case - Study 2: Read the following passage and answer the questions given below.

On a Sunday, your Parents took you to a fair. You could see lot of toys displayed, and you wanted them to buy a RUBIK's cube and strawberry ice-cream for you. Observe the figures and answer the questions-:

(i) The length of the diagonal if each edge measures 6cm is

(ii) Volume of the solid figure if the length of the edge is 7cm is-

(iii) What is the curved surface area of hemisphere (ice cream) if the base radius is 7cm?

OR

Find total surface area of cube if each side is 3 cm

38. Case - Study 3: Read the following passage and answer the questions given below.

On a weekend Rani was playing cards with her family. The deck has 52 cards. If her brother drew one card .

(i) Find the probability of getting a king of red colour.

(ii) Find the probability of getting a face card.

(iii) Find the probability of getting a jack of hearts.

OR

Find probability of getting a spade.

7 Sample Paper

LATEST PATTERN

BLUE PRINT

Ch. No.	Chapter Name	Per Unit Marks	Section-A (1 Mark)		Section-B (2 Marks)	Section-C (3 Marks)	Section-D (5 Marks)	Section-E (4 Marks)	Total Marks
			MCQ	A/R	VSA	SA	LA	Case-Study	
1	Real Number	6	2(Q6, 17)	1(Q19)		1(Q31)			6
2	Polynomials	20	1(Q1)			1(Q27)			4
3	Pair of Linear Equations in Two Variables		1(Q5)		1(Q21)	1(Q26)			6
4	Quadratic Equations		1(Q2)				1(Q32)		6
5	Arithmetic Progression							1(Q36)	4
6	Triangles	15	1(Q7, 9)		1(Q23)		1(Q33)		9
7	Circles		1(Q10)		1(Q24)	1(Q29)			6
8	Coordinate Geometry	6	1(Q3, 8)					1(Q37)	6
9	Introduction to Trigonometry	12	1(Q4)	1(Q20)	1(Q22)	1(Q28)			7
10	Some Applications of Trigonometry		1(Q18)					1(Q38)	5
11	Areas Related to Circles	10	2(Q11, 14)		1(Q25)				4
12	Surface Areas and Volumes		1(Q13)				1(Q34)		6
13	Statistics	11	1(Q12, 16)				1(Q35)		7
14	Probability		1(Q15)			1(Q30)			4
Total Marks (Total Questions)		**80**	**18(18)**	**2(2)**	**10(5)**	**18(6)**	**20(4)**	**12(3)**	**80(38)**

Note : The number given inside the bracket denotes question number, asked in the sample paper, while the number given outside the bracket are the number of questions from that particular chapter.

Time : 3 Hours **Max. Marks : 80**

General Instructions

1. *This Question paper contains - five sections A, B, C, D and E. Each section is compulsory. However, there are internal choices in some questions.*
2. *Section A has 18 MCQ's and 02 Assertion-Reason based questions of 1 mark each.*
3. *Section B has 5 Very Short Answer (VSA)-type questions of 2 marks each.*
4. *Section C has 6 Short Answer (SA)-type questions of 3 marks each.*
5. *Section D has 4 Long Answer (LA)-type questions of 5 marks each.*
6. *Section E has 3 case based/integrated units of assessment (4 marks each) with sub parts of values of 1, 1 and 2 marks each respectively.*

SECTION-A (Multiple Choice Questions)

Each question carries 1 mark.

1. The zeroes of the polynomial are
$p(x) = x^2 - 10x - 75$
(a) $5, -15$ (b) $5, 15$ (c) $15, -5$ (d) $-5, -15$

2. If one root of $5x^2 + 13x + k = 0$ be the reciprocal of the other root, then the value of k is
(a) 0 (b) 1 (c) 2 (d) 5

3. If P (x, y) is any point on the line joining the points A $(a, 0)$ and B $(0, b)$, then
(a) $\frac{x}{b} + \frac{y}{a} = 1$ (b) $\frac{x}{a} - \frac{y}{b} = 1$ (c) $\frac{x}{a} + \frac{y}{b} = 1$ (d) $\frac{x}{b} - \frac{y}{a} = 1$

4. $\sin^2\theta + \operatorname{cosec}^2\theta$ is always
(a) greater than 1 (b) less than 1 (c) greater than or equal to 2 (d) equal to 2

5. The pair of linear equations $x + 2y = 5$ and $3x + 12y = 10$ has
(a) unique solution (b) no solution (c) more than two solutions (d) infinitely many solutions

6. What is the largest number that divides 70 and 125, leaving remainders 5 and 8 respectively?
(a) 13 (b) 9 (c) 3 (d) 585

7. Which of the following statement is false?
(a) All isosceles triangles are similar. (b) All quadrilateral triangles are similar.
(c) All circles are similar. (d) None of the above

8. The point P on x-axis equidistant from the points A(–1, 0) and B(5, 0) is
(a) (2,0) (b) (0,2) (c) (3,0) (d) (2,2)

9. In the given figure, express x in terms of a, b and c.

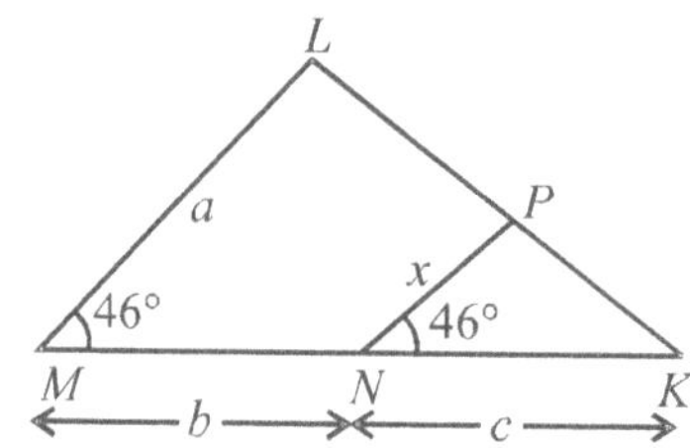

(a) $x = \frac{ab}{a+b}$ (b) $x = \frac{ac}{b+c}$ (c) $x = \frac{bc}{b+c}$ (d) $x = \frac{ac}{a+c}$

10. In the figure, ΔAPB is formed by three tangents to the circle with centre O. If ∠APB = 40°, then the measure of ∠BOA is

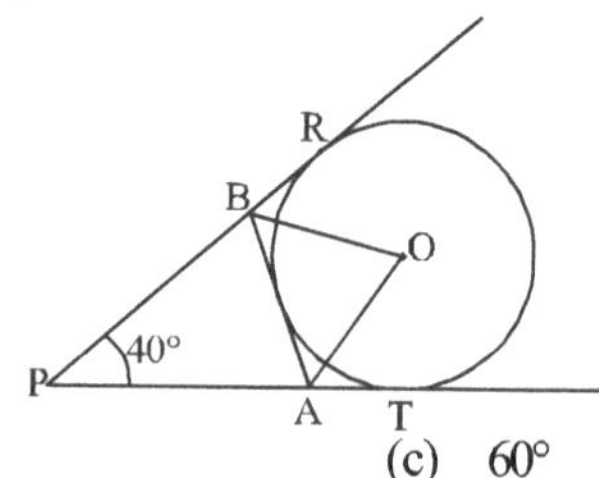

(a) 50° (b) 55° (c) 60° (d) 70°

11. The area of a sector of angle p (in degrees) of a circle with radius R is

(a) $\frac{p}{360°} \times 2\pi R$ (b) $\frac{p}{180°} \times \pi R^2$ (c) $\frac{p}{720°} \times 2\pi R$ (d) $\frac{p}{720°} \times 2\pi R^2$

12. For the data $(2, 9, x+6, 2x+3, 5, 10, 5)$ if mean is 7, then mode is

(a) 3 (b) 5 (c) 9 (d) 10

13. If a sphere and a cube have equal surface areas, then the ratio of the diameter of the sphere to the edge of the cube is

(a) $1:2$ (b) $2:1$ (c) $\sqrt{\pi}:\sqrt{6}$ (d) $\sqrt{6}:\sqrt{\pi}$

14. If the sector of a circle of diameter 10 cm subtends an angle of 144° at the centre, then the length of the arc of the sector is

(a) 2π cm (b) 4π cm (c) 5π cm (d) 6π cm

15. An unbiased die is rolled twice. Find the probability of getting the sum of two numbers as a prime

(a) $\frac{3}{5}$ (b) $\frac{5}{12}$ (c) $\frac{7}{12}$ (d) $\frac{4}{5}$

16. Find the mean of the following frequency distribution.

Class Interval	0–10	10–20	20–30	30–40	40–50
Frequency	8	12	10	11	9

(a) 25.3 (b) 25.2 (c) 24 (d) 25.5

17. If two positive integers p and q can be expressed as $p = ab^2$ and $q = a^3b$; where a, b being prime numbers, then LCM (p, q) is equal to

(a) ab (b) a^2b^2 (c) a^3b^2 (d) a^3b^3

18. If a pole 6 m high casts a shadow $2\sqrt{3}$ m long on the ground, then the sun's elevation is

(a) 60° (b) 45° (c) 30° (d) 90°

(ASSERTION-REASON BASED QUESTIONS)

In the following questions, a statement of Assertion (A) is followed by a statement of Reason (R). Choose the correct answer out of the following choices.

(a) ***Both A and R are true and R is the correct explanation of A.***
(b) ***Both A and R are true but R is not the correct explanation of A.***
(c) ***A is true but R is false.***
(d) ***A is false but R is true.***

19. **Assertion :** Denominator of 34.12345. When expressed in the form $\frac{p}{q}, q \neq 0$, is of the form $2^m \times 5^n$, where m, n are non-negative integers.

Reason : 34.12345 is a terminating decimal fraction.

20. **Assertion:** In a right angled triangle, if $\tan\theta = \frac{3}{4}$, the greatest side of the triangle is 5 units.

Reason: $(\text{greatest side})^2 = (\text{hypotenuse})^2 = (\text{perpendicular})^2 + (\text{base})^2$.

SECTION-B

This section comprises of very short answer type-questions (VSA) of 2 marks each.

21. Solve the system of equations : $ax + by = 1,\ bx + ay = \frac{2ab}{a^2 + b^2}$.

22. Prove that $\tan^2\theta + \cot^2\theta + 2 = \sec^2\theta + \text{cosec}^2\theta = \sec^2\theta\,\text{cosec}^2\theta$

OR

If $\frac{\cos\theta - \sin\theta}{\cos\theta + \sin\theta} = \frac{1-\sqrt{3}}{1+\sqrt{3}}$, then find the value of θ.

23. In the given figure, $PQ \parallel BA$ and $PR \parallel CA$. If $PD = 12$ cm, find $BD \times CD$.

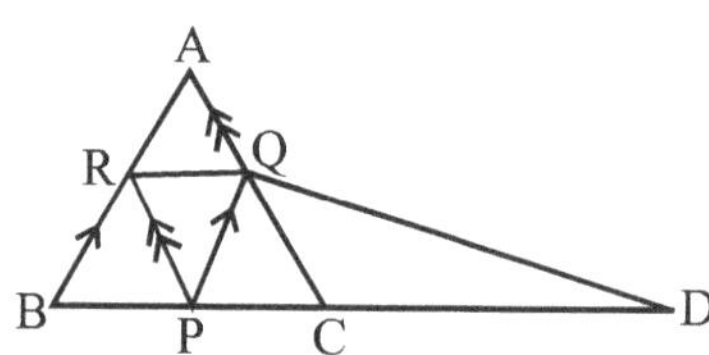

24. In the given figure, CP and CQ are tangents to a circle wih centre O. ARB is another tangent touching the cirlce at R. If CP = 11 cm and BC = 7 cm, then find the length of BR.

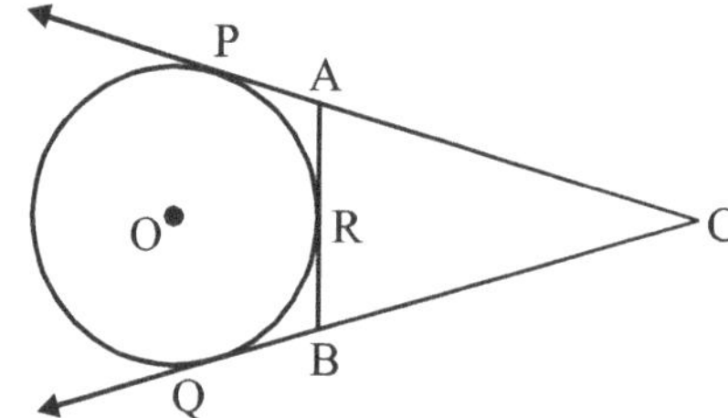

25. The area enclosed by the circumferences of two concentric circle is 346.5 cm^2. If the circumference of the inner circle is 88 cm, calculate the radius of the outer circle.

SECTION-C

This section comprises of short answer type questions (SA) of 3 marks each.

26. Determine the values of m and n so that the following system of linear equations have infinite number of solutions :
$(2m - 1)x + 3y - 5 = 0$
$3x + (n-1)y - 2 = 0$

27. If α and β are the zeroes of the polynomial $x^2 + 4x + 3$, find the polynomial whose zeroes are $1 + \frac{\beta}{\alpha}$ and $1 + \frac{\alpha}{\beta}$.

28. Solve $\frac{\cos^2\theta - 3\cos\theta + 2}{\sin^2\theta} = 1$; $(\theta < 90°)$.

29. PQ is a chord of length 8 cm of a circle of radius 5 cm. The tangents at P and Q intersect at a point T (see Fig.). Find the length of TP.

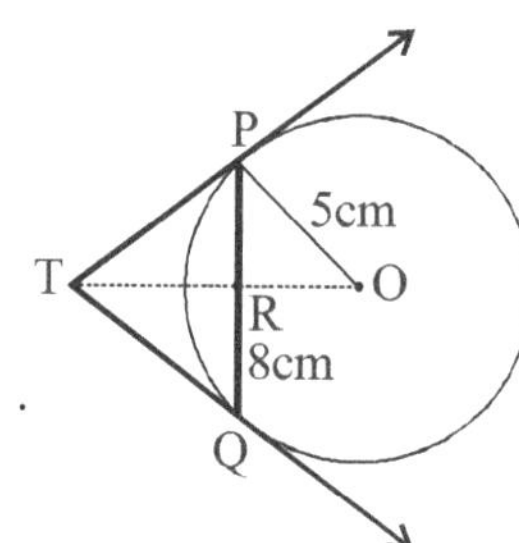

30. A card is drawn at random from a well shuffled pack of 52 playing cards. Find the probability of getting neither a red card nor a queen.

OR

Two different dice are tossed together. Find the probability that the product of the two numbers on the top of the dice is 6.

31. Find how many integers between 200 and 500 are divisible by 8.

OR

Find the greatest number of six digits exactly divisible by 18, 24 and 36.

SECTION-D

This section comprises of long answer-type questions (LA) of 5 marks each.

32. Solve the following quadratic equation for x :

$4\sqrt{3}x^2 + 5x - 2\sqrt{3} = 0$

33. ΔABC is right-angled at A. $DEFG$ is a square as shown in the figure. Prove that $DE^2 = BD \times EC$.

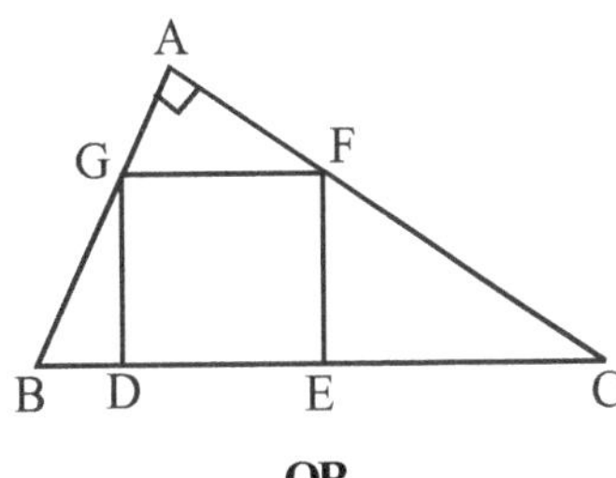

OR

In ΔABC, D is the midpoint of BC and $AE \perp BC$. If $AC > AB$, show that

$$AB^2 = AD^2 - BC \cdot DE + \frac{1}{4}BC^2$$

34. If h, c, v are respectively the height, the curved surface area and the volume of a cone, prove that $3\pi vh^3 - c^2h^2 + 9v^2 = 0$.

35. Find the mean of the following frequency distribution by Assumed Mean Method.

Class Interval	Frequency
0–4	6
4–8	3
8–12	6
12–16	16
16–20	3
20–24	14
24–28	10
28–32	8

OR

Calculate the mean for the following frequency distribution (By step deviation method).

Class interval	0 – 80	80 – 160	160 – 240	240 – 320	320 – 400
frequency	22	35	44	25	24

SECTION-E

This section comprises of 3 case study/passage - based questions of 4 marks each with three sub-parts (i), (ii), (iii) of marks 1, 1, 2 respectively.

36. Case - Study 1: Read the following passage and answer the questions given below.
Your friend Veer wants to participate in a 200m race. He can currently run that distance in 51 seconds and with each day of practice it takes him 2 seconds less.

(i) Which day he takes 31 seconds to complete

(ii) Which day he taks 27 seconds to complete

(iii) Find the time in 10th day

OR

Find the time in 15th day.

37. Case - Study 2: Read the following passage and answer the questions given below.

In order to conduct Sports Day activities in your School, lines have been drawn with chalk powder at a distance of 1 m each, in a rectangular shaped ground ABCD, 100 flowerpots have been placed at a distance of 1 m from each other along AD, as shown in given figure below. Niharika runs 1/4 th the distance AD on the 2nd line and posts a green flag. Preet runs 1/5 th distance AD on the eighth line and posts a red flag.

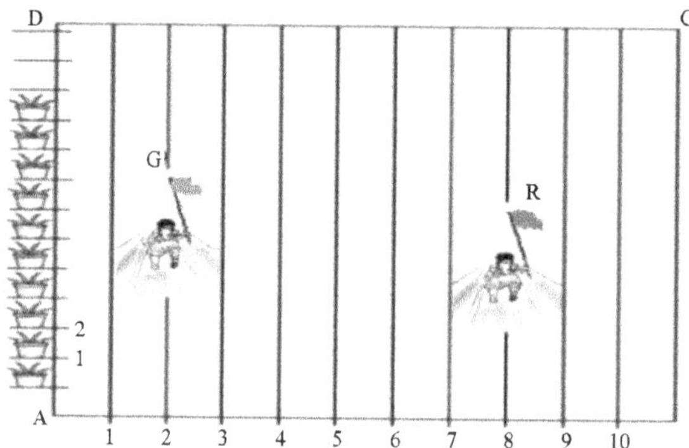

(i) Find the position of green flag

(ii) Find the position of red flag

(iii) What is the distance between both the flags?

OR

If Rashmi has to post a blue flag exactly halfway between the line segment joining the two flags, where should she post her flag?

38. Case - Study 3: Read the following passage and answer the questions given below.

A group of students of class X visited India Gate on an education trip. The teacher and students had interest in history as well. The teacher narrated that India Gate, official name Delhi Memorial, originally called All-India War Memorial, monumental sandstone arch in New Delhi, dedicated to the troops of British India who died in wars fought between 1914 and 1919. The teacher also said that India Gate, which is located at the eastern end of the Rajpath (formerly called the Kingsway), is about 138 feet (42 metres) in height.

(i) What is the angle of elevation if they are standing at a distance of 42m away from the monument?

(ii) They want to see the tower at an angle of 60°. So, they want to know the distance where they should stand and hence find the distance.

(iii) If the altitude of the Sun is at 60°, then find the height of the vertical tower that will cast a shadow of length 20 m.

OR

The ratio of the length of a rod and its shadow is 1:1. Find the angle of elevation of the Sun.

8 Sample Paper

LATEST PATTERN

BLUE PRINT

Ch. No.	Chapter Name	Per Unit Marks	Section-A (1 Mark)		Section-B (2 Marks)	Section-C (3 Marks)	Section-D (5 Marks)	Section-E (4 Marks)	Total Marks
			MCQ	A/R	VSA	SA	LA	Case-Study	
1	Real Number	6	1(Q1)		1(Q21)	1(Q31)			6
2	Polynomials	20	1(Q2)					(Q36)	5
3	Pair of Linear Equations in Two Variables		1(Q3)			1(Q26)			4
4	Quadratic Equations		2(Q4, 8)			1(Q28)			5
5	Arithmetic Progression		3(Q5, 6, 9)			1(Q29)			6
6	Triangles	15	1(Q7)	1(Q19)			1(Q32)	(Q38)	7
7	Circles		2(Q14, 13)		1(Q22)				8
8	Coordinate Geometry	6	1(Q10)		1(Q23)	1(Q27)			6
9	Introduction to Trigonometry	12	1(Q11)		1(Q24)	1(Q30)			6
10	Some Applications of Trigonometry		1(Q12)				1(Q33)		6
11	Areas Related to Circles	10	1(Q15)					(Q37)	5
12	Surface Areas and Volumes						1(Q34)		5
13	Statistics	11	1(Q17)	1(Q20)			1(Q35)		7
14	Probability		2(Q16, 18)		1(Q25)				4
Total Marks (Total Questions)		**80**	**18(18)**	**2(2)**	**10(5)**	**18(6)**	**20(4)**	**12(3)**	**80(38)**

Note : The number given inside the bracket denotes question number, asked in the sample paper, while the number given outside the bracket are the number of questions from that particular chapter.

Time : 3 Hours **Max. Marks : 80**

General Instructions

1. *This Question paper contains - five sections A, B, C, D and E. Each section is compulsory. However, there are internal choices in some questions.*
2. *Section A has 18 MCQ's and 02 Assertion-Reason based questions of 1 mark each.*
3. *Section B has 5 Very Short Answer (VSA)-type questions of 2 marks each.*
4. *Section C has 6 Short Answer (SA)-type questions of 3 marks each.*
5. *Section D has 4 Long Answer (LA)-type questions of 5 marks each.*
6. *Section E has 3 case based/integrated units of assessment (4 marks each) with sub parts of values of 1, 1 and 2 marks each respectively.*

SECTION-A (Multiple Choice Questions)

Each question carries 1 mark.

1. When 2^{256} is divided by 17, then remainder would be

(a) 1 (b) 16 (c) 14 (d) None of these

2. If the polynomials $ax^3 + 4x^2 + 3x - 4$ and $x^3 - 4x + a$ leave same remainder when divided by $(x - 3)$, find the value of a.

(a) –1 (b) 1 (c) $\frac{1}{2}$ (d) $-\frac{1}{2}$

3. The perimeter of a rectangle is 40 cm. The ratio of its sides is 2 : 3. Find its length and breadth.

(a) $l = 10$ cm, b = 8 cm (b) $l = 12$ cm, b = 8 cm (c) $l = 12$ m, b = 8 m (d) $l = 40$ m, b = 30 m

4. If the product of roots of the equation $x^3 - 3x + k = 10$ is –2, then the value of k is

(a) –2 (b) –8 (c) 8 (d) 12

5. Sanjay starts his job with a certain monthly salary and earns a fixed increment every year. If his salary was ₹ 4500 after four years of service and ₹ 5400 after 10 years, find his initial salary and annual increment.

(a) 4000, 200 (b) 3900, 150 (c) 4500, 100 (d) 3800, 250

6. In an A.P. if $a = 5$, $a_n = 81$ and $S_n = 860$, then n is

(a) 10 (b) 15 (c) 20 (d) 25

7. If in two ΔABC and ΔPQR, $\frac{AB}{QR} = \frac{BC}{PR} = \frac{CA}{PQ}$, then

(a) ΔPQR ~ ΔCAB (b) ΔPQR ~ ΔABC (c) ΔCBA ~ ΔPQR (d) ΔBCA ~ ΔPQR

8. If the equation
$(1 + m^2)x^2 + (2mc)x + (c^2 - a^2) = 0$ has equal roots, then

(a) $c^2 - a^2 = 1 + m^2$ (b) $c^2 = a^2(1 + m^2)$ (c) $c^2a^2 = (1 + m^2)$ (d) $c^2 + a^2 = 1 + m^2$

9. If eight times the 8th term of an A.P. is equal to 12 times the 12th term of the A.P. then its 20th term will be

(a) –1 (b) 1 (c) 0 (d) 2

10. The centroid of the triangle whose vertices are (3, –7), (–8, 6) and (5, 10) is

(a) (0, 9) (b) (0, 3) (c) (1, 3) (d) (3, 5)

11. cos 1° . cos 2°. cos 3° .... cos 179° is equal to

(a) –1 (b) 0 (c) 1 (d) $1/\sqrt{2}$

12. A tree 6 m tall casts a 4 cm long shadow. At the same time, a flag pole casts a shadow 50 m long. How long is the flag pole?

(a) 75m (b) 100m (c) 150m (d) 50m

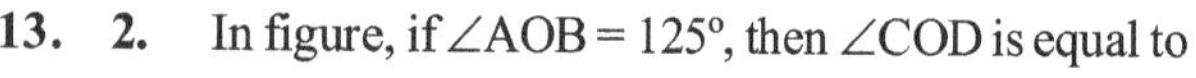

13. **2.** In figure, if ∠AOB = 125°, then ∠COD is equal to

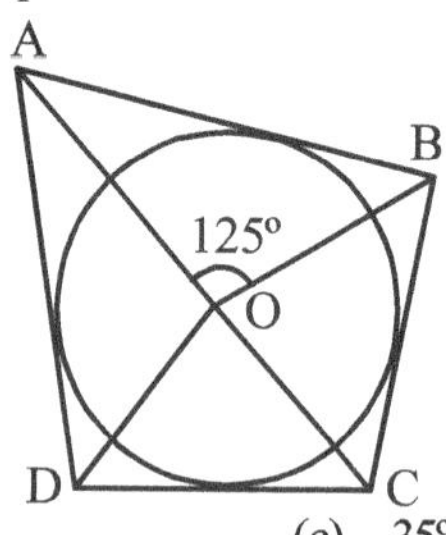

(a) 62.5° (b) 45° (c) 35° (d) 55°

14. Two circles with centres Oand P, and radii 8 cm and 4 cm touch each other externally. Find the length of their common tangent QR.

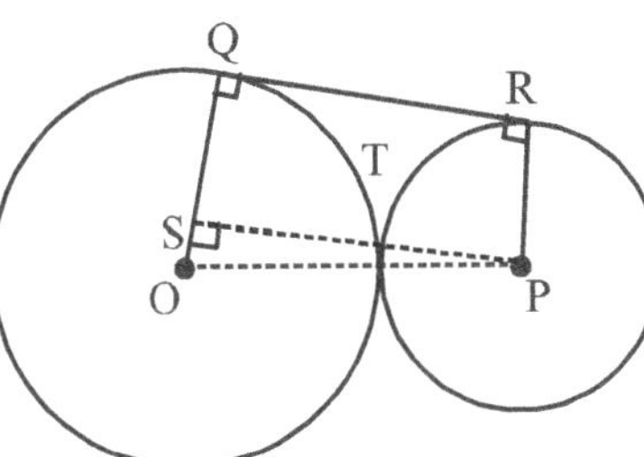

(a) 8 cm (b) 7 cm (c) $8\sqrt{2}$ cm (d) $7\sqrt{3}$ cm

15. A drain cover is made from a square metal plate of side 40 cm having 441 holes of diameter 1 cm each drilled in it. Find the area of the remaining square plate.
(a) 1250.5 cm^2 (b) 1253.5 cm^2 (c) 1240.2 cm^2 (d) 1260.2 cm^2

16. Two fair dice are thrown. Find the probability that both dice show different numbers.
(a) $\frac{1}{6}$ (b) $\frac{5}{6}$ (c) $\frac{32}{36}$ (d) $\frac{29}{36}$

17. In a frequency distribution, the mid value of a class is 10 and the width of the class is 6. The lower limit of the class is
(a) 6 (b) 7 (c) 8 (d) 12

18. A factory has 120 workers in January, 90 of them are female workers. In February, another 15 male workers were employed. A worker is then picked at random. Calculate the probability of picking a female worker.
(a) $\frac{3}{4}$ (b) $\frac{4}{9}$ (c) $\frac{2}{3}$ (d) $\frac{1}{2}$

(ASSERTION-REASON BASED QUESTIONS)

In the following questions, a statement of Assertion (A) is followed by a statement of Reason (R). Choose the correct answer out of the following choices.

(a) ***Both A and R are true and R is the correct explanation of A.***
(b) ***Both A and R are true but R is not the correct explanation of A.***
(c) ***A is true but R is false.***
(d) ***A is false but R is true.***

19. **Assertion :** If in a ΔABC, a line $DE \parallel BC$, intersects AB in D and AC in E, then $\frac{AB}{AD} = \frac{AC}{AE}$.

Reason : If a line is drawn parallel to one side of a triangle intersecting the other two sides, then the other two sides are divided in the same ratio.

20. **Assertion :** If the number of runs scored by 11 players of a cricket team of India are 5, 19, 42, 11, 50, 30, 21, 0, 52, 36, 27 then median is 30.

Reason : Median $= \left(\frac{n+1}{2}\right)^{th}$ value, if n is odd.

SECTION-B

This section comprises of very short answer type-questions (VSA) of 2 marks each.

21. Find how many integers between 200 and 500 are divisible by 8.

OR

Show that one and only one out of n, $n+2$, $n+4$ is divisible by 3, where n is any positive integer.

22. In the figure, PQ is tangent at a point R of the circle with centre O. If $\angle TRQ = 30°$, find $\angle PRS$.

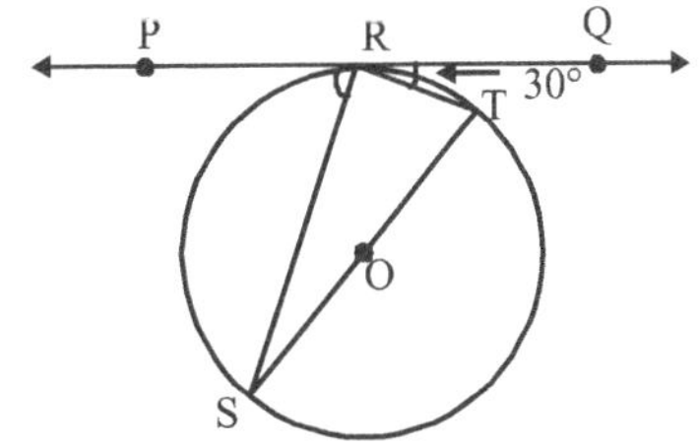

OR

In figure, BOA is a diameter of a circle and the tangent at a point P meets BA extended at T. If $\angle PBO = 30^\circ$, then what is the measure of $\angle PTA$?

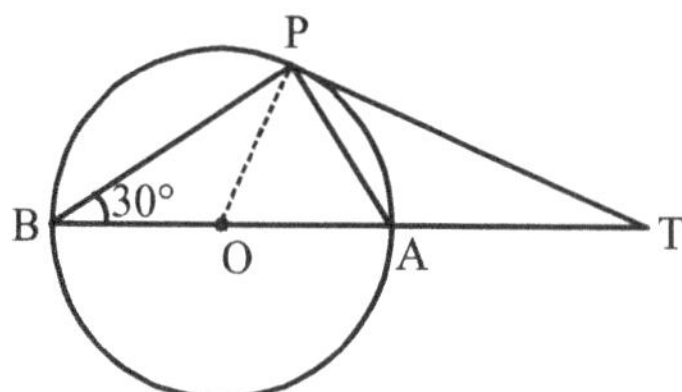

23. In what ratio is the line segment joining the points (3, 5) & (–4, 2) divided by y–axis?

24. Solve : $\sec^2\theta + \tan^2\theta = \frac{5}{3}; \theta < 90^\circ$

25. A bag contains 5 red balls and some blue balls. If the probability of drawing a blue ball is double that of a red ball, Find the number of blue balls in the bag.

SECTION-C

This section comprises of short answer type questions (SA) of 3 marks each.

26. Yash scored 40 marks in a test, getting 3 marks for each right answer and losing 1 mark for each wrong answer. Had 4 marks been awarded for each correct answer and 2 marks been deducted for each incorrect answer, then Yash would have scored 50 marks. How many questions were there in the test if Yash attempted every question?

OR

One hundred men in 10 days do one third of a piece of work. The work is then required to be completed in another 13 days. On the next day (the eleventh day) 50 more men are employed, and on the day after that, another 50. How many men must be relieved at the end of the 18th day so that the rest of the men, working for the remaining time, will just complete the work ?

27. Find the distance between each of the following pair of points :

(a) P(6, 8) and Q(–9, –12) (b) A(–6, –1) and B(–6, 11)

28. Roots of the quadratic equation $36x^2 - 12ax + (a^2 - b^2) = 0$ are $\frac{a+b}{c}$ and $\frac{a-b}{c}$. Then, find the value of c.

OR

Find the real roots of the equation $x^{2/3} + x^{1/3} - 2 = 0$.

29. If the ratio of the sum of first n terms of two A.P's is (7n + 1) : (4n + 27), find the ratio of their mth terms.

30. If $\tan\theta = \frac{x\sin\phi}{1 - x\cos\phi}$ and $\tan\phi = \frac{y\sin\theta}{1 - y\cos\theta}$, then the value of $\frac{x}{y}$ is ______.

31. Given that HCF (306, 657) = 9, find LCM (306, 657).

SECTION-D

This section comprises of long answer-type questions (LA) of 5 marks each.

32. From given fig. express 'x' in terms of a, b, c.

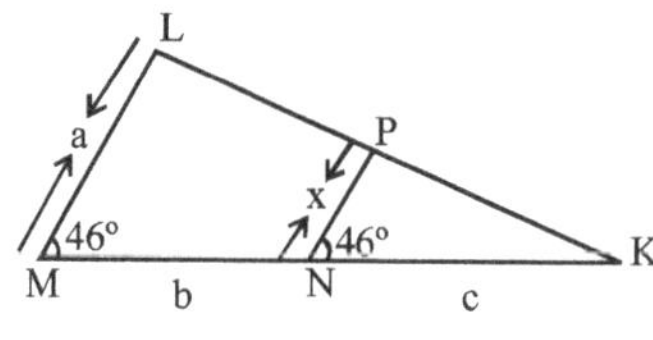

OR

In figure, two line segments AC and BD intersect each other at the point P such that PA = 6 cm, PB = 3 cm, PC = 2.5 cm, PD = 5 cm, $\angle APB = 50^\circ$ and $\angle CDP = 30^\circ$. Then, find the value of $\angle PBA$

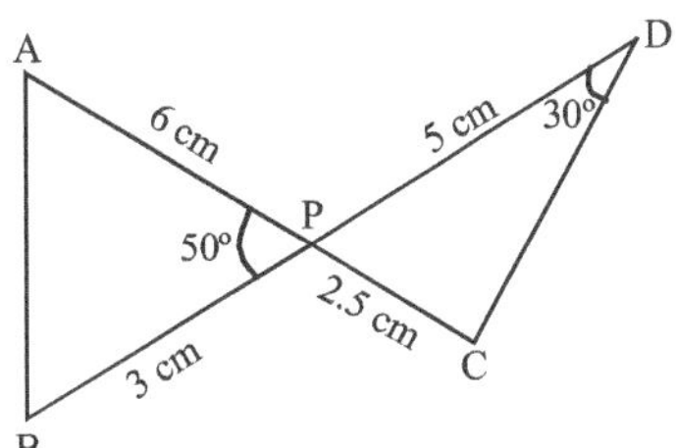

33. A boy on horizontal plane finds bird flying at a distance of 100 m from him at an elevation of 30°. A girl standing on the roof of 20 metre high building, finds the angle of elevation of the same bird to be 45°. Both the boy and the girl are on opposite sides of the bird. Find the distance of bird from the girl.

OR

A 1.2 m tall girl spots a balloon moving with the wind in a horizontal line at a height of 88.2 m from the ground. The angle of elevation of the balloon from the eyes of the girl at any instant is 60°. After sometime, the angle of elevation reduces to 30°. Find the distance travelled by the balloon during the interval.

34. A solid wooden toy is in the shape of a right circular cone mounted on a hemisphere. If the radius of the hemisphere is 4.2 cm and the total height of the toy is 10.2 cm, find the volume of the wooden toy.

35. Find the mean of the following frequency distribution by Assumed Mean Method.

Class Interval	Frequency
0–4	6
4–8	3
8–12	6
12–16	16
16–20	3
20–24	14
24–28	10
28–32	8

SECTION-E

This section comprises of 3 case study/passage - based questions of 4 marks each with three sub-parts (i), (ii), (iii) of marks 1, 1, 2 respectively.

36. **Case - Study 1:** Read the following passage and answer the questions given below.
The below picture are few natural examples of parabolic shape which is represented by a quadratic polynomial. A parabolic arch is an arch in the shape of a parabola. In structures, their curve represents an efficient method of load, and so can be found in bridges and in architecture in a variety of forms.

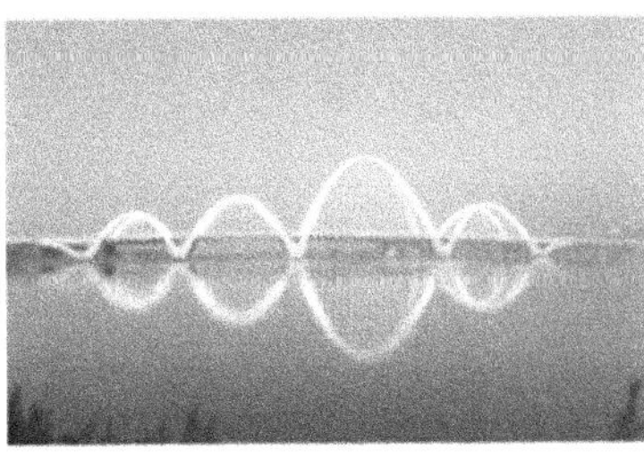

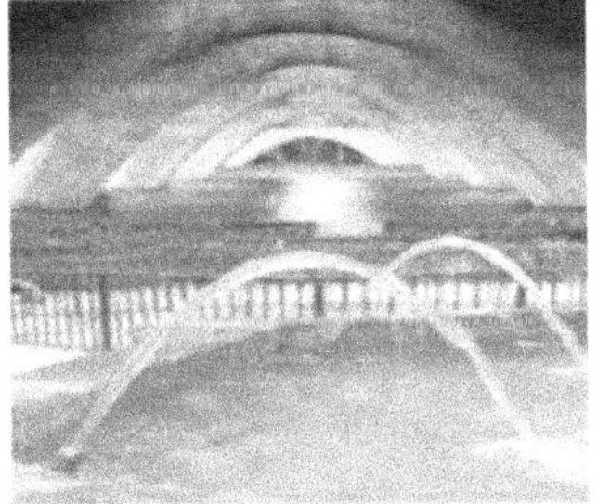

(i) Write in the standard form of quadratic polynomial.
(ii) If two zeros are 2 and 3 then find polynomial.
(iii) If α and $\frac{1}{\alpha}$ are the zeroes of the quadratic polynomial $2x^2 - x + 8k$, then find k.

OR

If the sum of the roots is $-p$ and product of the roots is $-\frac{1}{p}$, then find the quadratic polynomial.

37. **Case - Study 2:** Read the following passage and answer the questions given below.
Pookalam is the flower bed or flower pattern designed during Onam in Kerala. It is similar as Rangoli in North India and Kolam in Tamil Nadu.
During the festival of Onam, your school is planning to conduct a Pookalam competition. Your friend who is a partner in competition , suggests two designs given below.
Observe these carefully.

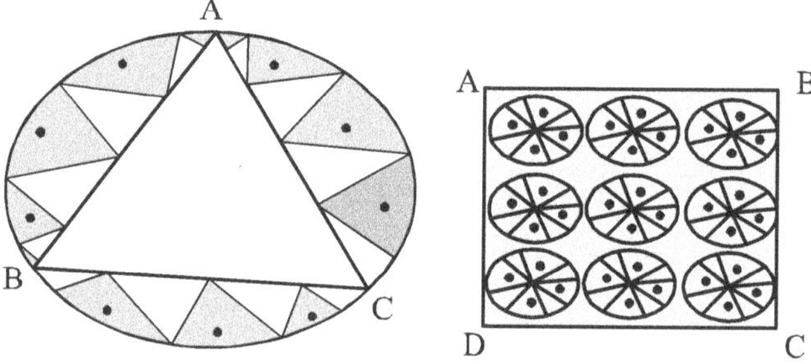

Design I: This design is made with a circle of radius 32cm leaving equilateral triangle ABC in the middle as shown in the given figure.
Design II: This Pookalam is made with 9 circular design each of radius 7cm.
Refer Design I:
(i) Find the side of equilateral triangle.
(ii) Find the altitude of the equilateral triangle is
Refer Design II:
(iii) Find the area of square is

OR

Find area of each circular design.

38. Rohan wants to measure the distance of a pond during the visit to his native. He marks points A and B on the opposite edges of a pond as shown in the figure below. To find the distance between the points, he makes a right-angled triangle using rope connecting B with another point C are a distance of 12m, connecting C to point D at a distance of 40m from point C and the connecting D to the point A which is are a distance of 30m from D such the $\angle ADC = 90°$.

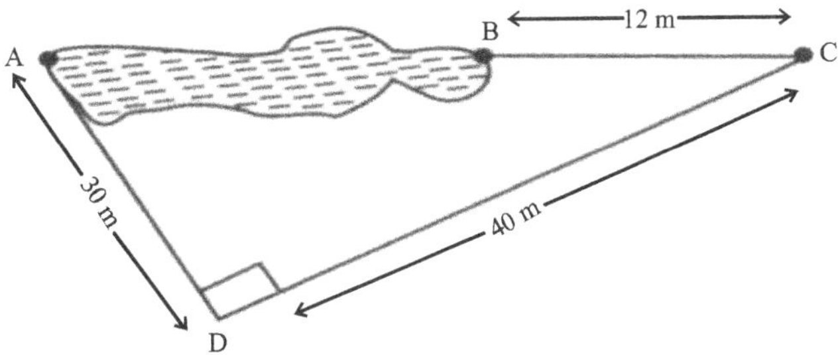

(i) What is the distance AC?

(ii) Which is the following does not form a Pythagoras triplet?

(iii) Find the length AB?

OR

Find the length of the rope used.

9 Sample Paper

LATEST PATTERN

BLUE PRINT

Ch. No.	Chapter Name	Per Unit Marks	Section-A (1 Mark)		Section-B (2 Marks)	Section-C (3 Marks)	Section-D (5 Marks)	Section-E (4 Marks)	Total Marks
			MCQ	A/R	VSA	SA	LA	Case-Study	
1	Real Number	6	1(Q1, 3)		1(Q21, 24)				**6**
2	Polynomials	20	1(Q4)		1(Q23)	1(Q28)			**6**
3	Pair of Linear Equations in Two Variables					1(Q26)		1(Q36)	**7**
4	Quadratic Equations								**0**
5	Arithmetic Progression					1(Q27)		1(Q38)	**7**
6	Triangles	15	4(Q2, 3, 7, 9)				1(Q32)		**9**
7	Circles		2(Q6, 8)	1(Q19)		1(Q30)			**6**
8	Coordinate Geometry	6	4(Q12, 14, 15, 17)		1(Q22)				**6**
9	Introduction to Trigonometry	12					1(Q33)	1(Q37)	**9**
10	Some Applications of Trigonometry					1(Q29)			**3**
11	Areas Related to Circles	10	1(Q10)			1(Q31)			**4**
12	Surface Areas and Volumes		1(Q13)				1(Q34)		**6**
13	Statistics	11	1(Q11)				1(Q35)		**6**
14	Probability		2(Q16, 18)	1(Q20)	1(Q25)				**5**
Total Marks (Total Questions)		**80**	**18(18)**	**2(2)**	**10(5)**	**18(6)**	**20(4)**	**12(3)**	**80(38)**

Note : The number given inside the bracket denotes question number, asked in the sample paper, while the number given outside the bracket are the number of questions from that particular chapter.

Time : 3 Hours **Max. Marks : 80**

General Instructions

1. *This Question paper contains - five sections A, B, C, D and E. Each section is compulsory. However, there are internal choices in some questions.*
2. *Section A has 18 MCQ's and 02 Assertion-Reason based questions of 1 mark each.*
3. *Section B has 5 Very Short Answer (VSA)-type questions of 2 marks each.*
4. *Section C has 6 Short Answer (SA)-type questions of 3 marks each.*
5. *Section D has 4 Long Answer (LA)-type questions of 5 marks each.*
6. *Section E has 3 case based/integrated units of assessment (4 marks each) with sub parts of values of 1, 1 and 2 marks each respectively.*

SECTION-A (Multiple Choice Questions)

Each question carries 1 mark.

1. If LCM(x, 18) = 36 and HCF(x, 18) = 2 then x is

(a) 2 (b) 3 (c) 4 (d) 5

2. $\Delta ABC \sim \Delta PQR$. If AM and PN are altitudes of ΔABC and ΔPQR respectively and $AB^2 : PQ^2 = 4 ; 9$, then AM : PN =

(a) 16 : 81 (b) 4 : 9 (c) 3 : 2 (d) 2 : 3

3. The ratio of LCM and HCF of the least composite and the least prime numbers is

(a) 1 : 2 (b) 2 : 1 (c) 1 : 1 (d) 1 : 3

4. The zeroes of the polynomial $x^2 - 3x - m(m+3)$ are

(a) $m, m+3$ (b) $-m, m+3$ (c) $m, -(m+3)$ (d) $-m, -(m+3)$

5. In ΔABC and ΔDEF, $\angle B = \angle E$, $\angle F = \angle C$ and AB = 3DE. Then, the two triangles are

(a) congruent but not similar (b) similar but not congruent

(c) neither congruent nor similar (d) congruent as well as similar

6. At one end A of a diameter AB of a circle of radius 5 cm, tangent XAY is drawn to the circle. The length of the chord CD parallel to XY and at a distance 8 cm from A, is

(a) 4 cm (b) 5 cm (c) 6 cm (d) 8 cm

7. If in fig. O is the point of intersection of two chords AB and CD such that OB = OD, then triangles OAC and ODB are

(a) equilateral but not similar

(b) isosceles but not similar

(c) equilateral and similar

(d) isosceles and similar

8. In figure, AT is a tangent to the circle with centre O such that OT = 4 cm and $\angle OTA = 30°$. Then, AT is equal to

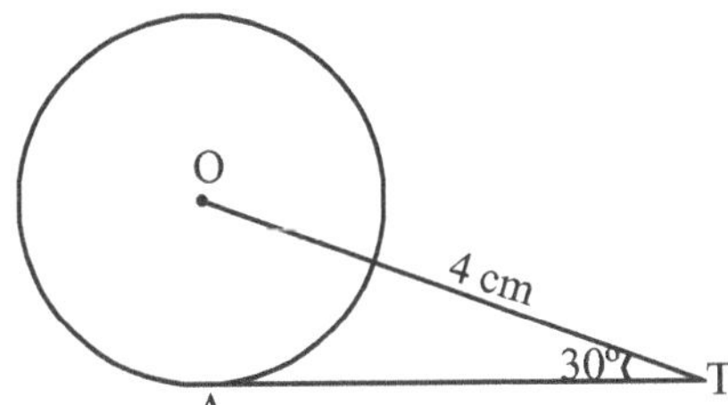

(a) 4 cm (b) 2 cm (c) $2\sqrt{3}$ cm (d) $4\sqrt{3}$ cm

9. If $\Delta ABC \sim \Delta DFE$, $\angle A = 30°$, $\angle C = 50°$, AB = 5 cm, AC = 8 cm and DF = 7.5 cm. Then, which of the following is true?

(a) DE = 12 cm, $\angle F = 50°$ (b) DE = 12 cm, $\angle F = 100°$ (c) EF = 12 cm, $\angle D = 100°$ (d) EF = 12 cm, $\angle D = 30°$

10. Given below is the picture of the Olympic rings made by taking five congruent circles of radius 1 cm each, intersecting in such a way that the chord formed by joining the point of intersection of two circles is also of length 1 cm. Total area of all the dotted regions assuming the thickness of the rings to be negligible is

(a) $4\left(\frac{\pi}{12}-\frac{\sqrt{3}}{4}\right)\text{cm}^2$ (b) $\left(\frac{\pi}{6}-\frac{\sqrt{3}}{4}\right)\text{cm}^2$ (c) $4\left(\frac{\pi}{6}-\frac{\sqrt{3}}{4}\right)\text{cm}^2$ (d) $8\left(\frac{\pi}{6}-\frac{\sqrt{3}}{4}\right)\text{cm}^2$

11. The mean of the following frequency table is 50.

Class	0-20	20-40	40-60	60-80	80-100	Total
Frequency	17	f_1	32	f_2	19	120

Which of the following is correct?
Consider the following.

(I) $f_1 - f_2 = 4$ (II) $f_1 + f_2 = 52$ (III) $f_1 = 24$ (IV) $f_2 = 28$

(a) I, II and III (b) II and IV (c) I and II (d) I and III

12. In what ratio is the line segment joining the points (3, 5) & (–4, 2) divided by y–axis?

(a) 3 : 2 (b) 3 : 4 (c) 2 : 3 (d) 4 : 3

13. A copper wire when bent in the form of an equilateral triangle has area $121\sqrt{3}\text{ cm}^2$. If the same wire is bent into the form of a circle, find the area enclosed by the wire.

(a) 345.5 cm^2 (b) 346.5 cm^2 (c) 342.5 cm^2 (d) 340.25 cm^2

14. A circle passes through the vertices of a triangle ABC. If the vertices are A(–2, 5), B(–2, –3), C(2, –3), then the centre of the circle is

(a) (0, 0) (b) (0, 1) (c) (–2, 1) (d) (0, –3)

15. If $\left(\frac{a}{3}, 4\right)$ is the midpoint of the line segment joining A(–6, 5) and B(–2, 3), then what is the value of 'a'?

(a) –4 (b) –12 (c) 12 (d) –6

16. An unbiased die is rolled twice. Find the probability of getting the sum of two numbers as a prime

(a) $\frac{3}{5}$ (b) $\frac{5}{12}$ (c) $\frac{7}{12}$ (d) $\frac{4}{5}$

17. If the mid point of the line joining (3, 4) and (k, 7) is (x, y) and $2x + 2y + 1 = 0$. Find the value of k.

(a) 10 (b) –15 (c) 15 (d) –10

18. Two fair dice are thrown. Find the probability that both dice show different numbers.

(a) $\frac{1}{6}$ (b) $\frac{5}{6}$ (c) $\frac{32}{36}$ (d) $\frac{29}{36}$

(ASSERTION-REASON BASED QUESTIONS)

In the following questions, a statement of Assertion (A) is followed by a statement of Reason (R). Choose the correct answer out of the following choices.

(a) ***Both A and R are true and R is the correct explanation of A.***
(b) ***Both A and R are true but R is not the correct explanation of A.***
(c) ***A is true but R is false.***
(d) ***A is false but R is true.***

19. **Assertion:** If in a circle, the radius of the circle is 3 cm and distance of a point from the centre of a circle is 5 cm, then length of the tangent will be 4 cm.

Reason: $(\text{hypotenuse})^2 = (\text{base})^2 + (\text{height})^2$

20. Assertion : If a die is thrown, the probability of getting a number less than 3 and greater than 2 is zero.

Reason : Probability of an impossible event is zero.

SECTION-B

This section comprises of very short answer type-questions (VSA) of 2 marks each.

21. Find the LCM of 66 & 486 by the Prime factorisation method. Hence find their HCF.

22. If the point A (0, 2) is equidistant from the points B (3, p) and C (p, 5), find p. Also find the length of AB.

OR

Find the ratio in which the line segment joining the points A (3, –3) and B (–2, 7) is divided by x-axis. Also find the coordinates of the point of division.

23. If zeroes of the polynomial $x^2 + 4x + 2a$ are α and $\frac{2}{\alpha}$, then find the value of a.

24. When 2^{256} is divided by 17 then find the remainder.

25. A girl calculates that the probability of her winning the first prize in a lottery is 0.08. If 6000 tickets are sold, how many tickets has she bought?

OR

A jar contains 54 marbles each of which is blue, green or white. The probability of selecting a blue marble and a green marble at random from the jar is $\frac{1}{3}$ and $\frac{4}{9}$ respectively. How many white marbles does the jar contain?

SECTION-C

This section comprises of short answer type questions (SA) of 3 marks each.

26. Find the value of a so that the point $(3, a)$ lies on the line represented by $2x - 3y = 5$.

OR

Solve the following pair of linear equations by substitution method:

$3x + 2y - 7 = 0$

$4x + y - 6 = 0$

27. The sum of the 5th and the 9th terms of an AP is 30. If its 25th term is three times its 8th term, find the AP.

28. Find the zeroes of the quadratic polynomial $\sqrt{3}x^2 - 8x + 4\sqrt{3}$.

29. Two ships are there in the sea on either side of a light house in such a way that the ships and the light house are in the same straight line. The angles of depression of two ships as observed from the top of the light house are 60° and 45°. If the height of the light house is 200 m, find the distance between the two ships. [Use $\sqrt{3} = 1.73$].

30. In fig., a circle inscribed in triangle ABC touches its sides AB, BC and AC at points D, E and F respectively. If AB = 12 cm, BC = 8 cm and AC = 10 cm, then find the lengths of AD, BE and CF.

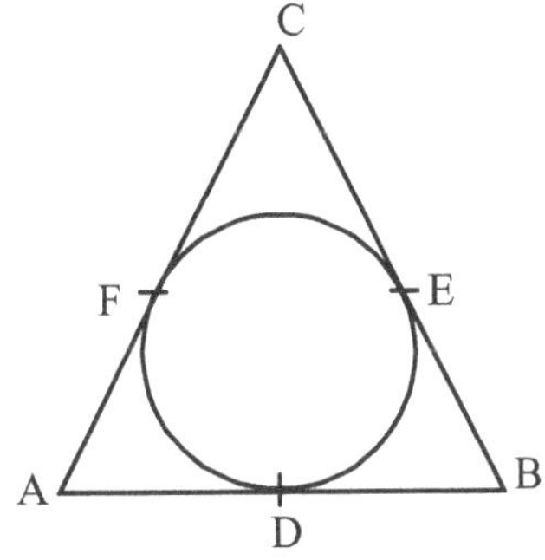

31. In fig., PSR, RTQ and PAQ are three semicircles of diameters 10 cm, 3 cm and 7 cm respectively. Find the perimeter of the shaded region. [Use $\pi = 3.14$]

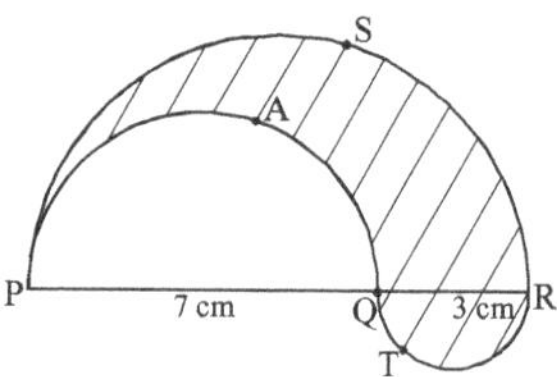

OR

In figure, $ABCD$ is a square of side 10 cm and semicircles are drawn with each side of the square as diameter. Find area of the shaded region.

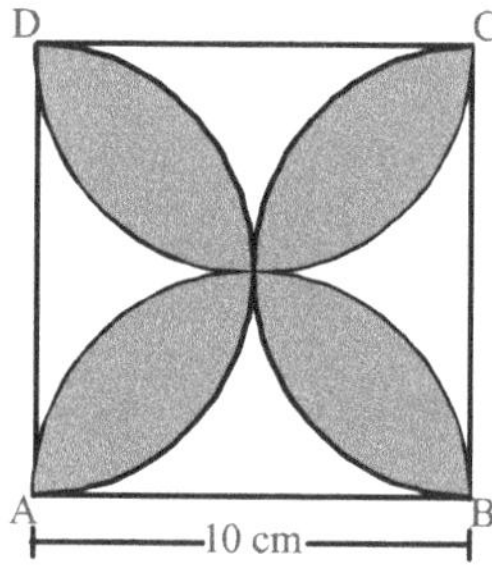

SECTION-D

This section comprises of long answer-type questions (LA) of 5 marks each.

32. In fig. $\angle BAC = 90°$, AD is its bisector. If $DE \perp AC$, prove that $DE \times (AB + AC) = AB \times AC$.

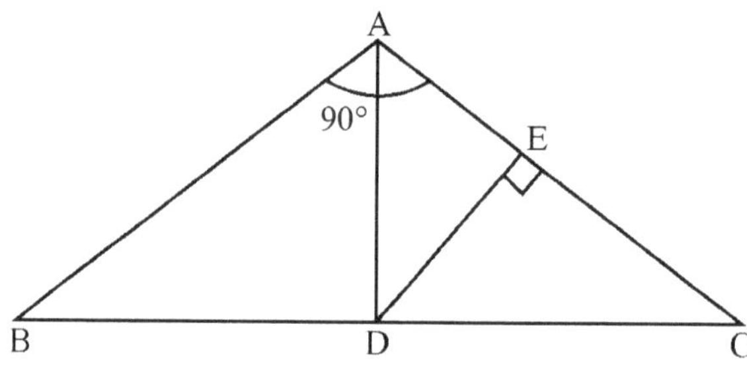

OR

1. In the figure, ABC is a right triangle, right angled at B. AD and CE are two medians drawn from A and C respectively. If $AC = 5$ cm and $AD = \frac{3\sqrt{5}}{2}$ cm, find the length of CE.

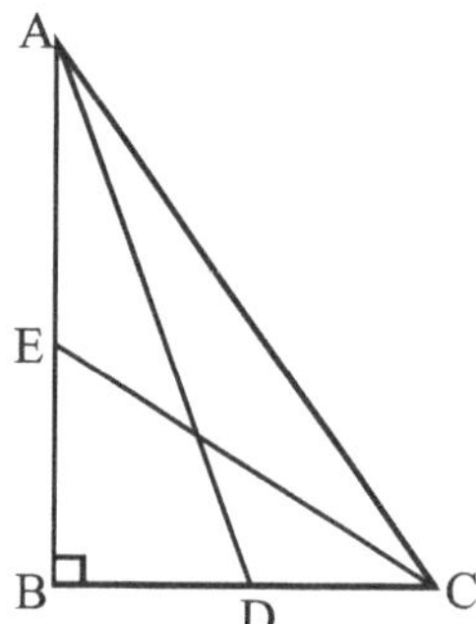

33. If $\sin\theta = \frac{c}{\sqrt{c^2 + d^2}}$ and $d > 0$, find the value of $\cos\theta$ and $\tan\theta$.

34. A container shaped like a right circular cylinder having diameter 12 cm and height 15 cm is full of ice × cream. The ice × cream is to be filled into cones of height 12 cm and diameter 6 cm, having a hemispherical shape on the top. Find the number of such cones which can be filled with ice cream.

35. 3. **The following data gives the distribution of total monthly household expenditure of 200 families of a village. Find the modal monthly expenditure of the families. Also, find the mean monthly expenditure :**

Expenditure (in ₹)	Number of families
1000 - 1500	24
1500 - 2000	40
2000 - 2500	33
2500 - 3000	28
3000 - 3500	30
3500 - 4000	22
4000 - 4500	16
4500 - 5000	7

OR

A student noted the number of cars passing through a spot on a road for 100 periods each of 3 minutes and summarised it in the table given below. Find the mode of the data :

Number of cars	0-10	10-20	20-30	30-40	40-50	50-60	60-70	70-80
Frequency	7	14	13	12	20	11	15	8

SECTION-E

This section comprises of 3 case study/passage - based questions of 4 marks each with three sub-parts (i), (ii), (iii) of marks 1, 1, 2 respectively.

36. **Case - Study 1:** Read the following passage and answer the questions given below.
A test consists of 'True' or 'False' questions. One mark is awarded for every correct answer while 1/4 mark is deducted for every wrong answer. A student knew answers to some of the questions. Rest of the questions he attempted by guessing. He answered 120 questions and got 90 marks.

Type of Question	Marks given for correct answer	Marks deducted for wrong answer
True/False	1	0.25

(i) If answer to all questions he attempted by guessing were wrong, then how many questions did he answer correctly?

(ii) How many questions did he guess?

(iii) If answer to all questions he attempted by guessing were wrong and answered 80 correctly, then how many marks he got?

OR

If answer to all questions he attempted by guessing were wrong, then how many questions answered correctly to score 95 marks?

37. Case - Study 2: Read the following passage and answer the questions given below.

In ΔABC, right angled at B $AB + AC = 9$ cm and $BC = 3$cm.

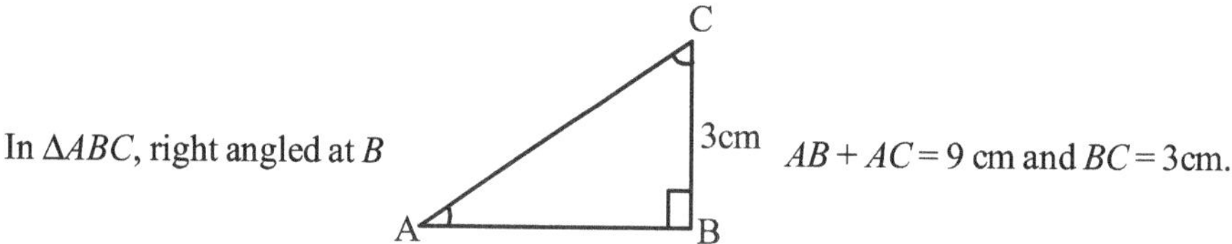

(i) What is the value of $\cot C$?

(ii) What is the value of $\sec C$?

(iii) Find the value of $\sin^2 C + \cos^2 C$.

OR

$1 + \tan^2 C$

38. Case - Study 3: Read the following passage and answer the questions given below.

Following two given series are in A.P.

2, 4, 6, 8 ....

3, 6, 9, 12 ....

First series contains 30 terms, while the second series contains 20 terms. Both of the above given series contain some terms, which are common to both of them.

(i) What is the last term of both the above given A.P. ?

(ii) What is the sum of both the above given A.P. ?

(iii) Find the no. of terms identical to both the above given A.P.

OR

Find the 15th term from the last term of both the above A.P.

10 Sample Paper

LATEST PATTERN

BLUE PRINT

Ch. No.	Chapter Name	Per Unit Marks	Section-A (1 Mark)		Section-B (2 Marks)	Section-C (3 Marks)	Section-D (5 Marks)	Section-E (4 Marks)	Total Marks
			MCQ	A/R	VSA	SA	LA	Case-Study	
1	Real Number	6	1(Q5)	1(Q19)				1(Q36)	6
2	Polynomials	20	1(Q2)			1(Q28)			4
3	Pair of Linear Equations in Two Variables		1(Q1)		1(Q21)	1(Q27)			6
4	Quadratic Equations		1(Q4)				1(Q32)		6
5	Arithmetic Progression		1(Q3)			1(Q26)			4
6	Triangles	15	1(Q8)		1(Q22)		1(Q33)		8
7	Circles		2(Q13, 17)		1(Q24)	1(Q30)			6
8	Coordinate Geometry	6	4(Q6, 8, 11, 15)		1(Q25)				6
9	Introduction to Trigonometry	12	2(Q7, 10)		1(Q23)	1(Q29)			7
10	Some Applications of Trigonometry		1(Q14)					1(Q37)	5
11	Areas Related to Circles	10	1(Q12)						1
12	Surface Areas and Volumes						1(Q34)	1(Q38)	9
13	Statistics	11	2(Q16, 18)				1(Q35)		7
14	Probability			1(Q20)		1(Q31)			4
Total Marks (Total Questions)		**80**	**18(18)**	**2(2)**	**10(5)**	**18(6)**	**20(4)**	**12(3)**	**80(38)**

Note : The number given inside the bracket denotes question number, asked in the sample paper, while the number given outside the bracket are the number of questions from that particular chapter.

Time : 3 Hours **Max. Marks : 80**

General Instructions

1. *This Question paper contains - five sections A, B, C, D and E. Each section is compulsory. However, there are internal choices in some questions.*
2. *Section A has 18 MCQ's and 02 Assertion-Reason based questions of 1 mark each.*
3. *Section B has 5 Very Short Answer (VSA)-type questions of 2 marks each.*
4. *Section C has 6 Short Answer (SA)-type questions of 3 marks each.*
5. *Section D has 4 Long Answer (LA)-type questions of 5 marks each.*
6. *Section E has 3 case based integrated units of assessment (4 marks each) with sub parts of values of 1, 1 and 2 marks each respectively.*

SECTION-A (Multiple Choice Questions)

Each question carries 1 mark.

1. For which value of p, will the lines represented by the following pair of linear equations be parallel

$3x - y - 5 = 0$ $\quad$ $6x - 2y - p = 0$

(a) all real values except 10 (b) 10 (c) 5/2 (d) 1/2

2. If one zero of the quadratic polynomial

$2x^2 - 8x - m$ is $\frac{5}{2}$, then the other zero is

(a) $\frac{2}{3}$ (b) $-\frac{2}{3}$ (c) $\frac{3}{2}$ (d) $\frac{-15}{2}$

3. The nth term of the A.P. a, $3a$, $5a$, ..., is

(a) na (b) $(2n - 1)a$ (c) $(2n + 1)a$ (d) $2na$

4. The condition for one root of the quadratic equation $ax^2 + bx + c = 0$ to be twice the other, is

(a) $b^2 = 4ac$ (b) $2b^2 = 9ac$ (c) $c^2 = 4a + b^2$ (d) $c^2 = 9a - b^2$

5. The rational number of the form $\frac{p}{q}$, $q \neq 0$, p and q are positive integers, which represents $0.1\overline{34}$ i.e., (0.1343434....) is

(a) $\frac{134}{999}$ (b) $\frac{134}{990}$ (c) $\frac{133}{999}$ (d) $\frac{133}{990}$

6. Ratio in which the line $3x + 4y = 7$ divides the line segment joining the points (1, 2) and (–2, 1) is

(a) 3 : 5 (b) 4 : 6 (c) 4 : 9 (d) None of these

7. If $x = p\sec\theta$ and $y = q\tan\theta$, then

(a) $x^2 - y^2 = p^2q^2$ (b) $x^2q^2 - y^2p^2 = pq$ (c) $x^2q^2 - y^2p^2 = \frac{1}{p^2q^2}$ (d) $x^2q^2 - y^2p^2 = p^2q^2$

8. If the mid point of the line joining (3, 4) and (k, 7) is (x, y) and $2x + 2y + 1 = 0$. Find the value of k.

(a) 10 (b) –15 (c) 15 (d) –10

9. In the given figure, $DE \parallel BC$. The value of EC is

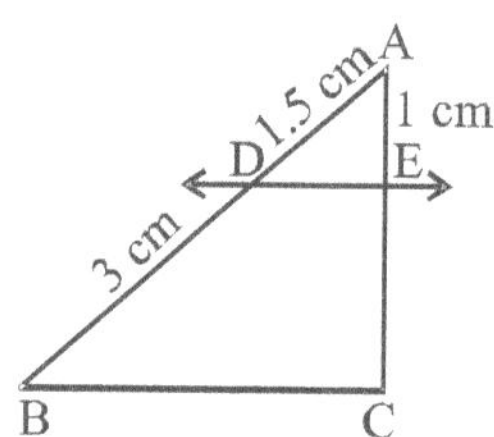

(a) 1.5 cm (b) 3 cm (c) 2 cm (d) 1 cm

10. $(\cos^4 A - \sin^4 A)$ is equal to
(a) $1 - 2\cos^2 A$ (b) $2\sin^2 A - 1$ (c) $\sin^2 A - \cos^2 A$ (d) $2\cos^2 A - 1$

11. In what ratio is the line segment joining the points (3, 5) & (–4, 2) divided by y–axis?
(a) 3 : 2 (b) 3 : 4 (c) 2 : 3 (d) 4 : 3

12. The perimeter of a sector of a circle with central angle 90° is 25 cm. Then the area of the minor segment of the circle is.
(a) 14 cm^2 (b) 16 cm^2 (c) 18 cm^2 (d) 24 cm^2

13. Two chords AB and CD of a circle intersect each other at P outside the circle. If AB = 5 cm, BP = 3 cm and PD = 2 cm, find CD.
(a) 4 cm
(b) 5 cm
(c) 8 cm
(d) 10 cm

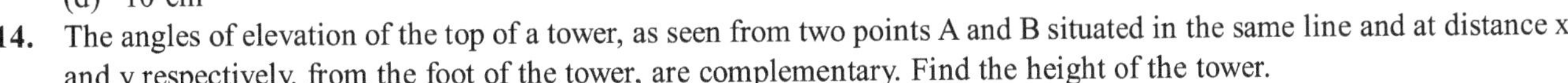

14. The angles of elevation of the top of a tower, as seen from two points A and B situated in the same line and at distance x and y respectively. from the foot of the tower, are complementary. Find the height of the tower.
(a) $\sqrt{x+y}$ (b) $\sqrt{xy}$ (c) xy (d) $\sqrt{x}+\sqrt{y}$

15. ABCD is a rectangle whose three vertices are B (4, 0), C (4, 3) and D (0, 3). The length of one of its diagonals is
(a) 5 (b) 4 (c) 3 (d) 25

16. What is the arithmetic mean of 20 fours, 40 fives, 30 sixes and 10 tens?
(a) 50 (b) 25 (c) 5.6 (d) 33

17. If radii of two concentric circles are 4 cm and 5 cm, then length of each chord of one circle which is tangent to the other circle, is
(a) 3 cm (b) 6 cm (c) 9 cm (d) 1 cm

18. The mean of discrete observations $y_1, y_2, ..., y_n$ is given by
(a) $\frac{\sum_{i=1}^{n} y_i}{n}$ (b) $\frac{\sum_{i=1}^{n} y_i}{\sum_{i=1}^{n} i}$ (c) $\frac{\sum_{i=1}^{n} y_i f_i}{n}$ (d) $\frac{\sum_{i=1}^{n} y_i f_i}{\sum_{i=1}^{n} f_i}$

(ASSERTION-REASON BASED QUESTIONS)

In the following questions, a statement of Assertion (A) is followed by a statement of Reason (R). Choose the correct answer out of the following choices.

(a) ***Both A and R are true and R is the correct explanation of A.***
(b) ***Both A and R are true but R is not the correct explanation of A.***
(c) ***A is true but R is false.***
(d) ***A is false but R is true.***

19. **Assertion :** 2 is a rational number.
Reason : The square roots of all positive integers are irrationals.

20. **Assertion :** If the probability of an event is P then probability of its complementary event will be $1 - P$.
Reason : When E and $\overline{E}$ are complementary events, then $P(E) + P(\overline{E}) = 1$

SECTION-B

This section comprises of very short answer type-questions (VSA) of 2 marks each.

21. Sum of the ages of a father and the son is 40 years. If father's age is three times that of his son, then find their respective ages.

22. S and T are points on sides PR and QR of ΔPQR such that ∠P = ∠RTS. Show that ΔRPQ ~ ΔRTS.

23. Find out the value of $\sqrt{\sec^2\theta + \text{cosec}^2\theta}$

24. In Fig. if TP and TQ are the two tangents to a circle with centre O so that $\angle POQ = 110°$, then find the measure of $\angle PTQ$.

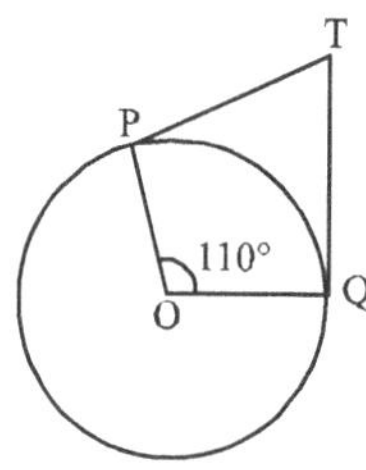

OR

In figure, a quadrilateral ABCD is drawn to circumscribe a circle, with centre O, in such a way that the sides AB, BC, CD and DA touch the circle at the points P, Q, R and S respectively. Prove that AB + CD = BC + DA.

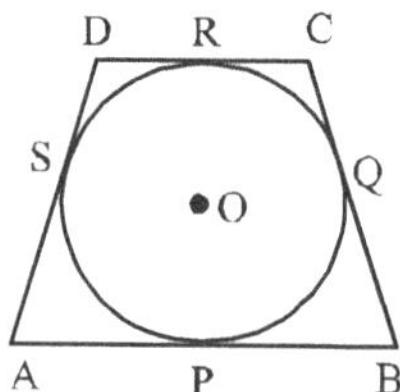

25. Find the coordinates of the point which divides the line segment joining the points (6, 3) and (– 4, 5) in the ratio 3 : 2 internally.

OR

Find the coordinates of points which trisect the line segment joining (1, – 2) and (– 3, 4).

SECTION-C

This section comprises of short answer type questions (SA) of 3 marks each.

26. The houses of a row are numbered consecutively from 1 to 49. Show that there is a value of x such that the sum of the numbers of the houses preceding the house numbered x is equal to the sum of the numbers of the houses fallowing it. Find this value of x. [Hint : $S_{x-1} = S_{49} - S_x$]

27. Find the sum of values of a and b for which the following system of linear equations has infinite number of solutions:
$2x + 3y = 7$
$(a + b + 1)x + (a + 2b + 2)y = 4(a + b) + 1$

28. Draw the graph of the quadratic polynomial $f(x) = 3 - 2x - x^2$. Also find its zeroes.

29. If $\frac{\cos\alpha}{\cos\beta} = m$ and $\frac{\cos\alpha}{\sin\beta} = n$, show that $(m^2 + n^2)\cos^2\beta = n^2$

OR

Find the value of 'x' such that $2\operatorname{cosec}^2 30° + x\sin^2 60° - \frac{3}{4}\tan^2 30° = 10$

30. A quadrilateral ABCD is drawn to circumscribe a circle, Prove that AB + CD = AD + BC.

31. Two dice are thrown simultaneously. What is the probability that the sum of the numbers appearing on the dice is a prime number?

OR

Cards marked with numbers 13, 14, 15, ..., 60 are placed in a box and mixed thoroughly. One card is drawn at random from the box. Find the probability that the number on drawn card is
(i) divisible by (ii) a number which is a perfect square.

SECTION-D

This section comprises of long answer-type questions (LA) of 5 marks each.

32. Find the roots of the equations $x^2 - 3x + 2 = 0$

33. If AD and PM are medians of triangles ABC and PQR, respectively where $\Delta ABC \sim \Delta PQR$, prove that $\frac{AB}{PQ} = \frac{AD}{PM}$.

34. In figure, a tent is in the shape of a cylinder surmounted by a conical top of same diameter. If the height and diameter of cylindrical part are 2.1 m and 3 m respectively and the slant height of conical part is 2.8 m, find the cost of canvas needed to make the tent if the canvas is available at the rate of ₹ 500/sq. metre. $\left(\text{Use } \pi = \frac{22}{7}\right)$

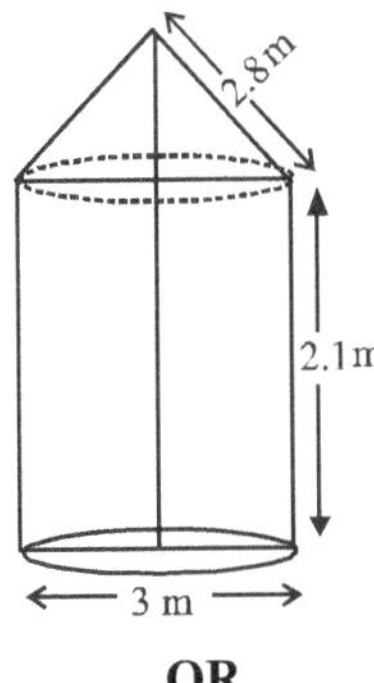

OR

A the largest possible sphere is carved out from a wooden solid cube of side 7 cm. Find the volume of the wood left.

$\left(\text{Use } \pi = \frac{22}{7}\right)$.

35. The following table shows marks secures by 140 students in an examination :

Marks	0-10	10-20	20-30	30-40	40-50
No. of Student	20	24	40	36	20

Calculation of mean by Step-deviation method.

OR

The following table shows the ages of the patients admitted in a hospital during a year:

Age (in years)	5 - 15	15 - 25	25 - 35	35 - 45	45 - 55	55 - 65
Number of patients	6	11	21	23	14	5

Find the mode and the mean of the data given above. Compare and interpret the two measures of central tendency.

SECTION-E

This section comprises of 3 case study/passage - based questions of 4 marks each with three sub-parts (i), (ii), (iii) of marks 1, 1, 2 respectively.

36. Case - Study 1: Read the following passage and answer the questions given below.

To enhance the reading skills of grade X students, the school nominates you and two of your friends to set up a class library. There are two sections-section A and section B of grade X. There are 32 students in section A and 36 students in section B.

(i) What is the minimum number of books you will acquire for the class library, so that they can be distributed equally among students of Section A or Section B?

(ii) If the product of two positive integers is equal to the product of their HCF and LCM is true then, the HCF (32, 36) is

(iii) $7 \times 11 \times 13 \times 15 + 15$ is a ______.

OR

If p and q are positive integers such that $p = ab^2$ and $q = a^2b$, where a, b are prime numbers, then the LCM (p, q) is ______.

37. **Case - Study 2:** Read the following passage and answer the questions given below.

Vijay is trying to find the average height of a tower near his house. He is using the properties of similar triangles.The height of Vijay's house if 20m when Vijay's house casts a shadow 10m long on the ground. At the same time, the tower casts a shadow 50m long on the ground and the house of Ajay casts 20m shadow on the ground.

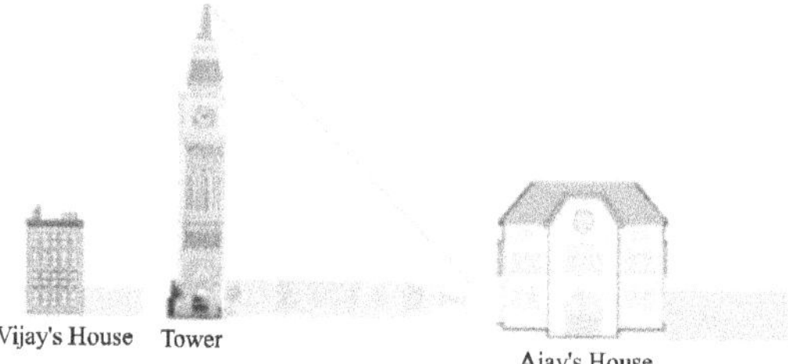

(i) What is the height of the tower?

(ii) What will be the length of the shadow of the tower when Vijay's house casts a shadow of 12m?

(iii) What is the height of Ajay's house?

OR

When the tower casts a shadow of 40m, same time what will be the length of the shadow of Ajay's house?

38. **Case - Study 3:** Read the following passage and answer the questions given below.

Adventure camps are the perfect place for the children to practice decision making for themselves without parents and teachers guiding their every move. Some students of a school reached for adventure at Sakleshpur. At the camp, the waiters served some students with a welcome drink in a cylindrical glass and some students in a hemispherical cup whose dimensions are shown below. After that they went for a jungle trek. The jungle trek was enjoyable but tiring. As dusk fell, it was time to take shelter. Each group of four students was given a canvas of area $551 m^2$. Each group had to make a conical tent to accommodate all the four students. Assuming that all the stitching and wasting incurred while cutting, would amount to $1 m^2$, the students put the tents. The radius of the tent is 7 m.

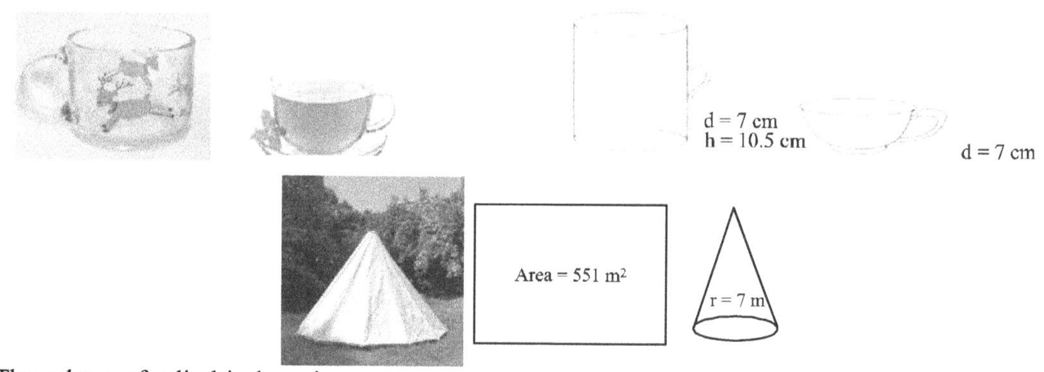

(i) The volume of cylindrical cup is ______.

(ii) The volume of hemispherical cup is ______.

(iii) The height of the conical tent prepared to accommodate four students is ______.

OR

How much space on the ground is occupied by each student in the conical tent ______.

SOLUTIONS

SAMPLE PAPER-1

1. (d) L.C.M × H.C.F = First number × second number

Hence, required number $= \frac{36 \times 2}{18} = 4$.

2. (a) Required equation is $x^2 - 6x + 6 = 0$.

3. (c) Here, $\frac{a_1}{a_2} = \frac{k}{12}, \frac{b_1}{b_2} = \frac{3}{k}, \frac{c_1}{c_2} = \frac{k-3}{k}$

For a pair of linear equations to have infinitely many solutions:

$\frac{a_1}{a_2} = \frac{b_1}{b_2} = \frac{c_1}{c_2}$

So, we have $\frac{k}{12} = \frac{3}{k} = \frac{k-3}{k}$ or $\frac{k}{12} = \frac{3}{k}$ which gives $k^2 = 36$ i.e., $k = \pm 6$

Also, $\frac{3}{k} = \frac{k-3}{k}$ gives $3k = k^2 - 3k$, i.e., $6k = k^2$, which means $k = 0$ or $k = 6$.

Therefore, the value of k that satisfies both the conditions, is $k = 6$. For this value, the pair of linear equations has infinitely many solutions.

4. (a) Since zeroes are reciprocal of each other, so product of the roots will be 1, so ,

$k^2 - k - 2 = 0 \Rightarrow (k-2)(k+1) = 0$

$k = 2, k = -1$, Since $k > 0 \therefore k = 2$

5. (a) H.C.F. (91, 126) $= \frac{91 \times 126}{\text{L.C.M.}(91, 126)}$

$= \frac{91 \times 126}{182} = 13$

6. (a) (By definition of similar triangles).

7. (d) $\sec\theta + \tan^3\theta \operatorname{cosec}\theta$

$= \sec\theta + \frac{\sin\theta}{\cos\theta} \tan^2\theta \operatorname{cosec}\theta = \sec\theta\,(1 + \tan^2\theta)$

$= (1 + \tan^2\theta)^{3/2} = [1 + (1 - a^2)]^{3/2}$

8. (b) Now, in ΔDEF and ΔPQR,

$\angle D = \angle Q, \angle R = \angle E$

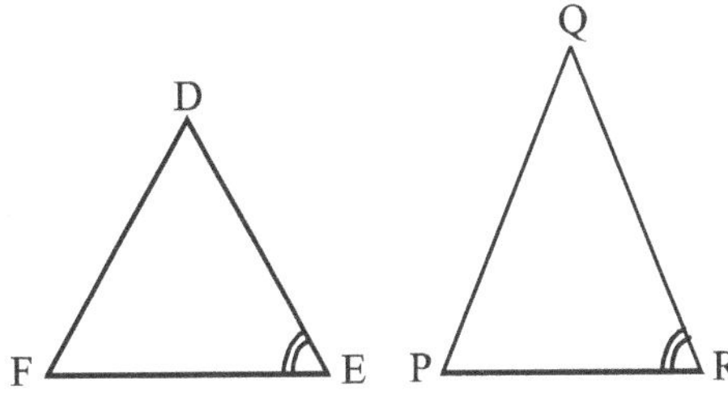

$\therefore$ ΔDEF ~ ΔQRP [by AAA similarity criterion]

$\Rightarrow \angle F = \angle P$ [corresponding angles]

$\therefore \frac{DF}{QP} = \frac{ED}{RQ} = \frac{FE}{PR}$ [corresponding sides]

9. (c) $PQ = 13 \Rightarrow PQ^2 = 169$

$\Rightarrow (x-2)^2 + (-7-5)^2 = 169$

$\Rightarrow x^2 - 4x + 4 + 144 = 169$

$\Rightarrow x^2 - 4x - 21 = 0 \Rightarrow x^2 - 7x + 3x - 21 = 0$

$\Rightarrow (x-7)(x+3) = 0 \Rightarrow x = 7, -3$

10. (d) Given, $\tan\theta = \frac{a}{b}$

$\therefore \frac{a\sin\theta - b\cos\theta}{a\sin\theta + b\cos\theta} = \frac{a\tan\theta - b}{a\tan\theta + b} = \frac{a^2 - b^2}{a^2 + b^2}$

11. (b) Suppose the required ratio is $m_1 : m_2$

Then, using the section formula, we get

$-2 = \frac{m_1(4) + m_2(-3)}{m_1 + m_2}$

$\Rightarrow -2m_1 - 2m_2 = 4m_1 - 3m_2$

$\Rightarrow m_2 = 6m_1 \Rightarrow m_1 : m_2 = 1:6$

12. (a) Area of the shaded region

$= \frac{40°}{360°} \times \frac{22}{7} \times (7)^2 - \frac{40°}{360°} \times \frac{22}{7} \times (3.5)^2$

$= \frac{1}{9} \times \frac{22}{7} \times (7^2 - 3.5^2) = \frac{1}{9} \times \frac{22}{7} \times \left(49 - \frac{49}{4}\right)$

$= \frac{1}{9} \times \frac{22}{7} \times \frac{49}{4} \times 3 = \frac{77}{6} \text{cm}^2$

13. (b) Exterior angle of a cyclic quadrilateral is equal to its interior opposite angle.

$\angle BAC = \angle DCA$ and proceed.

14. (a) Let the radii of the outer and inner circles be r_1 and r_2 respectively; we have

Area $= \pi r_1^2 - \pi r_2^2 = \pi(r_1^2 - r_2^2)$

$= \pi(r_1 - r_2)(r_1 + r_2)$

$= \pi(5.7 - 4.3)(5.7 + 4.3) = \pi \times 1.4 \times 10$ sq. cm

$= 3.1416 \times 14$ sq. cm. $= 43.98$ sq. cms.

15. (a) Let the mean weight of a class of 35 students be $\overline{x}_1$

and that of both students and a teacher be $\overline{x}_2$

Then $\overline{x}_1 = 45$ kg and

$\bar{x}_2 = 45 + \frac{500}{1000} = 45 + 0.5 = 45.5\text{kg}$

$\bar{x}_1 = \frac{\Sigma x_1}{n_1}, \ \bar{x}_2 = \frac{\Sigma x_2}{n_1}$

$\Rightarrow 45 = \frac{\Sigma x_1}{35}, \ 45.5 = \frac{\Sigma x_2}{36}$

$\Rightarrow$ $\Sigma x_1 = 1575$ kg, $\Sigma x_2 = 1638$ kg

$\Rightarrow$ Total weight = weight of students + weight of teacher

$\therefore$ Weight of teacher = Total weight – weight of students

$\therefore$ Weight of the teacher = $\Sigma x_2 - \Sigma x_1$
= 1638 – 1575 = 63 kg

16. **(d)** Volume of spherical shell

$= \frac{4}{3}\pi R^3 - \frac{4}{3}\pi r^3 = \frac{4}{3}\pi(R^3 - r^3)$

17. **(d)** Clearly, the number of families having income range (in ₹)
16000 – 19000 = 69 – 50 = 19.

18. **(d)** $\because \ P(E) + P(\bar{E}) = 1$

19. **(b)** Put $n = 1$ and $n = 2$.

20. **(a)** Both Assertion and Reason are correct and Reason is the correct explanation of the assertion.

greatest side = $\sqrt{(3)^2 + (4)^2} = 5$ units.

21. Comparing the given equations with $a_1x, + b_1y = c_1$ and $a_2x + b_2y = c_2$ we have

$\therefore \quad \frac{a_1}{a_2} = \frac{1}{2}; \frac{b_1}{b_2} = \frac{2}{1}; \frac{c_1}{c_2} = \frac{4}{5}$ [1 Mark]

Here, $\frac{a_1}{a_2} \neq \frac{b_1}{b_2}$ [½ Mark]

$\therefore$ The equations have consistent and unique olution. [½ Mark]

OR

Pair of lines are coincident if

$\frac{a_1}{a_2} = \frac{b_1}{b_2} = \frac{c_1}{c_2}$ ... (i) [½ Mark]

Given lines,
$3x - y + 8 = 0$
and $6x - ky + 16 = 0$

Here, $a_1 = 3, b_1 = -1, c_1 = 8$
$a_2 = 6, b_2 = -k, c_2 = 16$ [½ Mark]

Using equation (i) we have

$\frac{3}{6} = \frac{-1}{-k} = \frac{8}{16}$ [½ Mark]

$\Rightarrow \quad \frac{1}{k} = \frac{1}{2}$

$\therefore \quad k = 2$ [½ Mark]

22. Given : ΔABC and ΔPQR, in which,

$\frac{AB}{PQ} = \frac{BC}{QR} = \frac{AD}{PM}$

To Prove : $\Delta ABC \sim \Delta PQR$ [½ Mark]

Proof : $\frac{AB}{PQ} = \frac{BC}{QR}$ (Given)

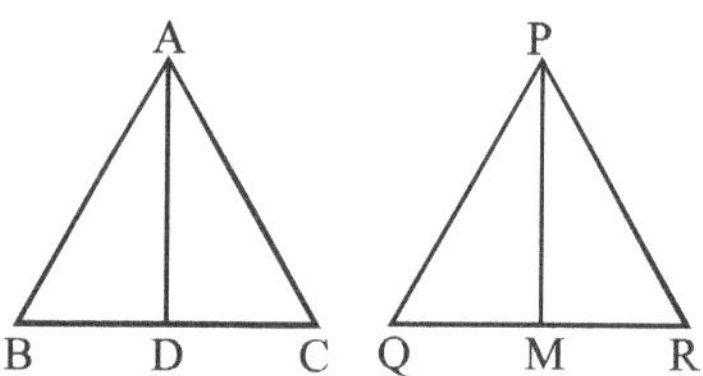

$\frac{2BD}{2QM} = \frac{BC}{QR} \therefore \frac{AB}{PQ} = \frac{BD}{QM} = \frac{AD}{PM}$

$\therefore$ $\Delta ABD \sim \Delta PQM$ (By SSS) [1 Mark]

$\therefore$ $\angle B = \angle Q$ (By corresponding angles of similar triangles)

Now, In ΔABC and ΔPQR, $\frac{AB}{PQ} = \frac{BC}{QR}$ and $\angle B = \angle Q$

$\therefore$ **$\Delta ABC \sim \Delta PQR$ (By SAS)** [½ Mark]

23. **LHS** $= \frac{\tan^2\theta}{\tan^2\theta - 1} + \frac{\text{cosec}^2\theta}{\sec^2\theta - \text{cosec}^2\theta}$

$= \frac{\frac{\sin^2\theta}{\cos^2\theta}}{\frac{\sin^2\theta}{\cos^2\theta} - 1} + \frac{\frac{1}{\sin^2\theta}}{\frac{1}{\cos^2\theta} - \frac{1}{\sin^2\theta}}$ [½ Mark]

$= \frac{\sin^2\theta}{\cos^2\theta} \times \frac{\cos^2\theta}{\sin^2\theta - \cos^2\theta} + \frac{1}{\sin^2\theta} \times \frac{\sin^2\theta\cos^2\theta}{\sin^2\theta - \cos^2\theta}$ [½ Mark]

$= \frac{\sin^2\theta}{\sin^2\theta - \cos^2\theta} + \frac{\cos^2\theta}{\sin^2\theta - \cos^2\theta}$ [½ Mark]

$= \frac{\sin^2\theta + \cos^2\theta}{\sin^2\theta - \cos^2\theta} = \frac{1}{\sin^2\theta - \cos^2\theta}$ = **RHS** [½ Mark]

24. In right Δ OSP,
$OP^2 = PS^2 + OS^2$ [1 Mark]
$\Rightarrow r^2 = 225 + (r - 10)^2$
$\Rightarrow r^2 = 225 + r^2 - 20r + 100$
$\Rightarrow 20r = 325$
$\Rightarrow 2r = 32.5$
Hence, diameter = 32.5 cm. [1 Mark]

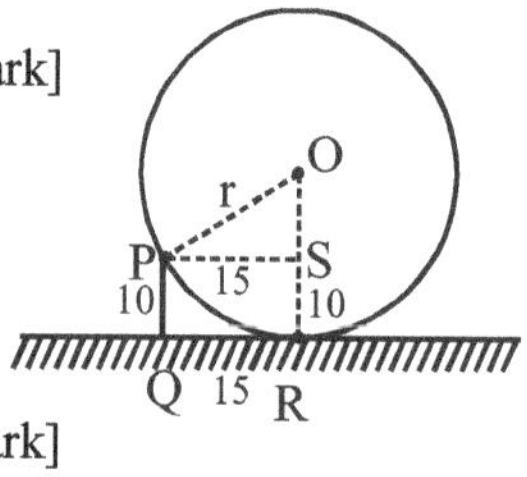

Answer : 32.5 cm

OR

$\angle POR + \angle PQR = 180°$
$\therefore \angle POR = 180° - 50° = 130°$

$\angle PSR = \frac{1}{2} \angle POR$ [½ Mark]

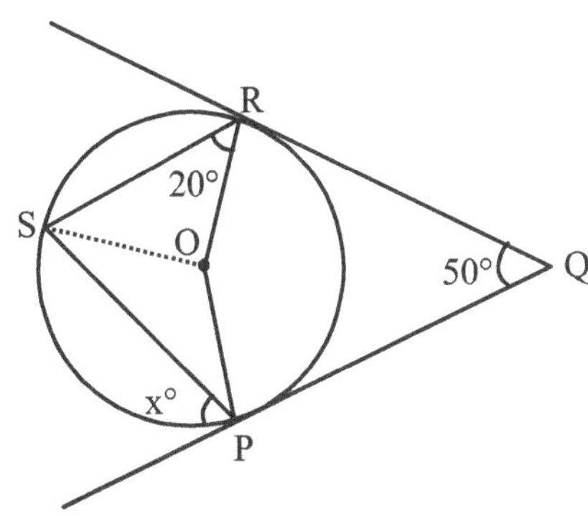

$\therefore \angle PSR = \frac{1}{2} \times 130° = 65°$ [½ Mark]

$\Rightarrow \angle PSR = \angle OSP + \angle OSR$

$\Rightarrow \angle PSR = \angle OSP + 20°$ [$\because \angle OSP = \angle OSR$]

$\Rightarrow 65° = \angle OSP = 20°$

$\Rightarrow \angle OSP = 45°$

$\Rightarrow \angle OPX = 90°$ [$\because$ PX is a tangent]

$\Rightarrow \angle SPX + \angle OPS = 90°$

$x° + \angle OSP = 90°$ [$\because \angle OPS = \angle OSP$]

$x° = 90° - 45° = 45°$

Answer : 45° [1 Mark]

25.

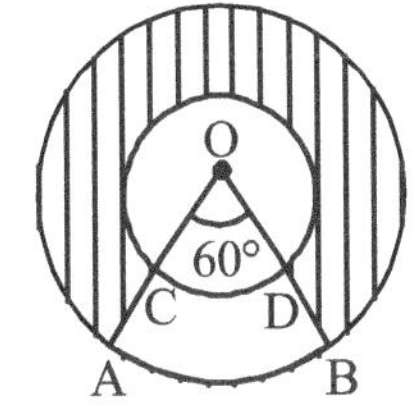

Radius of inner circle, r = 21 cm

Radius of outer circle, R = 42 cm

Area of (ABCD) = Area of sector (OAB) – Area of sector (OCD)

$= \frac{60}{360} \times \pi (42^2 - 21^2)$ [1 Mark]

$= \frac{1}{6} \times \frac{22}{7} \times (42+21)(42-21) = \frac{1}{6} \times \frac{22}{7} \times 63 \times 21$

$= 11 \times 21 \times 3 = 693 \text{ cm}^2$ [1 Mark]

Area of shaded region = Area of outer circle – Area of inner circle – Area (ABCD)

$= \pi(42)^2 - \pi(21)^2 - 693 = \frac{22}{7} \times 63 \times 21 - 693 = 4158 - 693$

$= 3465 \text{ cm}^2$ [1 Mark]

26. Let us assume on the contrary that $\sqrt{2} + \sqrt{5}$ is rational number. Then, there exist co-prime positive integers *a* and *b* such that

$\sqrt{2} + \sqrt{5} = \frac{a}{b} \Rightarrow \frac{a}{b} - \sqrt{2} = \sqrt{5}$ [½ Mark]

$\Rightarrow \left(\frac{a}{b} - \sqrt{2}\right)^2 = (\sqrt{5})^2$ [Squaring both sides] [½ Mark]

$\Rightarrow (a - \sqrt{2}b)^2 = 5b^2 \Rightarrow a^2 + 2b^2 - 2ab\sqrt{2} = 5b^2$ [½ Mark]

$\Rightarrow a^2 + 2b^2 - 3b^2 = 2ab\sqrt{2} \Rightarrow \frac{a^2 - 3b^2}{2ab} = \sqrt{2}$ [½ Mark]

$\Rightarrow \sqrt{2}$ is a rational number

$\left[\because a, b \text{ are integers} \Rightarrow \frac{a^2 - 3b^2}{2ab} \text{ is rational}\right]$ [½ Mark]

This contradicts the fact that $\sqrt{2}$ is irrational. So, our assumption is wrong.

Hence, $\sqrt{2} + \sqrt{5}$ is irrational. [½ Mark]

27. If α and β are the zeroes of $2x^2 - 3x + 1$,

then $\alpha + \beta = \frac{-b}{a} = \frac{3}{2}$ and $\alpha\beta = \frac{c}{a} = \frac{1}{2}$ [1 Mark]

New quadratic polynomial whose zeroes are 3α and 3β is given by

x^2 – (Sum of the roots)x + Product of the roots

$= x^2 - (3\alpha + 3\beta)x + 3\alpha \times 3\beta$ [1 Mark]

$= x^2 - 3(\alpha + \beta)x + 9\alpha\beta = x^2 - 3\left(\frac{3}{2}\right)x + 9\left(\frac{1}{2}\right)$

$= x^2 - \frac{9}{2}x + \frac{9}{2} = \frac{1}{2}(2x^2 - 9x + 9)$ [1 Mark]

Hence, required quadratic polynomial is $\frac{1}{2}(2x^2 - 9x + 9)$.

28. $\frac{4}{x} + 5y = 7$ and $\frac{3}{x} + 4y = 5$

$\frac{4}{x} + 5y = 7$ .....(i)

$\frac{3}{x} + 4y = 5$ .....(ii)

[1 Mark]

Multiply equation (i) by (3) and equation (ii) by (4) we get,

$\frac{12}{x} + 15y = 21$ .....(iii)

$\frac{12}{x} + 16y = 20$ .....(iv)

Subtract (iii) and (iv), we get, $-y = 1 \Rightarrow y = -1$ [1 Mark]

Now, putting the value of y = – 1 in equation (i)

$\frac{4}{x} + 5(-1) = 7 \Rightarrow \frac{4}{x} = 7 + 5 \Rightarrow \frac{4}{x} = \frac{12}{1} \Rightarrow 12x$

$= 4 \Rightarrow x = \frac{4}{12} \Rightarrow x = \frac{1}{3}$ [1 Mark]

Hence $x = \frac{1}{3}$ and $y = -1$

29. $\tan(A + B) = \sqrt{3} \Rightarrow \tan(A+B) = \tan 60°$

$\left(\because \tan 60 = \sqrt{3}\right)$

$\Rightarrow A+B = 60°$ ......(i)

$\tan(A - B) = \frac{1}{\sqrt{3}} \Rightarrow \tan(A-B) = \tan 30°$ [1 Mark]

$\left(\because \tan 30° = \frac{1}{\sqrt{3}}\right)$

$\Rightarrow A - B = 30°$ ......(ii)

Adding (i) and (ii), we get; [1 Mark]

$2A = 90° \Rightarrow A = 45°$

Then from (i), $45° + B = 60° \Rightarrow B = 15°$. [1 Mark]

30. **To Find :** Perimeter of ΔABC

Let AQ = 5 cm and

AQ = AR .....(i)

BQ = BP .....(ii) [1 Mark]

CP = CR .....(iii)

(Tangent drawn from an external points are equal)

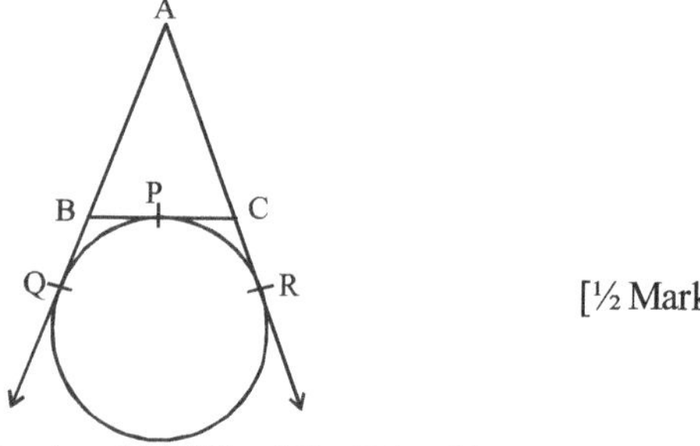

[½ Mark]

Since perimeter of $\Delta ABC = AB + BC + CA$

$\Rightarrow$ Perimeter of $\Delta ABC = AB + BP + PC + CA$

$[\because BC = BP + PC]$ [1 Mark]

$= (AB + BQ) + (CR + CA)$ from (ii) and (iii)

$= AQ + AR$ $[\because AQ = AR$ from (i)$]$

$= AQ + AQ = 2AQ = 2 \times 5 = 10$ cm [½ Mark]

$\therefore$ Perimeter of $\Delta ABC = 10$ cm.

OR

To prove: $\frac{AE}{DF} = \frac{AO}{DO}$

Construction : Draw $AE \perp BC$ and $DF \perp BC$.

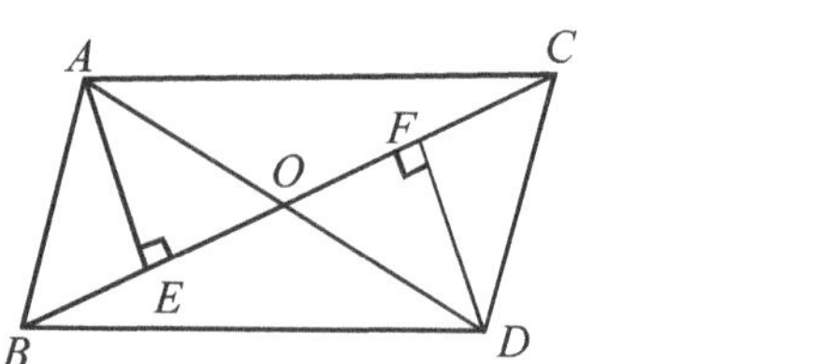

[1 Mark]

Proof :

In ΔAOE and ΔDOF,

$\angle AOE = \angle DOF$ (Vertically opposite angles)

$\angle AEO = \angle DFO = 90°$ (Construction)

$\Rightarrow$ $\Delta AOE \sim \Delta DOF$ (By AA Similarity) [1 Mark]

$\therefore \quad \frac{AO}{DO} = \frac{AE}{DF}$ ...(i) [1 Mark]

31. Total number of outcomes on throwing a pair of dice = 6 × 6 = 36

(i) Let E be the event of getting a prime number on each die.

So, favourable outcomes

= {(2, 2), (2, 3), (2, 5), (3, 2), (3, 3), (3, 5), (5, 2), (5, 3), (5, 5)}

Number of favourable outcomes = 9

Then, $P(E) = \frac{9}{36} = \frac{1}{4}$

Therefore, the probability of getting a prime number on each dice is $\frac{1}{4}$. [1½ Marks]

(ii) Let F be the event of getting a total of 9 or 11.

So, favourable outcomes

= {(3, 6), (4, 5), (5, 4), (6, 3), (5, 6), (6, 5)}.

Number of favourable outcomes = 6

Thus, $P(F) = \frac{6}{36} = \frac{1}{6}$

Hence, the probability of getting a total of 9 or 11 is $\frac{1}{6}$.

[1½ Marks]

OR

The possible outcomes of tossing three coins together : {HHH, HHT, HTH, THH, HTT, THT, TTH ,TTT}

$\Rightarrow$ Total number of outcomes = 8

(i) Outcomes of getting exactly two heads

= {HHT, HTH and THH}

Favourable number of outcomes = 3

Probability (getting exactly two heads) $= \frac{3}{8}$

[1 Mark]

(ii) Outcomes of getting at least two heads

= {HHH, HHT, HTH and THH}

Favourable number of outcomes = 4

Probability (getting atleast two heads) $= \frac{4}{8} = \frac{1}{2}$

[1 Mark]

(iii) Outcomes of getting at least two tails

= {HTT, THT, TTH and TTT}

Favourable number of outcomes = 4

Probability (getting atleast two tails) $= \frac{4}{8} = \frac{1}{2}$

[1 Mark]

32.

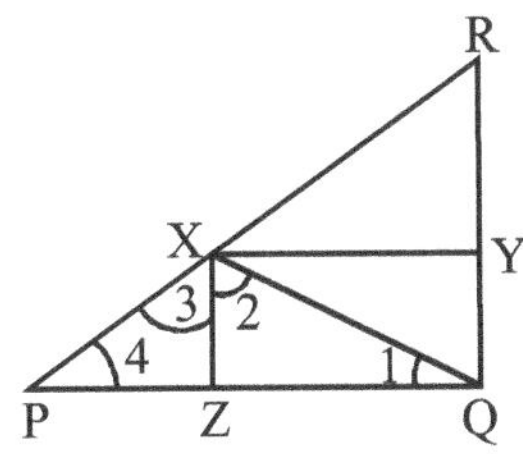

$RQ \perp PQ, XZ \perp PQ$

$\Rightarrow XZ \parallel YQ$

$\therefore XY \parallel ZQ$ ...(i)

$XYQZ$ is a rectangle. [1½ Marks]

In ΔXZQ, $\angle 1 + \angle 2 = 90°$ ...(ii)

In ΔPZX, $\angle 3 + \angle 4 = 90°$ ...(iii)

$XQ \perp PR \Rightarrow \angle 2 + \angle 3 = 90°$

From eqs. (i) and (iii)

$\angle 1 = \angle 3$ [1½ Marks]

From eqs. (ii) and (iii)

$\angle 2 = \angle 4$

$\Delta PZX \sim \Delta XZQ$ (*AA* similarity)

$$\frac{PZ}{XZ} = \frac{XZ}{ZQ}$$

$\Rightarrow XZ^2 = PZ \times ZQ$ [2 Marks]

33.

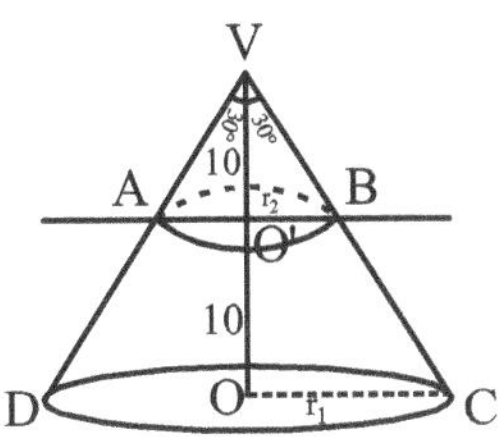

In ΔVO'A and ΔVOC [1 Mark]

$$\tan 30° = \frac{OC}{VO} \text{ and } \tan 30° = \frac{O'V}{VO'}$$

$$\frac{1}{\sqrt{3}} = \frac{r_1}{20} \text{ and } \frac{1}{\sqrt{3}} = \frac{r_2}{10}$$

$$r_1 = \frac{20}{\sqrt{3}} \text{ and } r_2 = \frac{10}{\sqrt{3}}$$ [2 Marks]

Volume of small cone

$$= \pi r_1 h = \frac{22}{7} \times \frac{10}{\sqrt{3}} \times 10$$

$$= \frac{2200}{7\sqrt{3}}$$ [2 Marks]

OR

Height of cylinder = 2.8 cm $= \frac{14}{5}$ cm

Radius of cylinder = 2.1 cm $= \frac{21}{10}$ cm

$l = \sqrt{(2.8)^2 + (2.1)^2} = 3.5\text{cm}$ [2 Marks]

According to question a conical cavity of same height and diameter is hollowed out.

Now, T.S.A of remaining solid = C.S.A of cone + C.S.A of cylinder + Area of base of cylinder

$= 2\pi r l + 2\pi r h + \pi r^2$ [1 Mark]

$= \pi r\,[l + 2h + r]$

$$= \frac{22}{7} \times \frac{21}{10}\left[\frac{7}{2} + \frac{28}{5} + \frac{21}{10}\right] = \frac{22}{10} \times 3\left[\frac{35+56+21}{10}\right]$$

$$= \frac{22}{10} \times 3 \times \frac{112}{10} = 73.92\text{cm}^2$$ [2 Marks]

34. Given equation is $36x^2 - 12ax + (a^2 - b^2) = 0$

$D = (-12a)^2 - 4(36)(a^2 - b^2)$ $[\because D = b^2 - 4ac]$ [1 Mark]

$= 144a^2 - 144(a^2 - b^2) = 144b^2$ [1 Mark]

Now, $= \dfrac{12a \pm 12b}{72} = \dfrac{a \pm b}{6}$ [2 Marks]

Hence, $c = 6$ [1 Mark]

OR

The given equation is $x^{2/3} + x^{1/3} - 2 = 0$

Put $x^{1/3} = y$, then $y^2 + y - 2 = 0$

$\Rightarrow y^2 + 2y - y - 2 = 0$ [1 Mark]

$\Rightarrow y(y+2) - 1(y+2) = 0 \quad \Rightarrow (y-1)(y+2) = 0$

$\Rightarrow y = 1$ or $y = -2$ [1 Mark]

$\Rightarrow x^{1/3} = 1$ or $x^{1/3} = -2$ [1 Mark]

$\therefore x = (1)^3$ or $x = (-2)^3 = -8$ [1 Mark]

Hence, the real roots of the given equations are 1, –8. [1 Mark]

35.

Height	Frequency	c.f.
100 – 120	12	12
120 – 140	14	26
140 – 160	8	34
160 – 180	6	40
180 – 200	10	50
Total	**50**	

[1 Mark]

Here, $N = 50 \Rightarrow \frac{N}{2} = \frac{50}{2} = 25$ [1 Mark]

So, Median Class = 120 – 140

Here, $l = 120$, $h = 20$, $c.f. = 12$, $f = 14$ [1 Mark]

$$\text{Median} = l + \left(\frac{\frac{N}{2} - c.f.}{f}\right) \times h = 120 + \left(\frac{25-12}{14}\right) \times 20$$

$$= 120 + \frac{260}{14} = 120 + 18.57$$

Median = 138.57 [2 Marks]

36. **(i)** Given that

$a_6 = a + 5d = 16000$ ..... (i)

$a_9 = a + 8d = 22600$ ..... (ii)

$- \quad - \quad -$

$-3d = -6600 \Rightarrow d = 2200$

$\Rightarrow$ $a = 5000$

$\therefore$ Production during first year = 5000 [1 Mark]

(i) Production during 8th year is $(a + 7d)$

$= 5000 + 2(2200) = 20400$ [1 Mark]

(ii) Production during first 3 year

$= 5000 + 7200 + 9400 = 21600$ [2 Marks]

OR

$5000 + (n - 1)\,2200 = 29200 \Rightarrow n = 12^{th}$ year [2 Marks]

37. $BD = 5 - 1.3 = 3.7m$

(i) $\sin C = \frac{BD}{BC} = \frac{3.7}{7.4} = \frac{1}{2}$

$\Rightarrow$ $\sin C = \sin 30° \angle \angle C = 30°$ [1 Mark]

(ii) $\angle D + B + \angle C = 180°$

$\Rightarrow$ $90° + \angle B + 30° = 180°$

$\angle B = 60°$ [1 Mark]

(iii) $\tan 30° = \frac{BD}{CD}$

$\Rightarrow \frac{1}{\sqrt{3}} = \frac{3.7}{CD}$

$\Rightarrow CD = 3.7\sqrt{3}m$ [2 Marks]

OR

$\sin^2 B + \sin^2 C = \sin^2 60° + \sin^2 30°$

$= \frac{3}{4} + \frac{1}{4} = 1$ [2 Marks]

38. **(i)** Centroid of ΔEHJ with E(2, 1), H(–2, 4) & J(–2, –2) is

Coordinates of centroid are

$\left(\frac{x_1 + x_2 + x_3}{3}, \frac{y_1 + y_2 + y_3}{3}\right)$

$\left(\frac{2 + (-2) + (-2)}{3}, \frac{1 + 4 + (-2)}{3}\right) = \left(\frac{-2}{3}, 1\right)$ [1 Mark]

(ii) If P needs to be at equal distance from A(3, 6) and G(1, –3), such that A, P and G are collinear, then P will be the mid-point of AG.

So coordinates of P will be $\left(\frac{3+1}{2}, \frac{6+(-3)}{2}\right) = \left(2, \frac{3}{2}\right)$

[1 Mark]

(iii) Let the point on x-axis equidistant from I(–1, 1) and E(2, 1) be (x, 0) then $\sqrt{(x+1)^2 + (0-1)^2}$

$= \sqrt{(x-2)^2 + (0-1)^2}$

$x^2 + 1 + 2x + 1 = x^2 + 4 - 4x + 1$

$6x = 3$

So $x = \frac{1}{2}$

$\therefore$ the required point is $\left(\frac{1}{2}, 0\right)$ [2 Marks]

OR

Let the coordinates of the position of a player Q such that his distance from K(–4,1) is twice his distance from E(2,1) be Q(x, y)

Then KQ : QE = 2 : 1

$Q(x, y) = \left(\frac{2\times 2 + 1\times(-4)}{3}, \frac{2\times 1 + 1\times 1}{3}\right) = (0, 1)$ [2 Marks]

SAMPLE PAPER-2

1. **(c)** H.C.F. of 20 and 15 = 5
So, 5 students are in each group.

$$\therefore \quad n=\frac{20+15}{5}=\frac{35}{5}=7$$

Hence, x = 4, y = 3 and n = 7

2. **(b)** The pair of linear equations in two variables is also known as simultaneous equations.

3. **(b)** Equate value of polynomial at $x = a$ with a
$a^2-27a+196=a \Rightarrow a^2-28a+196=0 \Rightarrow a=14$

4. **(d)** The roots of $5x^2-kx+1=0$ are real and distinct.
$\therefore \quad (k^2-4\times5\times1)>0 \Rightarrow k^2>20$

$\Rightarrow \quad k>\sqrt{20}$ or $k<-\sqrt{20} \Rightarrow k>2\sqrt{5}$ or $k<-2\sqrt{5}$.

5. **(b)** $a=5, t_{100}=-292$
$t_{100}-5+(100 \quad 1)d$ [using $t_n=a+(n-1)d$]
$\Rightarrow -292=5+99d$
$\Rightarrow -292-5=99d$

$$\Rightarrow d=\frac{-297}{99} \Rightarrow d=-3$$

$\therefore t_{50}=5+(50-1)(-3)=5+(-147)$
$=5-147 \Rightarrow t_{50}=-142$

6. **(c)** In ΔABC and ΔEDF,

$$\frac{AB}{DE}=\frac{BC}{FD} \quad \text{[Given]}$$

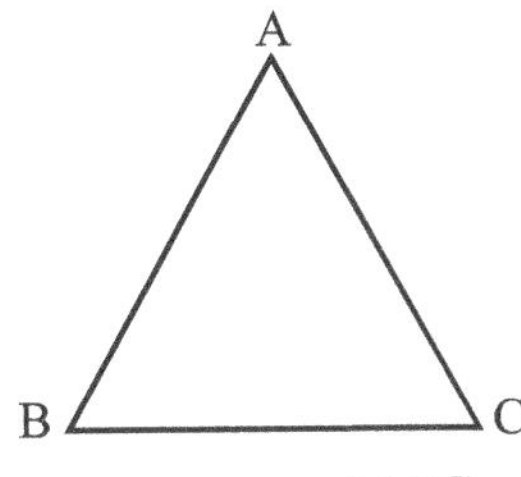

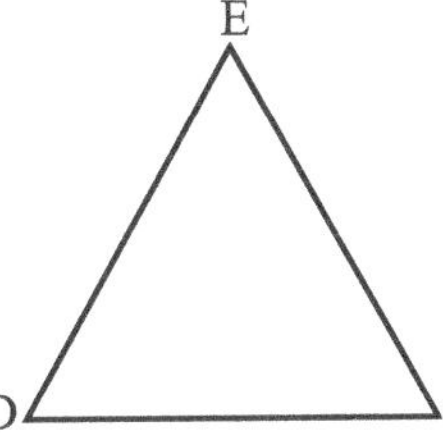

$\Delta ABC \sim \Delta EDF$
By converse of basic proportionality theorem
Then, $\angle B=\angle D, \angle A=\angle E$
$\angle C=\angle F$

7. **(b)** **Hint:** Using distance formula

8. **(b)** $a_n=a+(n-1)d=a+(n-1)2a$ [$\because d=3a-a=2a$]
$-a+2an \quad 2a=2an-a=(2n-1)a$

9. **(a)** We know that height of an equilateral triangle $\frac{\sqrt{3}}{2}a$, where a is the side of equilateral triangle

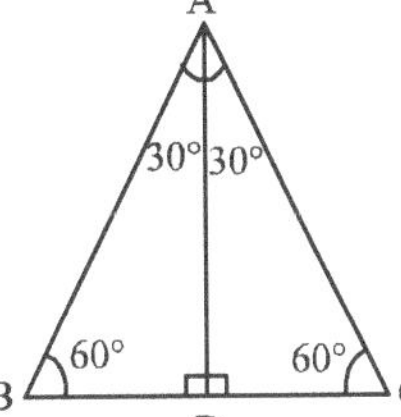

$$\therefore AD^2=\frac{3}{4}a^2=\frac{3}{4}BC^2$$

10. **(b)** [**Hint.** OP$\perp$PT, OQ$\perp$QT.
In quad. OPTQ, $\angle POQ+\angle OPT+\angle PTQ+\angle OQT=360°$
$\Rightarrow \quad 110°+90°+\angle PTQ+90°=360°$
$\Rightarrow \quad \angle PTQ=70°$]

11. **(d)** Let $\operatorname{cosec} x-\cot x=\frac{1}{3}$

$$\Rightarrow \quad \frac{1}{\sin x}-\frac{\cos x}{\sin x}=\frac{1}{3}$$

$$\Rightarrow \quad \frac{1-\cos x}{\sin x}=\frac{1}{3} \Rightarrow \frac{2\sin^2\frac{x}{2}}{2\sin\frac{x}{2}\cos\frac{x}{2}}=\frac{1}{3}$$

$$\Rightarrow \quad \tan\frac{x}{2}=\frac{1}{3}$$

Consider

$$\tan x=\frac{2\tan\frac{x}{2}}{1-\tan^2\frac{x}{2}}=\frac{\frac{2}{3}}{1-\frac{1}{9}}=\frac{3}{4}$$

Thus $\sin x=\frac{3}{5}, \cos x=\frac{4}{5}$

$$\therefore \quad \cos^2 x-\sin^2 x=\frac{16}{25}-\frac{9}{25}=\frac{7}{25}$$

12. **(b)** **Hint:** Using section formula

13. **(a)** The curved surface area of new solid
$=2\pi r^2+2\pi r^2=4\pi r^2$

14. **(d)** As $(a, 0)$, $(0, b)$ and $(1, 1)$ are collinear
By using distance formula,

we get, $1=\frac{1}{a}+\frac{1}{b}$

15. **(a)** Required probability $=\frac{4}{6}=\frac{2}{3}$.

16. **(c)** Total number of cards = 25
Prime number are 3, 5, 7, 11, 13, 17, 19, 23,

$\therefore$ Probability of prime number card $=\frac{8}{25}$

17. **(a)** **Hint:** Probability of head and tail.

18. **(c)** First join OA.

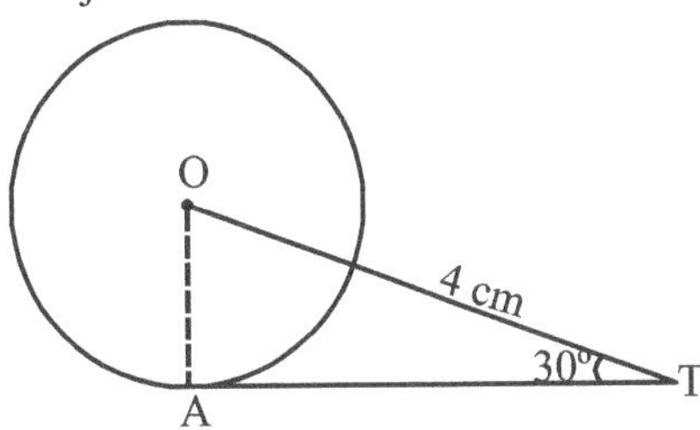

Then the tangent at any point of a circle is $\perp$ to the radius through the point of contact.

$\therefore \quad \angle OAT = 90^\circ$

In ΔOAT, $\cos 30^\circ = \frac{AT}{OT}$

$\Rightarrow \frac{\sqrt{3}}{2} = \frac{AT}{4} \Rightarrow AT = 2\sqrt{3}$ cm

19. **(d)** Here, reason is true [standard result]

Assertion is false. $\because \frac{3072}{16} = 192 \neq 162$

20. **(c)** Let $A(x_1, y_1)$, $B(x_2, y_2)$ & $C(x_3, y_3)$ are all rational coordinates of a triangle ABC.

According to question, $\frac{\sqrt{3}}{4}a^2 = \frac{1}{2} \times b \times h.$

Suppose AB as base which will provide us the rational number then, height would be irrational.
Hence, (x_1, y_1) (x_2, y_2) & (x_3, y_3) cannot be all rational.
Then, third coordinate would be irrational.

21. For the given quadratic polynomial $f(x) = ax^2 + bx + c$

Sum of roots $= (\alpha + \beta) = -\frac{b}{a}$

and product of roots $= \alpha\beta = \frac{c}{a}$

$$\therefore \frac{\alpha^4 + \beta^4}{\alpha^2\beta^2} = \frac{(\alpha^2+\beta^2)^2 - 2\alpha^2\beta^2}{\alpha^2\beta^2}$$

$$= \frac{\left[(\alpha+\beta)^2 - 2\alpha\beta\right]^2 - 2\alpha^2\beta^2}{\alpha^2\beta^2}$$ [1 Mark]

$$= \frac{\left[\left(-\frac{b}{a}\right)^2 - 2\left(\frac{c}{a}\right)\right]^2 - 2\left(\frac{c}{a}\right)^2}{\left(\frac{c}{a}\right)^2} = \frac{\left[\frac{b^2}{a^2} - 2\frac{c}{a}\right]^2 - 2\frac{c^2}{a^2}}{\frac{c^2}{a^2}}$$

$$= \frac{\frac{b^4}{a^4} + 4\frac{c^2}{a^2} - 4\frac{cb^2}{a^3} - 2\frac{c^2}{a^2}}{\frac{c^2}{a^2}}$$ [½ Mark]

$$= \frac{b^4 + 4a^2c^2 - 4acb^2 - 2a^2c^2}{a^4 \times \frac{c^2}{a^2}}$$

$$= \frac{b^4 + 2a^2c^2 - 4acb^2}{a^2c^2}$$ [½ Mark]

22. $\frac{x}{10} + \frac{y}{5} - 1 = 0$ and $\frac{x}{8} + \frac{y}{6} = 15$

i.e. $x + 2y = 10$ ... (1)

and $3x + 4y = 360$ ... (2)

Multiplying equation (1) by 2 and equation (2) by 1. We have

$2x + 4y = 20$ ... (3)

$3x + 4y = 360$ ... (4) [½ Mark]

Subtracting (3) from (4), we get

$x = 340$

and $y = -165$ (from (1)) [½ Mark]

Now, $y = \lambda x + 5$

$\Rightarrow \lambda = \frac{y-5}{x} = \frac{-165-5}{340} = \frac{-170}{340} = \frac{-1}{2}$ [1 Mark]

$x = 340, y = -165$ and $\lambda = -\frac{1}{2}$

OR

Let fixed charge be ₹ x and cost of food per day be ₹ y

$x + 20y = 3000$ ...(i)

$x + 25y = 3500$ ...(ii)

By using Elimination Method

$x + 25y = 3500$

$x + 20y = 3000$

$- \quad - \quad -$

$5y = 500$ [1 Mark]

$\Rightarrow y = 100$

$x + 20(100) = 3000$ From (i)

$\Rightarrow x = 1000$

$\therefore x = 1000$ and $y = 100$ [1 Mark]

Fixed charge and cost of food per day are ₹ 1000 and ₹ 100.

23. **Given:** In the fig., $BD \perp AC$ and $CE \perp AB$

To prove:

(i) $\Delta AEC \sim \Delta ADB$

(ii) $\frac{CA}{AB} = \frac{CE}{DB}$

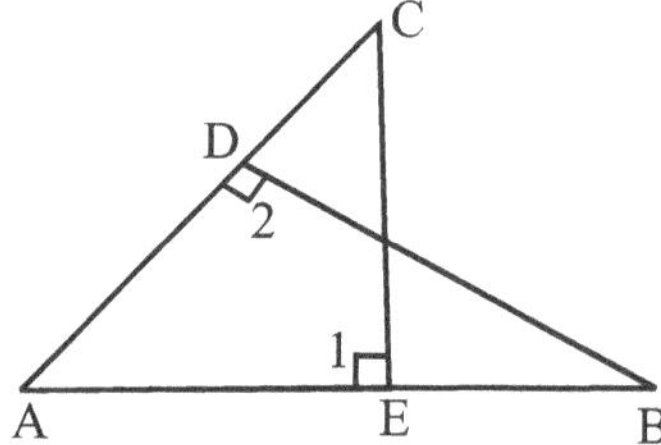

Proof:

(i) In ΔAEC and ΔADB

$\angle 1 = \angle 2$ (each 90°)

$\angle A = \angle A$ (common)

$\therefore \Delta AEC \sim \Delta ADB$ (by AA rule) [1 Mark]

(ii) $\Delta AEC \sim \Delta ADB$

$\frac{CA}{AB} = \frac{CE}{DB}$ ($\because$ Angles are similar) [1 Mark]

$\therefore$ corresponding sides are proportional

Hence proved

OR

Given : $\frac{OA}{OC}=\frac{OD}{OB}$

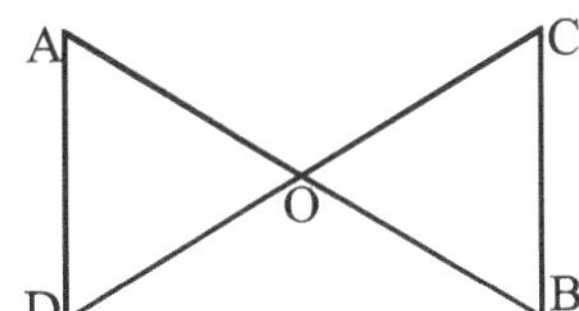

To prove: $\angle A=\angle C$ and $\angle B=\angle D$

Proof: In ΔAOD and ΔBOC

$\frac{OA}{OC}=\frac{OD}{OB}$ (Given)

and $\angle AOD=\angle BOC$ (Vertically opposite angles)

$\therefore \Delta AOD \sim \Delta BOC$ (by SAS) [1 Mark]

$\therefore \angle A=\angle C$ and $\angle B=\angle D$ (C.P.S.T.) [1 Mark]

24. Let the required ratio be K : 1

$\therefore$ The co-ordinates of the required point on the y-axis is

$x=\frac{K(-4)+1(3)}{K+1}$; $y=\frac{K(2)+1(5)}{K+1}$ [½ Mark]

Since, it lies on y-axis

$\therefore$ Its x-coordinates = 0

$\therefore \frac{-4K+3}{K+1}=0 \Rightarrow -4K+3=0 \Rightarrow K=\frac{3}{4}$ [1 Mark]

$\Rightarrow$ Required ratio $=\frac{3}{4}:1=3:4$ [½ Mark]

25. Given : Tangents AB and DC are parallel

Prove : PQ passing through centre O

Const : Draw EO || AB

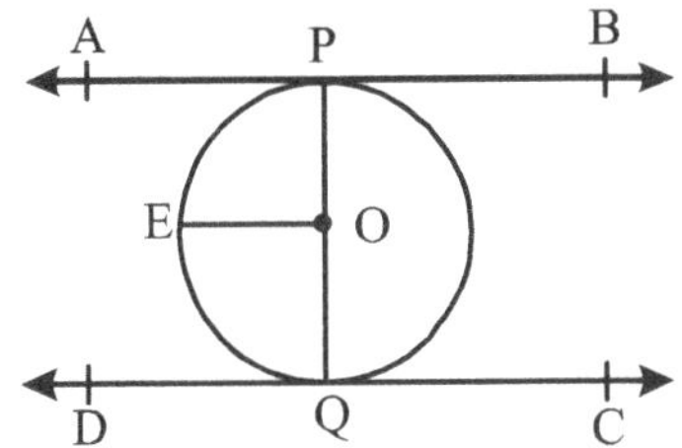

Proof : AB || DC

$\therefore$ Sum of the angles on the same side of transversal is 180°

$\angle APO+\angle EOP-180°$ [1 Mark]

$\angle EOP=180°-90°=90°$

Similarly, $\angle EOB=90°$ [1 Mark]

$\therefore \angle EOP+\angle EOB=90°+90°=180°$

$\therefore$ PQ is a straight line

Hence PQ passing through the centre O.

26. $\alpha+\beta=-\frac{5}{2}$ and $\alpha\beta=\frac{k}{2}$ [$\because$ Sum of roots $=-\frac{b}{a}$ and product of roots $=\frac{c}{a}$] [1 Mark]

$\alpha^2+\beta^2+\alpha\beta=\frac{21}{4}$

Now $\alpha^2+\beta^2+\alpha\beta=(\alpha+\beta)^2-\alpha\beta$

$\Rightarrow (\alpha+\beta)^2-\alpha\beta=\frac{21}{4}\Rightarrow\frac{25}{4}-\frac{k}{2}=\frac{21}{4}$

$\Rightarrow \frac{25-2k}{4}=\frac{21}{4}\Rightarrow 2k=4\Rightarrow k=2$ [2 Marks]

27. Since, $a\left(\frac{1}{b}+\frac{1}{c}\right), b\left(\frac{1}{a}+\frac{1}{c}\right)$ and $c\left(\frac{1}{a}+\frac{1}{b}\right)$ are in A.P.

So, $2b\left(\frac{1}{a}+\frac{1}{c}\right)=a\left(\frac{1}{b}+\frac{1}{c}\right)+c\left(\frac{1}{a}+\frac{1}{b}\right)$ [1 Mark]

$\Rightarrow \frac{2b}{a}+\frac{2b}{c}=\frac{a}{b}+\frac{a}{c}+\frac{c}{a}+\frac{c}{b}\Rightarrow\frac{2b}{a}-\frac{c}{a}+\frac{2b}{c}-\frac{a}{c}=\frac{a}{b}+\frac{c}{b}$

$\Rightarrow \frac{2b-c}{a}+\frac{2b-a}{c}=\frac{a+c}{b}$

$\Rightarrow [2bc-c^2+2ab-a^2]\,b=[a+b]\,ac$

$\Rightarrow 2b^2c-b^2c+2ab^2-a^2b=a^2c+ac^2$

$\Rightarrow 2b^2(a+c)=a^2(b+c)+c^2(a+b)$ [½ Mark]

$\Rightarrow 2b^2(a+c)=a^2c+c^2a+a^2b+c^2b$

$\Rightarrow 2b^2(a+c)=ac(a+c)+b(a^2+c^2+2ac-2ac)$ [½ Mark]

$\Rightarrow 2b^2(a+c)+2abc=ac(a+c)+b(a+c)^2$ [½ Mark]

$\Rightarrow 2b(ab+bc+ca)=(a+c)(ab+bc+ca)$ [½ Mark]

$\Rightarrow 2b=a+c\ (\because ab+bc+ca\neq 0)$

So, a, b, c are in A.P. (Hence proved.)

28. LHS $=\frac{\cot A+\operatorname{cosec} A-1}{\cot A-\operatorname{cosec} A+1}$

$=\frac{\cot A+\operatorname{cosec}A-(\operatorname{cosec}^2A-\cot^2 A)}{\cot A-\operatorname{cosec} A+1}$

$=\frac{\cot A+\operatorname{cosec}A-[(\operatorname{cosec} A+\cot A)(\operatorname{cosec} A-\cot A)]}{\cot A-\operatorname{cosec} A+1}$

[2 Marks]

$=\frac{(\cot A+\operatorname{cosec} A)[1-\operatorname{cosec} A+\cot A]}{\cot A-\operatorname{cosec} A+1}=\cot A+\operatorname{cosec}$

$$A = \frac{\cos A}{\sin A} + \frac{1}{\sin A} = \frac{1+\cos A}{\sin A}$$ [1 Mark]

Also $\frac{1}{\sin A} + \frac{\cos A}{\sin A} = \text{cosec } A + \cot A$

$\therefore \frac{\cot A + \text{cosec } A - 1}{\cot A - \text{cosec } A + 1} = \frac{1+\cos A}{\sin A} = \text{cosec } A + \cot A$

Hence LHS = RHS

29.

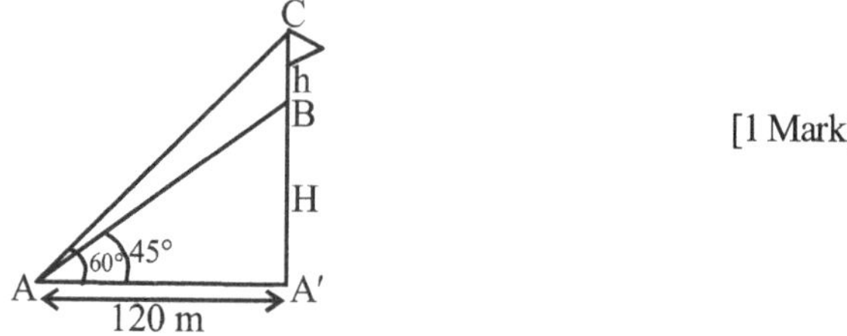

[1 Mark]

Let A'B is the tower of height 'H' and BC is the height of flag 'h'. A is the point on ground

Now, in ΔBA'A

$\tan 45° = \frac{H}{120} \Rightarrow H = 120\text{ m}$ [1 Mark]

Now, in ΔCA'A

$\tan 60° = \frac{h+H}{120} \Rightarrow \sqrt{3} = \frac{h+120}{120}$

$\Rightarrow h = 120\sqrt{3} - 120$

$\Rightarrow h = 120(\sqrt{3}-1) \Rightarrow h = 120\,(1.73-1)$

$\Rightarrow h = 120 \times 0.73 \Rightarrow h = 87.6\text{ m}$ [1 Mark]

Height of flag = 87.6 m

30. Suppose there is a circle with centre O and APB is tangent at the point of contact P.

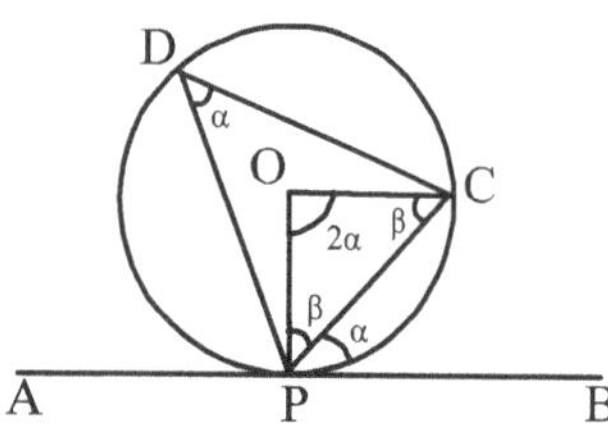

Let ∠CPB = α [1 Mark]

Then, ∠PDC = α = ∠CPB

[Angle made in remaining portion of circle]

Consider ∠OPC = β

⇒ ∠OCP = β (∵ OP = OC = radii of circle)

Now, ∠POC = 2∠PDC [Angle subtends on centre]

= 2α [1 Mark]

In ΔOPC,

∠OPC + ∠PCO + ∠POC = 180° [By angle sum property]

⇒ β + β + 2α = 180°

⇒ 2β + 2α = 180°

∴ α + β = 90° = ∠CPB + ∠OPC = ∠OPB [1 Mark]

Hence, tangent at any point of a circle is perpendicular to the radius through the point of contact.

OR

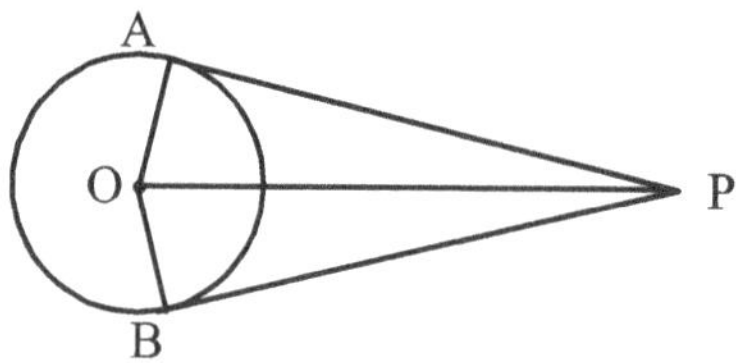

Given : PA and PB are two tangents from an external point P.

Prove : PA = PB

Const : Join OA, OB and OP.

Proof : We know that tangent is perpendicular to the radius of circle at point of contact.

∴ ∠OAP = ∠OBP = 90° [1 Mark]

In ΔAOP and ΔBOP

OP = OP (Common)

∠OAP = ∠OBP (each 90°) [1 Mark]

OA = OB (Radii)

ΔAOP ≅ ΔBOP (RHS)

∴ PA = PB (C.P.C.T) [1 Mark]

Hence Proved.

31. Number of 50 p coins = 100

Number of ₹ 1 coins = 50

Number of ₹ 2 coins = 20

Number of ₹ 5 coins = 10

Total number of coins = 180

⇒ Total no. of outcomes = 180 [½ Mark]

Then (i) $P(50\text{ p coin}) = \frac{100}{180} = \frac{5}{9}$ [1 Mark]

(ii) P (not a ₹ 5 coin) = 1 – P (a ₹ 5 coin) [½ Mark]

$= 1 - \frac{10}{180} = 1 - \frac{1}{18} = \frac{17}{18}$ [1 Mark]

OR

Here sample space is given as: S = {1, 2, 3, ..., 100}

∴ n(S) = 100 [1 Mark]

Let E be an event when doublet page is found.

E = {11, 22, 33, 44, 55, 66, 77, 88, 99} [1 Mark]

n(E) = 9 [½ Mark]

∴ required probability = $P(E) = \frac{9}{100}$ [½ Mark]

32. $(x+4)(x+5) = 3(x+1)(x+2) + 2x$

$\Rightarrow x^2 + 9x + 20 = 3(x^2 + 3x + 2) + 2x$ [½ Mark]

$\Rightarrow x^2 + 9x + 20 = 3x^2 + 9x + 6 + 2x$ [½ Mark]

$\Rightarrow x^2 - 3x^2 + 9x - 9x - 2x + 20 - 6 = 0$ [½ Mark]

$\Rightarrow -2x^2 - 2x + 14 = 0 \Rightarrow x^2 + x - 7 = 0$ [½ Mark]

We have

$$x = \frac{-b \pm \sqrt{b^2 - 4ac}}{2a} \Rightarrow x = \frac{-1 \pm \sqrt{1 - 4 \times 1(-7)}}{2 \times 1}$$ [1 Mark]

$$\Rightarrow x = \frac{-1 \pm \sqrt{1+28}}{2} \Rightarrow x = \frac{-1 \pm \sqrt{29}}{2}$$ [2 Marks]

OR

The equation

$(c^2 - ab)x^2 - 2(a^2 - bc)x + (b^2 - ac) = 0$

As, the roots are equal, D = 0 [½ Mark]

$\Rightarrow [-2(a^2 - bc)]^2 - 4(c^2 - ab)(b^2 - ac) = 0$ [½ Mark]

$\Rightarrow 4(a^4 + b^2c^2 - 2a^2bc - c^2b^2 + ac^3 + ab^3 - a^2bc) = 0$ [½ Mark]

$\Rightarrow a^4 + b^2c^2 - 2a^2bc - c^2b^2 + ac^3 + ab^3 - a^2bc = 0$ [½ Mark]

$\Rightarrow a^4 - 3a^2bc + ac^3 + ab^3 = 0$ [½ Mark]

$\Rightarrow a[a^3 - 3abc + c^3 + b^3] = 0$ [½ Mark]

Either a = 0 or $a^3 - 3abc + c^3 + b^3 = 0$ [1 Mark]

$\Rightarrow a^3 + b^3 + c^3 = 3abc.$ [1 Mark]

33. Let $\cos\theta + \sqrt{3}\sin\theta = 2\sin\theta$

$\Rightarrow \cos\theta = 2\sin\theta - \sqrt{3}\sin\theta = (2 - \sqrt{3})\sin\theta$ [1 Mark]

Multiplying both sides by $2 + \sqrt{3}$, we get

$(2+\sqrt{3})\cos\theta = (2+\sqrt{3})(2-\sqrt{3})\sin\theta$ [1 Mark]

$\Rightarrow (2+\sqrt{3})\cos\theta = \{(2)^2 - (\sqrt{3})^2\}\sin\theta$ [1 Mark]

$\Rightarrow 2\cos\theta + \sqrt{3}\cos\theta = (4-3)\sin\theta$ [1 Mark]

$\Rightarrow 2\cos\theta + \sqrt{3}\cos\theta = \sin\theta \Rightarrow \sin\theta - \sqrt{3}\cos\theta = 2\cos\theta$. [1Mark]

34. Median and altitude of an equilateral triangle are same and passing through the centre of incircle and centre divides the median in ratio 2 : 1.

$\therefore$ In ΔABD, $\angle D = 90°$

By Pythagoras theorem

$AD^2 = AB^2 - BD^2 \Rightarrow AD^2 = 12^2 - 6^2$

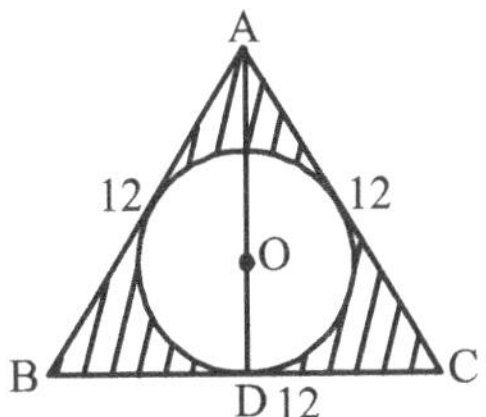

$\Rightarrow AD^2 = 144 - 36 \Rightarrow AD = \sqrt{108} = 6\sqrt{3}$cm

AO : OD = 2 : 1 [1 Mark]

$\therefore \quad OD = \frac{1}{3}AD = \frac{1}{3} \times 6\sqrt{3} = 2\sqrt{3}$ [½ Mark]

Now, radius of circle $= 2\sqrt{3} = 2 \times 1.73 = 3.46$cm [½ Mark]

Area of shaded region = Area of equilateral ΔABC – Area of circle [1 Mark]

$= \frac{\sqrt{3}}{4}(12)^2 - (2\sqrt{3})^2 \times \pi = 1.73 \times 36 - 12 \times 3.14$

$= 62.28 - 37.68 = 24.6$ cm². [2 Marks]

35. Here, maximum frequency = 9, so modal class is 60 – 90

Mode $= L + h\left(\frac{f_1 - f_0}{2f_1 - f_0 - f_2}\right)$ [2 Marks]

Here, $L = 60$, $f_1 = 9$, $f_0 = 6$, $f_2 = 6$ and $h = 30$. [1 Mark]

Mode $= 60 + 30\left(\frac{9-6}{2 \times 9 - 6 - 6}\right) = 60 + \frac{30 \times 3}{6} = 75$ [2 Marks]

OR

x_i	f_i	$x_i f_i$
3	10	30
9	p	$9p$
15	4	60
21	7	147
27	q	$27q$
33	4	132
39	1	39
Total	$\Sigma f_i = 26 + p + q$	$\Sigma x_i f_i = 408 + 9p + 27q$

[2 Marks]

Given $\Sigma fi = 40 \Rightarrow 26 + p + q = 40 \Rightarrow p + q = 14$ ...(i) [½ Mark]

$\therefore$ Mean, $\bar{x} = \frac{\Sigma x_i f_i}{\Sigma f_i} \Rightarrow 14.7 = \frac{408 + 9p + 27q}{40}$

$\Rightarrow 588 = 408 + 9p + 27q \Rightarrow p + 3q = 20$...(ii) [1 Mark]

Subtracting eq.(i) from eq. (ii),

$2q = 6 \Rightarrow q = 3$ [½ Mark]

Putting this value of q in eq. (i),

$p = 14 - q = 14 - 3 = 11$

$\therefore \ p = 11, q = 3$ [1 Mark]

36. **(i)** LCM of 60, 84, 108 is

$12 \times 5 \times 7 \times 9 = 3780$ [1 Mark]

(ii) $108 = 2 \times 2 \times 3 \times 3 \times 3 = 2^2 \times 3^3$ [1 Mark]

(iii) For maximum number of participants, taking HCF of 60, 84 and 108

$$\begin{array}{c|l} 12 & 60,84,108 \\ \hline & 5,7,9 \end{array}$$

[2 Marks]

= 12

OR

Minimum number of rooms required are

$5 + 7 + 9 = 21$ [2 Marks]

37. (i) $AC^2 = 30^2 + 40^2 = 2500 \Rightarrow AC = 50m$ [1 Mark]

(ii) 82m [1 Mark]

(iii) (21, 20, 28) $\because 28^2 \neq (21)^2 + (20)^2$ [2 Marks]

OR

$AB = 50 - 12 = 38m$ [2 Marks]

38. (i) Volume of hemispherical dome

$$= \frac{2}{3}\pi r^3 = \frac{2}{3} \times \frac{22}{7} \times 21 \times 21 \times 21 = 19404 \text{ cu. m}$$

[1 Mark]

(ii) $216 m^2$. [1 Mark]

(iii) Cloth required to cover hemispherical done = curved surface area of hemisphere

$= 2\pi r^2 = 1232$ sq. m [2 Marks]

OR

Surface area of combined figure

$= 2\pi r^2 + 2(l + b)h$

$= 1232 + 2(6 + 4)8 = 1392$ sq. m

SAMPLE PAPER-3

1. (c) Since, the sum of all the three prime numbrs is 100. Then, there are two cases
Case 1: All the three numbers should be even because 100 is an even number. But this case is not possible as there is only one even prime.
Case 2 : One prime is even and other two primes are odd. Since, 2 is only even prime, so it must be one of three primes. Let p and $p + 36$ be the other two primes.
Then, according to question
$2+p+(p+36)=100; 2p+38=100$
$2p=100-38=62; p=\frac{62}{2}=31$
So, all the three primes are 2, 31 and 67.
Hence, largest prime number is 67.
2. (d) Substitute $y = 1$
3. (c) $x^2-4=(x-2)(x+2)$ are the factors
$\therefore x=2,-2$ are roots of polynomial
$\therefore$ at $x=2; P(2)=2(2)^3+k_1(2)^2+k_2(2)+12=0$
$\Rightarrow 16+4k_1+2k_2+12=0 \Rightarrow 2k_1+k^2=-14$ ...(i)
at $x=2; P(-2)=2(-2)^3+k_1(-2)^2+k_2(-2)+12=0$
$\Rightarrow -16+4k_1-2k_2+12=0$
$\Rightarrow 2k_1-k_2=2$ ...(ii)
From (i) & (ii), $k_1=-3 \therefore k_1+k_2=-11$
4. (a) Let the two numbers be x and y ($x>y$). Then,
$x-y=26$ ... (i)
$x=3y$ ... (ii)
Substituting value of x from equation (ii) in (i)
$3y-y=26 \Rightarrow 2y=26 \Rightarrow y=13$
Substituting value of y in equation (ii), $x=3\times 13=39$
Thus, two numbers are 13 and 39.
5. (c) Let $x=0.\overline{235}$ ...(i)
$1000x=235.\overline{235}$ ...(ii)
Subtract (i) from (ii), $999x=235 \Rightarrow x=\frac{235}{999}$
6. (c) Let the no. of girls be 'x' and the no. of boys be 'y'.
Given, $0.50x+0.25y=49$
and $x+y=150$ ...(i)
$\Rightarrow \frac{x}{2}+\frac{x}{4}=49$ ...(ii)
From (i) & (ii), $x=46, y=104$
Hence, number of boys (y) = 104
7. (c) $x^2+y^2=25,\ xy=12$
$\Rightarrow x^2+\left(\frac{12}{x}\right)^2=25 \Rightarrow x^4+144-25x^2=0$
$\Rightarrow (x^2-16)(x^2-9) \Rightarrow x^2=16$ and $x^2=9$
$\Rightarrow x=\pm 4$ and $x=\pm 3$
8. (d) For given numbers,
$(55)^{725}$, unit digit = 5; $(73)^{5810}$, unit digit = 9
$(22)^{853}$, unit digit = 2
Unit digit in the expression
$55^{725}+735^{810}+22^{853}$ is 6
9. (c) Here, $a_1=\sqrt{2}, a_2=\sqrt{8}=2\sqrt{2}$
$\therefore\ d=2\sqrt{2}-\sqrt{2}=\sqrt{2}, a=\sqrt{2}$
$S_n=\frac{n}{2}[2a+(n-1)d]$
$=\frac{n}{2}[2\times\sqrt{2}+(n-1)\sqrt{2}]=\frac{n(n+1)}{\sqrt{2}}$
10. (c) $t_8=a+7d, t_{12}=a+11d$
According to question, $8t_8=12t_{12}$ (given)
$\Rightarrow 8(a+7d)=12(a+11d)$
$\Rightarrow 8a+56d=12a+132d$
$\Rightarrow 8a-12a+56d-132d=0$
$\Rightarrow -4a-76d=0$
$\Rightarrow a+19d=0$ ...(i)
$\therefore\ t_{20}=a+19d=0$ using (i)
$\therefore\ t_{20}=0$
11. (a) In ΔAFD & ΔFEB,
$\angle 1=\angle 2$ (V.O.A)
$\angle 3=\angle 4$ (Alternate angle)
$\therefore \Delta FBE \sim \Delta FDA$
So, $\frac{EF}{FA}=\frac{FB}{DF}$
12. (b) A(0, 4), B(0, 0), C(3, 0)
$AB=\sqrt{(0-0)^2+(0-4)^2}=4$
$BC=\sqrt{(3-0)^2+(0-0)^2}=3$
$CA=\sqrt{(0-3)^2+(4-0)^2}=5$
AB + BC + CA = 12
13. (d) $P(6,2)=\left(\frac{4\times 3+1\times 6}{3+1}, \frac{3\times y+1\times 5}{3+1}\right)$
$\because\ 6\neq\frac{18}{4}$ (Question is wrong)
$2=\frac{3y+5}{4} \Rightarrow 3y+5=8$
$3y=3 \Rightarrow y=1$
14. (b) Hint: Using distance formula
15. (c) We have, $\sin(A+B)=\frac{\sqrt{3}}{2}$
$\Rightarrow A+B=60°$ ...(i)
and $2B=30° \therefore B=15°$

Putting B in (i), we get
$A + 15° = 60° \Rightarrow A = 45°$

16. **(c)** We have, $\frac{\cos\theta}{1-\sin\theta}+\frac{\cos\theta}{1+\sin\theta}=4$

$$\Rightarrow \cos\theta\left(\frac{1+\sin\theta+1-\sin\theta}{1-\sin^2\theta}\right)=4$$

$$\Rightarrow \frac{2\cos\theta}{\cos^2\theta}=4 \Rightarrow \cos\theta=\frac{1}{2} \Rightarrow \theta=60°$$

17. **(c)**

18. **(c)** $n(S)=40$, let $n(C)=C$

$$P(C)=\frac{5}{8} \Rightarrow \frac{C}{40}=\frac{5}{8} \text{ or } C=25$$

Now, $\frac{25-x}{40-x}=\frac{1}{2} \Rightarrow x=10$

19. **(a)** Since, $a \times b = \text{HCF} \times \text{LCM}$ of (a, b).

20. **(b)** Both statements are individually correct.

21. $$\frac{1}{3+\sqrt{11}}=\frac{1}{3+\sqrt{11}}\times\frac{(3-\sqrt{11})}{(3-\sqrt{11})}=\frac{3-\sqrt{11}}{3^2-11}$$

[1 Mark]

$$=\frac{3-\sqrt{11}}{-2}=\frac{\sqrt{11}-3}{2}=\frac{\sqrt{11}}{2}-\frac{3}{2}$$

[1 Mark]

($\because$ Irrational number – Rational number = Irrational number)

Hence $\frac{1}{3+\sqrt{11}}$ is irrational.

22. In ΔADB, since DE is the bisector of $\angle ADB$

$\therefore \frac{BE}{EA}=\frac{BD}{AD}$ [Angle bisector theorem] ... (i)

In ΔADC, since DF is the bisector of $\angle ADC$

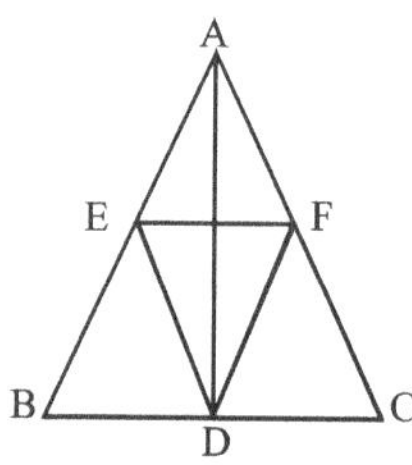

$\therefore \frac{CF}{FA}=\frac{DC}{AD}=\frac{BD}{AD}$ ......(ii) [1 Mark]

[$\because$ D is the mid-point of BC $\therefore$ BD = DC]

From (i) and (ii), we get $\frac{BE}{EA}=\frac{CF}{FA}$

In ΔABC, since $\frac{BE}{EA}=\frac{CF}{FA}$

$\therefore$ EF $\parallel$ BC [1 Mark]

(By the converse of Thale's theorem)

23. Given coordinates of vertices are (3, 0), (2, a) and (b, 6)
Centroid is (2, 5)

$\therefore \frac{x_1+x_2+x_3}{3}=2 \Rightarrow \frac{3+2+b}{3}=2 \Rightarrow 5+b=6 \Rightarrow b=6-5 \Rightarrow b=1$ [1 Mark]

and $\frac{y_1+y_2+y_3}{3}=5 \Rightarrow \frac{0+a+6}{3}=5$

$\Rightarrow a+6=15 \Rightarrow a=15-6 \Rightarrow a=9$ [1 Mark]

OR

$AB=\sqrt{(3-8)^2+(-4-1)^2}=\sqrt{50}=5\sqrt{2}$ [½ Mark]

$BC=\sqrt{(2-3)^2+(-5+4)^2}=\sqrt{2}$ [½ Mark]

$AC=\sqrt{(2-8)^2+(-5-1)^2}=\sqrt{72}=6\sqrt{2}$ [½ Mark]

Since, $AB+BC=5\sqrt{2}+\sqrt{2}=6\sqrt{2}=AC$ [½ Mark]

$\therefore$ given points are collinear

24. $m^2-n^2=(m+n)\times(m-n)$
$=\{(\tan\theta+\sin\theta)+(\tan\theta-\sin\theta)\}\times\{(\tan\theta+\sin\theta)-(\tan\theta-\sin\theta)\}$ [½ Mark]
$=\{2\tan\theta\}\times\{2\sin\theta\}=4\tan\theta\sin\theta$

$=4\sqrt{\tan^2\theta\sin^2\theta}=4\sqrt{(\sec^2\theta-1)\sin^2\theta}$

$=4\sqrt{\sec^2\theta\sin^2\theta-\sin^2\theta}$ $\left[\because \sec\theta=\frac{1}{\cos\theta}\right]$ [½ Mark]

$=4\sqrt{\tan^2\theta-\sin^2\theta}$

$=4\sqrt{(\tan\theta+\sin\theta)(\tan\theta-\sin\theta)}=4\sqrt{mn}$ [1 Mark]

OR

$$\frac{\cos^2\theta}{\cot^2\theta-\cos^2\theta}=3 \Rightarrow \frac{\cos^2\theta}{\frac{\cos^2\theta}{\sin^2\theta}-\cos^2\theta}=3$$ [½ Mark]

$$\Rightarrow \frac{\cos^2\theta\times\sin^2\theta}{\cos^2\theta-\sin^2\theta\cos^2\theta}=3$$

$$\Rightarrow \frac{\sin^2\theta\cos^2\theta}{\cos^2\theta(1-\sin^2\theta)}=3$$ [1Mark]

$$\Rightarrow \frac{\sin^2\theta}{\cos^2\theta}=3 \Rightarrow \tan^2\theta=3 \Rightarrow \tan\theta=\sqrt{3}$$

$\tan\theta=\tan 60° \Rightarrow \theta=60°$ (acute angle) [½ Mark]

25. In ΔOAB, OA = OB (radii of the circle)

$\therefore \angle OAB = \angle OBA$

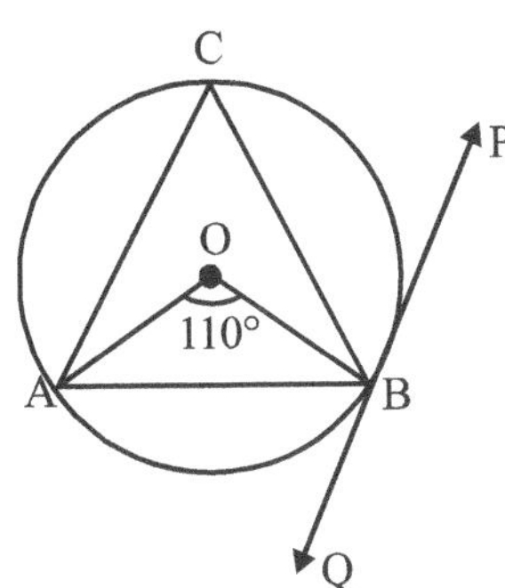

In ΔOAB, $\angle AOB + \angle OAB + \angle OBA = 180°$

$2\angle OBA = 180° - 110°$

$\Rightarrow \angle OBA = 35°$ [1 Mark]

Since BQ is a tangent at B

$\therefore \angle OBQ = 90°$

$\Rightarrow \angle OBA + \angle ABQ = 90° \Rightarrow 35° + \angle ABQ = 90°$

$\Rightarrow \angle ABQ = 90° - 35° = 55°$ [1 Mark]

26. $a_n = 3 + \frac{2n}{3}$. Here $T_n = a_n = 3 + \frac{2n}{3}$

$\Rightarrow T_1 = 3 + \frac{2(1)}{3} = \frac{11}{3}$ and $T_2 = 3 + \frac{2(2)}{3} = \frac{13}{3}$ [1 Mark]

$T_3 = 3 + \frac{2(3)}{3} = \frac{15}{3}$ ....

$\therefore \frac{11}{3}, \frac{13}{3}, \frac{15}{3}$, ... is an A.P.

Here $a = \frac{11}{3}$, $d = \frac{13}{3} - \frac{11}{3} = \frac{2}{3}$ [1 Mark]

Use, $S_n = \frac{n}{2}[2a + (n-1)d]$

$\therefore S_{24} = \frac{24}{2}\left[2 \times \frac{11}{3} + (24-1)\left(\frac{2}{3}\right)\right]$

$= 12\left(\frac{22}{3} + \frac{46}{3}\right) = 12 \times \frac{68}{3} = 272$ [1 Mark]

OR

$a = 5, l = 45$

Let d = common difference

$\therefore \quad l = a + (n-1)d$

$(n-1)d = 45 - 5 = 40$ ... (i)

[½ Mark]

also, $S_n = 400$

$\therefore \frac{n}{2}[2a + (n-1)d] = 400$ [1 Mark]

$n[10 + 40] = 800$

$n = 16$ [½ Mark]

$d = \frac{40}{n-1} = \frac{40}{15} = \frac{8}{3}$ [1 Mark]

27. (c) Given, $4\tan\theta = 3$

$\Rightarrow \tan\theta = \frac{3}{4}$ [1 Mark]

[divide by cos θ in both numerator and denominator]

$\therefore \frac{4\sin\theta - \cos\theta}{4\sin\theta + \cos\theta} = \frac{4\frac{\sin\theta}{\cos\theta} - 1}{4\frac{\sin\theta}{\cos\theta} + 1}$ [1 Mark]

$= \frac{4\tan - 1}{4\tan\theta + 1}\left[\because \tan\theta = \frac{\sin\theta}{\cos\theta}\right]$

$= \frac{4\left(\frac{3}{4}\right) - 1}{4\left(\frac{3}{4}\right) + 1} = \frac{3-1}{3+1} = \frac{1}{2}$ [1 Mark]

28.

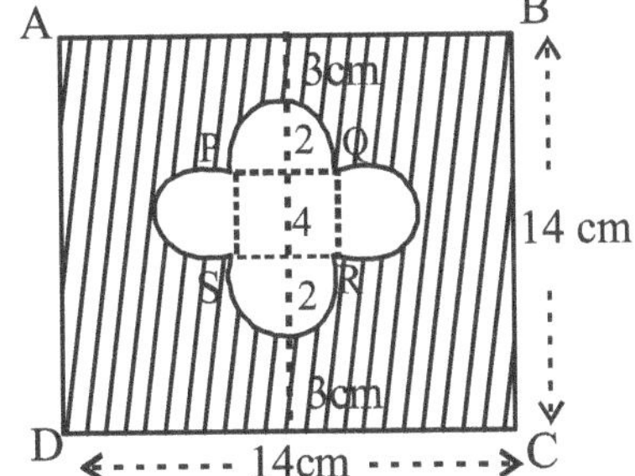

Area of sq. ABCD = $(\text{side})^2 = 196\ cm^2$ [1 Mark]

Area of small sq. = $(\text{side})^2 = 4^2 = 16\ cm^2$

Area of 4 semi-circles = $4 \times \frac{1}{2}\pi r^2 = \left[4.\frac{1}{2}(3.14)(2)^2\right] cm^2$

$= 25.12\ cm^2$ [1 Mark]

$\therefore$ Area of shaded region

$= (196 - 16 - 25.12)\ cm^2 = 154.88\ cm^2$ [1 Mark]

29. Canvas needed to make the tent = C.S.A of the conical part + C.S.A of the cylindrical part

Given that

Radius of the conical part = Radius of the cylindrical part

$= r = \frac{3}{2} m$

Slant height of the conical part = $l = 2.8$ m [1 Mark]

Height of the cylindrical part = h = 2.1m

C.S.A of the conical part $= \pi r l = \frac{22}{7} \times \frac{3}{2} \times 2.8\ m^2$

C.S.A of the cylindrical part $= 2\pi r h = 2 \times \frac{22}{7} \times \frac{3}{2} \times 2.1\ m^2$

$\therefore$ Total area of the canvas needed to make the tent

[1 Mark]

$= \frac{22}{7} \times \frac{3}{2} \times 2.8 + 2 \times \frac{22}{7} \times \frac{3}{2} \times 2.1$

$= \frac{22}{7} \times \frac{3}{2} \times (2.8 + 4.2) = \frac{22}{7} \times \frac{3}{2} \times 7 = 33m^2$

Cost of the canvas = ₹ 500/m²

So, total cost of the canvas needed to make the tent
= 500 × 33 = ₹ 16, 500 [1 Mark]

OR

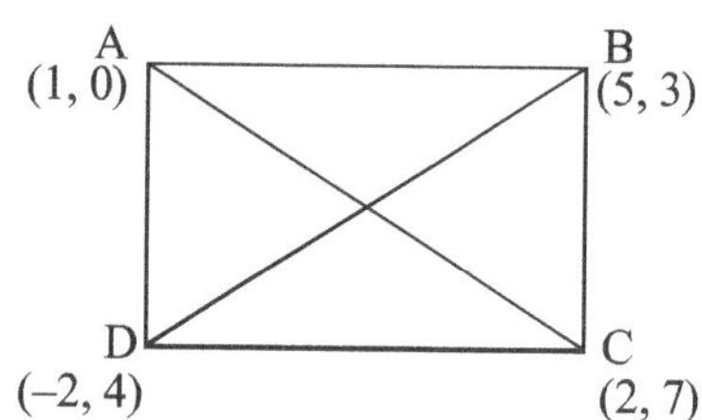

Coordinates of the mid-point of diagonal AC =

$\left(\frac{1+2}{2}, \frac{0+7}{2}\right) = \left(\frac{3}{2}, \frac{7}{2}\right)$ [1 Mark]

Coordinates of the mid-point of diagonal BD =

$\left(\frac{5-2}{2}, \frac{3+4}{2}\right) = \left(\frac{3}{2}, \frac{7}{2}\right)$ [1 Mark]

Since, the coordinates of the mid-points of diagonals AC and BD are same.

∴ They bisect each other.

Hence, ABCD is a parallelogram. [1 Mark]

30. Modal class is 30 – 35, $l = 30$, $f_1 = 25$, $f_0 = 10$, $f_2 = 7$, $h = 5$ [1 Mark]

Mode $= l + \left(\frac{f_1 - f_0}{2f_1 - f_0 - f_2}\right) \times h$ [1 Mark]

$\Rightarrow$ Mode $= 30 + \left(\frac{25 - 10}{50 - 10 - 7}\right) \times 5 = 32.27$ approx.

[1 Mark]

31. S = {S, M, T, W, Th, F, Sa} ⇒ n(S) = 7 [½ Mark]

A non-leap year contains 365 days, i.e., 52 weeks + 1 day.

E = {Sa}, n(E) = 1 [1½ Marks]

$\therefore$ $P(E) = \frac{n(E)}{n(S)} = \frac{1}{7}$ [1 Mark]

32. $\frac{1}{x+1} + \frac{3}{5x+1} = \frac{5}{x+4}, x \neq -1, -\frac{1}{5}, -4$

$\Rightarrow \frac{5x+1+3(x+1)}{(x+1)(5x+1)} = \frac{5}{x+4} \Rightarrow \frac{5x+1+3x+3}{5x^2+6x+1} = \frac{5}{x+4}$

[1 Mark]

$\Rightarrow (8x+4)(x+4) = 25x^2 + 30x + 5$

$\Rightarrow 8x^2 + 36x + 16 = 25x^2 + 30x + 5$ [1½ Marks]

$\Rightarrow 17x^2 - 6x - 11 = 0 \Rightarrow 17x^2 - 17x + 11x - 11 = 0$

$\Rightarrow 17x(x-1) + 11(x-1) = 0$

$\Rightarrow (x-1)(17x+11) = 0$ [1 Mark]

$\Rightarrow x = 1, \frac{-11}{17}$ [1½ Marks]

Hence, the value of x is 1 or $\frac{-11}{17}$.

33.

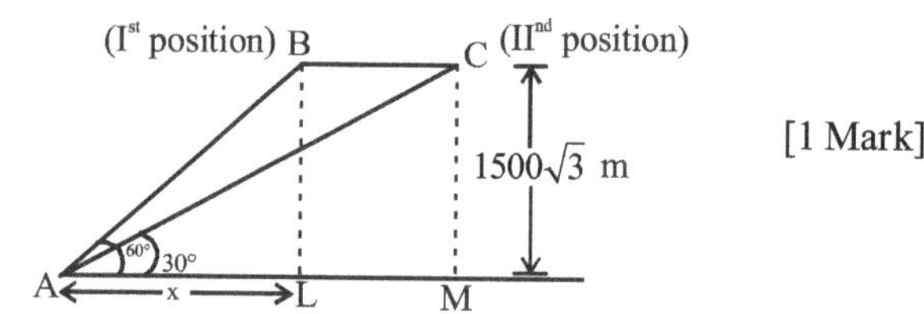

[1 Mark]

Suppose, AL = x m

$\therefore \frac{BL}{x} = \tan 60°$

So, $\frac{1500\sqrt{3}}{x} = \sqrt{3}$ [2 Mark]

$\therefore x = 1500$ m

Now, $\frac{CM}{AL + LM} = \tan 30° = \frac{1}{\sqrt{3}}$

$\therefore$ 1500 + LM = 1500 (3) = 4500

Therefore, LM = 3000 m.

Hence, speed $= \frac{3000}{15}$

$= 200$ m/s $= 720$ km/hr [2 Mark]

34. $x + 3y = 6 \Rightarrow y = \frac{6-x}{3}$ ...(i)

x	3	6	0
y	1	0	2

$2x - 3y = 12$ ...(ii)

$\Rightarrow y = \frac{2x - 12}{3}$ [1½ Marks]

x	0	6	3
y	– 4	0	– 2

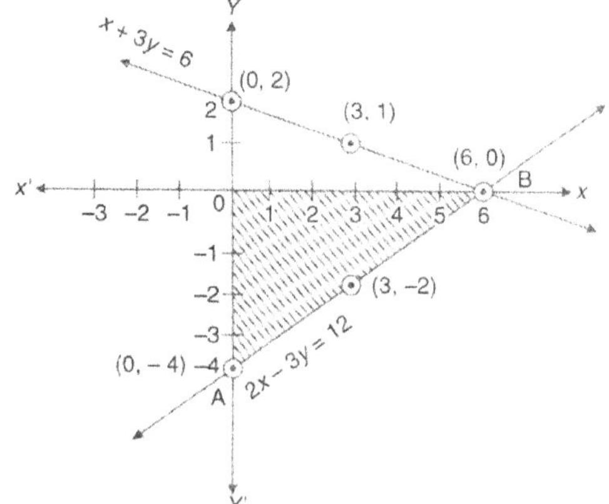

[2 Mark]

Clearly, the two lines intersect at point $B(6, 0)$. Hence, $x = 6$ and $y = 0$ is the solution of the system.

ΔOAB is the region bounded by the line $2x - 3y = 12$ and both the co-ordinate axes. [1½ Marks]

OR

$$3x - y = 7$$

$$\Rightarrow 3x - y - 7 = 0$$

$a_1 = 3, b_1 = -1, c_1 = -7$

$$2x + 5y + 1 = 0$$

$a_2 = 2, b_2 = 5, c_2 = 1$

$$\frac{a_1}{a_2} = \frac{3}{2}$$

$$\frac{b_1}{b_2} = \frac{-1}{5}$$

$$\frac{3}{2} \neq \frac{-1}{5}$$ [1 Mark]

Thus $\frac{a_1}{a_2} \neq \frac{b_1}{b_2}$

Hence, given linear equations has a unique solution.

Now, we have

$3x - y - 7 = 0 \Rightarrow y = 3x - 7$

x	0	2	3
y	−7	−1	2

and $2x + 5y + 1 = 0$ [2 Marks]

$$\Rightarrow y = \frac{-1-2x}{5}$$

x	− 1/2	2	−3
y	0	−1	1

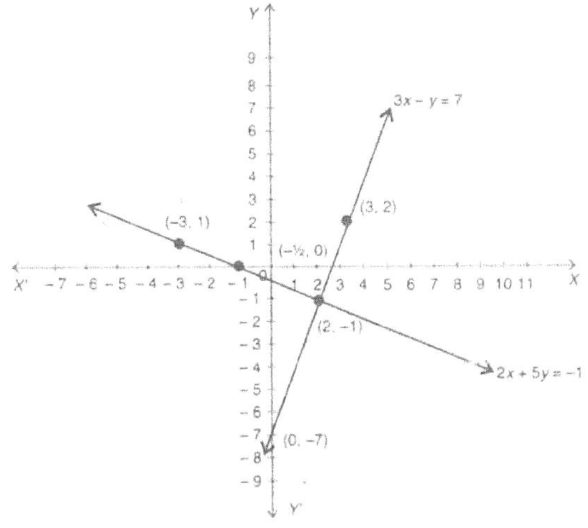

[2 Marks]

Hence, $x = 2$ and $y = -1$ is the solution.

35. $\because$ AB = 12 cm

So, AD + BD = 12 cm ...(i)

$\because$ BC = 8 cm

$\therefore$ BE + CE = 8 cm ... (ii) [1 Mark]

$\because$ CA = 10 cm

Therefore, AF + CF = 10 cm ...(iii)

Here CF and CE act as tangents to the circle from the external point C. [1 Mark]

Since, the lengths of tangents drawn from an external point to a circle are equal.

$\Rightarrow$ CF = CE ... (iv)

Now, AF and AD act as tangents to the circle from the external point A.

$\Rightarrow$ AF = AD ...(v)

As, BD and BE act as tangents to the circle from the external point B.

$\Rightarrow$ BD = BE ... (vi) [1 Mark]

By (iv) and (ii),

BE + CF = 8 cm ... (vii)

By (v) and (iii),

AD + CF = 10 cm ... (viii)

By (vi) and (i),

AD + BE = 12 cm ...(ix)

After adding (vii), (viii) and (ix),

BE + CF + AD + CF + AD + BE = 8cm + 10 cm + 12cm

$\therefore$ 2AD + 2BE + 2CF = 30 cm

So, AD + BE + CF = 15 cm ... (x)

After subtracting (vii) from (x),

AD + BE + CF – BE – CF = 15 cm – 8 cm

$\therefore$ AD = 7 cm [1 Mark]

After subtracting (viii) from (x),

AD + BE + CF – AD – CF = 15 cm – 10 cm

$\Rightarrow$ BE = 5 cm

After subtracting (ix) from (x),

AD + BE + CF – AD – BE = 15 cm – 12 cm

$\therefore$ CF = 3 cm [1 Mark]

Hence, the lengths of AD, BE and CF are 7 cm, 5 cm and 3 cm respectively.

OR

Since, AP and PB are tangents drawn to the given circle from an external point P. [1 Mark]

Since, the lengths of the tangents drawn from an external point to a circle are equal.

$\Rightarrow$ AP = PB [2 Marks]

In ΔPAB, sides AP and PB are of the equal length.

So, ΔPAB is isosceles, with AP = PB and $\angle$PAB = $\angle$PBA = x (say).

Now, $\angle$APB = 60° [2 Marks]

36.

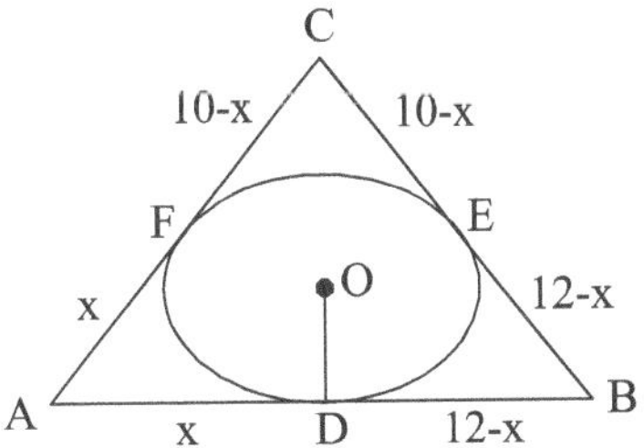

BC = 10 – x + 12 – x = 8 $\Rightarrow$ x = 7.

(i) $AD = 7$ cm [1 mark]
(ii) $BE = 12 - x = 12 - 7 = 5$ cm [1 mark]
(iii) $CF = 10 - x = 10 - 7 = 3$ cm [2 marks]

OR

$$\text{Ar } \Delta OAB = \frac{1}{2} \times AB \times OD$$

$$= \frac{1}{2} \times 12 \times 4 = 24 \text{ cm}^2$$ [2 marks]

37. (i) Radius of inner semicircular end [1 mark]

$$= \frac{60}{2} = 30 \text{ m}$$

(ii) Radius of outer semicircular end [1 mark]
$= 30 + 10 = 40$ m

(iii) The distance arounded the track along its inner edge
$= 106 \times 2 + 2 \times \pi r$ [1 mark]

$$= 212 + 2 \times \frac{22}{7} \times 30 = 212 + 188.57$$

$= 400.57$ m [1 mark]

OR

The distance arounded the track along its outer edge
$= 106 \times 2 + 2 \times \pi r$

$$= 212 + 2 \times \frac{22}{7} \times 40 = 212 + 251.43$$

$= 463.43$ m [2 marks]

38. (i) Let A be prime numbers from 1 to 25
$A = 2, 3, 5, 7, 11, 13, 17, 19, 23$

$$P(A) = \frac{9}{25}$$ [1 mark]

(ii) $P(C) = \frac{12}{25}$ [1 mark]

(iii) Let B is a multiply of 3 from 1 to 25.
$B = 3, 6, 9, 12, 15, 18, 21, 24$ [1 mark]

$$= \frac{8}{25}$$ [1 mark]

OR

$$P(d) = \frac{4}{25}$$ [2 marks]

SAMPLE PAPER-4

1. **(d)** $3^{13}-3^{10}=3^{10}(33-1)=3^{10}(26)=2\times 13\times 3^{10}$
Hence, $3^{13}-3^{10}$ is divisible by 2, 3 and 13.

2. **(c)** For a pair of linear equations having unique solution

$\frac{a_1}{a_2}\neq\frac{b_1}{b_2}\Rightarrow\frac{3}{2m-5}\neq\frac{-2}{7}$

or $-4m+10\neq 21$

or $-4m\neq 11$

or $m\neq -\frac{11}{4}$

3. **(a)** Since the roots are equal, we have $D=0$.

$\therefore\quad 4(k+2)^2-36k=0\Rightarrow(k+2)^2-9k=0$

$\therefore\quad k^2-5k+4=0\Rightarrow k^2-4k-k+4=0$

$\Rightarrow\quad k(k-4)-(k-4)=0$

$\Rightarrow\quad (k-4)(k-1)=0\Rightarrow k=4$ or $k=1$.

4. **(b)** $x^2-(m+3)x+mx-m(m+3)=0$

$\Rightarrow\quad x[x-(m+3)]+m[x-(m+3)]=0$

$\Rightarrow\quad (x+m)[x-(m+3)]=0$

$x+m=0\qquad x-(m+3)=0$

$x=-m\qquad x=m+3$

5. **(d)**

6. **(a)** In ABC, $\angle A=180°-(70°+50°)=60°$.

$\frac{BD}{DC}=\frac{AB}{AC}$. It means AD is the bisector of ÐA.

$\therefore\quad \angle BAD=\frac{1}{2}\times 60°=30°$

7. **(c)** We have, $x=a(\text{cosec}\,\theta+\cot\theta)$

$\Rightarrow\quad \frac{x}{a}=(\text{cosec}\,\theta+\cot\theta)$ ...(1)

and $y=b\left(\frac{1-\cos\theta}{\sin\theta}\right)\Rightarrow\frac{y}{b}=\frac{1}{\sin\theta}-\frac{\cos\theta}{\sin\theta}$

$\Rightarrow\quad \frac{y}{b}=\text{cosec}\,\theta-\cot\theta$ ...(2)

$\Rightarrow\quad \frac{x}{a}\times\frac{y}{b}=(\text{cosec}\,\theta+\cot\theta)(\text{cosec}\,\theta-\cot\theta)$

$\Rightarrow\quad \frac{xy}{ab}=(\text{cosec}^2\theta-\cot^2\theta)\qquad\therefore\quad xy=ab$

8. **(b)** Coordinates of mid-point are given by

$\left(\frac{x_1+x_2}{2},\frac{y_1+y_2}{2}\right)$

Here, coordinates of mid-point are $\left(\frac{a}{3},4\right)$

So, $\frac{a}{3}=\frac{-6-2}{2}$

$\therefore\quad a=-12$

9. **(c)** Let BD $=x$ cm
Since AC = BC, therefore ΔABC is an isoscele triangle.

$\Rightarrow\quad \angle B=\angle CAB=72°$

Since AD bisects ∠A

$\therefore\quad \angle DAB=36°$ so, In ΔADB, $\angle ADB=72°$

$\Rightarrow$ ADB is an isoscele triangle

$\therefore\quad$ AB = AD = 1cm

$\Rightarrow\quad$ AB = 1 cm

Similarly, ADC is also an isoscele triangle.

$\therefore\quad$ AD = CD $\Rightarrow$ AD = 1 cm

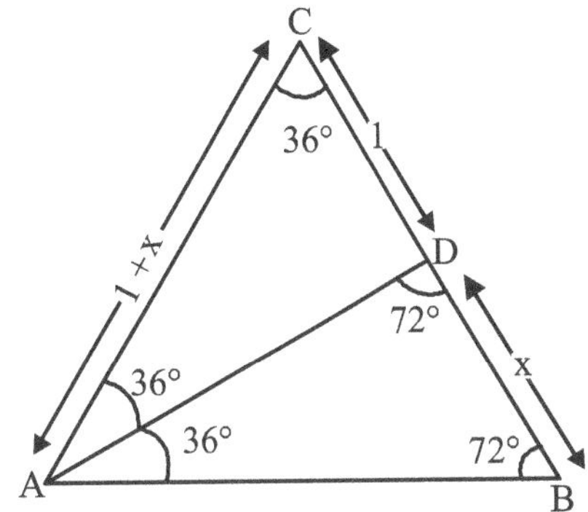

Now $\frac{AC}{AB}=\frac{CD}{BD}$

$\Rightarrow\quad \frac{1+x}{1}=\frac{1}{x}\Rightarrow x+x^2-1=0$

$\Rightarrow\quad x=\frac{-1\pm\sqrt{(1)^2-4(1)(-1)}}{2}=\frac{-1\pm\sqrt{5}}{2}$

$BD=\frac{\sqrt{5}-1}{2}$

10. **(b)** $\frac{(2+2\sin\theta)(1-\sin\theta)}{(1+\cos\theta)(2-2\cos\theta)}=\frac{2(1+\sin\theta)(1-\sin\theta)}{(1+\cos\theta)(2)(1-\cos\theta)}$

$=\frac{2(1-\sin^2\theta)}{2(1-\cos^2\theta)}=\frac{2\cos^2\theta}{2\sin^2\theta}=\cot^2\theta=\left(\frac{15}{8}\right)^2=\frac{225}{64}$

11. **(b)** $\frac{a-(a-a^1)}{b-(b-b^1)}=\frac{a^1}{b^1}$

12. **(b)** $\pi d_1+\pi d_2=\pi d\Rightarrow d_1+d_2=d$

13. **(a)** Since, OA ⊥ PA and OB ⊥ PB,

$\therefore$ In quadrilateral AOBP,

$\Rightarrow\quad 40°+90°+90°+\angle AOB=360°$

$\Rightarrow\quad \angle AOB=140°$

Also, $\angle AQB=\frac{1}{2}$ of $\angle AOB=70°$ and $\angle AMB=\frac{1}{2}$ of reflex $\angle AOB=\frac{1}{2}\times(360°-140°)=\frac{1}{2}\times 220=110°$

[∵ The angle subtended by an arc at the centre is double the angle subtended by the arc at any point on the remaining part of the cirlce.]

14. **(d)** Let AB be the chord of circle such that $\angle AOB=90°$
Let OA = 10 cm

$\therefore\ AB=10\sqrt{2}$ cm

Area of minor segment A X B
= Area of the sector AOB – Area of ΔAOB

$= \frac{90°}{360°} \times \pi(10)^2 - \frac{1}{2} \times 10 \times 10$

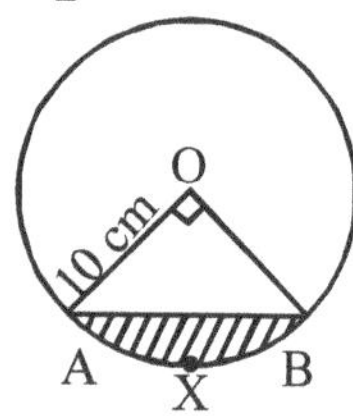

$= 25\,p - 50 = 25 \times 3.14 - 50 = 78.5 - 50 = 28.5\ cm^2.$

15. **(d)** $n_1 = 25 \quad \bar{x}_1 = 70\%$

$n_2 = 40 \quad \bar{x}_2 = 65\%$

$n_3 = 35 \quad \bar{x}_3 = 50\%$

$\bar{x} = \frac{n_1 \bar{x}_1 + n_2 \bar{x}_2 + n_3 \bar{x}_3}{n_1 + n_2 + n_3}$

$= \frac{(25 \times 70) + (40 \times 65) + (35 \times 50)}{25 + 40 + 35}$

$= \frac{1750 + 2600 + 1750}{100} = \frac{6100}{100} = 61\%$

16. **(a)** $r = \frac{1.4}{2} = 0.7$ m and $h = 2$ m

Area covered = C.S.A × number of revolutions
$= 2\pi h \times 5 = 10\pi rh$

$\Rightarrow \quad 10\left(\frac{22}{7}\right)(0.7)(2) = 44\ m^2$

17. **(b)** $n(S) = 6 \times 6 = 36$
E= {(1,2), (2,1), (2,3), (3,2), (3,4), (4,3), (4,5), (5,4), (5,6), (6,5)}
$n(E) = 10$

$\therefore \quad P(E) = \frac{n(E)}{n(S)} = \frac{10}{36} = \frac{5}{18}$

18. **(c)** Let a = 200

C.I.	f_i	x_i	$d_i = x_i - 200$	$f_i d_i$
0 – 80	22	40	– 160	– 3520
80 – 160	35	120	– 80	– 2800
160 – 240	44	200	0	0
240 – 320	25	280	+ 80	+ 2000
320 – 400	24	360	+ 160	+ 3840
	150			– 480

$\bar{x} = a + \frac{1}{n}\sum_{i=1}^{5} f_i d_i = 200 + \frac{1}{150}(-480)$

$= 200 - 3.2 = 196.8$

19. **(b)** Put n = 1 or 2.

20. **(a)** Both assertion and reason are correct and reason is the correct explanation of the assertion.

$\tan\theta = \frac{\sqrt{3}}{2} \times 2 = \sqrt{3}.$

21. The internal bisector of $\angle X$ meets YZ at P

$\frac{XY}{XZ} = \frac{YP}{PZ}$ [1 Mark]

Add 1 on both the sides ; we get

$\Rightarrow \frac{XY}{XZ} + 1 = \frac{YP}{PZ} + 1 \Rightarrow \frac{XY + XZ}{XZ} = \frac{YP + PZ}{PZ} = \frac{YZ}{PZ}$

[1 Mark]

22. $\frac{\text{cosec}^2\theta}{\text{cosec}\,\theta - 1} - \frac{\text{cosec}^2\theta}{\text{cosec}\,\theta + 1}$

$= \text{cosec}^2\theta\left[\frac{1}{\frac{1}{\sin\theta} - 1} - \frac{1}{\frac{1}{\sin\theta} + 1}\right]$ [1 Mark]

$= \text{cosec}^2\theta\left[\frac{\sin\theta}{1 - \sin\theta} - \frac{\sin\theta}{1 + \sin\theta}\right]$

$= \frac{1}{\sin\theta}\left[\frac{(1 + \sin\theta) - (1 - \sin\theta)}{(1 - \sin\theta)(1 + \sin\theta)}\right]$

$= \frac{1}{\sin\theta}\left[\frac{2\sin\theta}{1 - \sin^2\theta}\right]$

$= \frac{2}{\cos^2\theta} = 2\sec^2\theta$ [1 Mark]

= RHS

OR

$5\tan\theta = 4 \Rightarrow \tan\theta = \frac{4}{5} = \frac{\text{Perpendicular}}{\text{Base}}$

$(\text{Hypotenuse})^2 = (\text{Perp})^2 + (\text{Base})^2 = (4)^2 + (5)^2 = 41$

Hypotenuse $= \sqrt{41}$ [½ Mark]

$\sin\theta = \frac{\text{Perpendicular}}{\text{Hypotenuse}} = \frac{4}{\sqrt{41}};$

$\cos\theta = \frac{\text{Base}}{\text{Hypotenuse}} = \frac{5}{\sqrt{41}}$ [½ Mark]

Consider $\frac{5\sin\theta - 3\cos\theta}{5\sin\theta + 2\cos\theta} = \frac{5 \times \frac{4}{\sqrt{41}} - 3 \times \frac{5}{\sqrt{41}}}{5 \times \frac{4}{\sqrt{41}} + 2 \times \frac{5}{\sqrt{41}}}$

$= \frac{\frac{20}{\sqrt{41}} - \frac{15}{\sqrt{41}}}{\frac{20}{\sqrt{41}} + \frac{10}{\sqrt{41}}} = \frac{\frac{20-15}{\sqrt{41}}}{\frac{20+10}{\sqrt{41}}} = \frac{\frac{5}{\sqrt{41}}}{\frac{30}{\sqrt{41}}} = \frac{5}{\sqrt{41}} \times \frac{\sqrt{41}}{30} = \frac{1}{6}$

[1 Mark]

23. **Given :** PA and PB are tangents to the circle from an external point P. CD is another tangent at Q.
PA = 12 cm, QC = QD = 3 cm

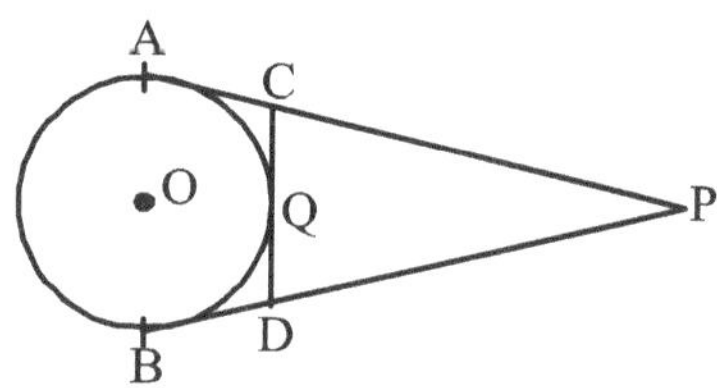

To find: PC + PD [½ Mark]

Proof : PA = PC + AC

12 = PC + 3

[∵ QC = AC = 3 cm, tangents from external point to a circle are equal in length]

PC = 9 cm ...(i) [½ Mark]

Similarly, BD = QD = 3 cm

and PB = PA = 12 cm [½ Mark]

PB = PD + BD ⇒ 12 = PD + 3 ⇒ PD = 9 cm

Now, PC + PD = 9 + 9 = 18 cm [½ Mark]

24. $r = \frac{10}{2}$ cm = 5 cm [2 Marks]

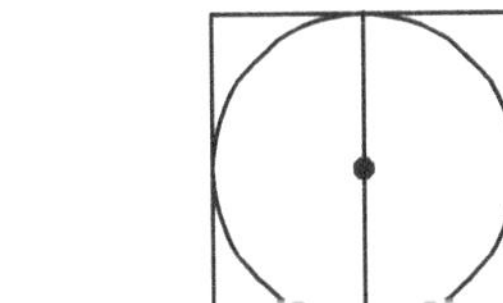

25. Substitute $\frac{1}{\sqrt{x}} = X$ and $\frac{1}{\sqrt{y}} = Y$

Then,

$2X + 3Y = 2$

$4X - 9Y = -1$

By elimination method

$4X - 9Y = -1$

$6X + 9Y = 6$

+ + +

$10X = 5$ [1 Mark]

$10X = 5 \Rightarrow X = \frac{5}{10} = \frac{1}{2} \Rightarrow \frac{1}{\sqrt{x}} = \frac{1}{2} \Rightarrow x = 4$ [½ Mark]

Now, $3Y = 2 - 2X = 2 - 2\left(\frac{1}{2}\right) = 1 = \frac{1}{3} \Rightarrow \frac{1}{\sqrt{y}} = \frac{1}{3} \Rightarrow y = 9$ [½ Mark]

Thus $x = 4, y = 9$ is the solution.

OR

$\frac{2}{x} + \frac{2}{3y} = \frac{1}{6}$ .....(i)

$\frac{3}{x} + \frac{2}{y} = 0$ .....(ii)

Multiplying (i) by 3 and equation (ii) by 2 we get,

$\frac{6}{x} + \frac{6}{3y} = \frac{3}{6}$ .....(iii)

$\frac{6}{x} + \frac{4}{y} = 0$ .....(iv)

Subtract (iii) and (iv), we get,

$-\frac{2}{y} = \frac{3}{6} \Rightarrow \frac{-2}{y} = \frac{1}{2} \Rightarrow y = -4$ [1 Mark]

Putting the value of $y = -4$ in (i) we get,

$\frac{2}{x} + \frac{2}{3(-4)} = \frac{1}{6} \Rightarrow \frac{2}{x} - \frac{2}{12} = \frac{1}{6}$

$\Rightarrow \frac{2}{x} = \frac{1}{6} + \frac{1}{6} \Rightarrow \frac{2}{x} = \frac{2}{6} \Rightarrow x = 6$ [½ Mark]

Given equation is $y = px - 4$

Putting the value of $x = 6$ and $y = -4$ we get $-4 = p \times 6 - 4$

$\Rightarrow -4 + 4 = 6p \Rightarrow p = 0$ [½ Mark]

26. Let if possible $\sqrt{5} = \frac{p}{q}$, where p and q are co-prime.

$\therefore \quad 5 \times q^2 = p^2$ ....(i)

$\Rightarrow$ 5 divides $p \Rightarrow p = 5 \times p_1$; p_1 is an integer. ......(ii) [½ Mark]

From (i) and (ii), we get :

$5 \times q^2 = (5 \times p_1)^2 = 5^2 \times p_1^2 \Rightarrow q^2 = 5 \times p_1^2 \Rightarrow$ 5 divides q [½ Mark]

$\Rightarrow q = 5 \times q_1$; q_1 is an integer .....(iii) [½ Mark]

From (ii) and (iii), we find 5 a common factor of p and q. It contradicts that p and q are co-prime.

Hence, $\sqrt{5}$ is an irrational number. [½ Mark]

27. $\sec\theta + \tan\theta = p$

since $\sec^2\theta - \tan^2\theta = 1 \Rightarrow (\sec\theta + \tan\theta) \times (\sec\theta - \tan\theta) = 1$ [½ Mark]

$\Rightarrow p \times (\sec\theta - \tan\theta) = 1 \Rightarrow \sec\theta - \tan\theta = \frac{1}{p}$ [½ Mark]

By elimination method

$\sec\theta + \tan\theta = p$ ...(i)

$\sec\theta - \tan\theta = \frac{1}{p}$ ...(ii)

+ + +

$2\sec\theta = p + \frac{1}{p} \Rightarrow 2\sec\theta = \frac{p^2+1}{p} \Rightarrow \sec\theta = \frac{p^2+1}{2p}$ [½ Mark]

$\because \sec\theta = \frac{1}{\cos\theta} \Rightarrow \cos\theta = \frac{2p}{p^2+1}$ [½ Mark]

Subtract equation (ii) from (i)

$\sec\theta + \tan\theta = p$

$\sec\theta - \tan 0 = \frac{1}{p}$ [½ Mark]

− + −

$2\tan\theta = p - \frac{1}{p} \Rightarrow \tan\theta = \frac{p^2-1}{2p}$ [½ Mark]

Now, $\tan\theta = \frac{\sin\theta}{\cos\theta} \Rightarrow \sin\theta = \tan\theta \cdot \cos\theta$

$= \frac{p^2-1}{2p} \times \frac{2p}{p^2+1} = \frac{p^2-1}{p^2+1}$ [½ Mark]

OR

In figure,

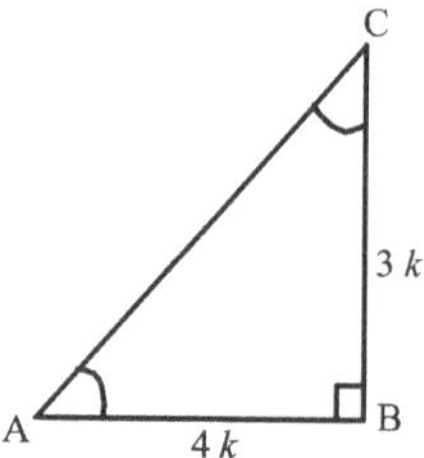

$3\cot A = 4$ (given) $\Rightarrow$ $\cot A = \frac{4}{3}$

$\Rightarrow \left(\frac{\text{Base}}{\text{Perpendicular}}\right) = \frac{AB}{BC} = \frac{4}{3}$ [½ Mark]

Let $AB = 4k$ and $BC = 3k$

In right angled ΔABC,

$AC^2 = BC^2 + AB^2$ (By pythagoras theorem)

$\Rightarrow AC = \sqrt{(4k)^2 + (3k)^2} = \pm 5k$

$\Rightarrow AC = 5k$ ($\because$ side cannot negative) [½ Mark]

Then, $\sin A = \frac{BC}{AC} = \frac{3}{5}$, $\cos A = \frac{AB}{AC} = \frac{4}{5}$ and

$\tan A = \frac{BC}{AB} = \frac{3}{4}$ [½ Mark]

Now, $\text{LHS} = \frac{1 - \tan^2 A}{1 + \tan^2 A} = \frac{1 - \left(\frac{3}{4}\right)^2}{1 + \left(\frac{3}{4}\right)^2} = \frac{7}{25}$ [½ Mark]

$\text{RHS} = \cos^2 A - \sin^2 A = \left(\frac{4}{5}\right)^2 - \left(\frac{3}{5}\right)^2 = \frac{7}{25}$

Therefore, LHS = RHS,

$\Rightarrow \frac{1 - \tan^2 A}{1 + \tan^2 A} = \cos^2 A - \sin^2 A$ [1 Mark]

28. If α and β are the zeroes of $2x^2 - 3x + 1$, then

$\alpha + \beta = \frac{-b}{a}$

$\Rightarrow \quad \alpha + \beta = \frac{3}{2}$

and $\quad \alpha\beta = \frac{c}{a}$

$\Rightarrow \quad \alpha\beta = \frac{1}{2}$ [1 Mark]

New quadratic polynomial whose zeroes are 3α and 3β is:

x^2 – (Sum of the roots)x + Product of the roots

$= x^2 - (3\alpha + 3\beta)x + 3\alpha \times 3\beta$

$= x^2 - 3(\alpha + \beta)x + 9\alpha\beta$

$= x^2 - 3\left(\frac{3}{2}\right)x + 9\left(\frac{1}{2}\right)$ [1 Mark]

$= x^2 - \frac{9}{2}x + \frac{9}{2}$

$= \frac{1}{2}(2x^2 - 9x + 9)$

Hence, required quadratic polynomial is

$\frac{1}{2}(2x^2 - 9x + 9)$. [1 Mark]

29. $a = 5, l = 45$

Let d = common difference

$S_n = 400$

$l = a + (n - l)d$

$(n - l)d = 45 - 5 = 40$ ...(i)

$S_n = 400$

$\frac{n}{2}[2a + (n - 1)d] = 400$

$n[10 + 40] = 800$

$n = 16$

$d = \frac{40}{n-1} = \frac{40}{15} = \frac{8}{3}$

OR

$a_7 = \frac{1}{9}, a_9 = \frac{1}{7}$

$\therefore \quad a + 6d = \frac{1}{9}$ [By term formula]

$a + 8d = \frac{1}{7}$

$- \quad - \quad -$

$-2d = \frac{1}{9} - \frac{1}{7}$

$-2d = \frac{-2}{63}$

$d = \frac{1}{63}$

$a + 6d = \frac{1}{9}$

$a + \frac{2}{21} = \frac{1}{9}$

$a = \frac{1}{9} - \frac{2}{21}$

$a = \frac{7-6}{63} = \frac{1}{63}$

$a_{63} = a + 62d$

$a_{63} = \frac{63}{63} = 1$

30. Let OP meet the circle at Q. Join AQ. As OP is equal to the diameter of the circle and OQ is radius,so OQ = QP i.e. Q is mid-point of OP. Since PA is tangent to the circle at A and OA is its radius, OA ⊥ AP i.e. ∠OAP = 90°. In right triangle OAP, Q is mid-point of hypotenuse,

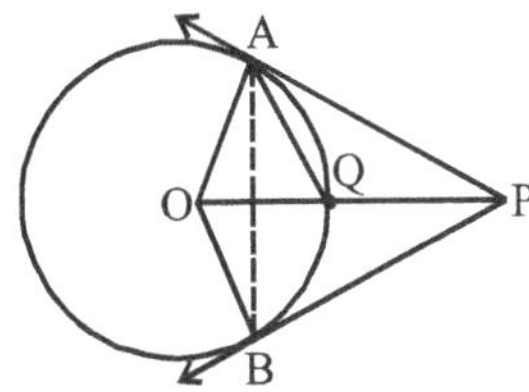

∴ AQ = OQ = QP

Also OA = OQ (radii of same circle)

⇒ OA = OQ = AQ ⇒ ΔOAQ is equilateral

⇒ ∠AOQ = 60° ⇒ ∠AOP = 60°. [1 Mark]

In ΔOAP, ∠OPA + ∠AOP + ∠OAP = 180°

⇒ ∠OPA + 60° + 90° = 180° ⇒ ∠OPA = 30°

⇒ ∠APB = 60° (∴ OP is bisector of ∠APB) [½ Mark]

Also PA = PB ⇒ ∠PAB = ∠PBA.

In ΔPAB, ∠PAB + ∠PBA + ∠APB = 180° [½ Mark]

⇒ 2 ∠PAB + 60° = 180° ⇒ ∠PAB = 60°

⇒ Triangle ABP is equilateral. [1 Mark]

31.

Class	f	$c.f.$
0 – 10	5	5
10 – 20	x	$x+5$
20 – 30	20	$x+25$
30 – 40	15	$x+40$
40 – 50	y	$x+y+40$
50 – 60	5	$x+y+45$
	$\Sigma f = 60$	

[1 Mark]

From table, $N = 60 = x + y + 45 \Rightarrow x + y = 60 - 45 = 15$ ... (i) [½ Mark]

Since, Median = 28.5

Median class = 20 – 30

$$\text{Median} = l + \frac{\left(\frac{N}{2} - c.f.\right)}{f} \times h$$ [½ Mark]

$$\Rightarrow 28.5 = 20 + \frac{[30 - (x+5)]}{20} \times 10 \Rightarrow 8.5 = \frac{25 - x}{2}$$

$\Rightarrow 25 - x = 17 \Rightarrow x = 25 - 17 = 8$ [½ Mark]

From (i), $y = 15 - 8 = 7$ [½ Mark]

32. Let the policeman catches the thief after t minutes.

∵ Uniform speed of the thief = 100 metres/minute

So, distance covered by thief in (t + 1) minutes = 100 (t + 1) metres [1 Mark]

∴ Distance covered by policeman in t minutes

= Sum of t terms of an AP whose first term 100 and common difference 10 [1 Mark]

$= \frac{t}{2}[2 \times 100 + (t-1) \times 10]$

$= t(5t + 95)$

$= 5t^2 + 95t$ [2 Marks]

If the policeman catches the thief, then :

$5t^2 + 95t = 100(t + 1)$

$5t^2 - 5t - 100 = 0$

∴ $t^2 - t - 20 = 0$

So, t = –4 and t = 5

Thus, t = 5 minutes (t > 0) [1 Mark]

Hence, the policeman catches the thief after 5 minutes.

33. **Proof**: $BC = 2BD$ (AD is the median)

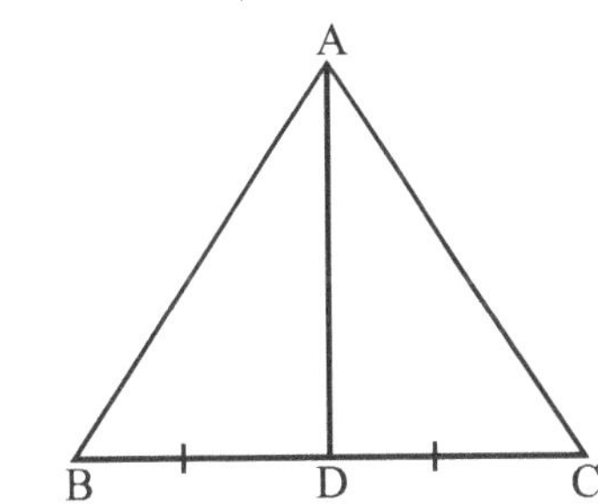

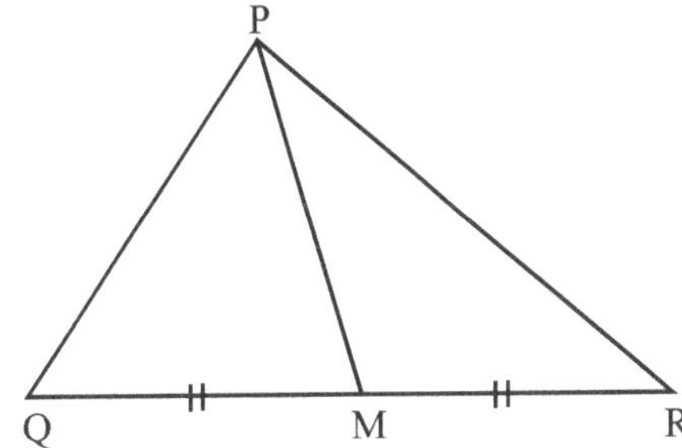

[1 Mark]

and $QR = 2QM$ (PM is the median)

Given, $\frac{AB}{PQ} = \frac{AD}{PM} = \frac{BC}{QR}$

$\Rightarrow \frac{AB}{PQ} = \frac{AD}{PM} = \frac{2BD}{2QM}$ [1 Mark]

In triangles ABD and PQM,

$\frac{AB}{PQ} = \frac{AD}{PM} = \frac{BD}{QM}$ [1 Mark]

∴ $\Delta ABD \sim \Delta PQM$ (SSS Similarity)

⇒ $\angle B = \angle Q$ (By CPST) [1 Mark]

In ΔABC and ΔPQR,

$\frac{AB}{PQ} = \frac{BC}{QR}$

and $\angle B = \angle Q$ (SAS Similarity)

∴ $\Delta ABC \sim \Delta PQR$ [1 Mark]

OR

Given : Two ΔABC and ΔDEF such that

$\frac{AB}{DE} = \frac{BC}{EF} = \frac{AC}{DF}$

To prove : $\Delta ABC \sim \Delta DEF$

Construction : Taking points P on DE and Q on DF such that $DP = AB$ and $DQ = AC$. Join PQ. [1Mark]

Proof : In ΔABC and ΔDEF, $\frac{AB}{DE} = \frac{AC}{DF} = \frac{BC}{EF}$

$\Rightarrow \frac{DP}{DE} = \frac{DQ}{DF}$ (By construction)

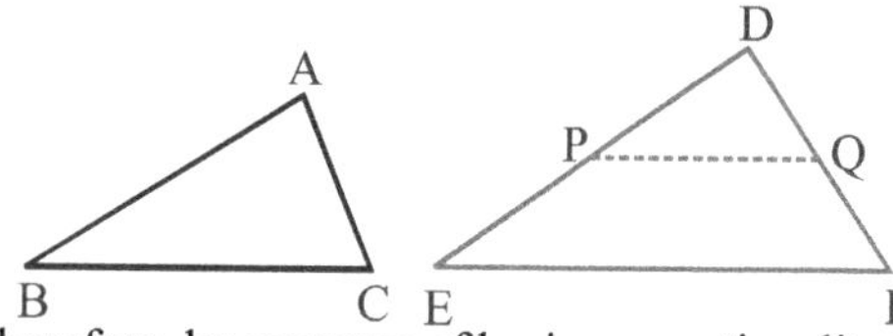

Therefore, by converse of basic proportionality theorem, $PQ \parallel EF$

So $\angle DPQ = \angle DEF$ and $\angle DQP = \angle DFE$ (corresponding angles)

Hence by AA similarity, $\Delta DPQ \sim \Delta DEF$ ...(i) [1 Mark]

Hence the corresponding sides of similar ΔDPQ and ΔDEF are proportional.

i.e., $\frac{DP}{DE} = \frac{PQ}{EF} \Rightarrow \frac{AB}{DE} = \frac{PQ}{EF}$ $(\because DP = AB)$

But, $\frac{AB}{DE} = \frac{BC}{EF} \Rightarrow \frac{PQ}{EF} = \frac{BC}{EF} \Rightarrow PQ = BC$ ...(ii)

Now, in ΔABC and ΔDPQ [1 Mark]

$AB = DP$ (By Construction)

$AC = DQ$ (By Construction)

$BC = PQ$ [From (ii)]

So by SSS congruence rule

$\Delta ABC \cong \Delta DPQ$ ...(iii) [1 Mark]

From (i) and (iii)

$\Delta ABC \sim \Delta DPQ \sim \Delta DEF$ [1 Mark]

34. Let the radius of spherical marble = 0.7 cm [1 Mark]

Volume of 1 marble $= \frac{4}{3}\pi r^3 = \frac{4}{3}\pi(0.7)^3$ cm^3 [1 Mark]

Volume of 150 marble $= 200\pi(0.7)^3$ cm^3 [1 Mark]

Let h be the rise in the height of water

$\therefore$ Volume of water raised = Volume of 150 marbles [1 Mark]

So, $\pi \times 7^2 \times h = 200\pi(0.7)^3 \Rightarrow h = \frac{200 \times 7 \times 7 \times 7}{7 \times 7 \times 10 \times 10 \times 10}$

$\Rightarrow h = 1.4$ cm [2 Marks]

OR

Let the radius of hemisphere = r

Now, volume of hemisphere $= \frac{2}{3}\pi r^3$ [1 Mark]

Surface area of hemisphere $= 3\pi r^2$ [1 Mark]

A.T.Q, volume of hemisphere = surface area of hemisphere

$\Rightarrow \frac{2}{3}\pi r^3 = 3\pi r^2 \Rightarrow r = \frac{9}{2}$ units [1 Mark]

So, the required diameter of hemisphere = 2r = 9 units.

35.

Class Interval	Frequency	Cumulative frequency
0–100	2	2
100–200	5	7
200–300	x	$7+x$
300–400	12	$19+x$
400–500	17	$36+x$
500–600	20	$56+x$
600–700	y	$56+x+y$
700–800	9	$65+x+y$
800–900	7	$72+x+y$
900–1000	4	$76+x+y$
	$N=100$	

Hence, $76 + x + y = 100$ [1 Mark]

$\Rightarrow x + y = 100 - 76 = 24$

Given, Median = 525,

$\Rightarrow$ Median class = 500 – 600 [1 Mark]

Here, $l = 500$

$h = 100$

$c.f. = 36 + x$

$f = 20$

Now, Median $= l + \frac{\frac{n}{2} - c.f.}{f} \times h$ [1 Mark]

$$525 = 500 + \left[\frac{\frac{100}{2} - (36 + x)}{20}\right] \times 100$$

$25 = (50 - 36 - x)\,5$ [1 Mark]

$(14 - x) = 5$

$x = 14 - 5 = 9$

Substituting the value of x in equation (i),

$y = 24 - 9 = 15$ [1 Mark]

36. (i) Volume of concrete required for the first step of terrace $= \frac{1}{4} \times \frac{1}{2} \times 50 = 6.25$ m^3 [1 Mark]

(ii) Volume of concrete required for the 8th| step of terrace $= 8 \times \frac{1}{4} \times \frac{1}{2} \times 50 = 50$ m^3 [1 Mark]

(iii) The A.P. formed by the volume of concrete required to build the first step, second step, third step,.........,fifteenth step

$= \frac{1}{4}\times\frac{1}{2}\times 50, \left(2\times\frac{1}{4}\right)\times\frac{1}{2}\times 50, \left(3\times\frac{1}{4}\right)$

$\times\frac{1}{2}\times 50, \ldots\ldots, \left(15\times\frac{1}{4}\right)\times\frac{1}{2}\times 50$

$= \frac{50}{8}, 2\times\frac{50}{8}, 3\times\frac{50}{8}, \ldots\ldots, 15\times\frac{50}{8}$

∴ The common difference of A.P. formed by volume of steps of terrace

$= 2\times\frac{50}{8} - \frac{50}{8} = \frac{50}{8} = \frac{25}{4}$ [2 Marks]

OR

Total volume of concrete required to build the terrace

$= 1\times\frac{50}{8} + 2\times\frac{50}{8} + 3\times\frac{50}{8} + \ldots\ldots + 15\times\frac{50}{8}$

$= \frac{50}{8}[1+2+3+\ldots+15]$

$= \frac{50}{8}\times\frac{15}{2}[2\times 1 + (15-1)\times 1]$

$= \frac{50}{8}\times\frac{15}{2}\times 16 = 750\ m^3$ [2 Marks]

37. (i) (0,0) [1 Mark]
(ii) (4,6) [1 Mark]
(iii) (6,5) [2 Marks]

OR

(16,0) [2 Marks]

38. (i) $x \tan 60° = (100 - x)\tan 30°$

$x\sqrt{3} = (100 - x)\frac{1}{\sqrt{3}} \Rightarrow x = 25$ [1 Mark]

∴ Distance of p from pillar making angle 60° = 25m

(ii) Distance of p from pillar making angle 30°
$= 100 - 25 = 75m$ [1 Mark]

(iii) Height = $x \tan 60° = 25\sqrt{3}$ m. [2 Marks]

OR

$\text{Sum} = \sqrt{(25\sqrt{3})^2 + (25)^2} + \sqrt{(25\sqrt{3})^2 + (75)^2}$ [2 Marks]

$= 50 + 50\sqrt{3} = 50\left(\sqrt{3+1}\right)$m.

1. **(d)** The L.C.M. of 16, 20 and 24 is 240. The least multiple of 240 that is a perfect square is 3600 and also we can easily eliminate choices (a) and (c) since they are not perfect number. Hence, the required least number which is also a perfect square is 3600 which is divisible by each of 16, 20 and 24.

2. **(b)** The diagonals of a rhombus are perpendicular bisector of each other.

Given, AC = 16 cm
and BD = 12 cm
∴ AO = 8 cm, BO = 6 cm
and ∠AOB = 90°

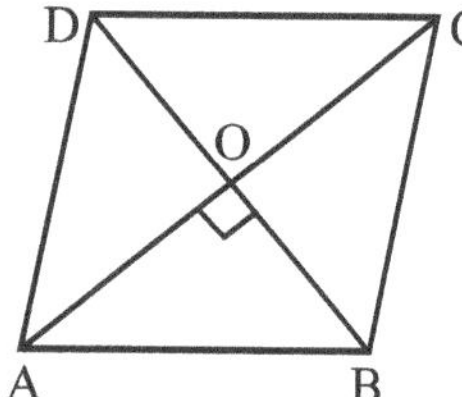

In right angled ΔAOB,

$$AB^2 = AO^2 + OB^2$$ [by Pythagoras theorem]

$$\Rightarrow AB^2 = 8^2 + 6^2 = 64 + 36 = 100 = 10^2$$

∴ AB = 10 cm

3. **(a) Hint:** Use distance formula.

4. **(b)** ∵ $m = n^2 - n = n(n-1)$

Now, $m^2 - 2m = m(m-2)$

$= n(n-1)(n^2 - n - 2) = n(n-1)(n-2)(n+1)$

Since we know that product of any four consecutive integers is always divisible by 24.

∴ $m^2 - 2m$ is divisible by 24.

5. **(d)** In ΔAPB and ΔCPD,

∠APB = ∠CPD = 50° [vertically opposite angles]

Now, $\frac{AP}{PD} = \frac{6}{5}$ ...(i)

and $\frac{BP}{CP} = \frac{3}{2.5} = \frac{6}{5}$ ...(ii)

∴ $\frac{AP}{PD} = \frac{BP}{CP}$ From Eqs. (i) and (ii)

∴ ΔAPB ~ ΔDPC [by SAS similarity criterion]

∴ ∠A = ∠D = 30° [corresponding angles of similar triangles]

In ΔAPB, ∠A + ∠B + ∠APB = 180° [sum of angles of a triangle = 180°]

⇒ 30° + ∠B + 50° = 180°

⇒ ∠B = 180° − (50° + 30°) = 100°

i.e., ∠PBA = 100°

6. **(c)** For reflection of a point with respect to x-axis change sign of y-coordinate and with respect to y-axis change sign of x-coordinate.

7. **(a)** $\operatorname{cosec} x - \sin x = a$ & $\sec x - \cos x = b$

$$\operatorname{cosec} x - \frac{1}{\operatorname{cosec} x} = a \;\&\; \sec x - \frac{1}{\sec x} = b$$

$$\Rightarrow \frac{\operatorname{cosec}^2 x - 1}{\operatorname{cosec} x} = a \;\&\; \frac{\sec^2 x - 1}{\sec x} = b$$

$$\Rightarrow \frac{\cot^2 x}{\operatorname{cosec} x} = a \;\&\; \frac{\tan^2 x}{\sec x} = b$$

$$\frac{\cos^2 x}{\sin x} = a \;\&\; \frac{\sin^2 x}{\cos x} = b$$

Now, $a^2 b = \frac{\cos^4 x}{\sin^2 x} \cdot \frac{\sin^2 x}{\cos x} = \cos^3 x$

⇒ $\cos x = (a^2 b)^{1/3} \Rightarrow \cos^2 x = (a^2 b)^{2/3}$

Similarly, $\sin^2 x = (ab^2)^{2/3}$

We know that, $\sin^2 x + \cos^2 x = 1$

⇒ $(ab^2)^{2/3} + (a^2 b)^{2/3} = 1$

8. **(a)** Since, $C(y, -1)$ is the mid-point of $P(4, x)$ and $Q(-2, 4)$.

P	C	Q
(4, x)	$(y_1, -1)$	(−2, 4)

We have, $\frac{4-2}{2} = y$ and $\frac{4+x}{2} = -1$

∴ $y = 1$ and $x = -6$

9. **(c) Hint:** $\tan 30° = \frac{AB}{OB}$

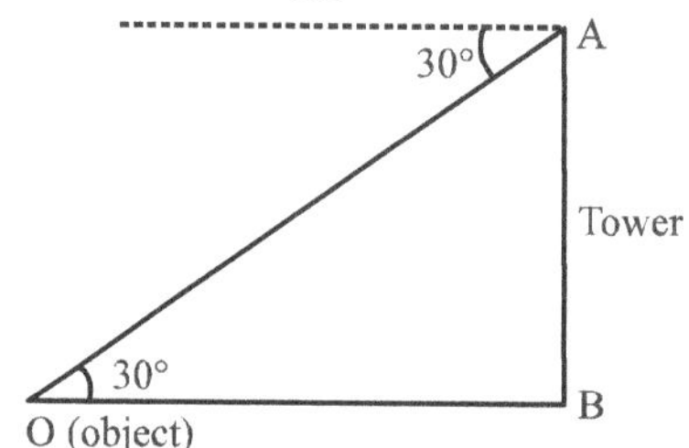

$$\Rightarrow \frac{1}{\sqrt{3}} = \frac{75}{OB} \Rightarrow OB = 75\sqrt{3}\text{ m}$$

10. **(d)** $\frac{1 + \tan^2 A}{1 + \cot^2 A} = \frac{(\sec^2 A - \tan^2 A) + \tan^2 A}{(\operatorname{cosec}^2 A - \cot^2 A) + \cot^2 A}$

$$= \frac{\sec^2 A}{\operatorname{cosec}^2 A} = \frac{\sin^2 A}{\cos^2 A} = \left(\frac{\sin A}{\cos A}\right)^2 = \tan^2 A.$$

11. **(b)** (i) APBC is a cyclic quadrilateral.
(ii) $\angle ABC$ is an angle in a semi circle.
(iii) ABQC is a cyclic quadrilateral.

12. **(b)** **Hint:** C.S.A of cylinder

13. **(d)** $(\sec A + \tan A)(1 - \sin A)$

$$= \left(\frac{1}{\cos A} + \frac{\sin A}{\cos A}\right) \times (1 - \sin A)$$

$$= \frac{(1+\sin A)(1-\sin A)}{\cos A}$$

$$= \frac{1-\sin^2 A}{\cos A} = \frac{\cos^2 A}{\cos A} \qquad (\because \cos^2 A = 1 - \sin^2 A)$$

$= \cos A$.

14. **(b)** All chords are of same length.

15. **(b)** Given that, total number of students = 23

Number of students in house A, B and C

= 4 + 8 + 5 = 17

$\therefore$ Remains students = 23 – 17 = 6

Hence, probability that the selected student is not from A, B and C

$$= \frac{\text{No. of possible outcomes}}{\text{Total no. of outcomes}} = \frac{6}{23}$$

16. **(d)** Total number of marbles = 38 – 18 + 1 = 21

The multiples of 3 from 18 to 38 are 18, 21, 24, 27, 30, 33, 36.

These are 7 in numbers

$\therefore$ Required probability $= \frac{7}{21} = \frac{1}{3}$

17. **(d)** Since $n = 9$, then middle term $= \left(\frac{9+1}{2}\right)^{th} = 5^{th}$ term.

Now, last four observations are increased by 2.

$\because$ The median is 5th observation, which is remains unchanged.

$\therefore$ There will be no change in median.

18. **(d)** Since, the mean of a group of eleven consecutive natural numbers is m, then

$$\frac{x + x + 1 + ... + x + 10}{11} = m$$

$11x + 55 = 11\,m; x + 5 = m; x = m - 5$

Let n be the mean when next six consecutive natural numbers are included in the group then

$$\frac{x + x + 1 + ... + x + 16}{17} = n;$$

$$17x + \frac{16 \times 17}{2} = 17n$$

$17x + 8 \times 17 = 17\,n$

$m - 5 + 8 = n$

$\Rightarrow\ n = m + 3 \qquad (\therefore x = m - 5)$

Hence, required percentage change in the mean

$$= \frac{n-m}{m} \times 100 = \frac{m+3-m}{m} \times 100 = \frac{300}{m}\%$$

19. **(d)** In right angled ΔABC,

$AB^2 = AC^2 + BC^2$ (By Pythagorus Theorem)

$= AC^2 + AC^2$ $[\because BC = AC]$

$= 2AC^2$

$\therefore$ $AB^2 = 2AC^2$

$\therefore$ Assertion is false.

Again since

$AB^2 = 2AC^2 = AC^2 + AC^2$

$= AC^2 + BC^2$ ($\because AC = BC$ given)

$\therefore \angle C = 90°$ (By converse of Pythagoras Theorem)

$\therefore$ Reason is true.

20. **(a)** Both assertion and reason are correct. Reason is correct explanation of assertion.

21. $\sin A + \operatorname{cosec} A = 3$

$$\Rightarrow \sin A + \frac{1}{\sin A} = 3 \Rightarrow \frac{\sin^2 A + 1}{\sin A} = 3 \qquad \text{[1 Mark]}$$

or $\sin^2 A + 1 = 3 \sin A$

Squaring both sides, we get

$$1 + \sin^4 A + 2\sin^2 A = 9\sin^2 A$$

$$\Rightarrow 1 + \sin^4 A = 7\sin^2 A \Rightarrow \frac{1 + \sin^4 A}{\sin^2 A} = 7 \qquad \text{[1 Mark]}$$

22. Let OT be a radius and OP be a tangent.

In a ΔOPT. [1 Mark]

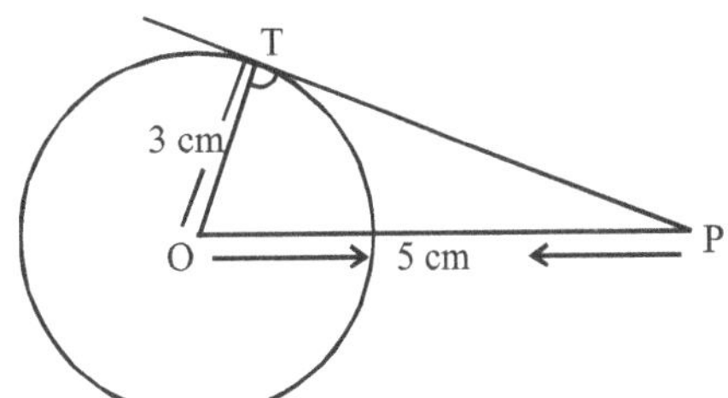

$OT^2 + PT^2 = OP^2$ (By Pythagoras theorem)

$$\Rightarrow (3)^2 + PT^2 = (5)^2 \Rightarrow PT^2 = 25 - 9$$

$$\Rightarrow PT^2 = 16 \Rightarrow PT = 4 \text{ cm.} \qquad \text{[1 Mark]}$$

23. Here, $r = 45$ cm

θ = sector angle between two consecutive ribs.

$= \frac{360}{8}$ degree ($\because$ there are 8 sectors of same size)

= 45 degrees [1 Mark]

Therefore, the area between two consecutive ribs of the umbrella

= The area of one sector $= \frac{45}{360} \times \pi r^2$

$\left[\because \text{area of sector} = \frac{\theta}{360} \times \pi r^2\right]$

$$= \frac{11}{28} \times 45 \times 45\,\text{cm}^2 = \frac{22275}{28}\,\text{cm}^2 \qquad \text{[1 Mark]}$$

24. Percentage of bad mangoes
= 100% – percentage of good mangoes
= 100% – 90% = 10% [1 Mark]

$\therefore$ probability of bad magoes = $\frac{10}{100}=\frac{1}{10}$ [1 Mark]

OR

Total number of coins = 40
let number of ₹ 2 coins is C.

$\because$ P(drawing a ₹ 2 coin) $=\frac{5}{8}\Rightarrow\frac{C}{40}=\frac{5}{8}\Rightarrow C=25$

[1 Mark]

Now, $\frac{25-x}{40-x}=\frac{1}{2}\Rightarrow x=10$ [1 Mark]

25. Since points are collinear,

Distance AB = $\sqrt{13}$ [1 Mark]

Distance BC = $\sqrt{4+k^2+1-2k}$

Put AB = BC
Then, k = 4 [1 Mark]

OR

Given that
Distance between A(–3, –14) and B(a, –5), AB = 9
$\therefore$ using distance formula

$$\sqrt{(a+3)^2+(-5+14)^2}=9$$ [½ Mark]

$$\Rightarrow \sqrt{(a+3)^2+(9)^2}=9$$ [½ Mark]

On squaring both the sides,
$(a+3)^2+81=81$ [½ Mark]
$\Rightarrow (a+3)^2=0$
$\Rightarrow a=-3$ [½ Mark]

26. $p(x)=2x^3-11x^2+17x-6$
$p(2)=2(2)^3-11(2)^2+17(2)-6$
$=16-44+34-6$
$=50-50=0$

Hence 2 is the zero of $p(x)$.

$p(3)=2(3)^3-11(3)^2+17(3)-6$
$=54-99+51-6$
$=105-105=0$ [1 Mark]

Hence, 3 is the zero of $p(x)$.

$$p\left(\frac{1}{2}\right)=2\left(\frac{1}{2}\right)^3-11\left(\frac{1}{2}\right)^2+17\left(\frac{1}{2}\right)-6$$

$$=\frac{1}{4}-\frac{11}{4}+\frac{17}{2}-6=0$$

Hence, $\frac{1}{2}$ is also the zero of $p(x)$. [1 Mark]

OR

Suppose $p(x)=5x^2+8x-4$ [1 Mark]
$=5x^2+10x-2x-4$
$=5x(x+2)-2(x+2)$
$=(x+2)(5x-2)$ [1 Mark]

Hence, zeroes of the quadratic polynomial

$5x^2+8x-4$ are -2 and $\frac{2}{5}$. [1 Mark]

Verification:

Sum of zeroes $=-2+\frac{2}{5}=\frac{-8}{5}$

Product of zeroes $=(-2)\times\left(\frac{2}{5}\right)=\frac{-4}{5}$

Again sum of zeroes $=-\frac{\text{Coeff. of }x}{\text{Coeff. of }x^2}=\frac{-8}{5}$

Product of zeroes $=\frac{\text{Constant term}}{\text{Coeff. of }x^2}=\frac{-4}{5}$

27. Since p, q, r are in A.P
$\therefore\ q-p=r-q$
$\Rightarrow 2q=r+p$ ... (i) [1 Mark]
$p^3+r^3-8q^3=(p^3+r^3)-(2q)^3$
$=(p+r)(p^2+r^2-rp)-(2q)^3$
$=(p+r)(p^2+r^2-rp)-(r+p)^3$ [From (i), $2q=r+p$]
[1 Mark]
$=(r+p)[(p^2+r^2-rp)-(r+p)^2]$
$=(r+p)[p^2+r^2-rp-r^2-p^2-2pr]$
$=(r+p)(-3pr)=(2q)(-3pr)=-6pqr$ [From (i), $2q=r+p$]
[1 Mark]

OR

The given AP is 18, $15\frac{1}{2}$, 13 ...., $-49\frac{1}{2}$.

Suppose the number of terms in given AP is n.
As, last term of an AP, $l=a+(n-1)d$ [1 Mark]

So, $-49\frac{1}{2}=18+(n-1)\left(15\frac{1}{2}-18\right)$

$\Rightarrow -\frac{99}{2}=18+(n-1)\left(-\frac{5}{2}\right)$ [½ Mark]

$\Rightarrow 99=-36+(n-1)5\Rightarrow 5(n-1)=99+36=135$

$\Rightarrow n-1=\frac{135}{5}=27\Rightarrow n=27+1=28$ [½ Mark]

Therefore, the number of terms in given AP is 28.
And, the sum of all 28terms

$=\frac{28}{2}\left(18-49\frac{1}{2}\right)=14\left(\frac{36-99}{2}\right)=-441$ [1 Mark]

Hence, the number of terms in given AP is 28 and the sum of all its terms is – 441.

28. $m=a\cos\theta+b\sin\theta$
$(m)^2=(a\cos\theta+b\sin\theta)^2$
$m^2=a^2\cos^2\theta+b^2\sin^2\theta+2ab\cos\theta\sin\theta$ ...(i)
[1 Mark]

also, $n = a \sin\theta - b\cos\theta$; $(n)^2 = (a\sin\theta - b\cos\theta)^2$

$n^2 = a^2\sin^2\theta + b^2\cos^2\theta - 2ab\cos\theta\sin\theta$ ...(ii)

[1 Mark]

On adding equation (i) and (ii), we get

$m^2 + n^2 = a^2\cos^2\theta + b^2\sin^2\theta + a^2\sin^2\theta + b^2\cos^2\theta$

$= a^2(\cos^2\theta + \sin^2\theta) + b^2(\sin^2\theta + \cos^2\theta)$

$m^2 + n^2 = a^2 + b^2$ [1 Mark]

(Hence proved.)

29. Let AB is the height of light house = 200m

Two ships are at points C and D on either side of AB (light house)

In ΔABC,

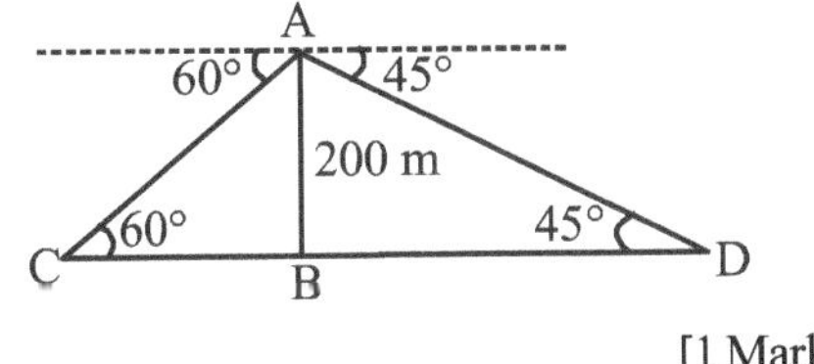

[1 Mark]

$\tan 60° = \frac{AB}{BC}$

$\Rightarrow BC = \frac{200\sqrt{3}}{3} = \frac{200\times1.73}{3} = 115.33$ m [1 Mark]

In ΔABD, $\tan 45° = \frac{AB}{BD} \Rightarrow$ BD = 200 [1 Mark]

Distance between both ships

= BC + BD = 115.33 + 200 = 315.33 m [1 Mark]

30. Let there be a circle with centre O whereas AB, BC, CD and DA are tangents at P, Q, R and S respectively.

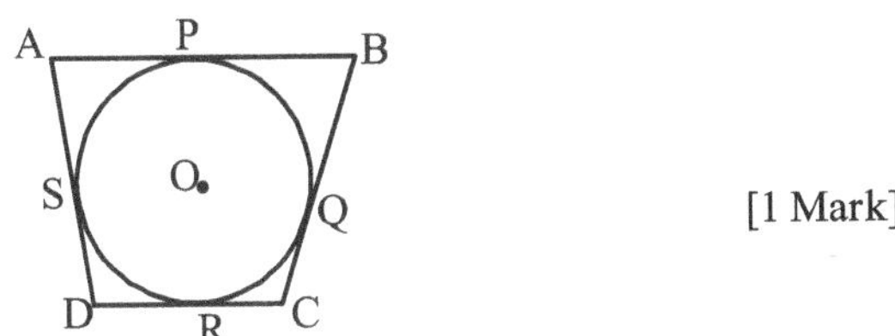

[1 Mark]

Here,

AP = AS ...(i)

BP = BQ ...(ii)

CR = CQ ...(iii)

DR = DS ..(iv)

[Tangents drawn from a point (outside the circle) on a given circle are equal in lengths]

From equations (i), (ii), (iii) and (iv), [1 Mark]

(AP + BP) + (CR + DR) = (BQ + CQ) + (DS + AS)

AB + CD = BC + DA (Hence proved.) [1 Mark]

31. Since, radius of circle with centre O is OR.

Suppose OR = x

$\therefore$ $x^2 + x^2 = (42)^2$ [By Pythagoras theorem]

$x = 21\sqrt{2}$m [1 Mark]

So, area of one flower bed = Area of segment of circle – Area of triangle POS

$= \pi r^2 \times \frac{90°}{360°} - \frac{1}{2} \times OR \times OR$

$= \frac{22}{7} \times 21\sqrt{2} \times 21\sqrt{2} \times \frac{90°}{360°} - \frac{1}{2} \times 21\sqrt{2} \times 21\sqrt{2}$ [1 Mark]

$= \frac{22}{7} \times 21 \times 21 \times 2 \times \frac{1}{4} - \frac{1}{2} \times 21 \times 21 \times 2$

$= 33 \times 21 - 21 \times 21 = 21[33 - 21] = 21 \times 12 = 252\text{m}^2$

[½ Mark]

Hence, area of two flower beds = 2 × 252 = 504 m^2

[½ Mark]

32. Let $\frac{2x-3}{x-1} = y$ then the given equation becomes

$\therefore y - 4 \times \frac{1}{y} = 3 \Rightarrow y^2 - 4 = 3y$ [1 Mark]

or $y^2 - 3y - 4 = 0 \Rightarrow y^2 - 4y + y - 4 = 0$

$\Rightarrow y(y-4) + 1(y-4) = 0 \Rightarrow (y+1)(y-4) = 0$ [2 Marks]

Either $y + 1 = 0 \Rightarrow y = -1$ or $y - 4 = 0 \Rightarrow y = 4$

Putting the value of y = – 1 then

$\frac{2x-3}{x-1} = -1 \Rightarrow 2x - 3 = -x + 1$

or $2x + x - 3 - 1 = 0 \Rightarrow 3x = 4 \Rightarrow x = \frac{4}{3}$ [1 Mark]

Putting the value of y = 4 in $\frac{2x-3}{x-1} = 4 \Rightarrow 2x - 3 = 4x - 4$

or $2x - 4x - 3 + 4 = 0$ or $-2x + 1 = 0 \Rightarrow -2x = -1$

$\Rightarrow x = 1/2$ [1 Mark]

x = {4/3, 1/2}

OR

Let the present age of Rehman be x years.

Rehman's age, 3 years ago = $(x - 3)$ years [1 Mark]

Rehman's age, 5 years later = $(x + 5)$ years

According to the question

$\frac{1}{x-3} + \frac{1}{x+5} = \frac{1}{3}$

$\Rightarrow 6x + 6 = x^2 + 2x - 15 \Rightarrow x^2 - 4x - 21 = 0$

On comparing with $ax^2 + bx + c = 0$,

we get $a = 1, b = -4, c = -21$

$D = b^2 - 4ac = (-4)^2 - 4(1)(-21) = 16 + 84 = 100$

$\Rightarrow \sqrt{D} = \sqrt{100} = 10$

$\therefore x = \frac{-b \pm \sqrt{D}}{2a} = \frac{4 \pm 10}{2} = \frac{14}{2}, \frac{-6}{2}$ [2 Marks]

$\Rightarrow x = 7, -3$ [1 Mark]

We reject $x = -3$ ($\because$ age cannot be negative)

$\therefore$ Rehman's present age = 7 years [1 Mark]

33. $\because$ Sum of p terms = q

$\therefore \frac{p}{2}[2a+(p-1)d] = q$ ...(i) [½ Mark]

Now, sum of q terms = p

$\therefore \frac{q}{2}[2a+(q-1)d] = p$ ...(ii) [½ Mark]

After solving (i) and (ii), we get

$d = \frac{-2(p+q)}{pq}$ ...(iii) [1 Mark]

$S_{p-q} = \frac{p-q}{2}[2a+(p-q-1)d]$

$= \frac{p-q}{2}[2a+(p-1)d-qd]$

$= \frac{p-q}{2}\left[\frac{2q}{p} - q\left\{\frac{-2(p+q)}{pq}\right\}\right]$ [From (i) and (iii)] [2 Marks]

$=(p-q)\left[\frac{q+(p+q)}{p}\right]$ [From (i) and (iii)]

$=(p-q)\left[\frac{p}{p}+\frac{2q}{p}\right] = (p-q)\left[1+\frac{2q}{p}\right]$

(Hence Proved). [1 Mark]

OR

Let 'a' be the 1st term and 'd' the common difference of an A.P.

S_1 = Sum of n terms of the A.P. $= \frac{n}{2}[2a+(n-1)d]$

[½ Mark]

S_2 = Sum of 2n terms of the A.P.

$= \frac{2n}{2}[2a+(2n-1)d] = n[2a+(2n-1)d]$ [½ Mark]

S_3 = Sum of 3n terms of the A.P.

$= \frac{3n}{2}[2a+(3n-1)d]$ .....(i) [1 Mark]

Now, **R.H.S.** = 3 ($S_2 - S_1$)

$= 3\left[n\{2a+2(n-1)d\} - \frac{n}{2}\{2a+(n-1)d\}\right]$ [2 Marks]

$3\left[an+\frac{3n^2d}{2}-\frac{nd}{2}\right] = 3n\left[\frac{2a+3nd-d}{2}\right]$

$= \frac{3n}{2}[2a+(3n-1)d] = S_3$ (from (i)) = **L.H.S.** [1 Mark]

34. In ΔABC, ℓ is drawn parallel to BC which intersects AB and AC at D and E respectively.

To prove : $\frac{AD}{DB} = \frac{AE}{EC}$

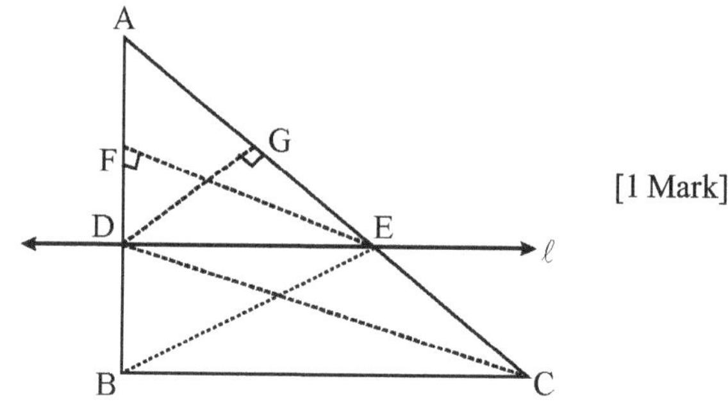

[1 Mark]

Construction : Join BE and CD and draw $EF \perp AB$ and $DG \perp AC$. [½ Mark]

Proof : ΔDBE and ΔCDE are on the same base DE and between the same parallel lines DE and BC.

$\therefore$ Area (ΔBDE) = Area (ΔCDE) .... (i)

[½ Mark]

Since, $EF \perp AB$ therefore the height of both triangles is EF.

$\therefore \frac{\text{Area }(\Delta ADE)}{\text{Area }(\Delta BDE)} = \frac{\frac{1}{2}\times AD\times EF}{\frac{1}{2}\times BD\times EF} = \frac{AD}{BD}$ ...... (ii)

[1 Mark]

Similarly,

$\frac{\text{Area }(\Delta ADE)}{\text{Area }(\Delta CDE)} = \frac{\frac{1}{2}\times AE\times DG}{\frac{1}{2}\times EC\times DG} = \frac{AE}{EC}$ ...... (iii)

[1 Mark]

Hence from (i), (ii) and (iii), we get $\frac{AD}{DB} = \frac{AE}{EC}$ [1 Mark]

35. Here, maximum frequency = 95,

So modal class = 11 – 13 [1 Mark]

$l = 11, f_1 = 95, f_0 = 41, f_2 = 36, h = 2$ [1 Mark]

$\text{Mode} = l + \left(\frac{f_1 - f_0}{2f_1 - f_0 - f_2}\right)\times h$

$= 11 + \left(\frac{95-41}{190-41-36}\right)\times 2 = 11 + \frac{54}{113}\times 2$ [2 Marks]

$\therefore$ Mode = 11 + 0.95 = 11.95 [1 Mark]

36. (i) (c) H.C.F. = 16 and Product = 3072

$\text{L.C.M.} = \frac{\text{Product}}{\text{H.C.F.}} = \frac{3072}{16} = 192$ [1 Mark]

(ii) (c) H.C.F. of two numbers is 27

So let the numbers are 27a and 27b

Now 27a + 27b = 135

$\Rightarrow$ a + b = 5 ...(i)

Also 27a × 27b = 27 × 162.

$\Rightarrow$ ab = 6 ...(ii)

$(a-b)^2 = (a+b)^2 - 4ab$

$\Rightarrow \quad a - b = 1$

Solving (i) and (iii), we get

$a = 3, b = 2$

So numbers are 27×3, 27×2 i.e., 81, 54 [1 Mark]

(iii) LCM=HCF

Let a_1 and a_2 be two numbers.

LCM $(a_1, a_2) = x$

HCF $(a_1, a_2) = x$

$\Rightarrow$ Then, two numbers are equal. [2 Marks]

OR

Clearly, LCM = (LCM of p and p^3) [2 Marks]

(LCM of q^2 and q) = p^3q^2

37. (i) **Hint:** Solve $(10x+y)$ [1 Mark]

(ii) **Hint:** Solve $(10x+y)=(x-y)\,13+2$ [1 Mark]

(iii) Use elimination method to solve the equations. [2 Marks]

38. (i) Volume of cylindrical cup = $\pi r^2 h$

$\frac{22}{7} \times \frac{7}{2} \times \frac{7}{2} \times 10.5 = 404.25 \text{ cm}^3$ [1 Mark]

(ii) Volume of hemispherical cup

$= \frac{2}{3}\pi r^3 = \frac{3}{2} \times \frac{22}{7} \times \left(\frac{7}{2}\right)^3 = 89.83 \text{ cm}^3$ [1 Mark]

(iii) Curved surface area of cone = 551 $\Rightarrow \pi rl = 441$

$\Rightarrow \frac{22}{7} \times 7 \times l = 551$

$\Rightarrow \quad l = 25.045$

$\therefore \; h = \sqrt{l^2 - r^2} = 24 \text{ m}$ [2 Marks]

OR

Space occupied by each student

$= \frac{\pi r^2}{4} = 38.5 \text{ m}^2$ [2 Marks]

1. **(b)** $196 = 2^2 \cdot 7^2$, sum of exponents $= 2 + 2 = 4$

2. **(b)** $10x = 7.\overline{7}$ or $x = 0.\overline{7}$

   Subtracting, $9x = 7 \therefore x = \dfrac{7}{9}$

   $2x = \dfrac{14}{9} = 1.555........ = 1.\overline{5}$

3. **(c)** $t_8 = a + 7d, t_{12} = a + 11d$

   According to question, $8t_8 = 12t_{12}$ (given)

   $\Rightarrow \quad 8(a + 7d) = 12(a + 11d)$

   $\Rightarrow \quad 8a + 56d = 12a + 132d$

   $\Rightarrow \quad 8a - 12a + 56d - 132d = 0$

   $\Rightarrow \quad -4a - 76d = 0$

   $\Rightarrow a + 19d = 0 \quad \ldots$(i)

   $\therefore \quad t_{20} = a + 19d = 0$ using (i)

   $\therefore \quad t_{20} = 0$

4. **(c)** Let the ages of father and son be $7x$, $3x$

   After 10 years,

   $\therefore (7x + 10) : (3x + 10) = 2 : 1$ or $x = 10$

   $\therefore$ Age of the father is $7x$ i.e. 70 years.

5. **(c)**

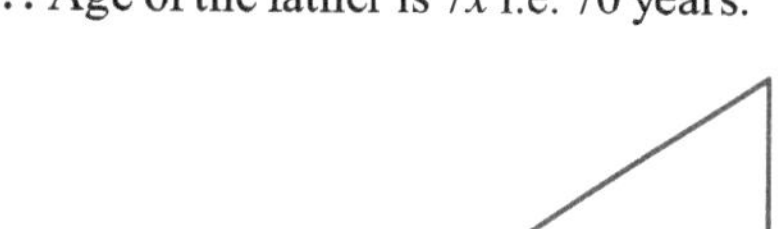

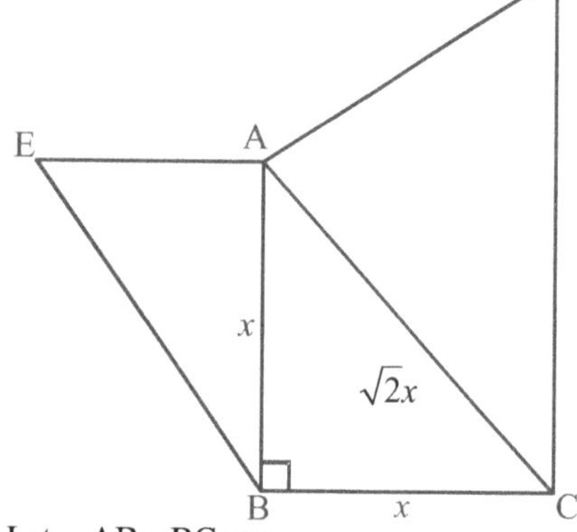

   Let $AB = BC = x$.

   Since, ΔABC is right-angled with $\angle B = 90°$

   $\therefore \quad AC^2 = AB^2 + BC^2 = x^2 + x^2 = 2x^2$

   $\Rightarrow \quad AC = \sqrt{2}x$

   Since, $\Delta ABE \sim \Delta ACD$

   Thus, $\dfrac{AB}{AC} = \dfrac{1}{\sqrt{2}}$

   Thus, required ratio is 1 : 2.

6. **(c)** For reflection of a point with respect to x-axis change sign of y-coordinate and with respect to y-axis change sign of x-coordinate.

7. **(d)** Out of n and $n + 2$, one is divisible by 2 and the other by 4, hence $n(n + 2)$ is divisible by 8. Also $n, n + 1, n + 2$ are three consecutive numbers, hence one of them is divisible by 3. Hence, $n(n + 1)(n + 2)$ must be divisible by 24. This will be true for any even number n.

8. **(b)** Hint $\cos 90° = 0$

9. **(a)** In ΔAFD & ΔFEB,

   $\angle 1 = \angle 2$ (V.O.A)

   $\angle 3 = \angle 4$ (Alternate angle)

   $\therefore \Delta FBE \sim \Delta FDA$

   So, $\dfrac{EF}{FA} = \dfrac{FB}{DF}$

10. **(b)** Probability lies from 0 to 1

11. **(b)** $2\pi r_1 = 503$ and $2\pi r_2 = 437$

    $\therefore \quad r_1 = \dfrac{503}{2\pi}$ and $r_2 = \dfrac{437}{2\pi}$

    Area of ring $= \pi(r_1 + r_2)(r_1 - r_2)$

    $= \pi\left(\dfrac{503 + 437}{2\pi}\right)\left(\dfrac{503 - 437}{2\pi}\right)$

    $= \dfrac{940}{2}\left(\dfrac{66}{2\pi}\right) = 235 \times \dfrac{66}{22} \times 7 = 235 \times 21 = 4935$ sq. cm.

12. **(a)** Since, $C(y, -1)$ is the mid-point of $P(4, x)$ and $Q(-2, 4)$.

    P ——— C ——— Q

    (4, x) $\quad (y_1, -1) \quad$ (–2, 4)

    We have, $\dfrac{4 - 2}{2} = y$ and $\dfrac{4 + x}{2} = -1$

    $\therefore y = 1$ and $x = -6$

13. **(c)** **Hint:** Add all entries then find mean

14. **(a)** From the right angled ΔACB,

    $AB^2 = AC^2 + CB^2$

    $= (20)^2 + (15)^2 = 400 + 225 = 625$

    $\therefore \quad AB = \sqrt{625} = 25$cm

    Again, from right angled ΔABD

    $AB^2 = AD^2 + BD^2$

    $\Rightarrow 625 = (24)^2 + (BD)^2$

    $\Rightarrow \quad (BD)^2 = 625 - 576 = 49$

    $\Rightarrow \quad BD = 7$ cm

15. **(a)** The number divisible by 15, 25 and 35 = L.C.M. (15, 25, 35) = 525

    Since, the number is short by 10 for complete division by 15, 25 and 35.

    Hence, the required least number = 525 – 10 = 515.

16. **(d)** $\dfrac{\tan 30°}{\cot 60°} = \dfrac{\frac{1}{\sqrt{3}}}{\frac{1}{\sqrt{3}}} = 1$

17. **(b)** Given, $\angle BPC = b°$ and $\angle ACP = a°$.

    Also, $\angle OPA = \angle OAP = b°$ (Angles in an isosceles triangle OAP, angle in alternate segment.)

    $\angle CPO = 90° \therefore \angle CPA = 90° + b°$

    In ΔACP, $\angle ACP = 180° - [(b° + 90°) + b°]$

    $\Rightarrow \quad a° + 2b° = 90°$

18. **(b)** Since $\cos A = \frac{4}{5}$

$\therefore$ $\sin A = \sqrt{1-\cos^2 A}$

$= \sqrt{1-\left(\frac{4}{5}\right)^2} = \sqrt{1-\frac{16}{25}}$

$= \sqrt{\frac{9}{25}} = \frac{3}{5}$

Now, $\tan A = \frac{\sin A}{\cos A} = \frac{\frac{3}{5}}{\frac{4}{5}} = \frac{3}{4}$

Hence, $\tan A$ is $\frac{3}{4}$.

19. **(a)** As $x = 3, y = 1$ is the solution

Then, $2x + y - q^2 - 3 = 0$

$2 \times 3 + 1 - q^2 - 3 = 0$

$q = \pm 2$

20. **(a)** Reason is true. [This is Thale's Theorem]

For Assertion

Since $DE \parallel BC$ $\therefore$ by Thale's Theorem

$\frac{AD}{DB} = \frac{AE}{EC} \Rightarrow \frac{DB}{AD} = \frac{EC}{AE}$

$\Rightarrow 1 + \frac{DB}{AD} = 1 + \frac{EC}{AE}$

$\Rightarrow \frac{AD+DB}{AD} = \frac{AE+EC}{AE}$

$\Rightarrow \frac{AB}{AD} = \frac{AC}{AE}$

$\therefore$ Assertion is true.

Since reason gives Assertion.

21. Since the given number ends in 5. which means it is a multiple of 5. Hence it is a composite number. [2 Marks]

22.

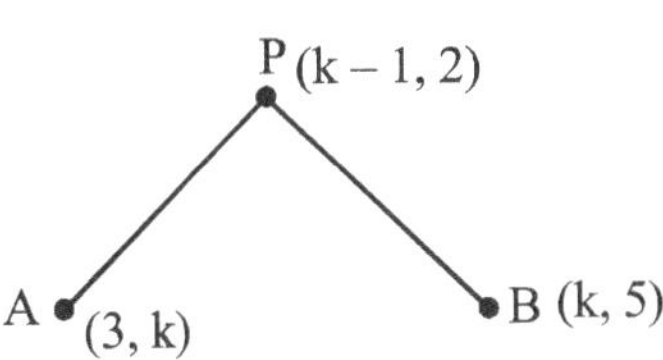

AP = BP

$\Rightarrow \sqrt{(k-1-3)^2+(2-k)^2} = \sqrt{(k-1-k)^2+(2-5)^2}$

[By Distance formula]

$\Rightarrow (k-4)^2 + (2-k)^2 = 1 + 9$ [1 Mark]

$\Rightarrow k^2 + 16 - 8k + 4 + k^2 - 4k = 10$

$\Rightarrow 2k^2 - 12k + 10 = 0 \Rightarrow k^2 - 6k + 5 = 0$

$\Rightarrow (k-5)(k-1) = 0 \Rightarrow k = 1, 5$ [1 Mark]

23. Since, the coordinates of given triangle are A (1, 3), B (–1, 0) and C (4, 0).

So, the area of triangle ABC [1 Mark]

$= \frac{1}{2}[1(0-0)+(-1)(0-3)+4(3-0)]$

$= \frac{1}{2}[3+12] = \frac{15}{2} = 7.5$ sq. units. [1 Mark]

OR

Given that

Distance between A(–3, –14) and B(a, –5), AB = 9

$\therefore$ using distance formula

$\sqrt{(a+3)^2+(-5+14)^2} = 9$ [½ Mark]

$\Rightarrow \sqrt{(a+3)^2+(9)^2} = 9$ [½ Mark]

On squaring both the sides, $(a+3)^2 + 81 = 81$

$\Rightarrow (a+3)^2 = 0 \Rightarrow a = -3$ [1 Mark]

Hence, the required value of a is –3.

24.

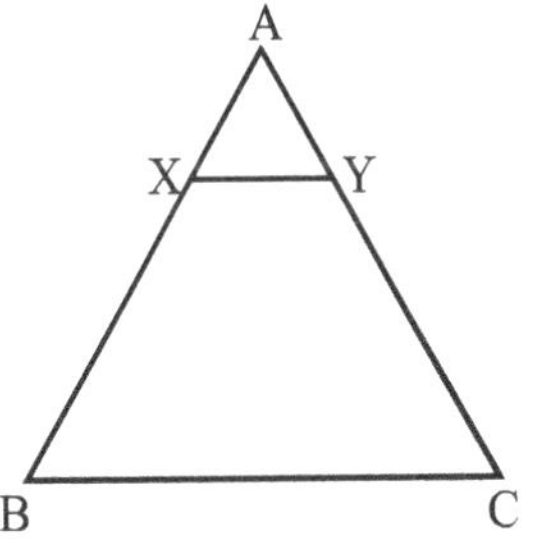

$\frac{AX}{XB} = \frac{3}{4}$, $AY = 5$, $YC = 9$ (Given) [1 Mark]

$\frac{AX}{XB} = \frac{3}{4}$ and $\frac{AY}{YC} = \frac{5}{9}$

$\frac{AX}{XB} \neq \frac{AY}{YC}$ (By B.P.T.)

Hence XY is not parallel to BC. [1 Mark]

OR

Consider ΔABC be an equilateral triangle of side 24 cm and AD is altitude which is also a perpendicular bisector of side BC.

Hence $BD = \frac{BC}{2} = 12$ cm

$AB = 24$ cm [1 Mark]

$\therefore$ $AD = \sqrt{AB^2 - BD^2}$

$AD = \sqrt{(24)^2 - (12)^2}$

$AD = \sqrt{576 - 144}$

$AD = \sqrt{432}$

$\therefore$ $AD = 12\sqrt{3}$ cm [1 Mark]

25. Since, the difference between the circumference and the radius of a circle is 37 cm.

So, $2\pi r - r = 37$

$r\left(\frac{44}{7} - 1\right) = 37$

$r \times \frac{37}{7} = 37$

$r = 7$ cm. [1 Mark]

Therefore, circumference of the circle $= 2\pi r$

$= 2 \times \frac{22}{7} \times 7 = 44$ cm^2

[1 Mark]

26. Suppose the sides of given two squares are a and b.
As, the sum of the areas of two squares is 400 cm^2.
So, $a^2 + b^2 = 400$ ...(i)
Now, the difference of their perimeters is 16 cm.
Therefore,
$4a - 4b = 16$ ...(ii)
$\therefore \quad a - b = 4$ ... (iii)
Putting a = b + 4 in the equation (i), we get,
$(b+4)^2 + b^2 = 400$ [1 Mark]
$b^2 + 16 + 8b + b^2 = 400$
$2b^2 + 8b - 384 = 0$
$b^2 + 4b - 192 = 0$
$b^2 + 16b - 12b - 192 = 0$
$b(b+16) - 12(b+16) = 0$
$(b-12)(b+16) = 0$ [1 Mark]
$b = 12$ cm [$\because$ b cannot be negative]
From equation (iii),
$a = 4 + b$
$= 4 + 12$
$= 16$ cm [1 Mark]
Hence, the sides of two squares are 12 cm and 16 cm.

OR

$3x + 2y - 7 = 0$ ... (i)
$4x + y - 6 = 0$ ... (ii)
From (ii), $y = 6 - 4x$
Value of y put in eqn. (i)
$3x + 2y - 7 = 0$
$\Rightarrow \quad 3x + 2(6-4x) - 7 = 0$
$\Rightarrow \quad 3x + 12 - 8x - 7 = 0$
$\Rightarrow \quad 5x = 5$
$\therefore \quad x = 1$ [2 Marks]
Substitute the value of x in eq(ii) to get value of y,
$4x + y - 6 = 0$
$\Rightarrow \quad 4(1) + y - 6 = 0$
$\Rightarrow \quad 4 + y - 6 = 0$
$\Rightarrow \quad y - 2 = 0$
$\therefore \quad y = 2$ [1 Mark]
Hence, values of x and y are 1 and 2.

27. Since DE || BC
$\therefore \quad \frac{AD}{AB} = \frac{AE}{EC}$ (By B.P.T.)
$\Rightarrow \quad \frac{3}{4} = \frac{6}{EC}$ [2 Marks]
$\therefore \quad EC = 8$ cm [1 Mark]

28. $\frac{5\cos^2 60° + 4\cos^2 30° - \tan^2 45°}{\sin^2 30° + \cos^2 60°}$

$= \frac{5\left(\frac{1}{2}\right)^2 + 4\left(\frac{\sqrt{3}}{2}\right)^2 - (1)^2}{\left(\frac{1}{2}\right)^2 + \left(\frac{1}{2}\right)^2}$ [2 Marks]

$= \frac{\frac{5}{4} + 3 - 1}{\frac{1}{4} + \frac{1}{4}} = \frac{\frac{5}{4} + 2}{\frac{1}{2}} = \frac{\frac{13}{4}}{\frac{1}{2}} = \frac{13}{2}$ [1 Mark]

29.

x_i	f_i	$x_i f_i$
3	10	30
9	p	$9p$
15	4	60
21	7	147
27	q	$27q$
33	4	132
39	1	39
Total	$\Sigma f_i = 26 + p + q$	$\Sigma x_i f_i = 408 + 9p + 27q$

Given $\Sigma fi = 40$, [1 Mark]
$\Rightarrow 26 + p + q = 40$
$\Rightarrow p + q = 14$

$\therefore$ Mean, $\bar{x} = \frac{\Sigma x_i f_i}{\Sigma f_i} \Rightarrow 14.7 = \frac{408 + 9p + 27q}{40}$

$\Rightarrow 588 = 408 + 9p + 27q \Rightarrow p + 3q = 20$
Subtracting eq.(i) from eq. (ii), $2q = 6$
$\Rightarrow q = 3$ [1 Mark]
Putting this value of q in eq. (i),
$p = 14 - q = 14 - 3 = 11$ [1 Mark]
$\therefore p = 11, q = 3$

OR

Here, maximum frequency = 95, so Modal class = 11–13
$l = 11, f_1 = 95, f_0 = 41, f_2 = 36, h = 2$ [1 Mark]

Mode $= l + \left(\frac{f_1 - f_0}{2f_1 - f_0 - f_2}\right) \times h$

$= 11 + \left(\frac{95 - 41}{190 - 41 - 36}\right) \times 2 = 11 + \frac{54}{113} \times 2$

$\therefore$ Mode $= 11 + 0.95 = 11.95$ [1 Mark]
Now, let us calculate Mean :

Age	x_i	f_i	$f_i x_i$
5–7	6	67	402
7–9	8	33	264
9–11	12	41	410
11–13	14	95	1140
13–15	16	36	504
15–17	18	13	208
17–19	5	15	270
		$\Sigma f_i = 300$	$\Sigma f_i x_i = 3{,}198$

Mean $= \frac{3198}{300} = 10.66$ [1 Mark]

30. $\tan^2 30° \sin 30° + \cos 60° \sin^2 90° \tan^2 60° - 2\tan 45° \cos^2 0° \sin 90°$

$= \frac{1}{3} \times \frac{1}{2} + \frac{1}{2} \times 1 \times 3 \times -2 \times 1 \times 1 \times 1 \;=\; \frac{1}{6} + \frac{3}{2} - 2 = -\frac{1}{3}$

[3 Marks]

31.

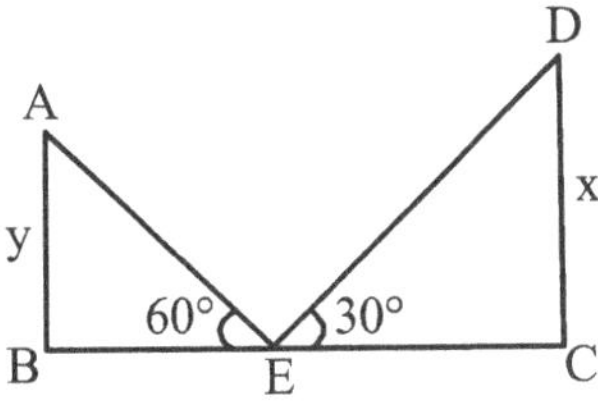

Given : BE = EC [1 Mark]

In ΔABE, $\tan 60° = \frac{y}{BE}$

$\Rightarrow \sqrt{3}BE = y$ ...(i)

In ΔDCE, $\tan 30° = \frac{x}{EC}$ [1 Mark]

$\Rightarrow \frac{1}{\sqrt{3}} = \frac{x}{BE}$

$\Rightarrow \frac{BE}{\sqrt{3}} = x$ ...(ii)

From (i) and (ii),

$x : y = \frac{1}{\sqrt{3}} : \sqrt{3} \Rightarrow x : y = 1 : 3$ [1 Mark]

32. $\frac{1}{x+1} + \frac{2}{x+2} = \frac{4}{x+4}, x \neq -1, -2, -4$

$\Rightarrow \frac{(x+2)+2(x+1)}{(x+1)(x+2)} = \frac{4}{x+4}$ [1½ Marks]

$\Rightarrow \frac{3x+4}{(x+1)(x+2)} = \frac{4}{x+4}$

$\Rightarrow (3x+4)(x+4) = 4(x+1)(x+2)$

$\Rightarrow 3x^2 + 16x + 16 = 4x^2 + 12x + 8 \Rightarrow x^2 - 4x - 8 = 0$

$x = \frac{-(-4) \pm \sqrt{(-4)^2 - 4 \times 1 \times (-8)}}{2}$ [1½ Marks]

[By quadratic formula]

$\Rightarrow x = \frac{4 \pm \sqrt{48}}{2} \Rightarrow x = \frac{4 \pm 4\sqrt{3}}{2} x = 2 \pm 2\sqrt{3}$ [1 Mark]

OR

Given : Speed of the boat in still water = 24 km/h

Let the speed of the stream be x km/h.

Now, speed of the boat upstream = (24 – x) km/h

and, speed of the boat downstream = (24 + x) km/h

Time taken in the upstream journey – Time taken in the downstream journey = 1 h

$\Rightarrow \frac{32}{(24-x)} - \frac{32}{(24+x)} = 1$ [1½ Marks]

$\Rightarrow \frac{32(24+x-24+x)}{(24-x)(24+x)} = 1 \Rightarrow \frac{64x}{576-x^2} = 1$ [2 Marks]

$\Rightarrow x^2 + 64x - 576 = 0 \Rightarrow x^2 + 72x - 8x - 576 = 0$

$\Rightarrow x(x+72) - 8(x+72) = 0 \Rightarrow (x-8)(x+72) = 0$

$\Rightarrow x = 8$ or $x = -72$ [1 ½ Marks]

[$x \neq -72$ as the speed cannot be negative]

So, the speed of the stream is 8 km/h.

33. According to the question,

A.P. = 4, 8, 12, ... 48. [1 Mark]

First term of A.P. = a = 4

Common difference of A.P. = d = 4

$a_n = 48 \therefore a + (n-1)d = 48$

$4 + (n-1)4 = 48$

$n = 12$ [2 Marks]

$S_{12} = \frac{12}{2}[4 + 48] = 12 \times 26 = 312$ [2 Marks]

Total 312 trees were planted by the students.

The value of planting trees is to reduce air pollution and increase the quantity of oxygen in air and reduces the soil erosion.

34. Given that :

$PR = PQ \Rightarrow \angle PRQ = \angle PQR = \frac{(180-30)°}{2} = 75°$ [1 Mark]

Now, SR || QP and QR is a transversal $\Rightarrow \angle SRQ = 75°$

$\therefore \angle ORQ = \angle RQO = 90° - 75° = 15°$ [2 Marks]

$\therefore \angle QOR = (180 - 2 \times 15)° = 150° \Rightarrow \angle QSR = 75°$

$\angle RQS = 180° - (\angle SRQ + \angle SQR) = 30°$ [2 Marks]

35. Volume of tank = $\pi r^2 h = \frac{22}{7} \times (1)^2 \times 3.5 = 11 \text{ m}^3$

[2 Marks]

So, rainfall $= \frac{11}{22 \times 20} \text{m} = \frac{11 \times 100}{22 \times 20} \text{cm} = 2.5 \text{ cm}$

[3 Marks]

Water conservation is required due to shortage of fresh water.

OR

Volume of earth taken out after digging the well $= \pi r^2 h$

$= \left(\frac{22}{7} \times 2 \times 2 \times 14\right) \text{cu.m} = 176 \text{ cu.m}$ ....(i) [2 Marks]

[where r = 2 and h = 14]

Let x be the width of embankment formed

Volume of embankment

$= \frac{22}{7}\left[(2+x)^2 - (2)^2\right] \times \frac{40}{100} = 176 \Rightarrow x^2 + 4x - 140 = 0$

$\Rightarrow (x + 14)(x - 10) = 0 \Rightarrow x = 10$

$x \neq -14$, ∵ Length can't be negative [3 Marks]

∴ Width of embankment = 10 m

36. **(i)** Parabola. [1 Mark]

(ii) $a < 0$, Graphs look like ⌒ open downwards

[1 Mark]

(iii) According to graph, there are two zeros one at (–2) and 2nd at 4, –2, 4 [2 Marks]

OR

(–2, 4)

37. **(i)** Length of diagonal $= \sqrt{3l^2} = 6\sqrt{3}$ [1 Mark]

(ii) Volume of cube = $(\text{side})^3$ = 343 cm^3 [1 Mark]

(iii) Curved surface area of hemisphere = $2\pi r^2 = 308 \text{ cm}^2$

[2 Marks]

OR

$6.3^2 = 54$ [2 Marks]

38. **(i)** P(king of red colour) $= \frac{2}{52} = \frac{1}{26}$ [1 Mark]

(ii) P(getting a face card) $= \frac{12}{52} = \frac{3}{13}$ [1 Mark]

(iii) P(getting a jack of hearts) $= \frac{1}{52}$ [2 Marks]

OR

There are 13 spactes of the cards hence porobality is P(S) $= \frac{1}{4}$ [2 Marks]

SAMPLE PAPER-7

1. **(c)** We have, $p(x) = x^2 - 10x - 75 = x^2 - 15x + 5x - 75$
$= x(x-15) + 5(x-15) = (x-15)(x+5)$
$\therefore\ p(x) = (x-15)(x+5)$
So, $p(x) = 0$ when $x = 15$ or $x = -5$. Therefore required zeroes are 15 and –5.

2. **(d)** Let the roots be α and $\frac{1}{\alpha}$. Then, product of roots
$= \left(\alpha \times \frac{1}{\alpha}\right) = 1.$
So, $\frac{k}{5} = 1 \Rightarrow k = 5.$

3. **(c)** As the point P (x, y) lies on the line joining the points A (a, 0) and B (0, b), the points A, B and P are collinear
$\Rightarrow\ a(b-y) + 0(y-0) + x(0-b) = 0$
$\Rightarrow\ ab - ay - bx = 0 \Rightarrow bx + ay = ab$
$\Rightarrow\ \frac{x}{a} + \frac{y}{b} = 1$

4. **(c)** Hint: [at $\theta = 90°$]

5. **(a)** The pair of linear equations are
$x + 2y - 5 = 0$ and
$3x + 12y - 10 = 0$
Here, $a_1 = 1, b_1 = 2, c_1 = -5$ and $a_2 = 3, b_2 = 12,$
$c_2 = -10$. Now, $\frac{a_1}{a_2} = \frac{1}{3}, \frac{b_1}{b_2} = \frac{2}{12} = \frac{1}{6}.$
As $\frac{a_1}{a_2} \neq \frac{b_1}{b_2}$
So, pair of equations has a unique solution.

6. **(a)** Required number = H.C.F. {(70 – 5), (125 – 8)}
= H.C.F. (65, 117) = 13.

7. **(a)** Statement given in option (a) is false.

8. **(a)** $P(x, 0) = \left(\frac{5-1}{2}, 0\right) = (2, 0)$
[$\because$ A and B both lies on x-axis]
Three or more points lies in same line are called collinear.

9. **(b)** In ΔKPN and ΔKLM, we have
$\angle KNP = \angle KML = 46°$
$\angle K = \angle K$ (Common)
$\therefore\ \Delta KNP \sim \Delta KML$ (By AA criterion of similarity)
$\Rightarrow \frac{KN}{KM} = \frac{NP}{ML} \Rightarrow \frac{c}{b+c} = \frac{x}{a}$

10. **(d)** We redraw the figure.

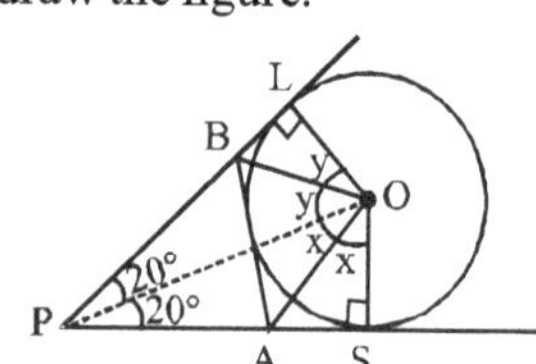

In ΔOPS, using Pythagoras theorem, $\angle POS = 70°$
and In ΔPOL, $\angle POL = 70°$
From figure, $2x + 2y = 140°$
$\angle BOA = x + y = 70°$

11. **(d)** Hint: Area of sector $= \frac{1}{2} r^2 \theta$

12. **(c)** Mean $= \frac{2+9+x+6+2x+3+5+10+5}{7} = 7$
$3x + 40 = 49 \Rightarrow x = 3$
$x + 6 = 9 \Rightarrow 2x + 3 = 9$
Data (2, 9, 9, 9, 5, 10, 5) and Mode = 9

13. **(d)** Let the diameter of the sphere be d units and the edge of the cube be a units, then
$4\pi\left(\frac{d}{2}\right)^2 = 6a^2 \Rightarrow \frac{d^2}{a^2} = \frac{6}{\pi} \Rightarrow \frac{d}{a} = \frac{\sqrt{6}}{\sqrt{\pi}}.$

14. **(b)** Length of arc $= \frac{114}{369} \pi\, 10 = 4\pi$

15. **(b)** The sum of the two numbers lies between 2 and 12.
So, the primes are 2, 3, 5, 7, 11.
No. of ways for getting 2 = (1, 1) = 1
No. of ways of getting 3 = (1, 2), (2, 1) = 2
No. of ways of getting 5
= (1, 4), (4, 1), (2, 3), (3, 2) = 4
No. of ways of getting 7
= (1, 6), (6, 1), (2, 5), (5, 2), (3, 4), (4, 3) = 6
No. of ways of getting 11 = (5, 6), (6, 5) = 2
No. of favourable ways = 1 + 2 + 4 + 6 + 2 = 15
No. of exhaustive ways = 6 × 6 = 36
$\therefore$ Probability of getting the sum as a prime
$= \frac{15}{36} = \frac{5}{12}$

16. **(b)**

C.I.	x_i	f_i	f_ix_i
0 – 10	5	8	40
10 – 20	15	12	180
20 – 30	25	10	250
30 – 40	35	11	385
40 – 50	45	9	405
		50	1260

We have $\bar{x} = \frac{\Sigma fx}{\Sigma f} = \frac{1260}{50} = 25.2$

17. (c) Given that, $p = ab^2 = a \times b \times b$
and $q = a^3b = a \times a \times a \times b$
$\therefore$ LCM (p, q) = LCM $(ab^2, a^3b) = a \times b \times b \times a \times a = a^3b^2$

18. **(a)** Suppose BC = 6 m be the height of the pole and AB = $2\sqrt{3}$ m be the length of the shadow on the ground. Suppose the sun's makes an angle θ on the ground.

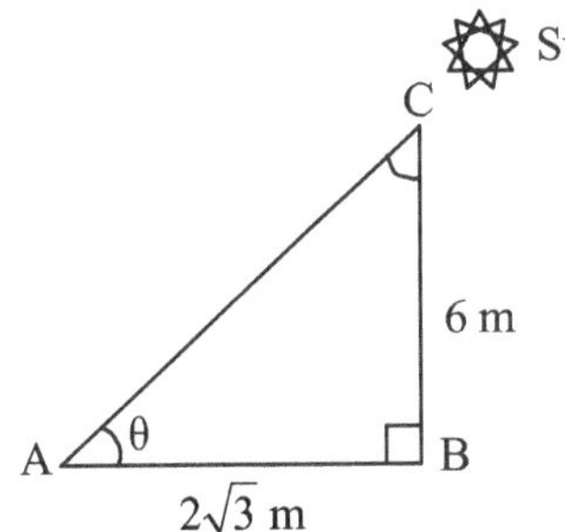

Now, in ΔBAC

$$\tan\theta = \frac{BC}{AB}$$

$$\Rightarrow \quad \tan\theta = \frac{6}{2\sqrt{3}} = \sqrt{3}$$

$$\Rightarrow \quad \tan\theta = \tan 60^\circ$$

$$\therefore \quad \theta = 60^\circ$$

So, sun's elevation is 60°.

19. **(a)** Reason is clearly true.

Again, $34.12345 = \frac{3412345}{100000} = \frac{682469}{20000} = \frac{682469}{2^5 \times 5^4}$

Its denominator is of the form $2^m \times 5^n$, where $m = 5, n = 4$ are non-negative integers

∴ Assertion is true. Since, reason gives assertion

∴ (a) holds.

20. **(a)** Both Assertion and Reason are correct and Reason is the correct explanation of the assertion.

greatest side = $\sqrt{(3)^2 + (4)^2} = 5$ units.

21. $ax + by = 1$ ...(i)

$bx + ay = \frac{2ab}{a^2 + b^2}$ ...(ii)

On adding (i) and (ii), we get

$$(a+b)x + (a+b)y = 1 + \frac{2ab}{a^2+b^2}$$

$$\Rightarrow (a+b)(x+y) = \frac{(a+b)^2}{a^2+b^2}$$

$$\Rightarrow x + y = \frac{a+b}{a^2+b^2} \quad ...(iii)$$ [½ Mark]

Subtracting (ii) from (i)

$$(a-b)x + (b-a)y = 1 - \frac{2ab}{a^2+b^2}$$

$$\Rightarrow (a-b)(x-y) = \frac{(a-b)^2}{a^2+b^2}$$

$$\Rightarrow x - y = \frac{a-b}{a^2+b^2} \quad ...(iv)$$ [1 Mark]

Adding (iii) and (iv),

$$2x = \frac{a+b}{a^2+b^2} + \frac{a-b}{a^2+b^2} = \frac{2a}{a^2+b^2} \Rightarrow x = \frac{a}{a^2+b^2}$$

Subtracting (iv) from (iii)

$$2y = \frac{a+b}{a^2+b^2} - \frac{a-b}{a^2+b^2} = \frac{2b}{a^2+b^2} \Rightarrow y = \frac{b}{a^2+b^2}$$

[½ Mark]

Therefore, the solution is : $x = \frac{a}{a^2+b^2}$, $y = \frac{b}{a^2+b^2}$

22. LHS = $\tan^2\theta + \cot^2\theta + 2 = (\tan^2\theta + 1) + (\cot^2\theta + 1)$ [½ Mark]

$= \sec^2\theta + \operatorname{cosec}^2\theta$

[∵ $\tan^2\theta + 1 = \sec^2\theta$ and $1 + \cot^2\theta = \operatorname{cosec}^2\theta$]

$= \frac{1}{\cos^2\theta} + \frac{1}{\sin^2\theta} = \frac{\sin^2\theta + \cos^2\theta}{\sin^2\theta\cos^2\theta}$ [1 Mark]

$= \frac{1}{\sin^2\theta\cos^2\theta} = \operatorname{cosec}^2\theta \sec^2\theta$ [½ Mark]

= RHS (Hence Proved).

OR

$$\frac{\cos\theta - \sin\theta}{\cos\theta + \sin\theta} = \frac{1-\sqrt{3}}{1+\sqrt{3}}$$

Dividing Nr. and Dr. in L.H.S. by cosθ

$\frac{1 - \tan\theta}{1 + \tan\theta} = \frac{1-\sqrt{3}}{1+\sqrt{3}}$ [1 Mark]

By comparison, we get $\tan\theta = \sqrt{3}$ [1 Mark]

23. $BA \parallel PQ$

$\Rightarrow$ $BR \parallel PQ$

and $PR \parallel CA$

$\Rightarrow$ $PR \parallel CQ$

In ΔBRD, $BR \parallel PQ$

$\Rightarrow$ $\frac{BD}{PD} = \frac{RD}{QD}$ (corr. of Thales) ...(1)

In ΔRPD, $PR \parallel CQ$ [1 Mark]

$\Rightarrow$ $\frac{RD}{QD} = \frac{PD}{CD}$ (corr. of Thales) ...(2)

From (1) and (2),

$$\frac{BD}{PD} = \frac{PD}{CD}$$

$\Rightarrow$ $PD^2 = BD \times CD$

∴ $BD \times CD = 144$ cm. [1 Mark]

24. CQ = CP = 11

[∵ length of tangents from C to the circle are equal]

∴ CQ = 11cm [1 Mark]

But BC = 7 cm ∴ 7 + BQ = 11 [∵ CQ = BC + BQ]

∴ BQ = 11 − 7 = 4

Since BR = BQ = 4

[∵ length of tangents from B to the circle are equal]

Thus BR = 4 cm. [1 Mark]

25. Let the radius of inner circle be r cm.
Then, its circumference = $(2\pi r)$ cm.

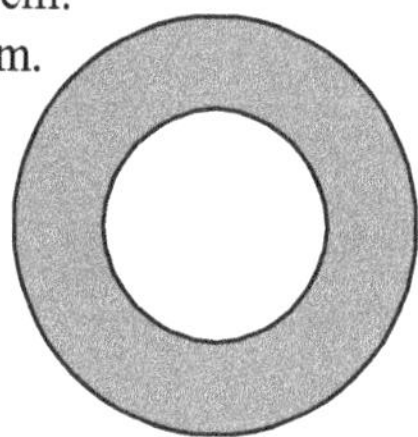

$\therefore 2\pi r = 88 \Rightarrow 2 \times \frac{22}{7} \times r = 88$

$\Rightarrow r = \left(88 \times \frac{7}{44}\right) = 14\text{cm}.$

$\therefore$ Radius of the inner circle is, r = 14 cm. [1 Mark]

Let the radius of the outer circle be R cm.
Then, area of the ring = $(\pi R^2 - \pi r^2)$ cm².

$= \left(\frac{22}{7}R^2 - 616\right) \text{cm}^2$

$\therefore \frac{22}{7}R^2 - 616 = 346.5 \Rightarrow \frac{22}{7}R^2 = 962.5$

$\Rightarrow R^2 = \left(962.5 \times \frac{7}{22}\right) = 306.25 \Rightarrow R = \sqrt{306.25} = 17.5\text{cm}$

[1 Mark]

26. $(2m-1)x + 3y - 5 = 0$ ...(i)
On comparing with $a_1x + b_1y + c_1 = 0$, we get :
$a_1 = 2m - 1, b_1 = 3, c_1 = -5$
$3x + (n-1)y - 2 = 0$ ...(ii)
On comparing with $a_2x + b_2y + c_2 = 0$, we get :
$a_2 = 3, b_2 = n - 1, c_2 = -2$ [1 Mark]
For a pair of linear equations to have infinite number of solutions

$\frac{a_1}{a_2} = \frac{b_1}{b_2} = \frac{c_1}{c_2} \Rightarrow \frac{2m-1}{3} = \frac{3}{n-1} = \frac{5}{2}$ [1 Mark]

$\Rightarrow 2(2m-1) = 15$ and $5(n-1) = 6 \Rightarrow m = \frac{17}{4}, n = \frac{11}{5}$

[1 Mark]

27. If α and β are the zeroes of the quadratic polynomial $x^2 + 4x + 3$ then, $\alpha + \beta = -4$ and $\alpha\beta = 3$

Sum of zeroes $= 1 + \frac{\beta}{\alpha} + 1 + \frac{\alpha}{\beta} = \frac{\alpha\beta + \beta^2 + \alpha\beta + \alpha^2}{\alpha\beta}$

$= \frac{\alpha^2 + \beta^2 + 2\alpha\beta}{\alpha\beta} = \frac{(\alpha+\beta)^2}{\alpha\beta} = \frac{(-4)^2}{3} = \frac{16}{3}$ [1 Mark]

Product of zeroes $= \left(1 + \frac{\beta}{\alpha}\right)\left(1 + \frac{\alpha}{\beta}\right) = 1 + \frac{\alpha}{\beta} + \frac{\beta}{\alpha} + \frac{\alpha\beta}{\alpha\beta}$

$= \frac{\alpha^2 + \beta^2 + 2\alpha\beta}{\alpha\beta} = \frac{(\alpha+\beta)^2}{\alpha\beta} = \frac{(-4)^2}{3} = \frac{16}{3}$ [1 Mark]

So, required polynomial
$= x^2 -$ (Sum of the zeroes) x + Product of the zeroes

$= x^2 - \left(\frac{16}{3}\right)x + \frac{16}{3} = \frac{1}{3}(3x^2 - 16x + 16)$ [1 Mark]

28. $\frac{\cos^2\theta - 3\cos\theta + 2}{\sin^2\theta} = 1 \Rightarrow \cos^2\theta - 3\cos\theta + 2 = \sin^2\theta$

[½ Mark]

$\Rightarrow \cos^2\theta - 3\cos\theta + 2 = 1 - \cos^2\theta$

$\Rightarrow 2\cos^2\theta - 3\cos\theta + 1 = 0$ [½ Mark]

$\Rightarrow 2\cos^2\theta - 2\cos\theta - \cos\theta + 1 = 0$

$\Rightarrow 2\cos\theta(\cos\theta - 1) - 1(\cos\theta - 1) = 0$ [½ Mark]

$\Rightarrow (2\cos\theta - 1)(\cos\theta - 1) = 0$ [½ Mark]

Either $2\cos\theta - 1 = 0 \Rightarrow 2\cos\theta = 1 \Rightarrow \cos\theta = ½$
$\Rightarrow \cos\theta = \cos 60° \Rightarrow \theta = 60°$ or $\cos\theta - 1 = 0$
or $\cos\theta = 1 = \cos 0°$
$\theta = 0°$ (impossible)
$\therefore \theta = 60°$ [1 Mark]

29. Join OT. Let it intersect PQ at the point R. Then Δ TPQ is isosceles triangle and TO is the angle bisector of $\angle$ PTQ. So, OT $\perp$ PQ therefore, OT bisects PQ which gives PR = RQ = 4 cm.

Also, OR $= \sqrt{OP^2 - PR^2} = \sqrt{5^2 - 4^2}$ cm = 3 cm.

[1 Mark]

Now, $\angle TPR + \angle RPO = 90° = \angle TPR + \angle PTR$

[1 Mark]

So, $\angle RPO = \angle PTR$
Therefore, right triangle TRP is similar to the right triangle PRO (by AA similarity).

This gives $\frac{TP}{PO} = \frac{RP}{RO}$ i.e., $\frac{TP}{5} = \frac{4}{3}$ or $TP = \frac{20}{3}$ cm.
[1 Mark]

30. Total number of events = 52
In a pack of 52 playing cards, there are 2 red queens and 2 black queens, respectively. [1 Mark]
$\therefore$ Number of cards that are neither red nor queen $= 52 - (26 + 2) = 24$ [1 Mark]
Now, favourable number of events = 24

So, required probability $= \frac{24}{52} = \frac{6}{13}$ [1 Mark]

OR

P (Product = 6) = P [(1, 6), (2, 3), (3, 2), (6, 1)]

[1½ Marks]

Probability $= \frac{4}{6^2} = \frac{4}{36} = \frac{1}{9}$ [1½ Marks]

Hence, the probability that the product of the two numbers on the top of the dice is 6, will be $\frac{1}{9}$.

31. First number divisible by 8 between 200 and 500 is 208.
If form an A.P. = 208, 216, 224, ..., 496.
Here, $a_n = 496, a = 208, d = 8$ [1 Mark]
$a_n = a + (n-1)d$
$496 = 208 + (n-1)8$
$(n-1)8 = 496 - 208$

$(n-1) = \frac{288}{8}$ [1 Mark]

$n - 1 = 36$
$n = 37$ [1 Mark]

OR

LCM of 18, 24 and 36 is 72.

$$72\overline{)999999}(13888$$
$$\underline{999936}$$
$$63$$
[1 Mark]

$\therefore$ Required number = 9,99,936. [2 Marks]

32. $\because \quad 4\sqrt{3}x^2 + 5x - 2\sqrt{3} = 0$

$4\sqrt{3}x^2 + 8x - 3x - 2\sqrt{3} = 0$ [1 Mark]

$4x(\sqrt{3}x + 2) - \sqrt{3}(\sqrt{3}x + 2) = 0$

$(\sqrt{3}x + 2)(4x - \sqrt{3}) = 0$ [1½ Marks]

So, $\sqrt{3}x + 2 = 0$ or $4x - \sqrt{3} = 0$

Therefore, $x = -\dfrac{2\sqrt{3}}{3}, \dfrac{\sqrt{3}}{4}$ [1½ Marks]

Hence, the values of x are $\dfrac{-2\sqrt{3}}{3}$ and $\dfrac{\sqrt{3}}{4}$. [1 Mark]

33. Given: ΔABC is right-angled at A. $DEFG$ is a square [½ Mark]

To prove: $DE^2 = BD \times EC$.

Proof : In ΔAGF and ΔDBG

$\angle GAF = \angle BDG = 90°$

$\angle AGF = \angle DBG$ (corres. angles)

$\therefore \quad \Delta AGF \sim \Delta DBG$ ... (i) (AA similarity) [1½ Marks]

In ΔAGF and ΔEFC,

$\angle GAF = \angle CEF = 90°$

$\angle AFG = \angle FCE$ (corres. angles)

$\therefore \quad \Delta AFG \sim \Delta EFC$ ... (ii) (AA similarity)

From (i) and (ii) [1½ Marks]

$\Delta DBG \sim \Delta EFC$

$\therefore \quad \dfrac{DB}{EF} = \dfrac{DG}{EC}$, But $EF = DG = DE$ (sides of a square)

$\therefore \quad \dfrac{DB}{DE} = \dfrac{DE}{EC} \quad \therefore \quad DE^2 = DB \times EC$ [1½ Marks]

OR

In ΔAEB, $\angle AEB = 90°$

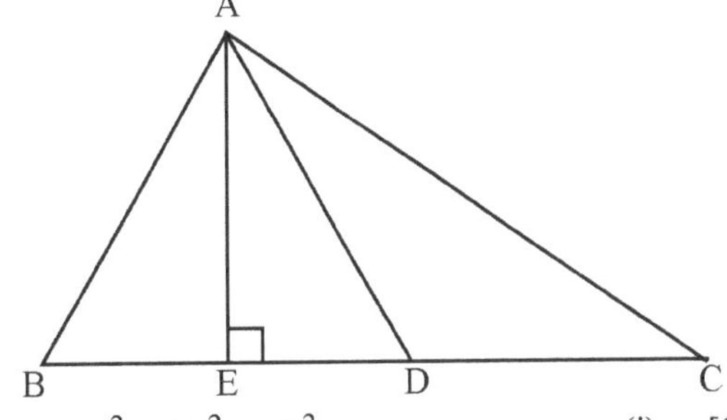

$\therefore AB^2 = AE^2 + BE^2$ ... (i) [1 Mark]

In ΔAED, $\angle AED = 90°$.

$\therefore AD^2 = (AE^2 + DE^2)$

$\Rightarrow AE^2 = (AD^2 - DE^2)$ [½ Mark]

$\therefore AB^2 = (AD^2 - DE^2) + BE^2$ [using (i)] [1 Mark]

$= (AD^2 - DE^2) + (BD - DE)^2$ [½ Mark]

$= (AD^2 - DE^2) + \left(\dfrac{1}{2}BC - DE\right)^2$ [1 Mark]

$= AD^2 + \dfrac{1}{4}BC^2 - BC \cdot DE$ [1 Mark]

34. We know that $\ell = \sqrt{r^2 + h^2}$, $v = \dfrac{1}{3}\pi r^2 h$, $c = \pi r \ell$ [1½ Marks]

LHS. $= 3\pi v h^3 - c^2h^2 + 9v^2$

$= 3\pi\left(\dfrac{1}{3}\pi r^2 h\right)h^3 - (\pi r \ell)^2 h^2 + 9\left(\dfrac{1}{3}\pi r^2 h\right)^2$ [1 Mark]

$= 3\pi\left(\dfrac{1}{3}\pi r^2 h\right)h^3 - \pi^2 r^2 (r^2 + h^2) \times h^2 + 9 \times \dfrac{1}{9}\pi^2 r^4 h^2$

$(\because \ell = \sqrt{h^2 + r^2})$ [1½ Marks]

$= \pi^2 r^2 h^4 - \pi^2 r^4 h^2 - \pi^2 r^2 h^4 + \pi^2 r^4 h^2 = 0 =$ **RHS** [1 Mark]

35.

[2 Marks]

[1 Mark]

Mean $= A + \dfrac{\Sigma f_i d_i}{\Sigma f_i} = 14 + \dfrac{252}{66} = 14 + 3.818 =$ **17.818** [2 Marks]

OR

Class Interval	Mid - value (x_i)	f_i	$u_i = (x_i - A)/h$	f_iu_i
0 – 80	40	22	–2	–44
80 – 160	120	35	–1	–35
160 – 240	200 (*A*)	44	0	0
240 – 320	280	25	1	25
320 – 400	360	24	2	48
Total		$\Sigma f_i = 150$		$\Sigma f_iu_i = -6$

Mean $(\bar{x}) = A + \frac{\Sigma f_iu_i}{\Sigma f_i} \times h = 200 + \left(\frac{-6}{150}\right) \times 80$

$= 200 - \frac{2 \times 8}{5} = 200 - \frac{16}{5} = \frac{1000 - 16}{5} = \frac{984}{5} = 196.8$

Remarks : (i) The mean obtained by all the there methods is the same.

(ii) The assumed mean method and step-deviation method are just simplified forms of the direct method.

(iii) If x_i and f_i are sufficiently small, then the direct method is an appropriate choice.

(iv) If x_i and f_i are numerically large numbers, then we can go for the assumed mean method or step-deviation method.

(v) If the class sizes are unequal, and x_i are large numberically, then we can go for the step-deviation method.

36. (i) $a_n = 51 - (n-1)2 = 31 \Rightarrow n = 11$ [1 Mark]

(ii) $a_n = 51 (n-1) 2 = 27 \Rightarrow n = 13$ [1 Mark]

(iii) $a_{10} = 51 - (10 - 1)2 = 33$ [2 Marks]

OR

$a_{15} = 51 - (15 - 1)2 = 23$ [2 Marks]

37. (i) (2, 25) $\left[\because x = 2, y = \frac{1}{4} \times 100 = 25\right]$ [1 Mark]

(ii) (8, 20) $\left[\because x = 8, y = \frac{1}{5} \times 100 = 20\right]$ [2 Marks]

(iii) $\sqrt{(8-2)^2 + (25-20)^2} = \sqrt{36 + 25} = \sqrt{61}$

OR

$\left(\frac{8+2}{2}, \frac{25+20}{2}\right) = (5, 22.5)$ [2 Marks]

38. (i)

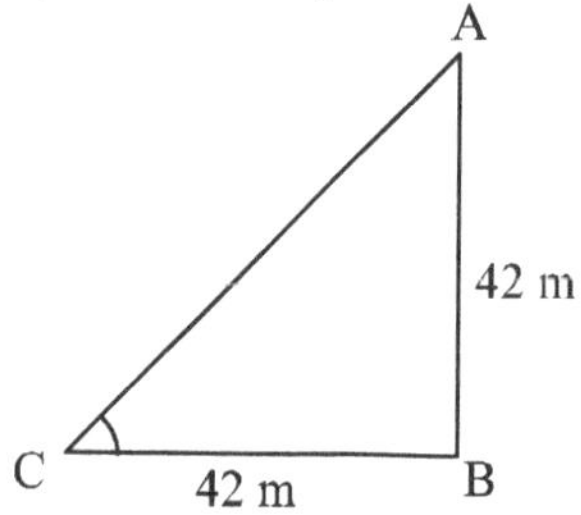

Since h = 42

d = 42

So $\theta = 45°$ [1 Mark]

(ii) $\tan 60° = \frac{42}{x}$

$x = \frac{42}{\sqrt{3}} = \frac{42}{3}\sqrt{3} = 14\sqrt{3} = 24.24$ m [1 Mark]

(iii)

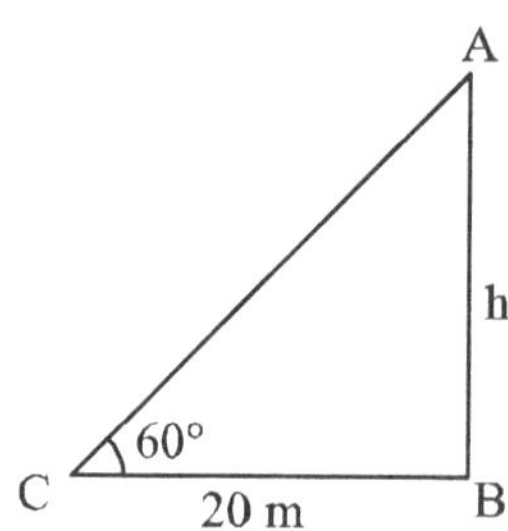

$\tan 60° = \frac{h}{20}$

$h = 20\sqrt{3}$ m [2 Mark]

OR

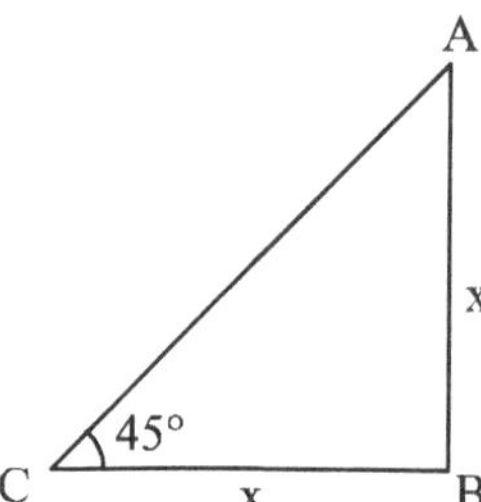

Since ratio of length of a rod: Shadow of rod = 1:1

so Angle = 45° [2 Marks]

SAMPLE PAPER-8

1. (a) When 2^{256} is divided by 17 then, $\frac{2^{256}}{2^4+1}=\frac{(2^4)^{64}}{(2^4+1)}$

By remainder theorem when $f(x)$ is divided by $x+a$ the remainder $=f(-a)$

Here, $f(a)=(2^4)^{64}$ and $x=2^4$ and $a=1$

$\therefore$ Remainder $=f(-1)=(-1)^{64}=1$

2. (a) Substitute $x=3$ in polynomial ax^3+4x^2+3x-4 and x^3-4x+a to obtain remainder and equate.

$a(3)^3+4(3)^2+3(3)-4=(3)^3-4(3)+a \Rightarrow a=-1$

3. (b) Let length and breadth be x cm and y cm respectively.

According to problem,

$2(x+y)=40$ ... (i)

and $\frac{y}{x}=\frac{2}{3}$ ... (ii)

on solving, $x=12, y=8$

$\therefore$ length = 12 cm and breadth = 8cm.

4. (c) Given equation is $x^2-3x+(k-10)=0$.

$\therefore$ Product of roots = $(k-10)$.

So, $k-10=-2 \Rightarrow k=8$.

5. (b) Let the annual increment be ₹ y and initial salary be ₹ x

$\therefore\ x+4y=4500$ ... (i)

and $x+10y=5400$ ... (ii)

Solving eqs. (i) and (ii), we get

$x=3900$ and $y=150$

$\therefore$ Initial salary = ₹ 3900

and increment = ₹ 150

6. (c) $S_n=(a+a_n)$

$\Rightarrow 860=(5+81)$

$n=860\div 43=20$

7. (a) Given that, ΔABC and ΔPQR,

$$\frac{AB}{QR}=\frac{BC}{PR}=\frac{CA}{PQ}$$

Therefore sides of one triangle are proportional to the side of the other triangle, then their corresponding angles are also equal. Hence, by SSS similarity, triangles are similar.

$\Rightarrow\ \Delta CAB \sim \Delta PQR$

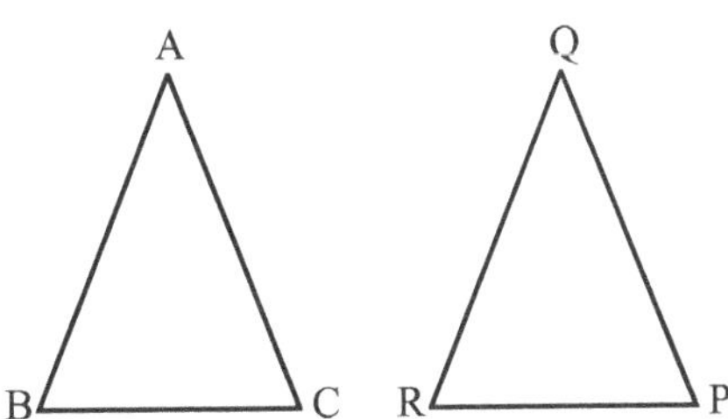

8. (b) Since the equation has two equal roots, D = 0

$\Rightarrow (2mc)^2-4(1+m^2)(c^2-a^2)=0$

$\Rightarrow 4m^2c^2-4c^2+4a^2-4m^2c^2+4m^2a^2=0$

$\Rightarrow -4c^2+4a^2+4m^2a^2=0 \Rightarrow 4c^2=4a^2+4m^2a^2$

$\Rightarrow 4c^2=4a^2(1+m^2) \Rightarrow c^2=a^2(1+m^2)$

9. (c) $t_8=a+7d, t_{12}=a+11d$

According to question, $8t_8=12t_{12}$ (given)

$\Rightarrow 8(a+7d)=12(a+11d)$

$\Rightarrow 8a+56d=12a+132d$

$\Rightarrow 8a-12a+56d-132d=0$

$\Rightarrow -4a-76d=0$

$\Rightarrow a+19d=0$ ...(i)

$\therefore\ t_{20}=a+19d=0$ using (i)

$\therefore\ t_{20}=0$

10. (b) Centroid is $\left(\frac{x_1+x_2+x_3}{3},\frac{y_1+y_2+y_3}{3}\right)$

i.e. $=\left(\frac{3+(-8)+5}{3},\frac{-7+6+10}{3}\right)=\left(\frac{0}{3},\frac{9}{3}\right)=(0,3)$

11. (b)

12. (a) Let h be the length of the pole.

By the given condition $\frac{6}{4}=\frac{h}{50}$

$\Rightarrow h=\frac{6\times 50}{4}=75$m

13. (d) The opposite sides of a quadrilateral circumscribing a circle subtend supplementary angles at the centre of the circle.

$\therefore\ \angle AOB+\angle COD=180°$

$\Rightarrow\ \angle COD=180°-\angle AOB$

$=180°-125°=55°$

14. (c) Join O to P and Q. Join P to R. Draw SP $\perp$ OQ.

Now SP = QR, as they are opposite sides of rectangle PRQS.

OP = 8 cm + 4 cm = 12 cm; OS = 8 cm − 4 cm = 4 cm

In right triangle POS,

$SP=\sqrt{OP^2-OS^2}=\sqrt{12^2-4^2}=8\sqrt{2}$ cm

$\therefore$ QR $=8\sqrt{2}$ cm

15. (b) We have,

Area of square metal plate $=40\times 40=1600$ cm^2

Area of each hole $=\pi r^2=\frac{22}{7}\times\left(\frac{1}{2}\right)^2=\frac{11}{14}$cm^2

$\therefore$ Area of 441 holes $=441\times\frac{11}{14}=346.5$cm^2

Hence, area of the remaining square plate

$=(1600-346.5)=1253.5$ cm^2

16. **(b)** S = {(1, 1), ..., (1, 6), (2, 1), ..., (2, 6), (3, 1), ..., (3, 6), (4, 1), ..., (4, 6), (5, 1), ..., (5, 6), (6, 1), ..., (6, 6)}

n(S) = 36

Let E be the event that both dice show different numbers.

E {(1, 2), (1, 3),...., (1, 6), (2, 1), (2, 3), (2, 4),...., (2, 6), (3, 1), (3, 2), (3, 4), (3, 5), (3, 6), (4, 1), (4, 2), (4, 3), (4, 5), (4, 6), (5, 1), (5, 2), (5, 3), (5, 4), (5, 6), (6, 1), (6, 2), (6, 3), (6, 4), (4, 5)}

n(E) = 30

$$\therefore \quad P(E) = \frac{n(E)}{n(S)} = \frac{30}{36} = \frac{5}{6}$$

17. **(b)** Let x be the upper limit and y be the lower limit.

Since, the mid value of the class is 10.

$$\therefore \frac{x+y}{2} = 10 \quad \Rightarrow \quad x + y = 20 \quad .....(i)$$

and $x - y = 6$ (width of the class = 6) .....(ii)

By solving equations (i) and (ii), we get $y = 7$.

Hence, lower limit of the class is 7.

18. **(c)** Initial number of workers = 120

When 15 male workers are added, then the total number of workers = 120 + 15 = 135

Number of female workers = 90

$$\therefore \quad \text{Probability of female workers} = \frac{90}{135} = \frac{2}{3}$$

19. **(a)** Reason is true. [This is Thale's Theorem]

For Assertion

Since $DE \parallel BC$ $\therefore$ by Thale's Theorem

Figure

$$\frac{AD}{DB} = \frac{AE}{EC} \Rightarrow \frac{DB}{AD} = \frac{EC}{AE}$$

$$\Rightarrow 1 + \frac{DB}{AD} = 1 + \frac{EC}{AE}$$

$$\Rightarrow \frac{AD + DB}{AD} = \frac{AE + EC}{AE}$$

$$\Rightarrow \frac{AB}{AD} = \frac{AC}{AE}$$

$\therefore$ Assertion is true.

Since reason gives Assertion.

20. **(d)** Arranging the terms in ascending order,

0, 5, 11, 19, 21, 27, 30, 36, 42, 50, 52

$$\text{median value} = \left(\frac{11+1}{2}\right)^{th} = 6^{th} \text{ value} = 27$$

21. First number divisible by 8 between 200 and 500 is 208.

It forms an A.P. = 208, 216, 224, ..., 496.

Here, $a_n = 496$, a = 208, d = 8

$a_n = a + (n-1)d \Rightarrow 496 = 208 + (n-1)\,8$ [1 Mark]

$(n-1)8 = 496 - 208$

$$(n-1) = \frac{288}{8} \Rightarrow n - 1 = 36 \quad \Rightarrow \quad n = 37$$ [1 Mark]

OR

Let q be the quotient and r be the remainder when n is divided by 3. [1 Mark]

Therefore, $n = 3q + r$, where r = 0, 1 , 2

$\Rightarrow \quad n = 3q$ or $n = 3q + 1$ or $3q + 2$

Case(i) if $n = 3q$, then n is divisible by 3, $n + 2$ and $n + 4$ are not divisible by 3.

Case (ii) if $n = 3q + 1$ then $n + 2 = 3q + 3$ $= 3(q + 1)$, which is divisible by 3 and $n + 4 = 3q + 5$, which is not divisible by 3.

So, only $(n + 2)$ is divisible by 3.

Case (iii) if $n = 3q + 2$, then $n + 2 = 3q + 4$, which is not divisible by 3 and $(n + 4) = 3q + 6$ $= 3(q + 2)$, which is divisible by 3.

So, only $(n + 4)$ is divisible by 3. [1 Mark]

Hence one and only one out of n, $(n + 2)$, $(x + 4)$ is divisible by 3.

22. **(d)** Since ST is a diameter of the circle with centre O, So $\angle SRT = 90°$. [Angle in a semicircle] [1 Mark]

Now, $\angle PRS + \angle SRT + \angle TRQ = 180°$ [Linear pair]

$\angle PRS + 90° + 30° = 180°$

$\angle PRS = 180° - 120° = 60°$ [1 Mark]

True. As $\angle$ BPA = 90°, $\angle$ PAB = $\angle$ OPA = 60°. Also, OP $\perp$ PT. Therefore, $\angle$ APT = 30° and [1 Mark]

$\angle$ PTA = 60° – 30° = 30°. [1 Mark]

23. **(b)** Let the required ratio be K : 1

$\therefore$ The co–ordinates of the required point on the y–axis is

$$x = \frac{K(-4) + 3(1)}{K+1}; \quad y = \frac{K(2) + 5(1)}{K+1}$$

Since, it lies on y – axis

$\therefore$ Its x–cordinates = 0

$$\therefore \frac{-4K + 3}{K+1} = 0 \Rightarrow -4K + 3 = 0$$

$$\Rightarrow K = \frac{3}{4}$$

$\Rightarrow$ Required ratio = $\frac{3}{4} : 1$ [1 Mark]

$\therefore$ ratio = 3 : 4

24. $\sec^2\theta + \tan^2\theta = \frac{5}{3}$ or $1 + \tan^2\theta + \tan^2\theta = \frac{5}{3}$

$2\tan^2\theta = \frac{2}{3}$ or $\tan^2\theta = \frac{1}{3}$ or $\tan\theta = \frac{1}{\sqrt{3}}$

$\Rightarrow \tan\theta = \tan 30°$ [1 Mark]

$\Rightarrow \theta = 30°$ [1 Mark]

25. Let the number of blue balls = x

$\therefore$ Total number of balls = 5 + x

P (blue ball) = $\frac{x}{5+x}$; P (red ball) = $\frac{5}{5+x}$ [1 Mark]

Given that P (blue) = 2 × P (red)

$\frac{x}{5+x} = 2\times\frac{5}{5+x} \Rightarrow \frac{x}{5+x} = \frac{10}{5+x}$

On solving we get x = 10 [1 Mark]

26. Let Yash make x correct and y wrong answers then $3x - y = 40$ and $4x - 2y = 50$.

So, equations are $3x - y - 40 = 0$ ...(i)

and $4x - 2y - 50 = 0$ [1 Mark]

or $2x - y - 25 = 0$ ...(ii)

Subtracting (ii) from (i), $3x - 2x - 40 + 25 = 0$ or $x - 15 = 0$ [1 Mark]

$\Rightarrow x = 15$ and putting $x = 15$ in eq. (i)

$3 \times 15 - y - 40 = 0 \Rightarrow -y + 5 = 0$. So, $y = 5$

$\therefore$ Total number of questions in the test $= x + y = 15 + 5 = 20$ [1 Mark]

OR

100 men do rd of work in 10 days. So, 100 men do complete work in 30 days.

So man-days for complete work = 100 × 30. Same work is completed by 100 men for 10 days + 150 men for 1 day + 200 men for 7 days + x men for 5 days. [1 Mark]

where x is the number of men who work from 19th to 23rd day.

So, $100 \times 10 + 150 \times 1 + 200 \times 7 + x \times 5 = 100 \times 30$

$\Rightarrow 5x = 2000 - 1400 - 150 \Rightarrow 5x = 450 \Rightarrow x = 90$

Hence, 200 – 90 = 110 men should be relieved. [1 Mark]

27. (a) Here the points are $P(6, 8)$ and $Q(-9, -12)$.

By using distance formula, we have

$PQ = \sqrt{(-9-6)^2 + (-12-8)^2}$

$= \sqrt{15^2 + 20^2} = \sqrt{225+400} = \sqrt{625} = 25$

Hence, $PQ = 25$ units. [1½ Marks]

(b) Here the points are $A(-6, -1)$ and $B(-6, 11)$

By using distance formula, we have

$AB = \sqrt{\{-6-(-6)\}^2 + \{11-(-1)\}^2} - \sqrt{0^2 + 12^2} = 12$

Hence, $AB = 12$ units. [1½ Marks]

28. Given equation is $36x^2 - 12ax + (a^2 - b^2) = 0$

$D = (-12a)^2 - 4(36)(a^2 - b^2)$ [$\because D = b^2 - 4ac$] [1 Mark]

$= 144a^2 - 144(a^2 - b^2) = 144b^2$ [½ Mark]

Now, $= \frac{12a \pm 12b}{72} = \frac{a \pm b}{6}$

Hence, $c = 6$ [½ Mark]

OR

The given equation is $x^{2/3} + x^{1/3} - 2 = 0$

Put $x^{1/3} = y$, then $y^2 + y - 2 = 0 \Rightarrow y^2 + 2y - y - 2 = 0$ [½ Mark]

$\Rightarrow y(y+2) - 1(y+2) = 0 \Rightarrow (y-1)(y+2) = 0$

$\Rightarrow y = 1$ or $y = -2$ [½ Mark]

$\Rightarrow x^{1/3} = 1$ or $x^{1/3} = -2$ [½ Mark]

$\therefore x = (1)^3$ or $x = (-2)^3 = -8$

Hence, the real roots of the given equations are 1, –8. [½ Mark]

29. Suppose a and a' be the first terms and d and d' be the common difference of the two AP's.

Now, $S_n = \frac{n}{2}[2a + (n-1)d]$ and $S'_n = \frac{n}{2}[2a' + (n-1)d']$ [½ Mark]

$\therefore \quad S_n : S'_n = \frac{\frac{n}{2}[2a + (n-1)d]}{\frac{n}{2}[2a' + (n-1)d']} = \frac{2a + (n-1)d}{2a' + (n-1)d'}$ [½ Mark]

Now, $\frac{S_n}{S'_n} = \frac{7n+1}{4n+27}$ (Given)

$\Rightarrow \frac{2a + (n-1)d}{2a' + (n-1)d'} = \frac{7n+1}{4n+27}$ ...(i)

We replace n by (2m – 1) in (i).

$\therefore \frac{2a + (2m-2)d}{2a' + (2m-2)d'} = \frac{7(2m-1)+1}{4(2m-1)+27}$

$\Rightarrow \frac{a + (m-1)d}{a' + (m-1)d'} = \frac{14m-6}{8m+23}$ [1 Mark]

So, the ratio of the mth terms of the two AP's is (14m – 6) : (8m + 23).

30. $x = \frac{\tan\theta}{\sin\phi + \tan\theta\cos\phi}$, $y = \frac{\tan\phi}{\sin\theta + \tan\phi\cos\theta}$ [1 Mark]

$\therefore \frac{x}{y} = \frac{\tan\theta}{\tan\phi}\left[\frac{\sin\phi\cos\theta + \sin\theta\cos\phi}{\sin\phi\cos\theta + \sin\theta\cos\phi}\right] \times \frac{\cos\theta}{\cos\phi}$

$= \frac{\sin\theta}{\cos\theta} \times \frac{\cos\phi}{\sin\phi} \times \frac{\cos\theta}{\cos\phi} = \frac{\sin\theta}{\sin\phi}$ [1 Mark]

31. We know that

HCF (a, b) × LCM (a, b) = a × b

$\Rightarrow$ LCM(a, b) $= \frac{a \times b}{\text{HCF}(a, b)}$ [1½ Marks]

$\therefore$ LCM (306, 657) $= \frac{306 \times 657}{\text{HCF}(306, 657)}$

$= \frac{306 \times 657}{9} = 34 \times 657 = 22338$ [1½ Marks]

32. $\Delta PNK \sim \Delta LMK$

[($\because \angle LMK = \angle PNK$ (each 46°) and $\angle K = \angle K$ (common)] [½ Mark]

$\therefore$ Corresponding sides are proportional

$\Rightarrow \frac{PN}{LM} = \frac{NK}{MK}$ [½ Mark]

$\Rightarrow \frac{x}{a} = \frac{c}{b+c} \Rightarrow x(b+c) = ac \Rightarrow x = \frac{ac}{b+c}$ [2 Marks]

OR

In ΔAPB and ΔCPD,

$\angle APB = \angle CPD = 50^\circ$ [vertically opposite angles]

Now, $\frac{AP}{PD} = \frac{6}{5}$ ...(i) [1 Mark]

and $\frac{BP}{CP} = \frac{3}{2.5} = \frac{6}{5}$ ...(ii) [1 Mark]

$\therefore \quad \frac{AP}{PD} = \frac{BP}{CP}$ [From Eqs. (i) and (ii)] [1 Mark]

$\therefore \quad \Delta APB \sim \Delta DPC$ [by SAS similarity criterion] [1 Mark]

$\therefore \quad \angle A = \angle D = 30^\circ$ [corresponding angles of similar triangles]

In ΔAPB, $\angle A + \angle B + \angle APB = 180^\circ$ [sum of angles of a triangle = 180°]

$\Rightarrow \quad 30^\circ + \angle B + 50^\circ = 180^\circ$

$\Rightarrow \quad \angle B = 180^\circ - (50^\circ + 30^\circ) = 100^\circ$ [1 Mark]

i.e., $\angle PBA = 100^\circ$

33. Let P, B and A be the positions of the bird, boy and girl respectively.

Given PB = 100 m, AC = 20 m, Let PM = x m.

In right-angled ΔPBO, we have,

$\sin 30^\circ = \frac{OP}{BP} \Rightarrow \frac{1}{2} = \frac{OP}{100} \Rightarrow OP = \frac{100}{2} = 50\,m$

[1 Mark]

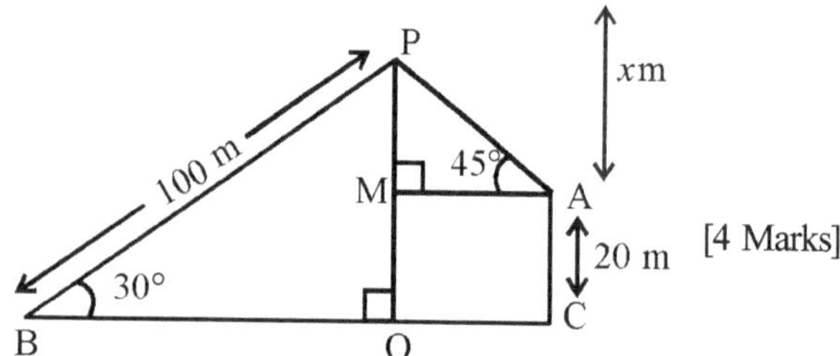

[4 Marks]

Now, $OP = OM + MP$

$\Rightarrow 50 = 20 + x \quad [\because OM = AC = 20 m]$

$\Rightarrow x = 30\,m$ [1 Mark]

In ΔPMA, $\sin 45^\circ = \frac{x}{PA} \Rightarrow \frac{1}{\sqrt{2}} = \frac{30}{PA}$

$\Rightarrow PA = 30\sqrt{2} m = 30 \times 1.41 = 42.3\,m$ [1 Mark]

Hence, required distance is 42.3 m.

OR

Suppose P be the position of the balloon if its angle of elevation from the eyes of the girl is 60° and Q be the position if angle of elevation is 30°.

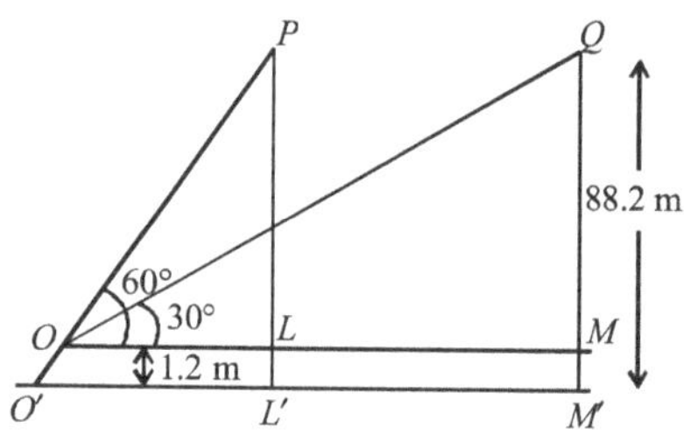

[2 Marks]

In ΔOLP, $\tan 60^\circ = \frac{PL}{OL}$

$\Rightarrow \sqrt{3} = \frac{PL' - LL'}{OL} = \frac{88.2 - 1.2}{OL} = \frac{87}{OL}$ [1 Mark]

So, $OL = \frac{87}{\sqrt{3}}$

In ΔOMQ, $\tan 30^\circ = \frac{QM}{OM} = \frac{QM' - MM'}{OM}$

$\Rightarrow \frac{1}{\sqrt{3}} = \frac{88.2 - 1.2}{OM} \Rightarrow OM = 87\sqrt{3}$ [1 Mark]

Therefore, distance covered by the balloon,

$PQ = OM - OL$

$= \left(87\sqrt{3} - \frac{87}{\sqrt{3}}\right) m = 87\left(\sqrt{3} - \frac{1}{\sqrt{3}}\right) m = \frac{174}{\sqrt{3}} m$

$= 58\sqrt{3}$ m [1 Mark]

34. We have, $VO' = 10.2$ cm, $OA = OO' = 4.2$ cm

Let r be the radius of the hemisphere and h be the height of the conical part of the toy.

Then, $r = OA = 4.2$ cm.

$h = VO = VO' - OO' = (10.2 - 4.2)$ cm $= 6$ cm

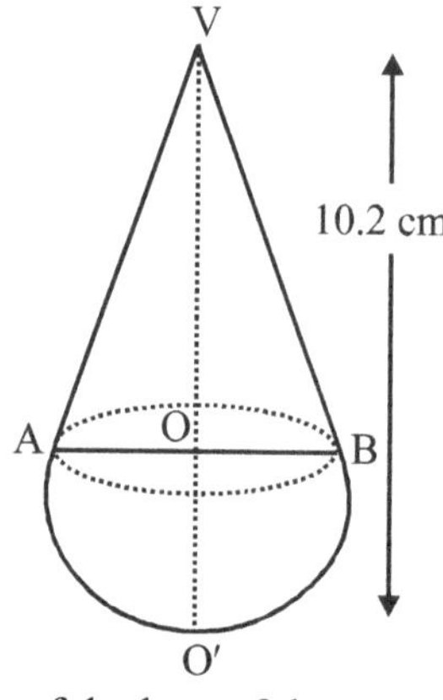

[2 Marks]

Also, radius of the base of the cone $= OA = r = 4.2$ cm

$\therefore$ Volume of the wooden toy

= Volume of the conical part + Volume of the hemispherical part

$= \left(\frac{1}{3}\pi r^2 h + \frac{2\pi}{3} r^3\right) cm^3 = \frac{\pi r^2}{3}(h + 2r)\ cm^3$ [1 Marks]

$= \frac{1}{3} \times \frac{22}{7} \times 4.2 \times 4.2 \times (6 + 2 \times 4.2)\ cm^3$

$= \frac{1}{3} \times \frac{22}{7} \times 4.2 \times 4.2 \times 14.4\ cm^3 = 266.11\ cm^3$ [2 Marks]

35.

Class interval	Mid values (x_i)	Frequency (f_i)	Deviation (d_i) $= x_i - A$	$f_i d_i$
0–4	2	6	–12	–72
4–8	6	3	–8	–24
8–12	10	6	–4	–24
12–16	14 (A)	16	0	0
16–20	18	3	4	12
20–24	22	14	8	112
24–28	26	10	12	120
28–32	30	8	16	128
		$\Sigma f_i = 66$		$\Sigma f_i d_i = 252$

[4 Marks]

Mean $= A + \frac{\Sigma f_i d_i}{\Sigma f_i} = 14 + \frac{252}{66} = 14 + 3.818 =$ **17.818** [1 Mark]

36. (i) $p(x) = ax^2 + bx + c$ [1 Mark]

(ii) $p(x) = k(x+2)(x-3)$

$= k(x^2 - 5x + 6)$ [1 Mark]

(iii) For value of k,

$\alpha . \frac{1}{\alpha} = \frac{c}{a}$ (Product of roots $= \frac{c}{a}$)

$1 = \frac{8k}{2}$ or $k = \frac{1}{4}$ [2 Marks]

OR

We know, for a quadratic polynomial

$k(x^2$ – (Sum of roots) x + Product of roots)

$k(x^2 - (-p) + (-1/p))$; $k(x^2 + p - 1/p)$ [2 Marks]

37. (i) $\cos 30° = \frac{BD}{32}$ $BD = 16\sqrt{3}$ cm. side $BC = 32\sqrt{3}$ cm

[1 Mark]

(ii) $AD = \sqrt{AB^2 - BD^2} = \sqrt{(32\sqrt{3})^2 - (16\sqrt{3})^2} = 48$ cm

[1 Mark]

(iii) Side of square $= 6 \times 7 = 42$ cm.

Area of square $= 42 \times 42 = 1764$ cm^2 [2 Marks]

OR

Area of each circular

$= \pi(7)^2 = \frac{22}{7} \times 49$

$= 154$ cm^2 [2 Marks]

38. (i) $AC^2 - 30^2 + 40^2 = 2500 \Rightarrow AC = 50$ m

(ii) (21, 20, 28) $[\because 28^2 \neq (21)^2 + (20)^2]$

(iii) $AB = 50 - 12 = 38$ m

OR

82m

1. **(c)** LCM × HCF = Product of two numbers

$36 \times 2 = 18 \times x$

$72 = 18x$

$4 = x$

$x = 4$

2. **(d)** Ratio of altitudes = Ratio of sides for similar triangles

So AM : PN = AB : PQ = 2 : 3

3. **(b)** Least composite number is 4 and the least prime number is 2. LCM (4, 2) : HCF(4, 2) = 4 : 2 = 2 : 1

4. **(b)** $x^2 - (m+3)x + mx - m(m+3) = 0$

$\Rightarrow x[x-(m+3)] + m[x-(m+3)] = 0$

$\Rightarrow (x+m)[x-(m+3)] = 0$

$\therefore x + m = 0 \qquad x - (m+3) = 0$

$x = -m \qquad x = m + 3$

5. **(b)** In ΔABC and ΔDEF, ∠B = ∠E, ∠F = ∠C and AB = 3DE

ΔABC ~ ΔDEF

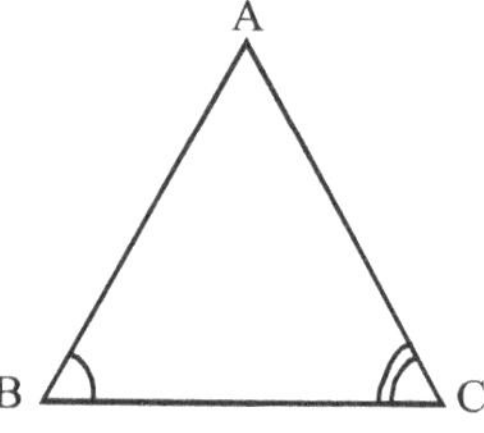

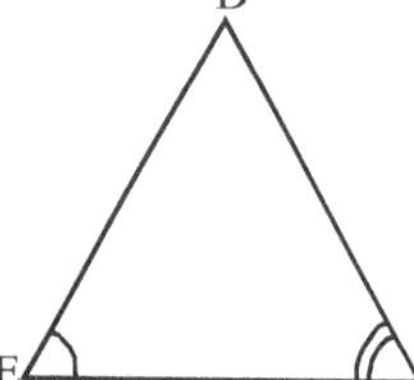

Also, ΔABC and ΔDEF do not satisfy any rule of congruency, (SAS, ASA, SSS), so both are not congruent.

6. **(d)**

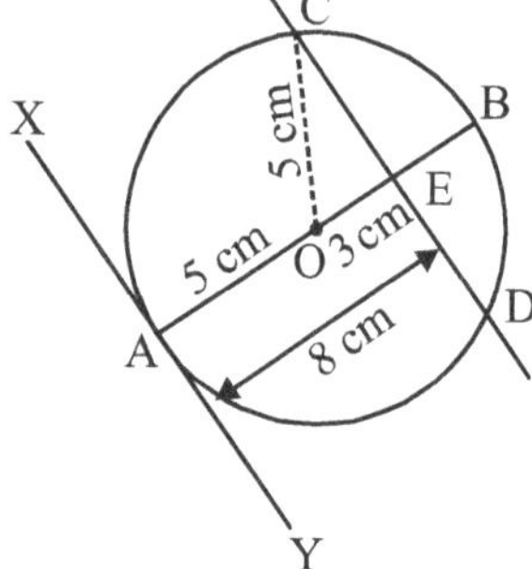

Now, in figure

∠OAY = 90°

[Tangent at any point of a circle is perpendicular to the radius through the point of contact]

ΔOAY + ΔOED = 180°

⇒ ΔOED = 90°

Also, AE = 8 cm.

Join OC

Now, in right angled ΔOEC,

$OC^2 = OE^2 + EC^2$

$\Rightarrow EC^2 = OC^2 - OE^2$

[by Pythagoras theorem]

$= 5^2 - 3^2 = 25 - 9 = 16$

$\Rightarrow$ EC = 4 cm

Hence, length of chord CD = 2CE

$= 2 \times 4 = 8$ cm

7. **(d)** isosceles and similar

8. **(c)** First join OA.

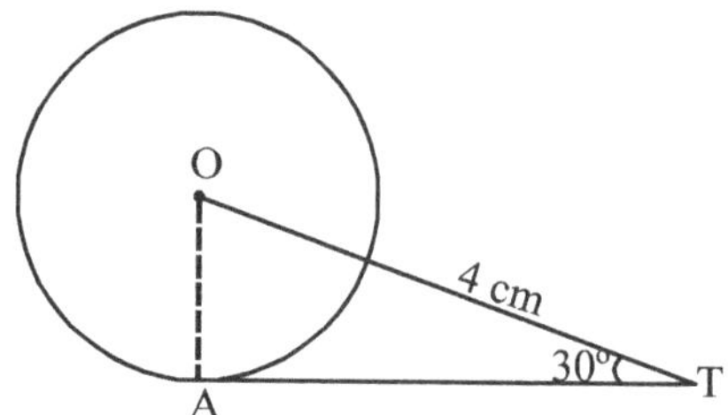

Then the tangent at any point of a circle is ⊥ to the radius through the point of contact.

∴ ∠OAT = 90°

In ΔOAT, $\cos 30^\circ = \frac{AT}{OT}$

$\Rightarrow \frac{\sqrt{3}}{2} = \frac{AT}{4}$

$\Rightarrow AT = 2\sqrt{3}$ cm

9. **(b)** Given, ΔABC ~ ΔDFE then ∠A = ∠D = 30°, ∠C = ∠E = 50°

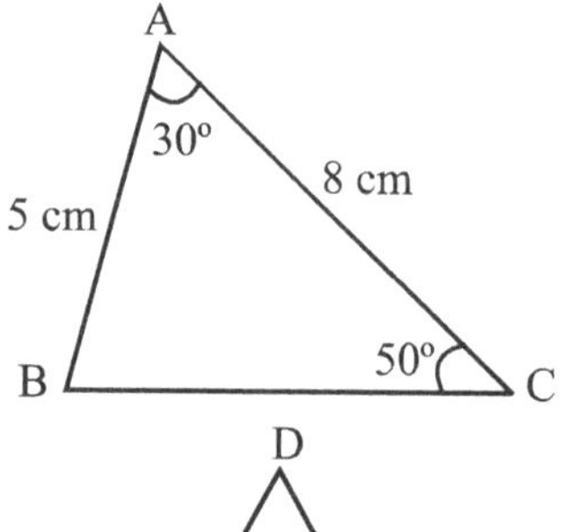

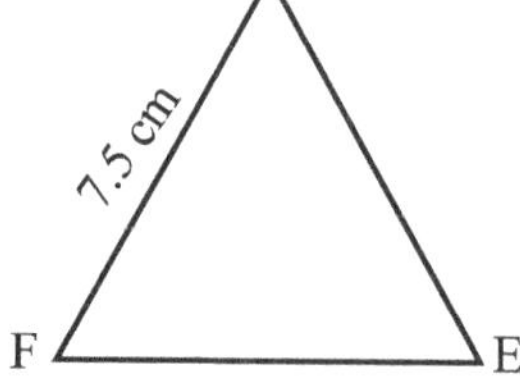

∠B = ∠F = 180° – (30° + 50°) = 100°

Also, AB = 5 cm, AC = 8 cm

and DF = 7.5 cm

Therefore $\frac{AB}{DF} = \frac{AC}{DE}$

[By property of similar triangles]

$$\Rightarrow \quad \frac{5}{7.5} = \frac{8}{DE}$$

$$DE = \frac{8 \times 7.5}{5} = 12 \text{ cm}$$

So, DE = 12 cm, $\angle F = 100°$

10. (d)

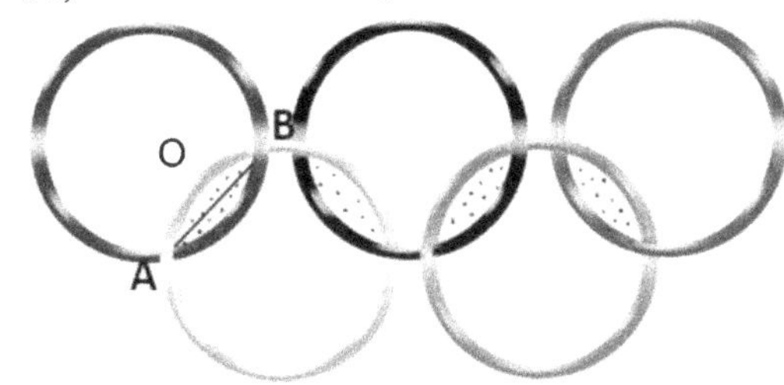

Let O be the centre of the circle OA = OB = AB = 1 cm.

So ΔOAB is an equilateral triangle and $\therefore \angle AOB = 60°$

Required area = 8x Area of one segment with r = 1cm, θ = 60°

Area of sector OAB – Area of an equilateral ΔOAB,

$$= 8x\left(\frac{60}{360} \times \pi \times 1^2 - \frac{\sqrt{3}}{4} \times 1^2\right)$$

$$= 8\left(\frac{\pi}{6} - \frac{\sqrt{3}}{4}\right) \text{cm}^2$$

11. (c)

Class	f_i	x_i	$f_i x_i$
0 – 20	17	10	170
20 – 40	f_1	30	$30f_1$
40 – 60	32	50	1600
60 – 80	f_2	70	$70f_2$
80 – 100	19	90	1710
	$\Sigma f_i = 68 + f_1 + f_2$		$\Sigma f_i x_i = 3480 + 30f_1 + 70 f_2$

We have $\Sigma f_i = 120$

$\Rightarrow 68 + f_1 + f_2 = 120 \Rightarrow f_1 + f_2 = 52$ ... (i)

Now, mean = 50

$$\Rightarrow \quad 50 = \frac{\Sigma f_i x_i}{\Sigma f_i} \Rightarrow 50 = \frac{3480 + 30f_i + 70f_2}{120}$$

$\Rightarrow 6000 = 3480 + 30f_1 + 70f_2 \Rightarrow 30f_1 + 70f_2 = 2520$ ... (ii)

Solving (i) and (ii) we get; $f_1 = 28$, $f_2 = 24$

12. (b) Let the required ratio be K : 1

$\therefore$ The coordinates of the required point on the y-axis is

$$x = \frac{K(-4) + 3(1)}{K+1}; \; y = \frac{K(2) + 5(1)}{K+1}$$

Since, it lies on y-axis

$\therefore$ Its x-cordinates = 0

$$\therefore \frac{-4K+3}{K+1} = 0 \Rightarrow -4K + 3 = 0$$

$$\Rightarrow K = \frac{3}{4}$$

$\Rightarrow$ Required ratio = $\frac{3}{4} : 1$

$\therefore$ ratio = 3 : 4

13. (b) Area of equilateral triangle $= \frac{\sqrt{3}}{4}a^2$

$$\Rightarrow \frac{\sqrt{3}}{4}a^2 = 121\sqrt{3}$$

$\Rightarrow a^2 = 484$

$\Rightarrow a = 22$ cm

Perimeter of equilateral $\Delta = 3a$

$= 3(22)$

$= 66$ cm

Since the wire is bent into the form of Q circle, So perimeter of circle = 66 cm

$\Rightarrow 2pr = 66$

$$\Rightarrow 2 \times \frac{22}{7} \times r = 66 \Rightarrow r = 66 \times \frac{1}{2} \times \frac{7}{22}$$

$\Rightarrow r = 10.5$ cm

So Area enclosed by circle = πr^2

$$= \frac{22}{7} \times 10.5 \times 10.5$$

$= 22 \times 1.5 \times 10.5$

$= 346.5 \text{ cm}^2$

14. (b)

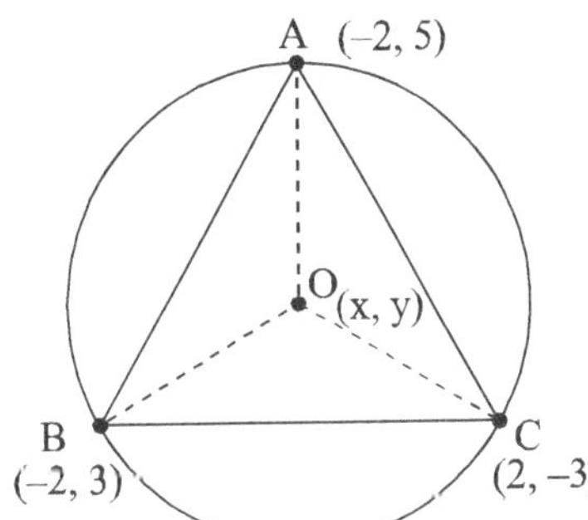

Let O(*x*, *y*) is the centre of the given circle.

Join OA, OB & OC.

$\because$ OA = OB = OC

$\therefore$ $OA^2 = OB^2$

$$\Rightarrow \sqrt{(x+2)^2 + (y-5)^2} = \sqrt{(x+2)^2 + (y+3)^2}$$

$\Rightarrow\ x^2 + 4 + 4x + y^2 + 25 - 10y = x^2 + 4 + 4x + y^2 + 9 + 6x$

$\Rightarrow\ 16y = 16 \Rightarrow y = 1$

Again: $OB^2 = OC^2$

$\Rightarrow\ \sqrt{(x+2)^2+(y+3)^2} = \sqrt{(x-2)^2+(y+3)^2}$

$\Rightarrow\ x^2 + 4 + 4x + (y + 3)^2 = x^2 + 4 - 4x + (y + 3)^2$

$\Rightarrow\ 8x = 0 \Rightarrow x = 0$

$\therefore$ centre of the circle is (0, 1).

15. **(b)** Coordinates of mid-point are given by $\left(\frac{x_1+x_2}{2}, \frac{y_1+y_2}{2}\right)$

Here, coordinates of mid-point are $\left(\frac{a}{3}, 4\right)$

So, $\frac{a}{3} = \frac{-6-2}{2}$

$\therefore\ a = -12$

16. **(b)** The sum of the two numbers lies between 2 and 12.

So the primes are 2, 3, 5, 7, 11.

No. of ways for getting 2 = (1, 1) = 1

No. of ways of getting 3 = (1, 2), (2, 1) = 2

No. of ways of getting 5 = (1, 4), (4, 1), (2, 3), (3, 2) = 4

No. of ways of getting 7

= (1, 6), (6, 1), (2, 5), (5, 2), (3, 4), (4, 3) = 6

No. of ways of getting 11 = (5, 6), (6, 5) = 2

No. of favourable ways = 1 + 2 + 4 + 6 + 2 = 15

No. of exhaustive ways = 6 × 6 = 36

Probability of the sum as a prime

$= \frac{15}{36} = \frac{5}{12}$

17. **(b)** Since (x, y) is midpoint of (3, 4) and (k, 7)

$\therefore\ x = \frac{3+k}{2}$ and $y = \frac{4+7}{2}$

Also $2x + 2y + 1 = 0$ putting values we get

$3 + k + 4 + 7 + 1 = 0$

$\Rightarrow\ k + 15 = 0 \Rightarrow k = -15$

18. **(b)** S = {(1, 1), ..., (1, 6), (2, 1),.....,(2, 6), (3, 1), ..., (3, 6), (4, 1), ..., (4, 6), (5, 1),...., (5, 6), (6, 1),....., (6, 6)}

n(S) = 36

Let E be the event that both dice show different numbers.

E {(1, 2), (1, 3),...., (1, 6), (2, 1), (2, 3), (2, 4),...., (2, 6), (3, 1), (3, 2), (3, 4), (3, 5), (3, 6), (4, 1), (4, 2), (4, 3), (4, 5), (4, 6), (5, 1), (5, 2), (5, 3), (5, 4), (5, 6), (6, 1), (6, 2), (6, 3), (6, 4), (4, 5)}

n(E) = 30

$P(E) = \frac{n(E)}{n(S)} = \frac{30}{36} = \frac{5}{6}$

19. **(a)** $(OA)^2 = (AB)^2 + (OB)^2$

$AB = \sqrt{25-9} = 4$ cm.

Both Assertion and Reason are correct.

Also, Reason is the correct explanation of the Assertion.

20. **(a)** Both statements are correct. Event given in Assertion is an impossible event.

21. The Prime factorisation of 66 & 486 gives

$66 = 2 \times 3 \times 11$

$486 = 2 \times 3 \times 3 \times 3 \times 3 \times 3 = 2 \times 3^5$ [½ Mark]

$\therefore$ The LCM of these two integer is : $2 \times 3^5 \times 11 = 5346$ [½ Mark]

$$HCF(66, 486) = \frac{66 \times 486}{LCM(66, 486)} = \frac{66 \times 486}{5346} = 6$$ [1 Mark]

22.

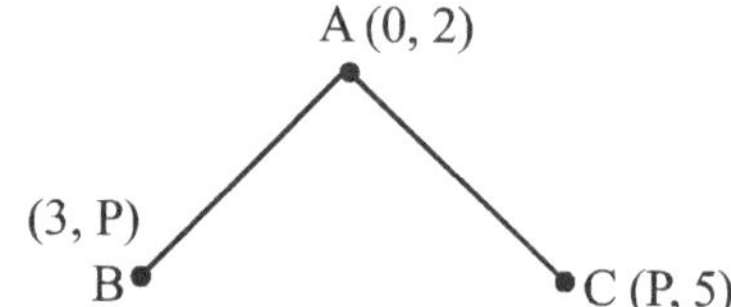

Given that : AB = AC

By distance formula :

$d = \sqrt{(x_2-x_1)^2+(y_2-y_1)^2}$ [1 Mark]

$\sqrt{(3-0)^2+(P-2)^2} = \sqrt{(P-0)^2+(5-2)^2}$

Squaring both sides

$9 + P^2 + 4 - 4P = P^2 + 9$

$\Rightarrow\ 4 - 4P = 0 \Rightarrow P = 1$ [1 Mark]

OR

A (3, –3) —— (h, 0), k : 1 —— B (–2, 7)

Let (h, 0) be point on x-axis which divides AB in k : 1.
By section formula :

$$h = \frac{-2k+3}{k+1}, 0 = \frac{7k-3}{k+1} \Rightarrow k = \frac{3}{7}$$ [1 Mark]

Now, $h = \frac{-2\left(\frac{3}{7}\right)+3}{\frac{3}{7}+1} = \frac{-6+21}{10} = \frac{3}{2}$

point on x-axis $= \left(\frac{3}{2}, 0\right)$ and ratio is 3 : 7. [1 Mark]

23. Given, α and $\frac{2}{\alpha}$ are the zeroes of $x^2 + 4x + 2a$.

Now

Product of the zeroes $= \frac{\text{Constant term}}{\text{Coefficient of } x^2}$ [1 Mark]

$\alpha \times \frac{2}{\alpha} = \frac{2a}{1}$

$2 = 2a$

$\therefore a = 1$ [1 Mark]

24. When 2^{256} is divided by 17 then, $\frac{2^{256}}{17} = \frac{2^{256}}{2^4+1} = \frac{(2^4)^{64}}{(2^4+1)}$

[½ Mark]

By remainder theorem when $f(x)$ is divided by $x + a$ the remainder $= f(-a)$ [½ Mark]
Here $f(x) = (2^4)^{64}$ and $x = 2^4$ and $a = 1$ [½ Mark]
$\therefore$ Remainder $= f(-1) = (-1)^{64} = 1$ [½ Mark]

25. P (winning) = 0.08
Total tickets sold = 6000
Let the number of tickets she bought be x, then probability

of winning $= \frac{x}{6000}$ [1 Mark]

$\Rightarrow \frac{x}{6000} = 0.08 \Rightarrow x = 6000 \times 0.08 \Rightarrow x = 480$ [1 Mark]

Thus the girl bought 480 tickets.

OR

Let there be x blue, y green and z white marbles in the jar.
Then, $x + y + z = 54$ ...(i) [½ Mark]

$\therefore P(\text{selecting a blue marble}) = \frac{x}{54} \Rightarrow \frac{x}{54} = \frac{1}{3} \Rightarrow x = 18$

[½ Mark]

Similarly, $P(\text{selecting a green marble}) = \frac{y}{54}$

$\Rightarrow \frac{y}{54} = \frac{4}{9} \Rightarrow y = 24$ [½ Mark]

Substituting the values of x and y in (i), $z = 12$
Hence, the jar contains 12 white marbles. [½ Mark]

26. Since, (3, a) lies on the line 2x – 3y = 5
So, $2 \times 3 - 3a = 5$ [1 Mark]
$\Rightarrow 6 - 3a = 5$
$= 6 - 5 = 3a$

$\Rightarrow a = \frac{1}{3}$ [1 Mark]

OR

$3x + 2y - 7 = 0$ ... (i)
$4x + y - 6 = 0$ ... (ii)
From (ii), $y = 6 - 4x$ [½ Mark]
Value of y put in eqn. (i)
$3x + 2y - 7 = 0$
$\Rightarrow 3x + 2(6 - 4x) - 7 = 0$
$\Rightarrow 3x + 12 - 8x - 7 = 0$
$\Rightarrow 5x = 5$
$\therefore x = 1$ [1 Mark]
Substitute the value of x in eq(ii) to get value of y,
$4x + y - 6 = 0$ [½ Mark]
$\Rightarrow 4(1) + y - 6 = 0$
$\Rightarrow 4 + y - 6 = 0$
$\Rightarrow y - 2 = 0$
$\therefore y = 2$
Hence, values of x and y are 1 and 2. [1 Mark]

27. Given : $a_5 + a_9 = 30$
$a_{25} = 3a_8$
Now, $a + 4d + a + 8d = 30 \Rightarrow 2a + 12d = 30$
$\Rightarrow a + 6d = 15$ ...(i) [½ Mark]
and, $a + 24d = 3a + 21d \Rightarrow 2a - 3d = 0$ ...(ii) [½ Mark]
From eqs. (i) and (ii)

$$\begin{aligned} 2a + 12d &= 30 \\ \underset{-}{}2a \underset{+}{-} 3d &\underset{-}{=} 0 \\ \hline 15d &= 30 \Rightarrow d = 2 \end{aligned}$$ [½ Mark]

Now, put d = 2 in eq. (i) : a + 12 = 15 $\Rightarrow$ a = 3
Required A.P. = 3, 5, 7, ... [½ Mark]

$\therefore 5 = 210 \times 5 + 55y \Rightarrow y = \frac{-1045}{55} = (-19)$ [1 Mark]

28. Let $p(x) = \sqrt{3}x^2 - 8x + 4\sqrt{3}$
$= \sqrt{3}x^2 - 6x - 2x + 4\sqrt{3}$ [1 Mark]
$= \sqrt{3}x(x - 2\sqrt{3}) - 2(x - 2\sqrt{3})$ [1 Mark]
$= (\sqrt{3}x - 2)(x - 2\sqrt{3})$
Put $P(n) = 0$

$\therefore$ Zeroes are, $x = \frac{2}{\sqrt{3}}, 2\sqrt{3}$ [1 Mark]

29.

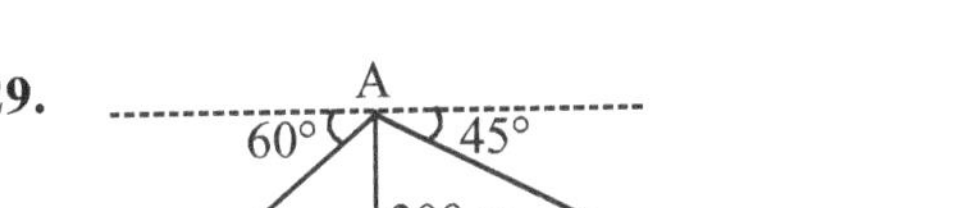

[1 Mark]

Let AB is the height of light house = 200m

Two ships are at points C and D on either side of AB (light house)

In ΔABC,

$\tan 60° = \frac{AB}{BC}$ [1 Mark]

$\Rightarrow BC = \frac{200\sqrt{3}}{3} = \frac{200 \times 1.73}{3} = 115.33$ m

In ΔABD,

$\tan 45° = \frac{AB}{BD}$

$\Rightarrow BD = 200$

Distance between both ships = BC + BD

= 115.33 + 200

= 315.33 m [1 Mark]

30. LET AD = X

∴ AF = AD = x

Then,

DB = AB – AD

= 12 – x (∵ AB = 12 cm)

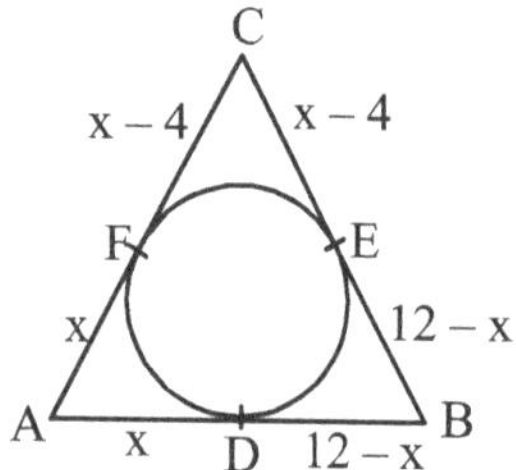

∵ BC = 8 cm

So, CE = BC – BE

= 8 – (12 – x)

= x – 4

⇒ CF = CE = x – 4 [1 Mark]

[∵ tangents drawn on a circle from an external point are equal in lengths]

Now, AC = 10 cm

AF + CF = 10

x + x – 4 = 10

2x – 4 = 10

2x = 14

x = 7 cm

∴ AD = x = 7 cm [1 Mark]

Now, BE = 12 – x

= 12 – 7 = 5 cm

And, CF = x – 4

= 7 – 4 = 3 cm [1 Mark]

Hence, the lengths of AD, BE and CF are 7 cm, 5 cm and 3 cm respectively.

31. Perimeter of shaded region = Perimeter (QTR + QAP + PSR) [1 Mark]

$= \pi\left[5 + \frac{3}{2} + \frac{7}{2}\right] = \pi\left[\frac{20}{2}\right] = 10\pi = 31.4$ cm [2 Marks]

OR

We mark the area of unshaded regions as $A_1, A_2\, A_3$ and A_4 as shown in the figure.

Area of the shaded region

= Area of the square *ABCD* – Area of the unshaded portion (A_1+A_2+ A_3+A_4).

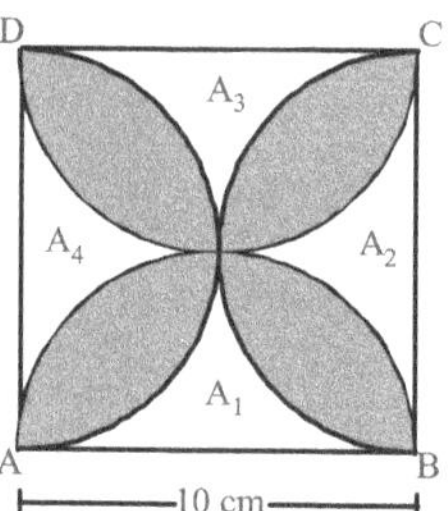

Area of unshaded region A_1+ A_3

= Area of square *ABCD* – Area of semi circle on BC as diameter– Area of semi-circle on *AD* as diameter.

$= 10^2 - \frac{\pi \cdot 5^2}{2} - \frac{\pi \cdot 5^2}{2} = 100 - 25\pi.$ [1 Mark]

Similarly, area of unshaded region $A_2 + A_4$ = Area of square *ABCD* – Area of the semi-circles on diameter *AB* and *DC*.

So, Area $A_2 + A_4 = 10^2 - 2 \times \frac{\pi \times 5^2}{2} = 100 - 25\pi.$

So, Area $A_1 + A_2 + A_3 + A_4 = 200 - 50\,\pi$.

Area of the shaded region = Area of square *ABCD* – Area ($A_1 + A_2 + A_3 + A_4$) [1 Mark]

$= 10^2 - (200 - 50\,\pi)$

$= (100 - 200 + 50\,\pi)$ sq. cm.

$= 50\,\pi - 100 = 50\,(\pi - 2)$ sq. cm.

$= 50\,(3.14 - 2) = 50 \times 1.14 = 57$ cm^2. [1 Mark]

32. It is give that AD is the bisector of ∠A of ΔABC.

$\therefore \frac{AB}{AC} = \frac{BD}{DC} \Rightarrow \frac{AB}{AC} + 1 = \frac{BD}{DC} + 1$ [Adding 1 on both sides]

[1 Mark]

$\Rightarrow \frac{AB + AC}{AC} = \frac{BD + DC}{DC}$ [½ Mark]

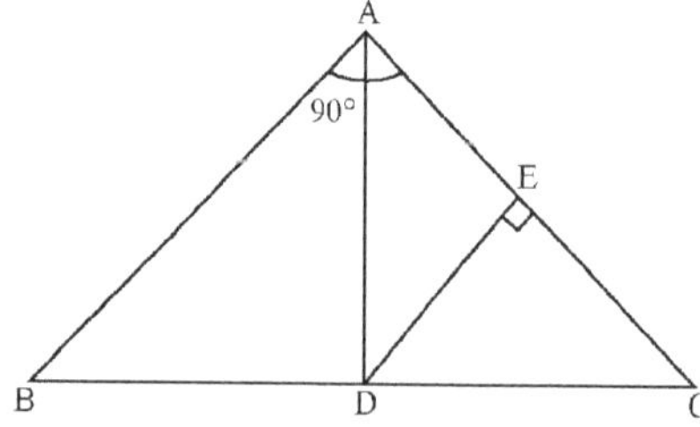

$\Rightarrow \frac{AB + AC}{AC} = \frac{BC}{DC}$ ... (1) [½ Mark]

In Δ's CDE and CBA, we have

∠DCE = ∠BCA = ∠C [Common]

$\angle BAC = \angle DEC$ [Each equal to 90°]

So, by AA-criterion of similarity, we have [1 Mark]

$\Delta CDE \sim \Delta CBA \Rightarrow \frac{CD}{CB} = \frac{DE}{BA} \Rightarrow \frac{AB}{DE} = \frac{BC}{DC}$ ... (2)

[1 Mark]

From (1) and (2), we have $\frac{AB+AC}{AC} = \frac{AB}{DE}$

$\Rightarrow DE \times (AB + AC) = AB \times AC$ [1 Mark]

OR

In ΔABC, $\angle B = 90°$ and AD and CE are two medians.

$\therefore \quad AC^2 = AB^2 + BC^2 = (5)^2 = 25$ ...(i)

(By Pythagoras theorem)

In ΔABD, $AD^2 = AB^2 + BD^2$

$\Rightarrow \left(\frac{3\sqrt{5}}{2}\right)^2 = AB^2 + \frac{BC^2}{4}$

$\Rightarrow \frac{45}{4} = AB^2 + \frac{BC^2}{4}$ ...(ii)

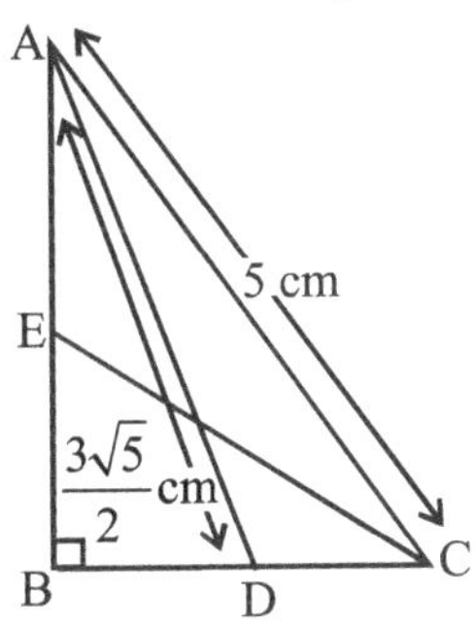

In ΔEBC, $CE^2 = BC^2 + \frac{AB^2}{4}$ ...(iii) [2 Marks]

Subtracting equation (ii) from equation (i),

$\frac{3BC^2}{4} = 25 - \frac{45}{4} = \frac{55}{4}$

$\Rightarrow BC^2 = \frac{55}{3}$ ...(iv) [1 Mark]

$AB^2 + \frac{55}{12} = \frac{45}{4}$ From equation (ii),

$\Rightarrow AB^2 = \frac{45}{4} - \frac{55}{12} = \frac{20}{3}$ [1 Mark]

$CE^2 = \frac{55}{3} + \frac{20}{3 \times 4}$

From equation (iii),

$= \frac{240}{12} = 20$ [1 Mark]

$\therefore \quad CE = 2\sqrt{5}$ cm.

33. Given $\sin\theta = \frac{c}{\sqrt{c^2+d^2}}$

$\cos^2\theta = 1 - \sin^2\theta$ [1 Mark]

$= 1 - \left(\frac{c}{\sqrt{c^2+d^2}}\right)^2$

$= 1 - \frac{c^2}{c^2+d^2}$

$= \frac{c^2+d^2-c^2}{c^2+d^2}$

$= \frac{d^2}{c^2+d^2}$ [2 Marks]

$\cos\theta = \frac{d}{\sqrt{c^2+d^2}}$

We know that, $\tan\theta = \frac{\sin\theta}{\cos\theta}$

$= \frac{\frac{c}{\sqrt{c^2+d^2}}}{\frac{d}{\sqrt{c^2+d^2}}}$

$\tan\theta = \frac{c}{d}$ [2 Marks]

34. Volume of one ice-cream cone as shown in figure

$= \frac{1}{3}\pi \times (3)^2 \times 9 + \frac{2}{3}\pi(3)^3 \text{ cm}^3 = 45\pi \text{ cm}^3$

Volume of the ice-cream in the cylindrical container (of height 15 cm and diameter 12 cm) [2 Marks]

$= \pi \times (6)_2 \times 15$

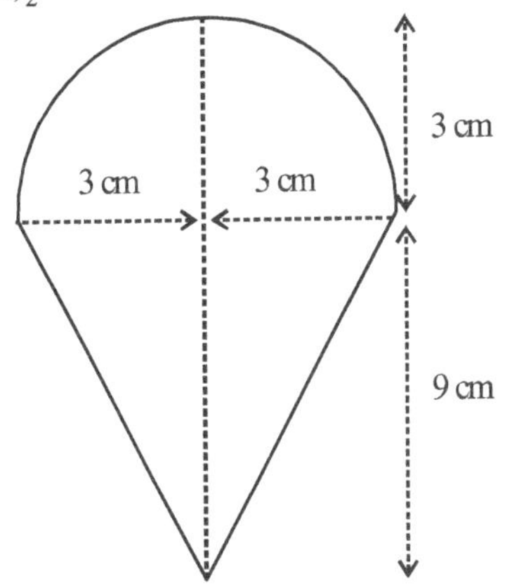

[2 Marks]

Let the number of cones made be n.

Then, $n \times 45\pi = \pi \times (6)^2 \times 15$

$\Rightarrow 45n = 36 \times 15 \Rightarrow n = 12$ [1 Mark]

35. The class 1500 – 2000 has the maximum frequency, therefore, this the modal class.

Here $l = 1500$, $h = 500$, $f_1 = 40$, $f_0 = 24$ and $f_2 = 33$

Now, let us substitute these values in the formula

Mode $= l + \left(\frac{f_1 - f_0}{2f_1 - f_0 - f_2}\right) \times h$ [1 Mark]

$= 1500 + \frac{40-24}{80-24-33} \times 500$ [1 Mark]

$= 1500 + \frac{16}{23} \times 500 = 1500 + 347.83 = 1847.83$

∴ Modal monthly expenditure = ₹ 1847.83

Let the assumed mean be A = 3250 and h = 500.

Exp. (in ₹)	f_i	x_i	$d_i = x_i - A = x_i - 3250$	$u_i = \frac{x_i - A}{h} = \frac{x_i - 3250}{500}$	$f_i u_i$
1000 – 1500	24	1250	–2000	–4	–96
1500 – 2000	40	1750	–1500	–3	–120
2000 – 2500	33	2250	–1000	–2	–66
2500 – 3000	28	2750	–500	–1	–28
3000 – 3500	30	3250	0	0	0
3500 – 4000	22	3750	500	1	22
4000 – 4500	16	4250	1000	2	32
4500 – 5000	7	4750	1500	3	21
	$N = \Sigma f_i = 200$				$\Sigma f_i u_i = -235$

We have, N = 200, A = 3250, h = 500 [2 Marks]

and $\Sigma f_i u_i = -235$

$$\text{Mean} = A + h\left(\frac{1}{N}\Sigma f_i u_i\right) = 3250 + 500 \times \frac{-235}{200}$$

= 3250 – 587.5 = 2662.5 [1 Mark]

Hence, the average expenditure is ₹ 2662.50.

OR

The class 40 – 50 has the maximum frequency, therefore, this is the modal class.

Here $l = 40$, $h = 10$, $f_1 = 20$, $f_0 = 12$ and $f_2 = 11$ [2 Marks]

Now, let us substitute these values in the formula

Mode =

$$l + \left(\frac{f_1 - f_0}{2f_1 - f_0 - f_2}\right) \times h = 40 + \left(\frac{20 - 12}{40 - 12 - 11}\right) \times 10$$

[2 Marks]

$$= 40 + \frac{8}{17} \times 10 = 40 + 4.7 = 44.7$$ [1 Mark]

Hence, mode = 44.7 cars

36. (i) No. of correct questions are 96 [1 Mark]

(ii) He guessed 24 questions. [1 Mark]

(iii) Marks $= 80 - \frac{1}{4}$ of $40 = 70$

OR

Here, x + y = 120 ...(i)

$$x - \frac{1}{4}y = 95$$ ...(ii) [2 Marks]

On solving (i) & (ii) x = 100

37. (i) $\cot C = \frac{BC}{AB} = \frac{3}{4}$ [1 Mark]

(ii) $\sec C = \frac{AC}{BC} = \frac{5}{3}$ [1 Mark]

(iii) $\sin C = \frac{4}{5}$, $\cos C = \frac{3}{5}$

$$\text{L.H.S} = \sin^2 C + \cos^2 C = \left(\frac{4}{5}\right)^2 + \left(\frac{3}{5}\right)^2$$

$$= \frac{16 + 9}{25} = 1 = \text{R.H.S}$$ [2 Marks]

OR

$$\tan C = \frac{4}{3}$$

$$1 + \tan^2 C = 1 + \frac{16}{9} = \frac{25}{9}$$ [2 Marks]

38 (i) 2, 4, 6, 8 ....

Last term, $t_{30} = 2 + (30 - 1)\,2 = 2 + 2(29) = 60$

3, 6, 9, 12 ....

Last term, $t_{20} = 3 + (20 - 1)3 = 3 + 57 = 60$ [1 Mark]

(ii) For 2, 4, 6, 8.........

$$S_{30} = \frac{30}{2}(2 + 60) = 930$$

For 3, 6, 9, 12 ....

$$S_{20} = \frac{20}{2}(3 + 60) = 630$$ [1 Mark]

(iii) Let m^{th} term of the first series is common with the nth term of the second series.

$$t_m = t_n$$

$$2 + (m - 1)\,2 = 3 + (n - 1)\,3$$

$$2 + 2m - 2 = 3 + 3n - 3 \Rightarrow 2m = 3n$$

$$\frac{m}{3} = \frac{n}{2} = k \text{ (let) } m = 3k, n = 2k$$

$1 \le m \le 30$	$1 \le n \le 20$
$1 \le 3k \le 30$	$1 \le 2k \le 20$
$\frac{1}{3} \le k \le 10$	$\frac{1}{2} \le k \le 10$

Hence, k = 1, 2, 3, ... 10. For each value of k, we get one identical term.

Thus, number of identical terms = 10. [2 Marks]

OR

As per part (i), the last term of both A.Ps is 60 and x = 15,

For first A.P d = – 2, a = 60

$a_{15} = 60 + (15 - 1)y - z$,

$= 60 + 14 \times -2 = 60 - 28$

$a_{15} = 32$

Similar for second A.P d = – 3

$a_{15} = 60 + (15 - 1) \times -3 = 60 - 42$

$= 18$ [2 Marks]

SAMPLE PAPER-10

1. **(a)** If the lines are parallel, then

$$\frac{a_1}{a_2}=\frac{b_1}{b_2}\neq\frac{c_1}{c_2}$$

Here, $a_1=3, b_1=-1, c_1=-5,$

$a_2=6, b_2=-2, c_2=-p$

$$\Rightarrow \frac{3}{6}=\frac{-1}{-2}\neq\frac{-5}{-p} \quad ...(i)$$

Taking II and III part of equation (i), we get

$$\Rightarrow \frac{1}{2}\neq\frac{-5}{-p} \Rightarrow -p\neq-10 \Rightarrow p\neq 10$$

So, option (a) is correct.

2. **(c)** Let α, β be two zeroes of $2x^2-8x-m$, where $a=\frac{5}{2}$.

$$\therefore a+b=\frac{(-\text{Coefficient of } x)}{\text{Coefficient of } x^2}$$

$$\Rightarrow \frac{5}{2}+b=\frac{8}{2}$$

$$\Rightarrow b=\frac{8}{2}-\frac{5}{2}=\frac{3}{2}.$$

3. **(b)** $a_n=a+(n-1)d=a+(n-1)2a$

$[\because d=3a-a=2a]$

$=a+2an-2a=2an-a=(2n-1)a$

4. **(b)** $\alpha+2\alpha=-\frac{b}{a}$ and $\alpha\times 2\alpha=\frac{c}{a} \Rightarrow 3\alpha=-\frac{b}{a}$

$$\Rightarrow \alpha=-\frac{b}{3a} \text{ and } 2\alpha^2=\frac{c}{a} \Rightarrow 2\left(\frac{-b}{3a}\right)^2=\frac{c}{a}$$

$$\Rightarrow \frac{2b^2}{9a^2}=\frac{c}{a} \Rightarrow 2ab^2-9a^2c=0 \Rightarrow a(2b^2-9ac)=0$$

Since $a\neq 0$, $\therefore 2b^2=9ac$

Hence, the required condition is $2b^2=9ac$

5. **(d)** $0.1\overline{34}=\frac{134-1}{990}=\frac{133}{990}$

6. **(c)** $-\frac{3(1)+4(2)-7}{3(-2)+4(1)-7}=-\frac{4}{-9}=\frac{4}{9}$

7. **(d)** We know that $\sec^2\theta-\tan^2\theta=1$ and $\sec\theta=\frac{x}{p}$,

$\tan\theta=\frac{y}{q}$

$\therefore \quad x^2q^2-p^2y^2=p^2q^2$

8. **(b)** Since (x, y) is midpoint of (3, 4) and (k, 7)

$$\therefore x=\frac{3+k}{2} \text{ and } y=\frac{4+7}{2}$$

Also $2x+2y+1=0$ putting values we get

$3+k+4+7+1=0$

$\Rightarrow \quad k+15=0 \Rightarrow k=-15$

9. **(c)** Since, $DE\parallel BC$ $\therefore \Delta ADE\sim\Delta ABC$

$$\therefore \frac{AD}{DB}=\frac{AE}{EC}\Rightarrow\frac{1.5}{3}=\frac{1}{EC}\Rightarrow EC=2 \text{ cm}$$

10. **(d)** $(\cos^4 A-\sin^4 A)=(\cos^2 A)^2-(\sin^2 A)^2$

$=(\cos^2 A-\sin^2 A)(\cos^2 A+\sin^2 A)$

$=(\cos^2 A-\sin^2 A)(1)=\cos^2 A-(1-\cos^2 A)$

$=2\cos^2 A-1$

11. **(b)** Let the required ratio be K : 1

$\therefore$ The coordinates of the required point on the y-axis is

$$x=\frac{K(-4)+3(1)}{K+1};y=\frac{K(2)+5(1)}{K+1}$$

Since, it lies on y-axis

$\therefore$ Its x-cordinates = 0

$$\therefore \frac{-4K+3}{K+1}=0\Rightarrow -4K+3=0$$

$$\Rightarrow K=\frac{3}{4}$$

$\Rightarrow$ Required ratio $=\frac{3}{4}:1$ $\quad\therefore$ ratio $=3:4$

12. **(a)** Perimeter of sector = 25 cm

$$\Rightarrow 2r+\frac{\theta}{360^\circ}\times 2\pi r=25$$

$$\Rightarrow 2r+\frac{90^\circ}{360^\circ}\times 2\times\frac{22}{7}\times r=25$$

$$\Rightarrow 2r+\frac{11}{7}r=25 \Rightarrow \frac{25}{7}r=25\Rightarrow r=7$$

Area of minor segment $=\left(\frac{\pi\theta}{360^\circ}-\frac{\sin\theta}{2}\right)r^2$

$$=\left(\frac{22}{7}\times\frac{90^\circ}{360^\circ}-\frac{\sin 90^\circ}{2}\right)(7)^2$$

$$=\left(\frac{11}{14}-\frac{1}{2}\right)\times 49=\frac{4}{14}\times 49=14\text{ cm}^2.$$

13. (d) Since, two chords AB and CD of the circle are intersecting at P, when produced.

$\therefore$ PA. PB = PC.PD

[Each = (length of the tangent from P)^2]

$\Rightarrow$ (AB + PB). (PB) = (PD + DC) $\cdot$ PD

$\Rightarrow$ $(5+3)(3)=(2+x)2$

$\Rightarrow$ $24=(2+x)(2)\Rightarrow 12=2+x$

$\Rightarrow$ $x=10\Rightarrow$ CD = 10 cm

14. (b) Let DC be the tower of height 'h' metres.

In rt. ΔACD, $\tan\theta=\dfrac{h}{x}$ ...(i)

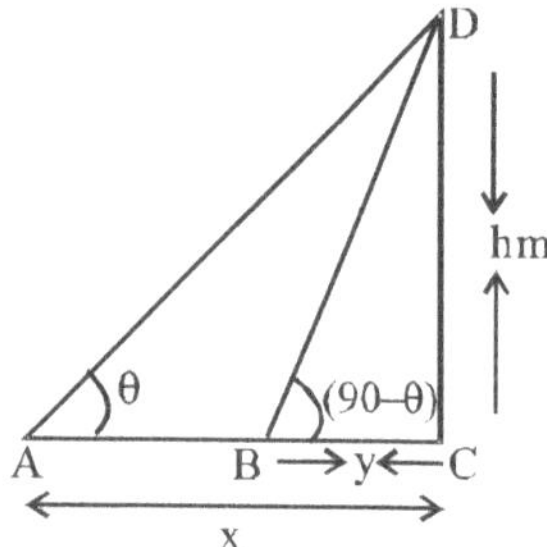

In rt. ΔBDC, $\tan(90-\theta)=\dfrac{h}{y}$

$\Rightarrow \cot\theta=\dfrac{h}{y}$ ...(ii)

Multiplying (i) by (ii), we get

$$\tan\theta\times\cot\theta=\frac{h}{x}\times\frac{h}{y}$$

$$\Rightarrow \tan\theta\times\frac{1}{\tan\theta}=\frac{h^2}{xy}$$

$$\Rightarrow 1=\frac{h^2}{xy}\Rightarrow h^2=xy$$

$$\Rightarrow h=\sqrt{xy}$$

15. (a)

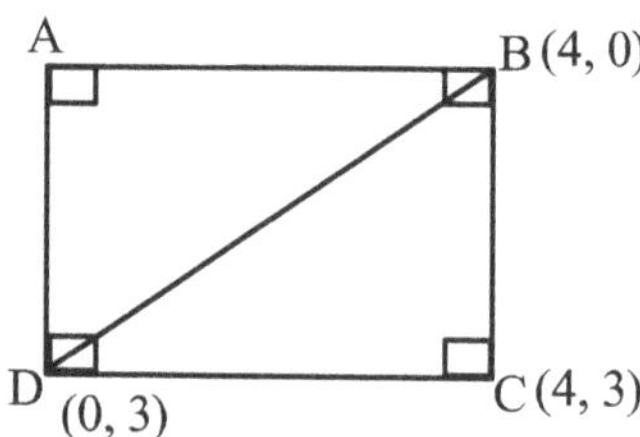

According to the figure

BD is the diagonal of ABCD.

By distance formula

$$BD=\sqrt{(x_2-x_1)^2+(y_2-y_1)^2}$$

$$=\sqrt{(4-0)^2+(0-3)^2}$$

$$=\sqrt{25}=5\text{ units}$$

16. (c) $\bar{x}=\dfrac{20(4)+40(5)+30(6)+10(10)}{20+40+30+10}$

$$=\frac{80+200+180+100}{100}=\frac{560}{100}=5.6$$

17. (b) Suppose O be the centre of two concentric circles C_1 and C_2, whose radii are $r_1=4$ cm and $r_2=5$ cm we draw a chord AC to circle C_2, which touches the circle C_1 at B. Then, join OB, which is perpendicular to AC.

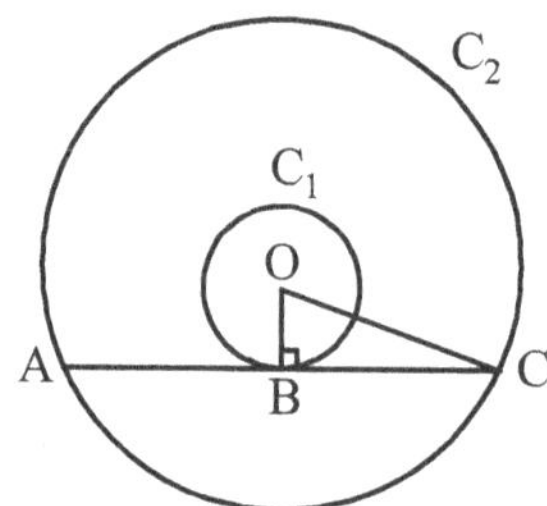

Now, in right angled ΔOBC,

$OC^2=BC^2+BO^2$

by using Pythagoras theorem

$\Rightarrow$ $5^2=BC^2+4^2$

$\Rightarrow$ $BC^2=25-16=9$

$\Rightarrow$ BC = 3 cm

So, length of chord AC = 2 BC = 2 × 3 = 6 cm

18. (a)

19. (c) Here, reason is not true.

$\because \sqrt{4}=\pm 2,$ which is not an irrational number.

$\therefore$ Reason does not hold. Clearly, assertion is true.

20. (a) Both statements are correct and Reason is the correct for Assertion.

21. Let ages of father and son be x and y respectively.

$x+y=40$ ...(i)

$x=3y$ ...(ii) [1 Mark]

By solving eqs. (i) and (ii)

$x=30$ and $y=10$

Ages are 30 years and 10 years. [1 Mark]

22. In figure,

We have ΔRPQ and ΔRTS in which

$\angle RPQ = \angle RTS$ (Given)

$\angle PRQ = \angle SRT$ (Each $= \angle R$) [1 Mark]

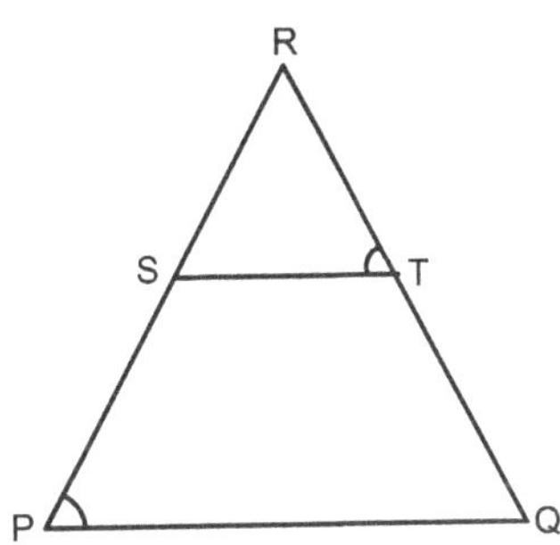

Then by AA similarity criterion, we have

$\Delta RPQ \sim \Delta RTS$ [1 Mark]

23. Consider $\sqrt{\sec^2\theta + \text{cosec}^2\theta} = \sqrt{\sec^2\theta + \text{cosec}^2\theta + 2 - 2}$

[1 Mark]

$= \sqrt{\sec^2\theta - 1 + \text{cosec}^2\theta - 1 + 2} = \sqrt{\tan^2\theta + \cot^2\theta + 2}$

$= \sqrt{(\tan\theta + \cot\theta)^2} = \tan\theta + \cot\theta$ [1 Mark]

24. In figure, TPOQ is a quadrilateral. Here, $\angle OPT = \angle OQT = 90°$

[$\because$ radius is perpendicular to tangent]

$\Rightarrow \angle PTQ + \angle POQ = 180°$ [1 Mark]

[$\because$ sum of all angles of quadrilateral is 360°]

$\Rightarrow \angle PTQ + \angle 110° = 180° \Rightarrow \angle PTQ = 70°$

OR

As, the tangents drawn from the exterior point to a circle are equal in length.

So, DR = DS ...(i)

AP = AS ...(ii)

BP = BQ ...(iii)

CR = CQ ...(iv) [1 Mark]

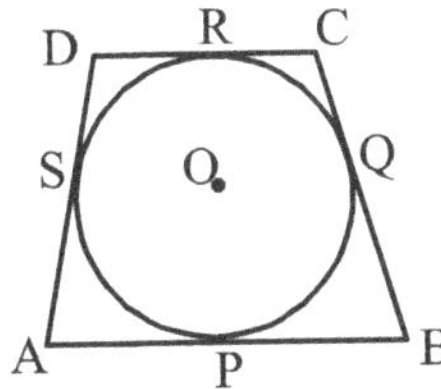

Adding (i), (ii), (iii) and (iv), we get

DR + AP + BP + CR = DS + AS + BQ + CQ

$\Rightarrow$ (DR + CR) + (AP + BP) = (DS + AS) + (BQ + CQ)

$\Rightarrow$ CD + AB = DA + BC $\Rightarrow$ AB + CD = BC + DA **(Hence Proved).** [1 Mark]

25. Let $P(x, y)$ be the required point. Then,

$$x = \frac{3 \times -4 + 2 \times 6}{3+2} \text{ and } y = \frac{3 \times 5 + 2 \times 3}{3+2}$$

$\Rightarrow x = 0$ and $y = \frac{21}{5}$ [1 Mark]

3 → ← 2

A(6, 3) — AP(x, y) — B(–4, 5)

So, the coordinates of P are (0, 21/5) [1 Mark]

OR

Let A (1, – 2) and B (– 3, 4) be the given points. Let the points of trisection be P and Q. Then, AP = PQ = QB = λ (say).

λ | λ | λ

A(1, –2) — P — Q — B(–3, 4)

$\therefore$ PB = PQ + QB = 2λ and AQ = AP + PQ = 2λ [1 Mark]

$\Rightarrow$ AP : PB = $\lambda : 2\lambda$ = 1 : 2 and AQ : QB = $2\lambda : \lambda$ = 2 : 1

So, P divides AB internally in the ratio 1 : 2 while Q divides internally in the ratio 2 : 1. Thus, the coordinates of P and Q are

$$P\left(\frac{1\times(-3)+2\times1}{1+2}, \frac{1\times4+2\times(-2)}{1+2}\right) = P\left(\frac{-1}{3}, 0\right) \text{ [1 Mark]}$$

$$Q\left(\frac{2\times(-3)+1\times1}{2+1}, \frac{2\times4+1\times(-2)}{2+1}\right) = Q\left(\frac{-5}{3}, 2\right)$$

respectively

Hence, the two points of trisection are (–1/3,0) and (–5/3,2)

[1 Mark]

26. Here, $a = 1$, and $d = 1$

$$\therefore \quad S_{n-1} = \frac{x-1}{2}[2\times1 + (x-1-1)\times1]$$

$$= \frac{x-1}{2}(2 + x - 2) = \frac{(x-1)(x)}{2} = \frac{x^2 - x}{2}$$

$$S_n = \frac{x}{2}[2\times1 + (x-1)\times1] = \frac{x}{2}(x+1) = \frac{x^2+x}{2} \text{ [1 Mark]}$$

and, $S_{49} = \frac{49}{2}[2\times1+(49-1)\times1]$

$$= \frac{49}{2}[2+48] = \frac{49}{2}\times 50 = 49\times 25$$

According to the question, [1 Mark]

$S_{n-1} = S_{49} - S_x$

i.e., $\frac{x^2-x}{2} = 49\times 25 - \frac{x^2+x}{2}$

$\Rightarrow \frac{x^2-x}{2} + \frac{x^2+x}{2} = 49\times 25$

$\Rightarrow \frac{x^2-x+x^2+x}{2} = 49\times 25$

$\Rightarrow x^2 = 49\times 25 \quad \Rightarrow x = \pm 7\times 5$ [1 Mark]

$\because$ x is a counting number, so taking positive square root, $x = 7\times 5 = 35$.

27. Here, $\frac{a_1}{a_2} = \frac{2}{a+b+1}$; $\frac{b_1}{b_2} = \frac{3}{a+2b+2}$;

$\frac{c_1}{c_2} = \frac{7}{4(a+b)+1}$

For Infinite number of solutions

$$\frac{a_1}{a_2} = \frac{b_1}{b_2} = \frac{c_1}{c_2} \text{ or } \frac{2}{a+b+1} = \frac{3}{a+2b+2} = \frac{7}{4(a+b)+1}$$

[½ Mark]

(I) (II) (III)

Taking I and II & taking II and III

$$\frac{2}{a+b+1} = \frac{3}{a+2b+2} \text{ and } \frac{3}{a+2b+2} = \frac{7}{4(a+b)+1}$$

[½ Mark]

$3a+3b+3 = 2a+4b+4$ and $12a+12b+3 = 7a+14b+14$

$a-b=1$ ... (i) [1 Mark]

and $5a-2b=11$ ... (ii)

Multiplying (i) by 2 and subtracting (ii) from (i)

$$2a-2b=2$$
$$5a-2b=11$$

$-3a = -9 \Rightarrow a = 3$

Putting the value of a in (i), we get

$a-b=1 \Rightarrow 3-b=1 \quad \Rightarrow b=2$ [1 Mark]

28. Let $y = f(x)$ or $y = 3-2x-x^2$

Let us list a few values of $y = 3-2x-x^2$ corresponding to a few values of x as follows :

x	–5	–4	–3	–2	–1	0	1	2	3
$y=3-2x-x^2$	–12	–5	0	3	4	3	0	–5	–12

Thus, the following points lie on the graph of polynomial $y = 3-2x-x^2$:

(–5, –12), (–4, –5), (–3, 0), (–2, 3), (–1, 4), (0, 3), (1, 0), (2, –5), and (3, – 12)

Let us plot these points on a graph paper and draw a smooth free hand curve passing through these points to obtain the graph of $y = 3-2x-x^2$. The curve thus obtained is a parabola. [2 Mark]

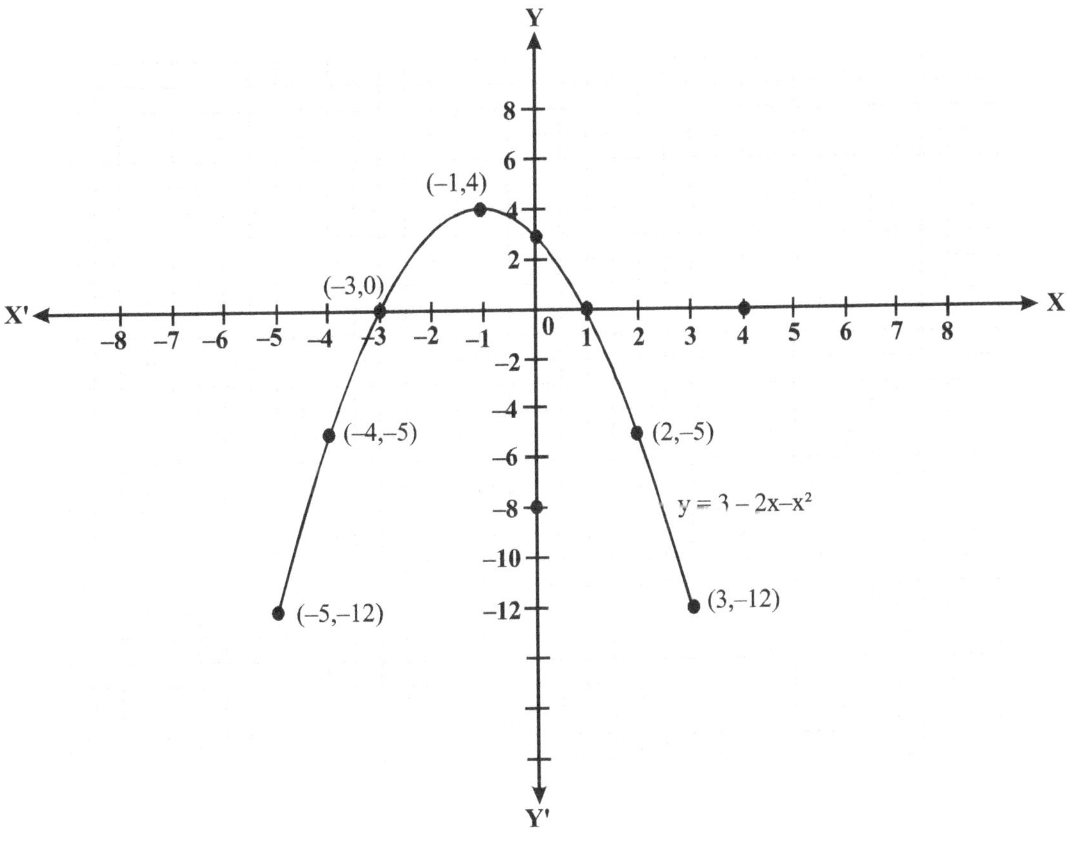

[1 Mark]

The parabola intersects X-axis at $x = -3$ and 1. Therefore, zeroes or roots of the polynomial are –3 and 1.

29. LHS = $(m^2+n^2)\cos^2\beta = \left(\frac{\cos^2\alpha}{\cos^2\beta}+\frac{\cos^2\alpha}{\sin^2\beta}\right)\cos^2\beta$ [1 Mark]

$$=\left(\frac{\cos^2\alpha\sin^2\beta+\cos^2\alpha\cos^2\beta}{\sin^2\beta\cos^2\beta}\right)\cos^2\beta$$

$$=\left(\frac{\cos^2\alpha\left(\sin^2\beta+\cos^2\beta\right)}{\sin^2\beta\cos^2\beta}\right)\cos^2\beta$$

[1 Mark]

$$=\left(\frac{\cos^2\alpha\cos^2\beta}{\sin^2\beta\cos^2\beta}\right)=\frac{\cos^2\alpha}{\sin^2\beta}=(n)^2=\text{RHS}$$

$\left(\because \frac{\cos\alpha}{\sin\beta}=n\right)$ [1 Mark]

Hence Proved.

OR

$$2\operatorname{cosec}^2 30^\circ + x\sin^2 60^\circ - \frac{3}{4}\tan^2 30^\circ = 10$$

$\Rightarrow 2(2)^2 + x\left(\frac{\sqrt{3}}{2}\right)^2 - \frac{3}{4}\left(\frac{1}{\sqrt{3}}\right)^2 = 10$ [1 Mark]

$\Rightarrow 8+\frac{3}{4}x-\frac{3}{4}\times\frac{1}{3}=10$ [½ Mark]

$\Rightarrow \frac{3}{4}x = 10-8+\frac{1}{4} \Rightarrow \frac{3}{4}x = \frac{40-32+1}{4}$ [½ Mark]

$\Rightarrow \frac{3}{4}x = \frac{9}{4} \Rightarrow 3x = 9 \Rightarrow x = 3$ [1 Mark]

30. **Given :** A quadrilateral ABCD circumscribes a circle with centre O.

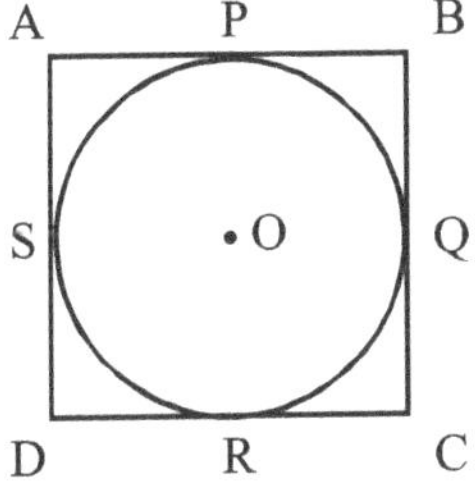

To prove : AB + CD = AD + BC

Proof : Since, tangents drawn to a circle from an exterior point are equal

AP = AS I

BP = BQ II

CR = CQ III

DR = DS .....IV [1 Mark]

By adding I, II, III and IV we get,

AP + BP + CR + DR = AS + BQ + CQ + DS

(AP + BP) + (CR + DR) = (AS + DS) + (BQ + CQ) [2 Marks]

AB + CD = AD + BC

Hence, proved.

31. Total number of possible outcomes when two dice are thrown simultaneously = 36 [1 Mark]

Sum of the numbers appearing on the dice is a prime number i.e., 2, 3, 5, 7 and 11

So, the possible outcomes are (1, 1), (1, 2), (2, 1), (1, 4), (2, 3), (3,2), (4, 1), (1, 6), (2, 5), (3, 4), (4, 3), (5, 2), (6, 1), (5, 6) and (6, 5).

Number of possible outcomes = 15 [1 Mark]

$\therefore$ required probability $= \frac{15}{36} = \frac{5}{12}$ [1 Mark]

OR

Total no. of cards = 60 – 12 = 48

$\Rightarrow$ Total no. of outcomes = 48

Numbers are 13, 14, 15, 16, ..., 60.

(i) Numbers divisible by 5 are 15, 20, 25, 30, 35, 40, 45, 50, 55, 60. [1 Mark]

$\therefore$ Favourable outcomes = 10

$\therefore$ P(no. is divisible by 5) $= \frac{10}{48} = \frac{5}{24}$ [½ Mark]

(ii) Perfect square numbers are 16, 25, 36, 49 [½ Mark]

$\therefore$ Favourable outcomes = 4

$\therefore$ P(perfect square) $= \frac{4}{48} = \frac{1}{12}$ [1 Mark]

32. Given equation is $x^2 - 3x + 2 = 0$ [1 Mark]

On comparing with $ax^2 + bx + c = 0$, we get $a = 1, b = -3, c = 2$

Now, Apply discriminant

$D = b^2 - 4ac = (-3)^2 - 4(1)(2) = 1 \Rightarrow \sqrt{D} = 1$ [2 Marks]

The two roots are given by $\frac{-b \pm \sqrt{D}}{2a}$, *i.e.*, $\frac{3 \pm 1}{2} = \frac{4}{2}$ and $\frac{2}{2}$

[2 Marks]

Hence, the two roots are 1 and 2.

33. $\Delta ABC \sim \Delta PQR$

(Given)

$\Rightarrow \frac{AB}{PQ} = \frac{BC}{QR} = \frac{AC}{PR}$;

$\angle A = \angle P, \angle B = \angle Q, \angle C = \angle R$ ...(1)

Now, $BD = CD = \frac{1}{2} BC$ and $QM = RM = \frac{1}{2} QR$ ...(2)

($\because$ D is mid-point of BC and M is mid-point of QR) [1 Mark]

From (1), $\frac{AB}{PQ} = \frac{BC}{QR}$

$\Rightarrow \frac{AB}{PQ} = \frac{2BD}{2QM}$ (By (2))

$\Rightarrow \frac{AB}{PQ} = \frac{BD}{QM}$ [2 Marks]

Thus, we have $\frac{AB}{PQ} = \frac{BD}{QM}$

and $\angle ABD = \angle PQM$ ($\because \angle B = \angle Q$)

$\Rightarrow \Delta ABD \sim \Delta PQM$

(By SAS similarity critetrion)

$\Rightarrow \frac{AB}{PQ} = \frac{AD}{PM}$ [2 Marks]

34. Canvas needed to make the tent = C.S.A of the conical part + C.S.A of the cylindrical part

Given that

Radius of the conical part = Radius of the cylindrical part

$= \frac{3}{2}$ m

Slant height of the conical part $= l = 2.8$ m

Height of the cylindrical part = h = 2.1m

C.S.A of the conical part $= \pi r l = \frac{22}{7} \times \frac{3}{2} \times 2.8\ m^2$ [1 Mark]

C.S.A of the cylindrical part $= 2\pi rh = 2 \times \frac{22}{7} \times \frac{3}{2} \times 2.1\ m^2$

[2 Marks]

$\therefore$ Total area of the canvas needed to make the tent

$= \frac{22}{7} \times \frac{3}{2} \times 2.8 + 2 \times \frac{22}{7} \times \frac{3}{2} \times 2.1$

$= \frac{22}{7} \times \frac{3}{2} \times (2.8 + 4.2) = \frac{22}{7} \times \frac{3}{2} \times 7 = 33\,m^2$ [2 Marks]

Cost of the canvas = ₹ 500/m^2

So, total cost of the canvas needed to make the tent = ₹ 500 × 33 = ₹16, 500 [1 Mark]

OR

Side of cube = 7 cm

Largest sphere carved out from cube with radius $= \frac{7}{2}$ cm

[1 Mark]

Vol. of wooden left = Vol. of cube – Vol. of sphere [2 Marks]

$= (\text{side})^3 - \frac{4}{3}\pi r^3 = 7^3 - \frac{4}{3} \times \frac{22}{7} \times \frac{7}{2} \times \frac{7}{2} \times \frac{7}{2}$

$= 343 - \frac{539}{3} = \frac{1029 - 539}{3} = \frac{490}{3} cm^3$ [2 Marks]

35. Let a = 25 (assumed mean) and h = 10 (class interval)

Marks	f_i	Mid-Point (x_i)	Deviation $\left(u_i = \frac{x_i - 25}{10}\right)$	f_iu_i
0 – 10	20	5	–2	–40
10 – 20	24	15	–1	–24
20 – 30	40	25	0	0
30 – 40	36	35	1	36
40 – 50	20	45	2	40
Total	140			12

[2 Marks]

Since, mean $= a + \left(\frac{\sum f_iu_i}{\sum f_i}\right) \times h$ [1 Mark]

$\Rightarrow$ mean $= 25 + \left(\frac{\sum f_iu_i}{\sum f_i}\right) \times 10 = 25 + \left(\frac{12}{140}\right) \times 10$

= 25.86 (Approximate) [2 Marks]

OR

From the given data, we have the modal class 35-40.

{$\because$ It has largest frequency among the given classes of the data}

So, $l = 35, f_m = 23, f_1 = 21, f_2 = 14$ and $h = 10$.

Mode $= l + \left\{\frac{f_m - f_1}{2f_m - f_1 - f_2}\right\} \times h$

$= 35 + \left\{\frac{23 - 21}{46 - 21 - 14}\right\} \times 10 = 36.8$ years

Now, let us find mean of the data : [2 Marks]

Age (in years)	Number of patients f_i	Class mark x_i	$u_i = \frac{x_i - 30}{10}$	$f_i \times u_i$
5-15	6	10	– 2	– 12
15-25	11	20	– 1	– 11
25-35	21	**30 = *a***	0	0
35-45	23	40	1	23
45-55	14	50	2	28
55-65	5	60	3	15
Total	$n = 80$			43

$a = 30, h = 10, n = 80$ and $\sum f_iu_i = 43$ [2 Marks]

Mean $= a + h \times \frac{1}{n} \times \sum f_iu_i =$

$30 + 10 \times \frac{1}{80} \times 43 = 30 + 5.37 = 35.37$ years.

Thus, mode = 36.8 years and mean = 35.37 years.

[1 Mark]

So, we conclude that the maximum number of patients admitted in the hospital are of the age 36.8 years (apporx.), whereas on an average the age of a patient admitted to the hospital is 35.37 years.

36. (i) For getting least number of books, taking LCM of 32, 36

4	32, 36
8	8, 9
9	1, 9
	1, 1

$\Rightarrow 4 \times 8 \times 9 = 288$ [1 Mark]

(ii) HCF of 32, 36 is

4	32, 36
	8, 9

[1 Mark]

= 4

(iii) $7 \times 11 \times 13 \times 15 + 15$

$\Rightarrow 15(7 \times 11 \times 13 + 1)$

so given no. is a composite number. [2 Marks]

OR

Given a, b are prime number. So

LCM of p, q, where $p = ab^2$, $q = a^2b$

$p = a \times b \times b$

$q = a \times b \times a$

$a \times b \times b \times a \Rightarrow a^2b^2$ [2 Marks]

37.

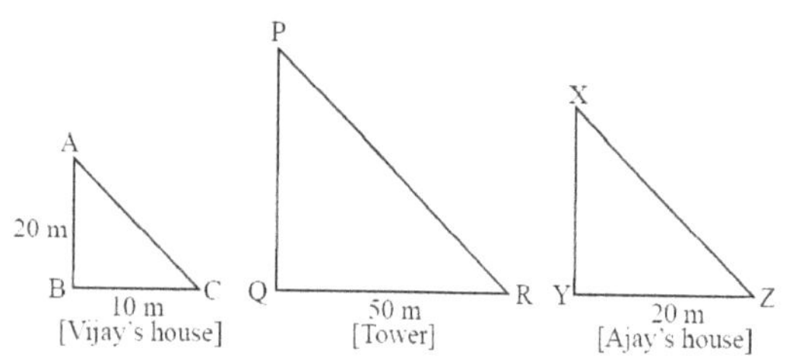

(i) $\because$ $\Delta ABC \sim \Delta PQR$

$\therefore$ $\frac{AB}{PQ} = \frac{BC}{QR} \Rightarrow \frac{20}{PQ} = \frac{10}{50}$

$\Rightarrow$ $PQ = 100$

$\therefore$ Height of the tower = 100 m [1 Mark]

(ii) Let $BC = 12$ m and $PQ = 100$ m

$\frac{AB}{PQ} = \frac{BC}{QR} \Rightarrow \frac{20}{100} = \frac{12}{QR}$

$\Rightarrow$ $QR = 60$ [1 Mark]

(iii) $\because$ $\Delta ABC \sim \Delta XYZ$

$\therefore$ $\frac{AB}{XY} = \frac{BC}{YZ} \Rightarrow \frac{20}{XY} = \frac{10}{20}$

$\Rightarrow$ $XY = 40$ [2 Marks]

OR

Let $QR = 40$ m, PQ = 100 m and $XY = 40$ m

$\therefore$ $\frac{PQ}{XY} = \frac{QR}{YZ} \Rightarrow \frac{100}{40} = \frac{40}{YZ}$ $\Rightarrow$ $YZ = 16$ m. [2 Marks]

38. (i) Volume of cylindrical cup = $\pi r^2 h$

$\frac{22}{7} \times \frac{7}{2} \times \frac{7}{2} \times 10.5 = 404.25 \text{ cm}^3$ [1 Mark]

(ii) Volume of hemispherical cup

$= \frac{2}{3}\pi r^3 = \frac{3}{2} \times \frac{22}{7} \times \left(\frac{7}{2}\right)^3 = 89.83 \text{ cm}^3$

(iii) Curved surface area of cone = 551 $\Rightarrow \pi rl = 441$

$\Rightarrow$ $\frac{22}{7} \times 7 \times l = 551 \Rightarrow l = 25.045$

$\therefore$ $h = \sqrt{l^2 - r^2} = 24$ m [2 Marks]

OR

Space occupied by each student = $\frac{\pi r^2}{4} = 38.5 \text{ m}^2$

[2 Marks]

www.ingramcontent.com/pod-product-compliance
Ingram Content Group UK Ltd.
Pitfield, Milton Keynes, MK11 3LW, UK
UKHW061958290726
14090UKWH00021B/1281